THE
ROMANCE
OF
ARTHUR
III

King Arthur's round Table

Preserved as a curious piece of Antiquity in the Castle of Winchester

The Round Table in the Great Hall of Winchester Castle. Once believed to be the work of Joseph of Arimathea, it has since been dated to the mid-13th century. In 1486, King Henry VII painted it white and green, and set a Tudor rose in the middle. The solar significance is obvious, with Arthur placed at Christmas or the winter solstice. (Courtesy of the British Tourist Authority)

THE ROMANCE OF ARTHUR III

*WORKS FROM RUSSIA TO SPAIN,
NORWAY TO ITALY*

edited by

James J. Wilhelm

GARLAND PUBLISHING, INC. · NEW YORK & LONDON
1988

LIBRARY OF CONGRESS
Library of Congress Cataloging-in-Publication Data

The Romance of Arthur III : works from Russia to Spain, Norway to
Italy / edited by James J. Wilhelm.
    p.   cm.
Includes index.
ISBN 0-8240-4103-8 (alk. paper)
1. Arthurian romances.   I. Wilhelm, James J.
PN6071. A84R63   1988
808.8′0351—dc19   88-11027
                                      CIP

Printed on acid-free, 250-year-life paper
Manufactured in the United States of America

CONTENTS

v

ARTHURIAN STUDIES FROM GARLAND

The Romance of Arthur
edited by James J. Wilhelm
and Laila Zamuelis Gross

The Romance of Arthur II
edited by James J. Wilhelm

The Arthurian Encyclopedia
edited by Norris J. Lacy et al.

The Arthurian Handbook
by Norris J. Lacy
and Geoffrey Ashe

"Arthur, the Greatest King":
An Anthology of
Modern Arthurian Poems
edited by Alan Lupack

Arthurian Legend and Literature:
An Annotated Bibliography
by Edmund Reiss,
Louise Horner Reiss
and Beverly Taylor

PREFACE

This third volume of the *Romance of Arthur* series is meant to provide some idea of the widespread dissemination of Arthurian myth in Europe and the literature evolving from it. We have therefore gone east to Russia, south to Italy and Spain, and north to Norway. In terms of time, we move to the 1500s with the Byelorussian *Tristan*, while most of the other selections can be dated from the 1100s to the 1400s, the period of florescence.

In selecting samples from the more commonly known languages—Middle English, French, and German—we decided to emphasize the lesser known but very interesting and important items that one cannot find in standard anthologies. We therefore chose *The Wedding of Sir Gawain and Dame Ragnell* rather than Chaucer's *Wife of Bath's Tale*. Mildred Leake Day's translation of the Latin *Rise of Gawain* has only lately come to assume the importance it deserves, after her splendid edition and translation in the Garland Library of Medieval Literature (Vol. 15, 1984), while Michael Resler's translation of the German *Daniel of the Blossoming Valley*, following his admirable edition published by Niemeyer of Tübingen in 1983, should make this highly innovative composition more popular than ever before. In many ways the anonymous *Knight of the Parrot*, translated by Thomas E. Vesce from his own edition of the Old North French, is as delightful because of its talking bird as Chrétien de Troyes's *Yvain*, with its humanized lion.

Although the ballad and lyric selections occupy less space than the narratives, these art forms are equally important for a well-rounded understanding of the spread of the material. The Italian *cantari* prefigure the passionate lyrics of later opera, while the Spanish ballads can be seen as companions for the longer romances, and the Norse mock-saga about the Telltale Mantle shows the humorous possibilities of Arthurian material.

As in the two preceding volumes, all of the selections, except the Spanish ballads, have been freshly translated. Most of them are printed in their entirety, although demands of space forced some condensation and abridgment in the longer narratives. The condensation usually involved little more than the elimination of repetitions, redundancies, and unpursued digressions. For the complete versions, one is referred to the editions of the Garland Library of Medieval Literature.

It is my hope that the reader will find these samples as interesting to read as the translators and the editor found them to create and assemble.

I would like to dedicate this work to my many good friends in Birmingham, especially those at Jefferson State College and the University of Alabama branch there, such as Mary Flowers Braswell, W. J. Dempsey, and Stephen O. Glosecki.

James J. Wilhelm

New York City

THE ROMANCE OF ARTHUR
III

chapter I
OLD NORTH FRENCH

THE KNIGHT OF THE PARROT

Thomas E. Vesce

Found only in a fifteenth-century manuscript, probably from around Lyons but now in the National Library in Paris (BN, fr. 2154), this romance about King Arthur has not known a very wide audience. Yet the motifs which are included (magic trees with protective blossoms, ghost-armies, a friendly unicorn, loss of real time when visiting an enchanted realm, and bridges to the other world) have apparent models in many earlier, popular medieval stories. These motifs continued to be imitated in later works in other lands, particularly in Germany (as in the *Wigalois* of Wirnt von Grafenberg).

As Chrétien de Troyes showed in *Erec et Enide*, birds of prey were the usual companions of noblemen, whose prowess was usually reflected in the stalking of falcons, hawks, and gyrfalcons. Yet here Arthur, who is the most noble of all knights, is content to be escorted on his various adventures not by a thrice-moulted goshawk but by a mere parrot. How-ever, this bird is endowed with powers which his more aggressive feathered peers could never match, for he speaks and plays the role of counselor and public relations adviser to the newly crowned king. Since the bird's bravery is non-existent, it is rather paradoxical that the dauntless Arthur should suffer his company. The broad comedy which appears so close to the surface of this relationship may well explain why critics generally have ignored this romance. On a more serious side, the work shows that the chivalric code imposed stricter obligations upon well-schooled knights than those bound to a more bureaucratic mode of aristocratic existence. The young King Arthur is forced to abandon the luxury of his newly gained power and to wander about in other domains assisting ladies in distress. Christian kindness is placed above self-indulgence.

The text is likewise of interest because it strays beyond the lofty customs of the castle and presents insights into the lives of members of other social classes. When Arthur fares badly in one of the adventures and almost drowns, the fisherman who finds his armor and leads his lord to rescue him fears for his life in having meddled in the affairs of aristocrats. Women also are not always paid with kindness for the ready offer of their charms, as Arthur proves when he savagely beats his paramour, the Lady of the Blonde Hair. And when the sworn men of the villain of the piece, the Wicked Marshal, change their allegiance out of fear of losing their lives to the invincible Arthur, we see the true politics of medieval times.

One of the charms of this miniature of chivalric manners is the adroit blending of the real with the fantastic and the acceptable with the forbidden which the anonymous author presents to his audience. This strange but fascinating story may finally be revealed as a worthy tale about the youthful adventures of Arthur the King.

Bibliographic note: The first English translation of *Le Chevalier du papegau* was done by me in 1986 (New York: Garland) based upon the only modern edition of the manuscript, accomplished by Ferdinand Heuckenkamp (Halle: Niemeyer) in 1896. For an updated bibliography, see my translation (pp. xxi–xxv), which likewise has an appendix on its folklore elements (pp. 97–101). The passages that follow are somewhat revised and briefly abbreviated from the original publication.

The Knight of the Parrot

He who delights in hearing of beautiful adventures and deeds of chivalry should listen now and hear about the first adventures that befell good King Arthur in the early days of his reign, which unfold below.

On the feast of Pentecost, on the very day that King Arthur was crowned, there were great joy and merrymaking in the city of Camelot. And when mass was celebrated, as was proper on such a high holiday, the king and all his barons went up to the palace. After a while there appeared a damsel, alone and unescorted, who, traveling at a brisk pace on her mule, came to the court while the feasting was going on. When she had dismounted at the foot of the palace steps and tied the mule's rein to a post, she went into the great hall to the place where she saw the king, who was already at table; she greeted him very courteously and said: "My good lord, one of the most beautiful, most worthy, and most gentle ladies whom one may ever encounter anywhere sends me here to you, and begs you to send her a knight of your court, fearless and true, who may give her aid against a knight who every day comes to destroy her people and her land, and who has already killed sixty of her best knights, so that no one comes forward to answer his challenge. This is the first adventure which has come to your court, and she prays you, for God and for your own honor, to grant it for her."

When he had returned her greeting, King Arthur answered her very softly: "My good damsel, I have very well understood what you have said. May good adventure come to your lady who sent you here, for gladly will I do what she requires!" And then he commanded a young lord to aid her in whatever she asked, and as the case might be, look after her needs. The young lord did what the king commanded, for he conducted her to the home of one of the most refined bourgeois in the town, who was also among the very richest, who directed that she be deferred to even in the least of her wishes. The young lady stayed with him for as long as the court lasted, which was a space of seven full days.

After the octave of Pentecost, the nobles of foreign lands took their leave, and like one who is knowledgeable about such things, the king distributed gold and silver to each one of them, according to his rank, so that they all left for their lands happy and promising their services to the king whenever he might have need of them. The king remained at Camelot together with his trusty barons. There then appeared the young lady who recalled the case of her mistress to the king. The knights and barons all offered to go to serve her lady but the king would not allow it, saying: "This adventure is mine by right; for it is the first which has been asked in my court, and, since I am a newly made king, I do not wish that any should go to serve the lady but myself." Nor could the barons sway Arthur from this: he then entrusted his kingdom and his court to one of his barons who was known as Lord Lot, and he caused it to be announced throughout his lands that all should do Lot's bidding, until such time as he himself returned. When he had accomplished this, he had himself clad in armor, mounted his charger, and left the city with the young damsel and his barons as escort. When they were about to enter the forest of Camelot, King Arthur commanded his barons to turn back. When they knew his pleasure, these headed back to Camelot, grieved and upset to see their lord, young and untried, go into strange lands. He was, beyond all doubt, the finest knight for his age that anyone knew anywhere.

After the king parted from his barons, he and the damsel continued riding alone and speaking to one another as the mood moved them. When they had ridden for a while, they heard a voice crying very loudly which seemed to be in need of help. It said: "My good and sweet lord, have pity on me!" This it cried three times. On hearing these cries, the king looked to one side and saw approaching on a mule a very beautiful and richly dressed lady who was fleeing before an armed knight, mounted on a charger, who was pursuing her closely with a drawn sword in his hand. When the lady saw the king riding with his young damsel companion, she went right up to him and said: "Ah, noble knight, for God's sake, take pity on me! Help me so that this knight does not kill me; he has already wrongly killed my companion and now seeks to kill me!" Just as she was ending her plea, the knight raised his sword to strike the lady.

But the king advanced and shouted: "My lord knight, do not harm this lady; for no praise is given a knight for the killing of young or old ladies in such a manner!"

When the knight saw the king was taking up the lady's defense, he told him very wrathfully: "Sir vassal, if you intend to defend her, beware of me; for I believe that you will badly defend both yourself and her." Then the knight sheathed his sword and went back a piece for a lance of his that he had left at the foot of a tree. When he had taken it up again, he spurred his mount fiercely and charged at the king, who prepared to defend himself. Having charged the whole distance between them, the knight struck the king's shield so hard that he broke both shield and hauberk on the right side, and if his lance had not broken, he would have badly abused the king. The king struck back at him with all his might, and for all that his spear was worth, neither shield nor hauberk could withstand it, so that the knight fell to the ground and was so stunned that he did not know where he was. After a while, when the shock wore off, he saw the king, who had dismounted, coming toward him with drawn sword and intent on striking him. As best he could, the knight said to him: "Noble sir, have mercy, for God's sake; do not kill me and pay no heed to my discourtesy."

When the king heard the knight begging for mercy, he answered him: "If you desire mercy from me I require you to place yourself at the mercy of this lady and to do all that she shall ask of you."

"Ha, my lord," said the knight. "By God, I would have you kill me before she should have me in her service!"

Then the king asked him why he had put her friend to death, and the knight answered him: "Sire, I will truly tell you why. It is true that she is the most beautiful lady in the world, as you can well see, and that her beauty slays me; for I have loved her more than a knight should ever love a lady, but she has preferred another's love to mine, and for this reason I sought to destroy her, since it did not please her to be with me. Her companion, then, I killed because he served her in spite of me and against my wishes and warnings."

"Knight," said the king, full of chagrin, "what is your name?" When this one said he was known as the Knight of the Wasteland, the king said: "You must place yourself completely in the service and at the mercy of this lady now or I shall kill you; but I believe that she will have mercy on you for my account."

"Ah, sire," said the knight, "a lady's mercy is dangerous; but since I see it would please you, I will do it."

The lady, who had heard these words, said to the king: "Sire, I have no desire to keep my enemy in my power, since I have no means of taking my revenge on him; prison is the place for an evil man, and I will tell you why: for if the evil man is not kept in prison, he will practice his evil ways so much that he will be dead and confounded by his own works. For this reason, my good lord, I leave it up to you to accomplish your pleasure in this matter here." Then the king had the knight pledge that he would go to Camelot and give himself up to Lord Lot and that he would stay at his mercy until such time as Arthur returned to court.

After Arthur dispatched the Knight of the Wasteland, he asked the lady in what direction she would travel, and the lady answered him: "My good lord, I would like to lead you, if it pleases you, to one of the most beautiful courts you could ever hope to see anywhere, which is quite close by here. There are some five hundred knights, the best in all the land, who have already come to attend that court, where the rule is that he who claims its beautiful damsel and proves this by exercise of arms shall gain a parrot that a dwarf brings there every year, the best bird in all the world, who sings sweet, pleasant songs of love and converses cleverly about matters which warm the hearts of men and women. But a knight has come there who has conquered by arms all the others of the land, to whom he does the greatest wrongs that ever a knight may do."

"What wrongs does he do, lady?" asked the king.

"Sire," said the lady, "once a month he has all the knights, ladies, damsels, and young fellows of the district come to the open field of Causuel, and has them swear homage to him, by force and not by reason, and afterwards he makes them do the same to his female friend, the most ugly creature you can see anywhere; and then by force he has them declare that she is the most beautiful, the most courteous, and the best-dressed lady in all the world. My good lord, it would be a very great courtesy to deliver the knights, ladies, and damsels from the bondage they wrongly suffer. Indeed you can deliver them, if you so wish, and for the reason that I shall explain to you: since you have defeated the Knight of the Wasteland by jousting, I will join together with you against the knight, and you will thus be able to demonstrate to him why I am more beautiful a woman and richer in wealth and goods than his lady-friend; and yet you do not know who I am, nor to whom you have given aid."

"Truly, lady, no," said the king, "except that you are, I do believe, the most beautiful lady I have ever seen. Love directs me to seek your service and do all that you may require. If it is the wish of this damsel here, in whose service I have placed myself, there will be nothing that can prevent me from accomplishing what you command."

Then the lady turned to the damsel and said: "Damsel, I pray you to come with this knight to that court, and know that you will have the best trip ever, once he vanquishes the knight there."

"Lady," said the damsel, "if it were up to me, I would do all I could to please you, since I see that you are courteous and well mannered. But I am in the service of a lady who sent me to seek out this knight, and so I do not command him but am only here to show him the way. If it pleases him to go there, it would not displease me, nor will I advise him, but will go wherever it pleases him to go."

When the king saw that the damsel was not against it, all three of them prepared to set out for the court together. They did not ride too far before they saw tents and pavilions in a beautiful, open field; and they also saw richly dressed ladies and damsels on mules and palfreys, who were joyously romping about on their mounts and making many strange noises. At the approach of the king and his party, they ceased their noise-making and started to cry out to the king, whom they saw was a stranger: "Sir, you come here wrongly and in an evil hour! Now your valor will be put to a test!" The others made fun of his companions. When the king heard himself spoken against like this, he said to them: "Spiteful people with no courtesy or grace, I have come here to deliver you from the servitude you suffer, and is this the way you shame me? In truth, no one should help you!"

When the knights among them heard what he had said, they repented for having so poorly and wrongly received him and his party. Then the king asked them where the knight was to whom they were forced to pay homage. He had scarcely finished asking when he saw a knight approaching, fully armed on a black destrier, who led a damsel on a very richly appareled mule. I would not know how to describe her beauty to you since there was none to be seen in her; nor would I be pleased to describe her ugliness, for I could not say all that had to be said about it. There also came around her ladies and damsels, joyously playing on harps and viols; and these were followed by a dwarf, dressed in scarlet lined with vair, who goaded before him a palfrey which carried a cage in which was the parrot previously mentioned.

When the knight saw that the king, who was speaking to the knights and ladies, was armed, he quickly surmised that he had come to fight with him. Without any other warning, and full of anger and bad intention, he took his shield and lance and ordered the place cleared, and his command was obeyed quickly. Then the king, who rightly perceived he was being required to joust, put his shield before him and took up his sword, as did the knight. They then spurred their horses onward and clashed with such great force that the impact smashed each shield to bits. But their hauberks were strong enough to safeguard the two knights from death, while their mounts, which had struck hard against each other, fell dead beneath their jousting lords. But the men were so strong and nimble that they quickly rose up, seized their battered shields, took up their swords, and ran at each other with great wrath.

The battle between the king and the knight lasted such a long time that no one knew who got the worst of it. All those men and women who were there were greatly amazed that the king, who was so young, was able to stand up so well against their lord; and because of the knightly worth they saw in him, and in order to be delivered from the servitude in which their lord unjustly held them, they all willingly prayed to God that He confound their master and cause him to be killed. The two knights fought so long with one another that it annoyed the knight that the king should last that long against him; his shame was great since he saw that the king was so young. And so, full of anger, he lunged forward and struck the king on the front of his helmet with such force that he shattered it and delved so deeply with his sword that he wounded him on the face. When the king saw the blood flowing beneath his ventail, he was stirred to great anger. The wrath he felt doubled his strength; for truly by anger strength is increased in men of worth, but it produces cowardice and base action in unworthy men. Full of fierce boldness, he ran up to the knight and dealt him such a mighty blow, between his helmet and shield, that he cut off his right arm and caused it to drop to the ground as it still clutched the shield. When all the onlookers saw that blow, they cried out with one voice: "Our master has more than found his match!" When he lost his arm, the knight felt himself sink to the ground from pain. The king went over to him and tore off his helmet, and the knight, as best he could, cried for mercy that he not kill him. As the king had found him to be such a valiant knight, he was inclined to show him pity, but all who were there urged the king to kill him, and the king did not know what he should do. Then he said to the knight: "Before I decide whether to show you mercy or not, I would have you tell me your name and lineage; then I will know what honor is fitting for you."

The knight answered him: "Since it is your pleasure, I will do so willingly. My good lord, my father was a poor vavasor who owned nothing in this world but this castle which is here before you, which is called Causuel. As I was an unruly child, he named me 'Bad Boy,' which did not bother me while I was an untried knight, but which was changed later when I became known as 'Merciless Lion,' since I took the lives of all those knights who jousted against me. After I overpowered them, I would have them acknowledge their personal debt to me and promise that all their honor was totally at my disposal."

"What did you do to those who would not submit to this?" asked the king.

"Sire," answered the knight, "I killed them, and took their women, children, possessions, and whatever else there was."

"What about those," said the king, "who submitted to your mercy; what did you do with them?"

"Sire, I took half of everything they owned at the moment when I spared them, and I caused them, their women, their young and old children to come before me once a month to do homage to me, just as they have been doing to this very day, according to my will."

"How long, then, have you enjoyed this power?" asked the king.

"My good lord, it has been a full fifteen years and more, for I have never met a knight who could best me, except for yourself, who now hold me and these others at your command. And so I beg you, my good lord, for God's sake, not to take my life."

"Lion," said the king, "you have followed the conventions of chivalry very badly, for chivalry requires reason and justice for all kinds of people; instead you have truly lived up to the name given you by your father and not the one given to you when you became a knight. And I will tell you why: with great wrong, you stripped goods away from knights who were not able to defend themselves, then you held them subject, together with their followers, against all reason and justice, and so you have well deserved the name of Bad Boy and not the name of Lion. For the lion is the noblest beast in the world; because he does not know how to harbor anger against any beast whatever once it grovels on the earth before him and displays humility, the lion does not bother it again. So you do not deserve the name of Lion. Still, since I do not wish to have your poor conduct trouble my generous spirit, I shall show you mercy as it befits you; do you know what I demand? You will relinquish your hold over all the people who are gathered here and will surrender to them all the goods that you stripped them of, if you have them, and you will right all the wrongs you did to them because of your pride. Furthermore, I command you to remain in this very place in a charterhouse that you will have built here. Also, I want all the people, young and old, who used to come to pay you homage here to come once a month to visit you until King Arthur of Britain calls you to his court to speak to him in the manner I will now describe to you: you will be dressed in all your finery and will ride in a cart, richly adorned, as a knight must do who cannot go on horseback, and you will command all those knights who were accustomed to serve you to accompany you to the court, each one helping the other. I wish them also to bear this penalty because of their cowardice and baseness."

The Merciless Lion, as well as all the other knights, then promised to do all that the king had described. All these knights marveled how the young king knew how to exact such retribution from the Merciless Lion. Since it was to their liking, they all agreed to carry out his commands. But no one can possibly describe to you the noise the parrot made; for he told the dwarf to lead him to the highest place he could, and he cried out: "Dwarf, my dwarf, bring me to see the best knight in the whole world! It is he about whom Merlin spoke in his prophecy when he said that the son of the ewe would subdue the Merciless Lion full of pride, felony, and anger. Oh, dwarf, do not tarry any longer! Bring me quickly to him, for he has won me!"

When the parrot came near the king, he began to relate sweetly all the events which had come to pass from the time of Merlin up to the present moment in such a way that the king and the others there marveled greatly about all he said. Then he said to the king: "Sire, why do you not take me? Truly I am yours; for you are the best knight in all the world, and the best instructed, and you have the most beautiful lady to be found anywhere, even if you do not know her name or her station."

"Sire," said the Lady Without Pride, "I am the sister of Morgan the Fay of Montgibel."

The king derived much joy indeed from what the parrot told him, as well as what the lady revealed to him. And so he came forward and took possession of the parrot, the dwarf, and all their equipment. After this, he thanked the Lady Without Pride for having led him to that court; and all the people of the district showed him great honor and beseeched him very kindly to remain at Causuel for as long as he pleased, but he answered that he could not because of an adventure which he had to conclude for the love of a certain lady. A Greek, Darsenois, who had come there to the court, presented the king with a handsome, sturdy charger that was well equipped, as was fitting for such a knight as he. The king accepted it very willingly, as would any whose service is rewarded; then the king mounted, as did the lady and the dwarf, who followed the palfrey that carried the parrot. The Lady Without Pride and all the other people also mounted in order to accompany the one who had freed them from their bondage. With great joy, to the sound of viols and harps, they ambled forth from the place.

After they had ridden for a good English league, the king asked all the men and women to turn back. Since they knew that this was his pleasure, they agreed, but they asked by what name he who had delivered them from their bondage should be spoken of. The king answered: "By the Knight of the Parrot." Then he said goodbye, and requested that his damsel companion should not address him by any other name than that. The Lady Without Pride took her leave of the king, and, promising him her service, should the need arise, went back to Causuel with the others, who were overjoyed by the good adventure that had come to them. Together with the Merciless Lion, these all did what the Knight of the Parrot had asked of them.

In this manner the Knight of the Parrot and his damsel went off riding, rejoicing marvelously over the adventure that had come to them. He glanced very often at the damsel, who was beautiful, white, and pink of color like a rose in the month of May. Thus they rode on, one next to the other, speaking about whatever pleased them. But when the parrot noticed the glances each of them were exchanging, he could not help saying: "You should be, the two of you, the most beautiful couple in the world; for you are, sir, the most handsome and best knight anyone could find in any land, no matter where, and she is so beautiful, well-mannered, and accomplished that no one could improve anything in her; and both of you are of the same age, and she is high-born, too."

"Parrot," said the damsel, "how do you know who I am?"

The parrot answered: "My lady, do you remember when you were at the court of our queen for schooling from the Damsel of the Love Castle? Since that time, my lady, I have heard of your lineage and learned your name, and I have always held you in esteem, as I shall for as long as I live because of your great beauty and your gracious name." He then turned toward the king: "Sire, would you like to hear the most gentle name of a damsel that may be found anywhere?"

"Yes, willingly," said the king.

"This damsel here with us," continued the parrot, "is properly called the Beauty Without Villainy, whom you should know is a noble countess of high rank and very rich in wealth and honor; her deceased father was the Count of Valsin, who had no other heir but her."

The Knight of the Parrot, who was made wondrously joyous by these words about the damsel and her lineage, rode onward with his joyful party until vespers. When the parrot sensed the air turning cold, he told the dwarf that he was cold, and the dwarf took a coverlet, fashioned of silk and very richly worked, from a sack and covered the parrot's cage, which was the most beautiful one could ever hope to see, for it was made of pure gold, engraved with all sorts of beasts and birds, each of which carried nineteen of the finest rubies to be found anywhere. Also, at the four corners of the cage were four carbuncles worth a great treasure, for at night they cast such a luminous brightness that a hundred knights and ladies could very honorably use it to see by. After the cage was covered, they had not gone too far when they saw looming to the right a very imposing castle. The knight turned to the Beauty Without Villainy to ask if she knew to whom the castle belonged and if they could safely spend the night there, and she assured him that they could. They had not progressed much further when the lord of the castle came toward them on a very richly caparisoned palfrey. After they exchanged greetings, the lord of the castle very politely asked them if they would be pleased to lodge that night with him, since it was the hour for it. The Knight of the Parrot and the Beauty Without Villainy both agreed to grant him his wish, for which the lord thanked them greatly. But why should I make a long story of all this? The lord of the castle caused them to be made comfortable and had all their needs attended to as soon as they told him what they wished done.

In the morning, at break of day, the parrot began to speak in song, saying: "Sire, wake up now, for the day has come in which you will receive high honor!" Those within the castle marveled greatly at the voice they heard so sweetly and clearly. As soon as he heard this, the Knight of the Parrot got up, as did the Beauty Without Villainy; the dwarf had already saddled their horses so they could ride away from there. After they had commended their host to God, they mounted and rode off in the direction indicated by the Beauty Without Villainy, straight to the lands belonging to the lady who was a fay of wisdom, whom the Knight of the Parrot intended to aid. The parrot accompanied them all the while by singing pleasant and amorous songs.

When high noon passed, they heard before them a great noise made by people fleeing before a knight who was laying waste to the whole district. It was the very same knight on whose account the Beauty Without Villainy had gone to court seeking aid for her lady and against whom she was leading the Knight of the Parrot. It was not long at all before they saw approaching on horseback far off the most hideous knight who could ever be seen, causing a commotion around him as great as any storm. They saw people fleeing before him in every direction to such an extent that when the dwarf and the damsel spotted the knight, they were also struck with fear and started to flee. And no wonder too; for his horse was as big as an elephant, and the knight was as large as was needed to ride upon it. He approached, shouting so loudly that the mere sound of his yelling caused the rocks, trees, and the earth to resound all around him. When the parrot saw his dwarf and the damsel fleeing, he believed that he was about to die there, and so he cried: "Dwarf, do not leave me here to die! Remember the high honors which have come to you in foreign lands because of me!" But the dwarf wished only to escape, he in one direction and the damsel in another, for they were so overwhelmed by great fear that they felt they could not manage to stay together.

When the parrot lost his dwarf and could not see where he was any more, he began to entreat the knight to let him fly out of his cage in order to find a high perch on some tree so that the devil could not kill him. But the knight laughed and cried: "Parrot, have you so quickly forgotten the song which you began a while back? Remember it and do not be afraid; for we shall both sing it again tonight, if it pleases God, in our lodgings."

While both the parrot and his knight were speaking in this manner, there approached the creature who was the most hideous thing that mortal man could ever see! When the knight saw him coming, he crossed himself and commended himself to God and then went forward bravely to meet him, his shield at his neck and his lance in hand; and so they lunged head-on against each other without speaking a word. The Knight of the Parrot struck him with such great force that he pierced both the shield and the hauberk and put a part of the wood of his lance in his body. But the devil struck back at him with such a blow that, were he not protected by his shield, which made the blow glance off, the knight would have been in danger; but God protected him from it. The parrot, when he saw his knight survive the first encounter, was much encouraged, although he still did not feel like singing.

After the knights completed the first charge of the joust, they unsheathed their swords and struck mighty blows on each other's helm. The Knight of the Parrot was trained in fencing and knew how to turn and hold his guard, as he proved there, for he fought without a shield with the greatest monster ever seen anywhere. Know then that he was so noble that every blow he planned landed on the helmet of his opponent. Also, the Knight of the Parrot took great care to keep his own helmet safe, for he knew only too well he would surely die if the other struck even one blow upon it. When he hit his opponent's shield, the Knight of the Parrot saw hot, red blood gush forth, which made him marvel greatly, for he was not aware of having struck anything other than wood or iron. Again, he was careful to take aim and strike the arm that wielded the sword, and he measured the thing well and dealt the knight many arm blows. So the dangerous battle lasted two-thirds of the afternoon until sunset. At that time the Knight of the Parrot wounded that devil, for he cut off his right arm, which was holding his sword. Immediately, the parrot began to sing: "Who is it who has delivered me from the fear I have known?"

When the Knight of the Parrot heard him, he began laughing and felt encouraged, and continued to strike his opponent on the helm, shield, and hauberk. From each place where he struck, there poured out so much blood that it was a marvel to see how the knight could endure it all. Finally, that one was so weakened by this loss of blood and the loss of his right arm that he could hold the field no longer, and so he fled, as fast as his horse could carry him, toward his stronghold. The Knight of the Parrot gave him hot pursuit, striking him wherever he could, and so greatly weakened him further that he could no longer hold himself erect, but fell to the ground like one in the grips of death; and he fought with death so hard that, if the Knight of the Parrot had not pulled back a bit, this last struggle could have been far worse than the first. But prudent judgment was worth more then than prowess, and so the Knight of the Parrot reined in his horse and fell back a little, since he saw that his opponent could not get up again. From a distance, he observed a feat that was one of the greatest marvels in the world, for the opposing knight ferociously cut down more than twenty trees, so big that four oxen would have had their work cut out to drag the thinnest away; and the knight moaned so loudly all the while that he caused the entire land about him to resound. The palfrey of the parrot, frightened by the murmurings of the trees, went straight over to the destrier of his knight, but the adversary expired and was dead.

When the Knight of the Parrot saw his opponent no longer moving, he went over to study the workmanship of his harness. He found him astride his horse, just as he was when alive, and studied his arms, which looked smoked and black. After he had looked him all over, he took hold of his helmet in order to see how light it was, inasmuch as it was so huge, and he found it to be hot to the touch. Afterwards, when he wanted to remove the helmet, he was amazed to find that he could not do so. After examining it well, he discovered that the helmet was held fast to the head and that everything was all of one piece—that the head was made like a helmet all round, and the leather on the ouside was black and very much like the skin of a snake. The hauberk was also the same, except that it seemed to be made of mail on the outside, just like any other hauberk. The Knight of the Parrot studied the dead knight so carefully that he soon discovered that the knight, destrier, hauberk, helmet, shield, sword, and lance were all one and the same thing. He marveled greatly at what had happened to the knight and wondered where he came from. After he looked the body all over, he turned to the direction where he first had seen the knight come from, chasing the palfrey that carried his parrot. He discovered the trail of the Beauty Without Villainy, and he rode off furiously, both he and his parrot, for fear that night would overtake them.

They had scarcely gone far along the road when they met four knights on four good destriers, armed at all points, whom the gracious fay had dispatched to assist the Knight of the Parrot. These recognized him, for the dwarf and the damsel, whom they had encountered, had told them at length about his adventure and the palfrey that carried the cage in which the parrot was to be found. When they came up to him, they greeted him gaily and with great honor, as he did them. Then they asked him about the huge knight, and he told them about the adventure from start to finish. No one could ever tell you about the joy and happiness the knights displayed when they heard that the wicked knight was dead. After they had sufficiently disported, they asked the Knight of the Parrot to lead them to where the battle had taken place, so that they could see the one who had been so feared by the people of the district.

After they had their fill of looking around, they left the place happy and joyous, and made their way toward the city. They were quite amazed that this young knight was endowed with such courage and prowess. They asked the Knight of the Parrot to please allow one of their number to go on ahead of them to bring the news to the lady. He told them they could do as they wished. So one of them made a dash for the city, riding as fast as his horse could carry him. On reaching the city, he found his lady in the middle of the palace and recounted the adventure of the Knight of the Parrot from start to finish. No one can ever describe how happy the lady was from it all! Quickly she had silken draperies, all very richly worked in gold, taken from her chambers, and she commanded the palace to be decked out with them. Then she mounted on a mule, fully caparisoned and covered by a rich silken cloth. She ordered the barons, knights, ladies, and damsels to mount also, and commanded that all the people of the city should go out in a procession with a cross to meet the best knight in all the world, who had delivered them from the knight who had ravaged the land and its people. She commanded that all the bells of the city should ring, and everyone did as she bade, and more. They all streamed out of the city, on horse and on foot, and they had not gone too far when they met the Knight of the Parrot and his party, who were giving him much praise.

When the Knight of the Parrot saw the procession, he dismounted before the cross; but the noise of the instruments, and the bravos and gaiety were so great that not even the thunder of God could have been heard then. In order to do him more honor, the lady herself dismounted, as did the others, and they all said with one voice: "Well met are you, who today have proved to be the best knight that may be found in all the world of chivalry!" He thanked the lady and the assembly for all the honor they were bestowing on him. Then the lady remounted, as did all the barony, and they made their way toward the city with great joy and delight. The Knight of the Parrot and the lady rode side by side—the lady on her mule and the Knight of the Parrot on a palfrey white as snow, which the lady had given him when she had greeted him. At his order, a squire carried his helmet and shield while another led his destrier on his right.

In the Amorous City, the feasting and the clamor of both the humble and the great was so spectacular that no one could ever hope to describe it to you. None could get their fill of looking at the Knight of the Parrot; in great joy, they had him dismount at the foot of the palace, and they led him up into the hall where they removed his armor with honor. When they had relieved him of his arms, they dressed him in a cloak made of costly silk cloth which the lady had sent to him. Then the Beauty Without Villainy came before him, together with two other damsels of her company, and obtained his pardon, after she very sweetly pleaded with him, for having fled with the dwarf. They conversed with one another until it was time to take supper.

While the Beauty Without Villainy was able to make her peace with the knight, the dwarf was not able to do the same with the parrot; for as soon as the knight had dismounted, the dwarf ran to serve the parrot, just as he was accustomed to, but the parrot did not want anything to do with him or his service, telling him: "Flee from here, you bad, cowardly dwarf, for you are not in the least worthy to touch me, nor do I desire to be served by you any longer." He cried this aloud again and again so that all those who heard it spoke about nothing else, although they did not understand the reason for this strife. The parrot then cried out even more loudly for his lord, so that the knight had to hear him: "Where is the best knight in all the world? Why does he not have me carried around with him? Does he not know that I lost my dwarf today in the forest?" The knight finally heard him and ordered a young squire to bring the parrot to him, which was done immediately. When the parrot came before his knight, he was so joyful that everyone was pleased. They were also comforted by what he said about his dwarf and about the Beauty Without Villainy; and his knight so pleaded with the parrot that he forgave the other his ire and bad temper.

Then the Beauty Without Villainy entered her chamber to find waiting the beautiful fay to whom all knowledge is given, to tell her about the praise which the parrot paid his new master and lord. Then she described the worth of her knight, recounting all that she had seen on the road; and in this way, she caused him to be more highly esteemed and served. But there was no need for this; for the lady had hardly seen him when love for him had entered her heart so deeply that she could not think of anything else, except to do all those things that might be his pleasure and will. When supper was ready, the tables were set throughout all the chambers of the palace, and beautifully white, very richly worked tablecloths were placed upon them, together with bread, wine, salt, and knives. When the water had been poured, they sat the Knight of the Parrot down at the most beautiful place in the hall, and all the barony of the Amorous City sat around him. The ladies were seated throughout the chambers in great comfort and delight, for a master of the viol, who knew how to perform very well indeed, sang them a courtly lay in a voice of very good tone that was in harmony with the viol. On the other side of the hall, there was such a feast and such light that no one could ever describe it; for the four carbuncles of the parrot's cage threw off such splendor throughout the palace that it was a miracle to behold. The parrot himself was so clever in describing in song all the deeds his knight had done, from the time he had boldly won him, that it gave heart to the knights who heard it. Such were the joy and delight of those who took supper there at court.

I do not wish to spend time in describing all the dishes they had. They supped happily, and after they had finished and the tables were removed and they had washed their hands, they all began to speak about what the parrot had said about his knight. Then the lady came down from her chamber into the hall, as did the Beauty Without Villainy, and well over twenty other ladies and damsels. The knights all got up when they saw their lady approach with her followers. She sat down on a cloth of silk that was spread in the middle of the hall in front of the Knight of the Parrot. The others sat down around the hall, some here, others there with the knights, and they spoke about love and whatever else pleased them. The lady looked very hard and long at the Knight of the Parrot to discover how his eyes, mouth, forehead, chin, and the rest of his body were made and was so eager in doing this that she did not tire of looking at him. After she had looked him all over very well, she said: "May good fortune come to the land where such knights are born, from whom we have such joy and comfort! And may good fortune also be given to him who made you a knight, for such a calling is very well exercised by you! And may the mother have good fortune and be blessed who carried such a child, who is considered the best knight in all the world, as his deeds well prove!"

When the Knight of the Parrot heard himself thus praised by the lady, he thanked her most kindly for it, and answered: "My lady, I would be, for your sake, the best knight in all the world, for you seem to me to be truly the most beautiful and the most courteous lady ever fashioned by Nature. And were I the best in all the world, so would I serve and honor you as the best lady in all the world, and most willingly I would do this before all else; but I have within me so little goodness that no lady as beautiful or as courteous as yourself should accept my service."

"What?" said the lady. "You have no lady?"

"In truth, no."

"And why," said she, "have you not wanted to take one?"

"Lady," he answered, "I will take none except her who has pierced my heart, if I may have her, to whom my heart is given over to do all her bidding."

"My good lord," said the lady,"who is this then? Tell me who, if you please."

He answered: "Lady, it is she who speaks to me of my death."

"Of your death? And why so?" asked the lady.

"Because she wants me to tell her that which will cause my death."

While they were conversing thus, the parrot had well understood what they were saying—for no one might ever move his lips so cleverly that he could not learn what was being said—and so he began to sing a lay of love so sweetly that the lady broke off speaking to the knight to listen and note in her heart what the parrot was recounting. The parrot sang right up to bedtime. Then the lady ordered the wine to be brought and served. When they had all drunk deeply, the lady retired to her chamber, as did her followers, and all her barony, who each went his separate way. Then a beautiful and rich bed was made in the hall itself for the Knight of the Parrot, who went to it willingly, like one who had worked enough that day. After he got into bed, his parrot began to tell him the story of an adventure he knew very well, about a lady who was imprisoned wrongly, and he told the tale so sweetly that it moved the knight to great pity.

In such fashion, the Knight of the Parrot soon fell asleep and rested all night long. In the morning, when the breaking day was being greeted by the songs of birds, the Knight of the Parrot was dressed in robes richly worked in gold that the lady sent to him. After he was dressed and adorned, as were the other people of the court and the city, both humble and great, the lady ordered horses saddled and commanded all the barons, as well as every lady and maiden, to mount, for she wished to go and see the body of the knight who had given trouble for a very long time to both her people and land. With great joy and mirth, each and every one of them mounted and very joyously cantered off to the sound of viols and harps. The Knight of the Parrot and the Lady of the Blonde Hair, for such was the name of the fay who had jurisdiction over the Amorous City, rode out in front of all the others, talking about anything that pleased their fancy; and the other knights and ladies followed them very sweetly singing *chansons doubles* in a low key. They all continued riding until they came to the place where the battle had occurred, right up to the spot where the knight was lying dead on the ground. But why should I prolong the story? They looked and searched all around until they all agreed that it was the most horrible thing that could ever be seen the whole world over. Then the lady commanded her seneschal to have the body skinned and the hide brought to the Amorous City and put in a place where it could always be viewed and known to all as a marvel; all of which was done according to her instructions. When the body was skinned, only one hide was to be had from both horse and knight. Nor was this something to be amazed at, for the body was all of a piece. Anyone may find things like this written in the book known as *Mapemundi*, wherein is described a monster who has its home in the sea and is named the Fish-Knight, who seems to have a mount, helmet, hauberk, lance, shield, and sword, but who is made into one being, just like this dead knight.

Afterwards, they traced the path the knight had made when he entered the district, and discovered that his trail led straight to the sea. When they reached the shore and could go no further, they stopped and looked about, both up and down, some towards the sea, and some towards land. Not too much later, they saw waves rising in the sea that seemed they could touch the sky. Then they heard the wind pick up, and it began to thunder so loudly that they all believed themselves lost. This storm lasted for a long time. When it finally passed, they heard shouting, crying, and moaning, but they did not know who was doing this, nor could they hear anything but the crying, shouting, and the rustlings of the reeds. So they wondered greatly about what this all could mean. There were some who said that it was coming from the clan of the Fish-Knight, while others claimed that the noise was made by devils who were exercising their powers. What one person said was not at all accepted by other persons, so that no one really understood where the truth of the matter was to be found. After they had stayed there a while, they all turned back toward the city.

At that point, they saw riding toward them a damsel who was crying and shouting for all she was worth, which made her quite hoarse; she rushed toward them, hitting her hands and twisting her fingers, and tearing her bright and shining hair, and comporting herself like an enraged woman. When she got close to them, she dismounted from her mule and, crying very loudly, demanded: "Where is the Knight of the Parrot?" With the Lady of the Blonde Hair at his side, the knight rode up to her very quickly to learn what she wanted and what was the matter. The parrot cried out to his dwarf to bring him up to his lord so that he could also hear what the damsel was saying. When the damsel saw the Knight of the Parrot, she fainted right on the spot. As soon as the knight saw her lying on the ground, he got down from his horse in order to pick her up. When she recovered from her swoon, she said: "My good sweet lord, I beg you, in the name of God, to have pity on me!"

He asked her why he should do this, and she responded by saying she would not tell him anything at all, nor would she budge from that place, until he promised to give her his aid and assistance. She then pleaded with him so sweetly that he granted her wish and said he would do everything he could for her, which made the damsel get on her knees before him and recount her plight: "My good sweet lord, the fame of your chivalry, which is known in every place, moved me to search for you until I finally found you at last, thanks be to God! Nor have I looked for you for myself, but on behalf of the best damsel that can be found anywhere and to whom the greatest honor should be shown, but who is instead imprisoned most grievously and unjustly, as I shall now explain to you. The fact is that the damsel about whom I am speaking is none other than the daughter of King Beauvoisin of Ile Fort, whose name is Flor de Mont. Now her father was mortally wounded in a tournament, and since he had no other son or daughter but Flor de Mont, he entrusted her, together with all his lands, to one of his marshals who had served him well during his lifetime. When the marshal got his hands on the kingdom, he made all the barons do homage to him and made them promise him Flor de Mont as his wife. They did this because he was a mighty man-of-arms; later, he took hold of all the castles and fortresses, except for one high keep which is very strong and beautiful. This keep was held by the queen and her daughter, as it is still, with the help of a very small number of people, against the marshal, who seeks to wed the princess by force. Because of the great reputation you have of possessing chivalry, loyalty, courtesy, prudence, and mercy, I came to search you out in great peril of losing my life. For had I been discovered by the marshal's people, all the world's riches would not have been enough to save me. They would have delivered me up to shameful martyrdom, but I will never return there, except with your help." She continued: "Do you understand now what you have promised me?" He answered that he did indeed. When she asked him what he believed it was, he told her that he had promised to do everything within his power to fulfill her wishes.

"And so I required," she answered, "on behalf of Flor de Mont, who sent me here to you, that you come with me directly to the keep, to the place where she is with her mother, and liberate them from the prison in which they find themselves so unjustly."

"Damsel," the Knight of the Parrot said, "I will do your bidding since I have promised you I would, and I shall be very happy if I can bring to pass what your lady wishes. Now then, mount, and let us go with these people to the Amorous City, for in this way we shall begin our journey." All of which was done as he told her. All there praised the Knight of the Parrot for having promised to go to the damsel's rescue, except for the Lady of the Blonde Hair. Instead of sharing everyone's opinion, she was so upset when she heard of the knight's promise to go off with the damsel that she thought she would go mad with grief. Nonetheless, she dissembled her feelings so well that none of her people suspected anything, and accordingly, she showed herself even more prettily to the Knight of the Parrot than she had done previously. And with good reason too, for he well deserved it.

Thus they all rode along together until they reached the city, where they dismounted in front of the palace. As soon as they had done this, the ruling lady had the cry made for a tournament, to be held eight days hence, with the rule that whoever earned the prize of the tournament would be permitted to kiss her once out of love before the entire assembly of barons, and also that she would hold him as her friend for an entire year. She then turned and entreated the damsel of Flor de Mont to stay with her and the Knight of the Parrot until the conclusion of the tournament, which the damsel had to agree to do, much against her wishes.

All the barons were highly delighted when they heard that the lady had promised her kiss to whoever would prove to be the most worthy of the tournament, for everyone believed that she would take as her husband the one who won her kiss, and so everyone equipped himself as best he could with beautiful chargers and the finest of arms. From all over there came barons and knights to the tourney in order to have the love of the lady, and the lady's love caused each one to believe in his heart that he would be the best knight of the whole tournament and that he would win the kiss before all the assembled lords; truly, however, only one of them could win it. During the tournament, the Lady of the Blonde Hair and the Knight of the Parrot enjoyed each other's company greatly, dining often together, both in chambers and in the gardens. The day before the tournament was to take place, all the barony of the land assembled together in the field outside the Amorous City. The lady had already ordered that a stand be built on the site in the meadow where she and her ladies would stay to view the tourneying and, in this way, spur on towards more bravery and daring any knight who saw her. On this very day, the eve of the tournament, the lady prepared a bed of silken sheets with precious gems of great brilliance in a room craftily built by cunning artists so that any who peered into it from the outside could not understand why it was so white and bright, nor could look at it except with much trouble. Inside, it was high and bright, made with vaulting, with all manner of gems displayed on the ceiling of the room and fashioned into beasts, birds, flowers, all explaining stories of ancient deeds. In the middle of the room there was a gem carved in the shape of a falcon in whose beak there hung a thin gold chain a whole span long, on which was fixed a carbuncle which at night gave forth such great splendor that the room seemed to be all ablaze. Within the falcon's breast there was a glass vial filled with balm that gave off such a great odor from the falcon's beak, and in such quantity, that the entire room was so filled with it that all those who were there were led to believe the place was a Paradise. Moreover, the falcon held a marble table in his talons which was easily as long as an ell and as wide as a span, and which was gilded over and had letters engraved on it so that anyone could easily read them.

The Lady of the Blonde Hair informed the Knight of the Parrot to come and speak to her in that room, and he came there most willingly and happily, for it was what he most desired to do in the whole world. When she saw him coming, she went to greet him at the threshold, and smiling, took his bare hand, and gave him a good welcome; he bowed before her very sweetly while looking at her lovingly. Then they sat down together on the bed, looking at one another in such a way as to steal one another's hearts, and they began to speak of those things which most pleased them. "Sire," said the lady, "Love has stricken me to the heart and commands that I do everything according to his dictates, but I do not know if you would do likewise."

"My sweet lady," said the knight,"I do not know if Love has touched you for me or for someone else, unless you tell me. But if Love advises that you favor me with some good or other, he does not do it because I can command him in any way—indeed I have not as yet done so much for him that I am worthy enough for him to repay me; he does it through courtesy and by his mercy, and for this I have placed my heart entirely at his disposal and I pray him, night and day, that he make me do and say whatever may be his pleasure."

"Sire," said the lady, "what it is that you pray to Love? Do you pray that he may teach you how to speak to me?"

"My lady," said he, "I pray him that he may turn your heart toward me so that you take pity for what I feel for you."

"My heart, my lord, by faith! I do not have it," said she, "at all."

"Who then has it, lady?" asked the Knight of the Parrot. The lady did not answer him and instead went to lean against him, all the while fixing him with a look so lovingly that he was set afire, and he embraced her with such ardor that they fell onto the bed, and they kissed and pressed one another against each other's breast, as they wished, and without anyone to forbid them. In truth, I believe the lady would have lost her chaste name then, but for a damsel whom they heard approaching the chamber door, and so they got up and were not discovered. Then the lady asked the knight if he knew how to read. When he answered yes, she said, "Well then read the writing that is engraved on that table there above in the falcon's talons."

He did this. When he finished, the lady asked him about the meaning of the writing. "Lady," he said, "it reads thus: 'You, sir knight, who is below me, give up happily whatever will be asked of you by the lady with whom you speak.'"

"Sire," said the lady, "would it please you to grant what the writing says? Then you will have my heart ready to do your bidding."

"Lady," said the knight, "there is nothing in all the world I would not do in exchange for this promise."

"How can I be certain of this?"

"My lady," said the knight, "truly, it is so. Tell me what you wish and I will do it if I can."

"My lord," she answered, "I wish you to go for me to the tournament tomorrow and to serve me there as the worst knight to be found in all the world, for I wish your bad reputation to be known throughout the world, balanced against the high esteem you now enjoy."

"God's mercy!" answered the knight; "ask instead that I serve you tomorrow as the best knight before making me serve you as the worst!"

"That is not what I wish at all!" said the lady. "Indeed, I insist that you keep the promise you have given me."

"In truth," said the knight, "I will, since I have promised you to do so, although it would give me more pleasure if you would permit me to serve you as the best, rather than the worst, knight. But let it not be said that I wish to do anything other than what may please you; for no one can better serve his lord than by doing whatever may please and delight him." With this, he quit the chamber and very pensively entered the great hall. And despite everything, he put on such a display of good cheer that no one noticed anything was awry. Then the parrot began to sing very sweetly to his lord: "You will dispose of the anger you are feeling with such great honor that no one will ever know about it." All those within hearing of these words were greatly amazed, except the knight himself, who felt reassured by what the parrot said; and taking heart from the parrot's words, he rested the better for them the whole night through.

On the morning of the tournament day, the Lady of the Blonde Hair awoke and adorned herself very richly with a dress and mantle of linen, white as the snow, which appeared tinted and was well suited to her fine complexion. Its mantle was so light that it could easily be carried in an alms purse without lining which was made of costly satin, richly worked in gold and precious stones. All dressed up and turned out in this fashion, she and her ladies and young maidens went to the tournament site outside the city. Once there, they went up into the stand the lady had ordered set up in the middle of the field, so that they could more easily see the tournament and so that those taking part in it would act more bold and hearty than they otherwise might. When they all settled down in the stand, the knights broke from the lists and spurred toward one another, and all together caused such a stir and such a great noise of splitting lances that it was marvelous to behold. After breaking their lances, they drew out their swords, and so commenced a very fierce and dangerous struggle. The Knight of the Parrot was very closely watched by the ladies and damsels, and although no one's lance had touched him, he was nonetheless thrown to the ground. When those on his side saw him thrown down, they raised him up, and he allowed himself to be struck, taken, and led before each and every knight without putting up much of a fight at all. What more can I tell you? He showed this day such poor knightly prowess that all who were there at the tournament said that there never was seen such a poor figure of a knight as this one in this tournament, all of which caused them, one and all, to marvel how he could have vanquished the Fish-Knight, and which moved them to say to one another: "He must have killed him by some enchantment or other." And they said that if he really knew magic, he would not, for anything in the world, permit himself to be so meanly shamed before such a noble company. Several of the court were much aggrieved because of the courtesy they had perceived in him. When the tournament was over, Count Doldays of Chastel d'Amours, who for a long time had loved the Lady of the Blonde Hair (for whom he had struck down the Knight of the Parrot twice that day) believed he had won the prize of her kiss and that she would hold him as her friend for a year's time. So he boasted before all the noble assembly and the Lady of the Blonde Hair too that he was the best knight in all the world, for there could be found no knight in that place who, man to man, could prove otherwise, all of which no one there challenged.

When the Knight of the Parrot saw this person vaunt himself so, and no one opposed him, he said: "If it pleases my lady, tomorrow, at the conclusion of the tournament, I shall show you all too clearly that you are not the best knight in the world." When Count Doldays heard himself being contradicted by the Knight of the Parrot, he said: "You poor simpering knight, who today have been struck down by all the knights in the tournament, and by myself twice, how do you act so bold as to speak to me about chivalry?"

"Indeed," said the Knight of the Parrot, "I say the truth, and if it may please my lady, I shall surely show this to you tomorrow!" After this,

Count Doldays came forward to give his pledge to the Lady of the Blonde Hair, who together with all the others had come down from the stand because of the argument between Count Doldays and the Knight of the Parrot. When she saw he was offering his gage against the Knight of the Parrot, the lady took it and gave it to four barons of Count Doldays' clan. Then she said that he had committed great folly and great brashness in saying villainous things to the person who finally killed the knight whom neither he nor any other dared even look at. She turned and asked the Knight of the Parrot: "Sire, who will take up your gage?"

"Lady," he answered, "your sweet mercy and my parrot."

"By all means," said the lady, "and very willingly, if it pleases the parrot."

At that point, the parrot began to cry out loudly to his knight: "Sire, is it your wish that I die?"

"Parrot," answered the knight, "that is not my wish at all."

"Lady," continued the parrot, "know surely, by this covenant, that tomorrow at the tournament my knight will prove himself in such a manner to Count Doldays that the count will repent what he has said to you."

"Why? Was he not at the tournament today?" said the lady to the parrot.

"No, my lady."

"Where was he then?"

"In prison."

"And where was this?"

"In this field where we are now."

"In prison?" asked the lady. "How can this be? I have seen him this day gallop about the field without any guards around him; what prison was he in then, parrot? God help you, tell me now!"

"Lady, he was in the worst prison that was ever known to man, for he had stripped himself of his valor."

"Why and for what purpose?" asked the lady.

"For the worst and most villainous command," said the parrot, "that was ever given to such a knight."

"Who gave it to him?"

"You know it was a bad person; for never would any good person have given him such a miserable order."

"Who was this person?" asked the lady.

The parrot answered: "Please let me be, for what is going to be said here will be more eagerly listened to than what I have already said."

"If you do not say it," said the lady, "I will tomorrow do all that I please with you when your knight is beaten."

"Lady," said the parrot, "I shall live a long time before a knight defeats him!"

They broke off their parley then to return to the city. The Knight of the Parrot was greatly shamed by his poor performance at the tournament that day and by what Count Doldays of Chastel d'Amours had told him. But just the same, he took heart in the belief that he would be avenged on the morrow. And his parrot continued singing good and pleasant songs to him in order to encourage him. When they arrived at the city, the Lady of the Blonde Hair and the Knight of the Parrot went into the great hall together with all the others, but she was not at all calm nor composed; for Love caused her to blanch, and so troubled and afflicted her because of the Knight of the Parrot that she could not stay still, but got up and went into one of her chambers where she had spoken with the Knight of the Parrot the day before; and since she felt unsettled, she did not want anyone to accompany her. Then she began to fight with Love in the following way: Love assaulted her and told her the Knight of the Parrot was the most handsome, best, and most loyal knight to be found in all the world, and that he was a most faithful lover, for if he did not love her loyally, he never would have subjected himself to the great shame he knew at the tournament. Love praised him so very much that she herself said she would truly not be able to reward him for what he had done for love of her, nor would she ever be able to repay him honor in sufficient exchange for the dishonor he had received that day for her sake. Thus she said she would send for him that very night and would abandon herself completely to him. But then she also told herself he would not want her any more at all. But Love told her that she would do well to keep to her resolve, and that she was so beautiful and so fair that never would any knight in all the world, no matter how valiant, refuse to put his life in peril for the chance to kiss her once upon the mouth. Still, she insisted he would not come for this; for she had placed him at her disposal to do her bidding yesterday, and he would have done so, "were it not for a girl who came upon us."—"For this reason," said Love, "he will come even more willingly; for he has known the sweetness of the kiss and the embrace, and because of this is so greatly in your power that there is nothing in the whole world he will refuse you, if you but command him to do it for you."—"Ah, for me!" said the lady. "The brave figure I cut for him yesterday has done me in; for he has stolen my heart so much by the sweetness we knew together, that never shall I have it back while I live."— "But if you really do love him so," said Love, "why did you give him the order which caused him to win such dishonor that will be almost impossible for him to escape from?"—"I gave him the command," she answered, "in order to find out if he loved me faithfully or not. I believed he would go and do that much for me. I shall be sad and sorrowful for as long as I live for this deed of mine. If I could amend that act in any way, I would do it more quickly than when I commanded him, and if I thought he would come to me, I would send for him. But I do not believe he would want to come, for I could not have given him a worse command than the one I gave him yesterday."—"The fact is," Love answered, "there is no other way his lot could be made worse; nonetheless, in no way will this deter him from coming to you. Inasmuch as this is possible, I advise you to go to him and show him good cheer with the most alluring comportment you are capable of. Also tell him: 'Sir, I love you more than myself, just as you have loved me more than yourself. I am quite convinced of this since today you have done deeds out of love for me which you never would have done for yourself alone; instead, you would have died, and so I must belong only to you for all the days of my life. I wish you to come to my chamber, and also to be more valiant in tomorrow's tournament against Count Doldays, who has made such shameless boasts.' Then lead him," Love continued, "to your chamber and allow him to use you as he wants."

Why do I prolong the telling of all this to you? All that Love advised, the lady did; for she led the knight to her chamber and acted in the most enticing way that ever a woman can show a man, and was completely disposed to follow the dictates of his will. When the Knight of the Parrot saw that he could do whatever he wished with the lady, without any restraints, he grabbed her by her tresses and threw her down to the floor, saying: "Most evil whore, full of every filthy wile, take this and that! See how well I follow your orders! Today you stripped me of my reputation and honor, for which I shall be shamed all the days of my life. Abandon yourself to me so that I can take my pleasure from you, and let you thus judge me as the worst knight in the whole world. It would have been better for you if you had taken me for the best knight of all. Now I want to render my service as the most vile knight in all the world, as is fitting for you." Then he dragged her by the hair all through the chamber, hitting her and kicking her, and she yelled to him then in tears, "God's mercy!" entreating him to have pity on her. She lamented and did this so softly that she could not be heard either by those in the hall or by her damsels in the other chambers. After the knight had hit and kicked her well, he dropped her and left her chamber and entered the hall, joining the knights and nobles who were scattered all over the place, playing at gaming tables and at checkers, and they received him joyfully. He put on as good a face as possible, so that they would not suspect him of being angry about anything.

Shame-ridden and greatly angry was the Lady of the Blonde Hair when the knight left her. Still, so that no one might learn the state she was in, as best she could, she wiped away the tears streaming down her face, redid her hair, and said to herself: "Alas, miserable fool that I am! How shamed I have become because of a strange, unfortunate knight whose name I do not even know, except that he is the most outrageous knight in the whole world!" But when she repeated this in her heart, she said that he was not at all outrageous, but was courteous, brave, worthy, loyal, indeed braver than any other knight to be found in the world. "If he did not have great courtesy and great loyalty also, he would not have followed my bidding, as he did, which caused him such shame that no other knight in the world would have endured it, not for any amount of wealth, nor for any fine words. Then following that, he received as much shame today. If he was not as well-schooled as he is, he would not have suffered what he did from the hands of Count Doldays, and if he was not more proud and more brave than any other person, he would not have dared touch me the way he did.

"But then," she continued, "he was very foolhardy to have struck me; indeed, he committed great folly; for had he not struck me, he would have had from me whatever he wanted and would have been proclaimed a rich and powerful king." Then she said once more to herself: "He paid me the greatest courtesy that a baron ever did, for he paid me well for my baseness. Alas, wretch that I am! Would it not have served me better to have had him obey me as the best knight rather than the worst? Surely, yes; for everyone would have said: 'It is good that this one should have such a lady as ours.' He would have pleased everyone on account of his prowess and courtesy, and it would not have displeased me, for he is fair and attractive. Alas, I do not know what I can do. I know he is the most noble and brave man in all the world. Today, because he has been a vile knight at my mean bidding, he has also demonstrated the greatest nobility ever shown anywhere; for he did not lower himself to take from me what he could well have had without opposition. Wretch, what have I said? I should have given him a better reward for the great pains he undertook for me when I gave him my order, for which I shall die. Ah, God, good father Jesus Christ! Counsel me now by your grace! For the sin which is within me has shamed me today. The devil has me so in his thrall that he caused me to do what will shame me if you do not come to my aid. If the Knight of the Parrot goes off without making peace with me, I will die from the shame he has given me today, if anyone else should learn of it. What have I said? Shall I conceal it from him who has treated me worse than any lady in the world? Surely, I would first have him torn apart, so that he will not be able to brag about this, no matter where he may go!" After this, she told herself: "What will the people of this land say who have seen all the honors you have given him and who know what he has done to you? They will say: 'Our lady gives a fine reward to him who has killed the Fish-Knight!' This would create a great scandal, and no one would then enter your service." Such was the mood she foundered in, not knowing what she would do about all this.

A bit later, she called to one of her ladies and told her to call the marshal, and when he came, she told him: "I want you to arm one hundred of the best knights of our city tomorrow, for I fear that when the Knight of the Parrot comes to the tournament, Count Doldays may conspire to have him killed. It would be too great a shame for me if the person who has delivered me from the Fish-Knight should be so betrayed at my court. And so I beg and command you to keep the Knight of the Parrot in your care from this moment on and to bring him to me when I ask you to do so. If you do not accomplish this, I will have you hanged together with all your relatives." All that the lady commanded, the marshal did, and the Knight of the Parrot was well aware of it, and so he was more deft, valiant, and brave.

Now we shall tell you what Count Doldays did as soon as he returned from the tournament after he had twice defeated the Knight of the Parrot. He held full and open court and dispensed gold, silver, palfreys, chargers, and everything, as much as he could, both of his own and others' goods, and made such great gifts that everyone considered him seized with madness. He did this because he was sure of winning the Lady of the Blonde Hair. Many who otherwise would not care to see him showed him kind smiles because of these gifts. But Love often quickly causes fools to believe in folly. I do not say that Love counsels one to do folly; but anguish, which the fool takes for love, causes him to say those things for which he is considered foolish. Since he does not know Love, he does such things at times which bring him neither honor nor good. Nor is this at all pleasing to Love; for Love requires suffering and control, of which Count Doldays had none at all. So, everyone rested the entire night until the next day, when the knights who were to go to the tournament mounted their chargers, armed and ready for the tournament. The Lady of the Blonde Hair and her damsels took their seats on their stand with the little turrets, bedecked in the most beautiful and most rich garments they had, in order to please the knights in the tournament even more.

When the ladies were seated in their places, the tournament was assembled, and there was such great noise at the breaking of the lances that not even God's thunder could be heard; for everyone was intent on the display of great prowess. But this was nothing next to what the Knight of the

Parrot did: every knight he hit with his lance was thrown to the ground, both the knight and horse in a heap, so that the place before him was cleared of everyone in a very short time. All gave way before him and cried out in one voice: "This knight has the devil in him!" and, "Who has ever seen such bold lance thrusts as these?" Indeed those whom he struck could not remount their horses and continue in the tournament. But despite all these words, the Knight of the Parrot did not let up; instead, he accomplished so much with his lance that there were none that day who did not look at him with amazement. When his lance split, he put his hand to his sword, which was called Chastiefol, and threw himself into the thickest part of the press, much like a hungry wolf among sheep. He struck out to the right and the left, and he did so much that, in a short space of time, all fled before him and there was no one who dared wait upon him.

Then the parrot told the Lady of the Blonde Hair: "My lady, my knight is presently in the tournament, and now you may see him if you wish. He is not now in prison; instead, I believe that he will release me easily from your pledge."

The speech of the parrot so stirred the knight that he did feats of arms that caused every baron, lady, and damsel to speak of him. All said: "What this knight did yesterday was done only to have his worth recognized, which he has fully demonstrated today." What more should I tell you besides this? No one there believed himself strong enough to brave the knight's blows; instead, those who were formerly ranged against him slyly slipped out of the lists, with the effect that the tournament was over before midday, so great was the fear all had of the Knight of the Parrot. When the tournament was won, the Knight of the Parrot came forward to the stand of the ladies and said: "My lady, I stand ready to acquit myself of your mercy, and my parrot from the pledge you have bound him to for my sake and against Count Doldays." What he said comforted the lady greatly, and she turned to the count and said: "My lord count, have you heard what this knight has said?"

"Lady," said the count, "indeed I have."

"And so? What do you say of this?"

"Lady, I say that I am ready to deliver up my hostages."

Then the lady told her marshal to have the place cleared, which was done according to her command. The knights then went off a bit to give themselves room to charge. They rode as hard toward one another as their spurs could prick their mounts, and they clashed with all their power and skill. Count Doldays, who was full of anger and malice, struck the Knight of the Parrot so hard that neither shield not hauberk was of any use to avoid his receiving a great wound on his left side; still, he did not budge from the saddle. The Knight of the Parrot struck Count Doldays between the shield and the hauberk so hard that his lance hit his body a good three times over and cast him down to the ground with his legs straight up, wounded, though not dead. When the Knight of the Parrot saw the count on the ground, he dismounted and went to him with his sword drawn in order to prevent him from getting up again. But the count was not frightened by this; instead, he cried for mercy from the Knight of the Parrot and pardon for the villainy he had done against him. When the Knight of the Parrot saw the count unable to move, he knew that for any knight who values anything, there is no honor in killing another knight who cries for mercy, and so he said: "I wish to have you know, my lord, that there are three types of fools in the world: one is he who so disesteems his enemy that he fears him neither too much nor too little. The next is he who says so many words that he is not believed, neither for the truth nor the lies. The third is he who gives so much of his goods to others that he saves nothing for his heir. My lord, had you known this lesson when you left the tournament yesterday, you would have done and said things that could still be done and spoken of, but I shall not say anything more about this. Since you beg for mercy, I am willing to show it to you on the condition that you place yourself at the mercy of the Lady of the Blonde Hair and quit me honorably from this contest."

The count agreed, as one who could do nothing less. Then he rose up as best he could and went to place himself at the mercy of the Lady of the Blonde Hair. Well would the lady have paid him back for the villainy he had shown the Knight of the Parrot, were it not for the Knight of the Parrot himself, who prevented her from doing this. So that the court would be full of joy and happiness, the lady granted the wish of the Knight of the Parrot. Then the count took his leave and rode off to his castle and had himself healed of the wound he had received in the battle.

Without dallying further, the Knight of the Parrot went up to the lady and before all the assembly of nobles kissed her as the best knight of the tournament. Afterwards, they all went back in joy and merriment to the city and stopped at the chief palace, which the lady had bedecked with silken cloth richly embroidered with gold. The tables were already set, and water was given to all as soon as they entered the hall. The lady sat down at the highest table and took the Knight of the Parrot by the right hand and sat him down between herself and the Duke de Valfort. But why should I prolong the story? When they had eaten their fill, in great ease and comfort, and the tables were taken away, there started up in the hall marvelous carols to the accompaniment of viols, harps and other instruments. The marshal, who wished to follow out the orders of his lady, had rugs and cloth of silk spread out so that any guest who wished to mingle and chat with any other one could do so to his heart's content. Then the Knight of the Parrot took the Lady of the Blonde Hair by the hand, and they sat by themselves on one side of the hall. They spoke so long to one another that they forgave the anger and maliciousness each had borne the other, and turned their thoughts entirely toward different wishes, earnestly desiring what the other wanted. They decided that night to explore their delight together, for which they eagerly awaited nightfall. On the other side of the hall, the ladies, damsels, and knights likewise were chatting about pleasant things, and each wished to take a friend, just as the Knight of the Parrot had done with their lady. They continued in this manner until supper was set, and they all supped with great joy. When it was time to go to bed, they all left the hall and went to their own lodgings.

The Lady of the Blonde Hair went to her chamber, together with two of her damsels, who put her to bed as daintily as they could. The Knight of the Parrot also found servants to assist him so that he would be bedded down to his heart's content. When everyone was asleep, the Knight of the Parrot got up, threw a mantle over his shoulders, and went to the door of the chamber in which the Lady of the Blonde Hair was lying, just as they had arranged the previous day. He found it unlocked, went inside, and when he locked the door behind him, smelled such a fragrance that it seemed to him that he had entered Paradise. He approached the bed of the lady, who was waiting for him with great desire, and she received him in her arms with great satisfaction and delight. Now the Knight of the Parrot knew great joy and delight with the Lady of the Blonde Hair. They delighted in each other and gave each other comfort and sport, just as young people are accustomed to do when they have the leisure and the place for it. Why should I go on describing this to you? They spent the best night that two young people could ever know, and they wished fervently that the night could last a year, which was not possible, of course.

A little before dawn, the Knight of the Parrot went back to his bed so that no one would know about this adventure. He fell asleep quickly, like one who had not slept the whole night through, and he slept practically up to the third hour [9 a.m.]. He got up then and dressed happily and joyously in marvelous spirits, like one who has received from the day and night all the delight and leisure which any mortal man could ever dream of putting into words. He remained in this kind of joy and contentment for a full eight days, during which time he thought of nothing else in the world except how to explore his delight with the Lady of the Blonde Hair so secretly that no one would notice it.

The day arrived when, after they had gotten up from dinner, the damsel of Flor de Mont came before the Knight of the Parrot and asked him, for God's sake, to remember her lady and to honor the promise he had made to her. This caused the Knight of the Parrot, who was ashamed at having delayed so long in going to the damsel's aid, to plead greatly with the Lady of the Blonde Hair to give him his leave. When she saw it could be no other way, she granted it, although it grieved her very much. The Knight of the Parrot then armed himself and mounted up on his charger, as did his dwarf and the parrot. The Lady of the Blonde Hair and all her court also mounted to give him escort, and they all rode off, according to the damsel's directions, conversing with one another for the distance of a league or more beyond the Amorous City. Then the Knight of the Parrot asked the lady and all her barony to return to the city. The lady took him by the hand and told him softly so that no one else could hear: "My good and sweet lord, will I ever see you again?"

"My lady," said the knight, "if it pleases God, you shall indeed."

"My good lord," she answered, "you are going, happy and joyous, to this damsel's country while I stay here sorrowful and in anguish, since you are carrying the heart from my bosom, and so I pray you, by God, to return as quickly as you can." The Knight of the Parrot commended the lady and all her barony to God, and gave them leave to turn back, and they for their part also commended him to God, praying Him to defend him from evil and entrapment, for he was the most courteous knight they had ever seen. So the Knight of the Parrot rode off with his party, thinking much about the lady; but the parrot diverted him from such thoughts by singing the best and sweetest songs to be heard the world over. But here we will leave off telling you about the Knight of the Parrot, and instead will tell you another story, inasmuch as it suits our business well here, and when it is fitting and proper, we shall easily know how to return to the matter at hand.

Now this story says that a certain duchess, who was called the Duchess d'Estrales, convened a tournament around her city, as well as all through very distant lands, for she wished that every worthy knight who heard tell of it would come to it, since it was her wish to marry the one who would best prove his mettle. A great many people assembled at the time when the tournament was to take place. News of the Knight of the Parrot was brought there also, and all agreed he was the best knight in the whole world. They spoke about him so much that the duchess and her damsels heard about it. When the duchess heard how he had put the Fish-Knight to death and freed the people of the Lady of the Blonde Hair, it penetrated her heart so deeply that she thought she would die if she did not have the knight. Therefore, she caused the tournament to be delayed almost a whole month, for she believed that Fortune would lead the Knight to her. As for the knights of the tournament, when they heard that the lady had delayed the contest for almost a month, they were not at all happy about it, for each one secretly hoped to have her as his wife. So they began to prance and jostle one another on their chargers in front of the duchess when they came to the duchess to take their leave. The duchess thanked them very much and prayed them to return at the appointed time, and they answered that they wished that the appointed time had already come. Then a great baron told the duchess: "Lady, if it pleases God, I shall be the best one at the tournament. I proclaim also I shall be not only the best of the whole court but also in the whole world. For I have never found a knight anywhere so strong and able to oppose me in the field who, seeing me grow angry, did not beg mercy of me. And so I pray you to command me as your own; for there is nothing in all the world which can be done by valor or by force that I would not do for you."

"Sir," said the duchess, "why do you say things that you can not do?"

"In truth, my lady, I would do just as I have said most willingly, as it may please you to prove at any and all times."

Again, the duchess said to him: "If you are as good a knight as you tell me, I grant you my love, but I wish you would freely fight a joust with the Knight of the Parrot, for all my damsels tell me that no one should speak of chivalry who has not jousted with the Knight of the Parrot, since he is the one who now carries the esteem of all the knights in the world."

"My lady, since this is your wish, I shall go and bring back to you his right hand as proof of battle, and thus you will know for certain that I have become the best knight in all the world." Then the knight called for his arms, which were the best to be found in all the world. For he had a hauberk not equalled anywhere, and no iron or steel could damage it. He also had a round helm which carried on the front visor-handle a jewel in the shape of a lady that gave forth such a great light that by night a good one hundred knights could be guided by it; and he had a very fine sword and a shield from the skin of a sea-fish. When he was armed with all these, he took leave of the duchess and set out on the road alone, on foot without iron boots; for he was so big that he could not find a horse that could carry him so armed.

After he left the duchess, he went searching for the Knight of the Parrot, and inquired about him from everyone he met. In the same way a famished lion goes after his prey, so the knight went looking for the Knight of the Parrot, and he asked after him so much that he heard he was to be found with the Lady of the Blonde Hair in the Amorous City. When he learned of this, so swift was his journeying that he arrived in the Amorous City the day after the Knight of the Parrot's departure. When he reached the palace, he asked: "Where is the Knight of the Parrot, who has made me so troubled?"

They told him he had gone off to aid a lady, and they showed him the road he had taken. So, without more ado, he took up the chase and persisted so much in his affair that where the Knight of the Parrot lodged one night, there the knight lodged the next; and he forced himself forward in the pursuit until he reached the Knight of the Parrot one evening about night-fall in a forest, under a large tree, together with his damsel, dwarf and parrot. When the Knight of the Parrot heard the great noise he was making in coming through the forest, he rose up armed to see what it was all about. The invader cried out loudly, "The Knight of the Parrot must not flee before the challenge of a lone knight," and the Knight of the Parrot answered him that he was not fleeing. "What?" said the other one; "you do not call this fleeing when I have chased you fifteen days and have only now caught up with you?"

"But why have you chased me?" asked the Knight of the Parrot. The other answered him that he wanted to do battle with him. When the Knight of the Parrot asked why, he told him he had promised to bring his right hand to a lady who had told him that, should he accomplish this, she would make him her husband and would give him her lands. Then the Knight of the Parrot told him: "You have made such a promise as will bring you, God willing, great grief and sorrow; nonetheless, I pray you, if indeed it can be done, that you put off this battle until I have concluded an adventure I have undertaken in the service of a damsel who is imprisoned most wrongfully and most unjustly. I promise you that as soon as I have brought it to an end, I shall be where you tell me."

To all of which, the other answered: "I do not wish this at all, since I have come to you to give you my challenge here and now." Without further ado, he ran up and struck him such a great blow on the helmet that he all but overwhelmed him. The Knight of the Parrot struck him back with such power that he clearly showed him he was not his friend and that he had every intention of protecting his right hand. From the outset, the battle the knights fought was thick indeed. They struck one another blows on the helmet, hauberk, and landed heavy blows, often and quickly, on both their shields, and did so for so long that they soon came to know one another's blows, for they did not strike at one another, except according to the rules of fencing. He who was battling with the Knight of the Parrot pranced about like a leopard when stalking the roebuck, and had the Knight of the Parrot not known how to guard himself well, he never could have lasted against him. They fought in this manner by the light of the jewel that was in the helmet of the Knight of the Parrot's enemy, until midnight and beyond, when the Knight of the Parrot struck such a blow on the nasal of the other's helmet that he cut off as much as he hit, so that the jewel fell down on the thick turf and they had to postpone the battle until daybreak. And so they dragged themselves up against one another to take their rest. But of sleep, there was none; for when either one wished to fall asleep, it seemed that a blow would be given from the other, and so neither went to sleep the whole night long.

When daybreak came, the birds began to sing throughout the woods. The parrot then said to his dwarf: "Take the cover off my cage so I may see my knight and the other one who is fighting with him." The dwarf did as he was ordered. Then the parrot asked his knight how he had done in the battle. When he wanted to answer him, his enemy ran toward him, and they both ran at each other, and without further ado, struck one another such blows that the whole forest resounded from them; the noise could be heard for well over a league. They fought so hard that the Knight of the Parrot was convinced he would never know another such bloody battle, for he was sorely wounded in more than seven places. The battle lasted up to and beyond the hour of nones [3 p.m.]. The Knight of the Parrot marveled greatly that, no matter how much he was able to strike his enemy on the hauberk, he did not hurt him at all. He then gave him a blow with all of his might on his shield which split off as much as was hit; the blow glanced onto the left knee so that his leg, right down to his foot, was chopped off by it. It fell on the ground at the feet of the Knight of the Parrot, and made such noise in the falling that it sounded as though one of the trees of the forest was being felled. The Knight of the Parrot went over to his opponent as quickly as he could, and that one said to him: "My good lord, for God's sake, mercy! You are surely one of the best knights in the world. For this reason, I pray you to please take the hauberk I am wearing on my back before I die. It is the best one you ever saw because no matter what blow, either by lance or sword, it cannot be damaged one bit, and yet it is so light a little boy can wear it all day long. Know also that you can cut away from it a great length I had added on to it, although I think it will be more than long enough for you."

When the Knight of the Parrot heard the man who had been his adversary speak in such sweet terms, he took pity on him. So he asked him his name, lineage, and rank. That one answered he was a count, a very rich and very noble man, and that he owned fourteen strong, beautiful castles, overflowing with all kinds of goods, riches, and people; after which he told him that his father had been a giant who had deflowered his mother forcibly, but she took him as her husband since he was so valorous and bold, and also because he was feared by the people of the land. "And so I am named the Knight-Giant after him." Then he told the Knight of the Parrot: "My good lord, my father taught me a precept I want you to know. He told me that there are three truths in the world and that no one could be a worthy man if he did not recognize them. The first truth is to recognize one's savior. The next is to understand the bad and the good one can do with one's hands and mouth. The third is to know oneself, for if I had known my capacities before I set myself to fighting with you, I would have lived much longer than I now will. For I know full well I shall not live much longer. So I pray you to pardon me for having done battle with you without cause and very wrongly too, and I also pray, for God's sake, that you hear my sins so that God may have mercy on my soul when I have passed from this world." After he had fully confessed himself to the Knight of the Parrot, he said his culpas and died on the spot before him. The Knight of the Parrot took his hauberk and tied it to the back of the dwarf and prayed God to have mercy on his soul; then he covered him with branches and grass against the sun's rays, and would have very willingly buried him but could not because of his great weight. The knight then resumed his journey, together with his damsel, dwarf, and parrot, who sang most sweetly, praying God for the grace that would bring a good night's lodging.

They went through the forest at a gentle gait since the knight was wounded in several places. After they left the forest behind them, they entered a most beautiful meadow, and they saw a castle upon a fine hillock. They directed themselves toward the castle in hope of lodging there, and had gone but a little way toward it when they saw issue forth four damsels who rode toward them at a gallop. When they got closer, they greeted one another gently and the damsels entreated the Knight of the Parrot, in the name of their lady, to take lodging that night in the castle. He told them that he would lodge there willingly, but for the fact that he was grievously wounded. The damsels answered that their lady was so noble that she would rather have herself destroyed before anyone should come to shame or villainy while in her house. "And who is your lady?" said the knight.

"Sire," said one of the damsels, "our lady is truly a noble countess who is the last of her line and who has well over three thousand silver marks in yearly rents, without counting the wheat and wine sent her. She is the lady of a land well over thirty leagues wide from end to end, abounding with good and beautiful castles. Since she is the wisest, most courteous, most beautiful, and most just damsel in her land, she is known as the Noble Maiden. Sire," she continued, "do come in all surety, for on our souls, you will be well received. She willingly pays more honor to strange knights than any other lady anywhere, and she also has more knowledge of medicines for wounds than any surgeon anywhere can ever hope to learn."

The parrot told his knight: "Sire, I advise you to do what the damsels ask you to do." The knight did so willingly, since he had greater need for rest than for traveling on account of the great amount of blood he had lost. So they went riding toward the castle together. The damsels stared long at the Knight of the Parrot and listened very willingly to the words of the parrot, and said to one another: "This bird will be good for our lady." Then they also told one another: "This must be the Knight of the Parrot." "It could not be," answered one of them, "for such a knight as he would not go about with so small a party as this."

In this manner they rode onward until they entered the castle. When they came to the palace, they dismounted and went up into the hall. But why should I tell you a long story? Never was a man better received by friend or relative than the knight and his party were by the Noble Maiden. When she learned that he was indeed that Knight of the Parrot, she so put herself to the task of easing his pain and healing his wounds that at the end of fifteen days, she actually brought him back to a better state of health and greater vigor to carry arms than he had ever before known in his life. When he felt himself fully restored, he took his leave of the lady, offered her his service, and said that no matter where he might be when he heard she was in need of his attendance, he would leave there and come to her immediately. The Noble Maiden thanked him very much for this and commended him to God, and together with the others in his party, he went riding forth, joyously and happy, like one who is driven toward a good port by Fortune.

The parrot continued to sing to him very sweetly of the chivalries he had done, right up to the edge of the forest.

After they had entered the forest, they saw approaching from the left a fully armed knight, mounted on a black charger, who rode with such haste that he made the land shake under the hooves of his mount. When he saw the Knight of the Parrot, he recognized him immediately because of the damsel and the parrot, and so rushed forward as quickly as possible to joust with him. When the Knight of the Parrot perceived him coming so furiously, he did not tarry but turned straight toward him, as should any knight in such matters. They hit each other with such strength on their shields that their slings and cinches broke, and their saddles were hurled to the ground right from under their legs; but they got up straightaway and, putting their hands to their swords, struck each other with such force that each one feared for his life; and they struck great blows on their shields and helmets until they were both grievously wounded. The fearsome battle that was so perilous for each one of them lasted from the hour of prime [6 a.m.] until the setting of the sun, and still no one knew who had the better part of it. Then the Knight of the Parrot struck his enemy squarely on the helm with all his might so that he split his helmet right in half, and his sword entered three-fingers deep into his skull; so greatly did he strike this blow that the man fell stunned to the ground and did not know where he was. The Knight of the Parrot ran up to him, but this one saw that he could not defend himself further, and so he cried out for mercy and pleaded not to be killed. The Knight asked what was his name, and that one answered: "I am the brother of the one whom you killed in the forest, who was called the Knight-Giant, and my name is the Redoubted Giant of the Sure Keep."

When the Knight of the Parrot heard he was the brother of the Knight-Giant, who had so nobly confessed to him, he felt much great pity for him, and so pardoned him all of his wrongdoings because of his brother. After this, the Redoubted Giant begged him to lodge in one of his keeps and to rest there until his wounds were healed, which was done. Never was a man better welcomed, either by father or mother, as was the Knight of the Parrot by the giant.

When the Knight of the Parrot departed, he rode through the forest in the company of his damsel, dwarf, and parrot in great joy and pleasure. They rode far on their journey until they came to a most beautiful castle belonging to a knight in the service of my lady Flor de Mont. This knight did not help her in any way against the usurping marshal, nor did he war against her in the marshal's cause. When he recognized his lady's damsel, he greeted her openly and welcomed the knight and the other members in his party and provided them with everything they required. In the evening, after they had supped, he led them to a very beautiful garden for their rest and relaxation. He had gathered all of his children, who were very handsome, among whom were five boys and one maid; of his five sons, one was a knight while the other four were squires, and they all sought to please the knight for the love of their lady. Then the Knight of the Parrot said to his host: "I am greatly puzzled about how you could have allowed the marshal to treat your lady so badly."

To which his host answered: "I shall tell you the whole truth of it. Her father was a very rich and powerful king who once went to war against the

King of Marioch and the Duke of Cité Fort, who ravaged the lands of his kingdom so much that they seized four of his castles and so greatly overwhelmed him in this war that he could not defend himself against them. When I heard my sire was reduced to such straits, I assembled all the chivalry I could, and we were three hundred knights, and we went off to serve the king. So much did we do that, out of fear of us, his enemies quit his land and jurisdiction and gave him, for each of the castles they had taken from him, land in damages, and swore by all the saints that they would never join against him again, as indeed they have not since. When the war was over, my lord king gave great gifts to the foreign knights who had helped him but, to me and to those of his knights who had come to his aid, he showed no largess at all; on the contrary, when asked why he had not rewarded any of us, as he had the foreign knights who had helped bring an end to the war, he stated that we were all his men and so had only performed our duty. As for me, he said that, were I not as rich as I was, he would have gotten even better service from me than the service I had given him.

"My good lord," continued the host of the Knight of the Parrot, "that was all the reward I got from my king for the service I had given him. Indeed, I tell you truly I have nothing from him worth one whit, other than the fact that I am his man, which I much regret. For I could not do anything that earned his favor, even though I served him more loyally than most other knights. In fact, he gave control over his lands and his only daughter not to me but to one of his marshals who was not better than I, neither in riches nor in anything else, except for the fact that my sire hated me more than any other person in his court. Because of all this, I have allowed to happen what I would not have permitted even on the pain of death, had the king not been so very harsh with me. On the other hand, she remains my lady, even though she is the daughter of a bad father, and so I have no wish to serve the marshal against my lady Flor de Mont. My good lord," said the chastelain, "now you know the truth of the matter, and your damsel knows well if I speak truly or not." Then the Knight of the Parrot so entreated his host for the service due the lady that his host promised he would help her with all the riches and friends at his command. After that, the host had wine brought and they all drank together. When they had their fill, it was time to go to bed, and so they went off to sleep.

At daybreak, the next morning, the Knight of the Parrot got up and dressed, and when he was fully armed, mounted his charger. In the company of his dwarf and damsel, he set out on the road with his host, who accompanied him well as an escort for a good two leagues. The Knight of the Parrot entreated him not to forget his lady but to come to her aid, and he answered that he would. After commending one another to God, they each went their own way. When the Knight of the Parrot asked his damsel their host's name, she replied that he was called Andois and that he was the most loyal and honest man in the kingdom, and that he had spoken the truth about the king and himself.

They continued riding and speaking together until the Knight of the Parrot and his damsel entered a region which by right belonged to Flor de Mont, and before her, to her father, King Belnain; now, however, it was held by a knight in the service of the marshal. They continued riding until they came to the foot of a mountain where the path was so narrow that no one could leave that region to enter the land of Flor de Mont, except by way of a castle which was on the other side of the mountain, at the entrance of Ile Fort. The marshal had placed the best of his knights as guards at this entrance, especially against the Knight of the Parrot, for they feared him greatly because of the things they had heard about him. When the Knight of the Parrot went up to that entrance, the knight who was guarding it began to cry aloud, "Sir vassal, turn back, for you may not pass beyond!"

The Knight of the Parrot asked why, and the other told him his lord had commanded him to allow no one to pass if he did not know who he was. "Let the matter, then, not rest on this," said the Knight of the Parrot, "for I shall quickly tell you who I am. I am from Britain and am called the Knight of the Parrot, and I wish to go to Ile Fort to correct the wrong which your sire has done to Lady Flor de Mont."

The knight looked at him and pitied him greatly, for he believed he had spoken so because his mind was not working right, and so he replied: "My good friend, turn around and go back."

"My good lord," said the Knight of the Parrot, "I have not come this far just to turn back; I have come this far, and shall go further, until I have accomplished the matter that has brought me here!"

The other answered him that goodness and courtesy are of little value to those who do not wish to hear them. "I have said things to you which I have not told any other person since my lord sent me here, but now I say to you that, if you wish to pass over to Ile Fort, you will have to joust with me for your passage. If I can knock you down right here without doing anything more on horseback, you will be entirely at my mercy. But if you knock me down, you will pass safely; nor shall you pass otherwise, so do what you will."

The Knight of the Parrot replied: "Since I cannot pass by any other way, I will joust with you." So they armed themselves for a joust, and after they had set their marks, they came against one another with great speed and broke their lances on their shields, without doing any other damage to one another. When they had broken their lances, the knight who was guarding the passage had many others brought out, and said that they had to joust until one of them was knocked down. Each of them broke four thick, strong lances before either one was moved from the saddle. The damsel and the dwarf became greatly alarmed, but the parrot comforted them by singing a song which caused his knight to be renewed in strength and daring, and, with a strong lance, he struck a blow against the Knight of the Passage's shield that knocked him and his mount to the ground. When he realized he had been thrown to the ground, this one got up very quickly and went to the Knight of the Parrot to plead, very courteously, that he and all those with him should take lodgings that night with him, which could be done as safely as if they were in their fathers' or mothers' houses, and the Knight of the Parrot granted this because of the great courtesy he saw in him. So the Knight of the Passage honored and lodged them to much satisfaction and great pleasure, and they were well served that night. In the morning, about daybreak, the Knight of the Parrot got up and dressed, and together with the others in his party, took leave of the Knight of the Passage, and rode onward, according to the damsel's directions, up to the keep where Lady

Flor de Mont was imprisoned with her mother, the queen. When they were one league along the way, the damsel accompanying the Knight of the Parrot began to cry. When the knight asked why she was crying, she answered him: "Sir, I cry because of the pity I have for you, because I see over there a knight against whom you must do battle and who is the best knight in the whole world." Our knight asked her where he was and she answered: "See him there, on that hillock, carrying that red pennant. He is the best knight in all this kingdom, as well as in all the world. Since I know only too well that he is full of pride and has no mercy in him, I am crying. Because he is such a good knight, the marshal has made him his chief standard-bearer."

"Damsel," said the Knight of the Parrot, "it is of no matter that he is so strong. God, Who is powerful, can easily protect us against him."

There appeared then the knight they were talking about, who had spied them approaching at the foot of the mountain. When he saw them drawing nearer to him, he charged furiously at the Knight of the Parrot, because he was riding with the damsel, for he had heard that she had gone off to search for a champion for her lady against the marshal. Seeing him approach, the Knight of the Parrot did not at all give way and flee; on the contrary, he veered toward him, prepared to defend himself vigorously, and they charged so mightily against one another that they struck each other down at the first pass without knowing who had acquitted himself better in the encounter. They quickly got to their feet and drew their swords, and so began such a bitter struggle that both were convinced they had never known such a strong opponent. After having continued for a goodly while in this fashion, on foot and with swords drawn, the one fighting against the Knight of the Parrot said: "My lord, let us do this properly; let us mount our chargers and go up to the mountain, before the gate of this castle, and joust there, so that the lady for whom you are fighting may see you, and may also come to learn which one of us has better use of the lance; for this will bring much more honor to us."

"Indeed," said the Knight of the Parrot, "that would suit me fine." So they mounted their chargers, and each one, holding a lance in his fist, entered the most beautiful meadow in all the world, which was right in front of the castle's keep, where they began the hard and bitter clash again. After they had broken their lances, they struck one another blows with their swords and strove to outdo each other because of Lady Flor de Mont, who was leaning on the window-sill, watching the battle with some twenty other damsels, all daughters of princes and barons. These were all wondering greatly if the stranger could be the Knight of the Parrot. The damsel who had accompanied the Knight of the Parrot drew up so close to them that they recognized her from the windows where they were watching. Thus they knew he was indeed the Knight of the Parrot, and felt great joy from this because they had heard much about his chivalry, and they greatly praised the restraint he was exercising in the battle, and spoke so loudly about him that he could hear all of it. When he grew aware of all this, he was so encouraged that he struck his adversary a marvelous blow squarely on his helmet, which split it entirely apart, so that his sword was able to hit him soundly on the head. This caused such hurt that he could not sit in his saddle, but instead fell to the ground so stunned that he did not know whether it was day or night. When the Knight of the Parrot went up to him, he saw the sword that had dropped next to him, picked it up, and put it in his scabbard next to his. After a while, the knight who had fallen to the ground opened his eyes and saw the Knight of the Parrot approaching him with a naked sword in his hand, and he was overcome with such fear for his life that he cried for mercy. The Knight of the Parrot said to him: "If you wish me to show mercy to you, then you must place yourself entirely at the mercy of my Lady Flor de Mont." The other agreed to do this immediately, like one who could do little else.

Then they glanced toward the keep and saw Flor de Mont and her damsels approaching to welcome the Knight of the Parrot. They received him with the greatest honor that a knight ever had from any lady or damsel. The marshal's knight placed himself at the mercy of the lady; she accepted him and ordered that he be treated honorably, out of love for the Knight of the Parrot, and also because he was courteous and a cousin to Flor de Mont. So they went into the palace in a spirit of great joy and good cheer that had not been seen there since the time of King Belnain. The damsels themselves, who were all of the same age, disarmed him, and they thought of nothing but laughter and play and of smiling nicely at him.

When the parrot saw the damsels, who were all fifteen years old, showing so much joy to his lord, he began to sing of the chivalrous deeds his lord had performed. After he had sung about his lord for a while, he began to sing about the damsels in this manner: "I would rather be a whole two months with you than anywhere else in the world." After this, he began to sing a lay of love so cleverly and sweetly that all the damsels took up the round with him; they had begun to give themselves up to great joy when they beheld the mother of Flor de Mont, with the long face and dreary expression of a lady who has lost her husband. When the damsels saw the queen approach, they stopped their singing and good cheer, but the parrot was not pleased by this, for he did not want to do anything but sing, dance, and have a good time. Nonetheless, he fell silent when he saw the queen because she did not seem to be at all happy. When the Knight of the Parrot learned that she was the queen, he went up to her and greeted her, as one who is full of courtesy should, and she took him by the hand, crying very tenderly, and said: "Good sire, you are truly welcome!" Then she asked him his name and country.

"Lady," said he, "I am from Britain." And she asked him if he were a friend of King Arthur, and he said: "In truth, yes, more than any other man in the world." Then the queen began to tell him: "Your fame is such that it caused us to seek you out all through the world, so that you might come here, by God's mercy and your goodness, to deliver us from this prison in which we find ourselves on account of the disloyalty of our marshal."

At which the knight said: "Lady, I am ready to do all that you may wish, if not more, and so I pray you to please show me, if you know it, the most direct way to the marshal's."

When he finished saying this, the queen kissed him and told him, crying: "My good lord, it is too sudden for that, for you are tired and exhausted from traveling, and he is one of the best knights in all the world; so I pray you to pause and rest, both you and your steed, for eight days, since I have heard from the damsel who sought you out that you have done many a feat of arms since leaving the Amorous City."

"My lady," said the Knight of the Parrot, "I have not come here to rest, but to increase my fame and reputation. Please know that a young knight should not refrain from exercising himself according to his capacities. Therefore, I wish to pursue my adventure now, if you please."

The queen felt great pity for what the knight said to her and was convinced that he was valiant and brave. Also, she found great comfort in that her destiny had once been foretold that a Briton would be the one to deliver her and her daughter from prison and be the cause for their return to joy and happiness. So she answered him: "My good lord, since you do not wish to rest, there will arrive here tomorrow one who will lead you surely on the right road." So they remained together the entire day. When they had supped and it was time to go to bed, four damsels came for the Knight of the Parrot. They bedded him down in the queen's chamber with great comfort, and you should know that the queen and her daughter did not leave his presence, but honored him as much as they could. They were not there long when a varlet came and called the queen, and she went out very quietly because it seemed to them that the knight wanted to fall asleep. After she had spoken with the varlet, she went back into her chamber and said to the Knight of the Parrot: "My good lord, are you sleeping or not?"

And he answered her: "No, my lady. What is it that you wish?"

Then she said: "I see that it is God's wish that you ride off on the most perilous adventure there ever was, for the messenger who is to lead you has arrived, who every three days has the custom of appearing only once, and who has not been here since we have been imprisoned; and so he had gone away last evening, and should not be here today, except that it is the will of our Lord Jesus Christ. Therefore, you must get up and arm yourself, and I shall have your horse saddled. I advise you, in good faith, to have yourself confessed by my chaplain, for then you will be more fortified, for you have to know that where you are going, I have sent more than fifteen men, none of whom has ever come back, and each of whom was, both in age and size, greater than you."

The Knight of the Parrot was very pleased by what the queen had told him, except for the fact that none of her knights had returned, and for this reason he had himself confessed by the chaplain, as she had asked him. After he was confessed and the chaplain had given him his penance, he descended the steps of the palace with the queen, Flor de Mont, and her damsels, and found his charger being led to the foot of the stairs by a varlet, as the queen had ordered. On the bow of the saddle, she had put two barrels of wine and a sack full of enough food for three days. Then she told him: "My good lord, you will have to ride through many places where you will find nothing to drink or eat, and will be all alone without company."

He answered her: "Lady, may everything be according to God's will." Then he mounted his charger, fully armed, except for his helmet, which my lady Flor de Mont held in her hands because she had attached to it a beautiful, rich silken cloth she herself had embroidered with gold and silver, and when she saw that he was mounted on his horse, she said to him: "Here, take this, beautiful, sweet friend, and may God grant you return in health and joy." After this, she tied it on his head. When she had turned away from him, the queen led him to a most beautiful meadow, near the keep, where they found a very beautiful beast, as big as a bull, who had a slender dragon-like neck with a small head like a deer's with two horns as white as snow, striped with gold on his crown and whose fur was redder than any scarlet. When the beast saw the Knight of the Parrot, it bent down low before him, as if he were a man of reason, and showed him a humble mien, all of which caused the Knight of the Parrot to be greatly amazed. But when the queen saw the beast go before the knight and bow at his feet, she tearfully told the knight: "My good lord, here then is the beast who must show you the way, and may God grant you a joyous return." The beast placed itself in front of the knight and looked into his face, as though it wished to speak to him which, I think, it would well have done if only it could, and then it began to walk off with small steps. After the knight had taken leave of the queen, he followed the beast, all the while greatly wondering what kind it could be, for it had such a scarlet color that it seemed to have been roasted. The splendor which was reflected by the light of the moon that glanced upon its horns was so bright that it really could have been the light of a clear day.

By means of this brightness, he followed the beast, and they traveled so much that midnight had already passed them when they entered a beautiful field. Then the beast went to a tree in the middle of the field and seemed ready to go to sleep. As he thought that the beast wished both him and his mount to rest, the Knight of the Parrot dismounted and tied his horse to a tree; then he cut some grass as best he could, and put it before his horse. After this, he fell asleep, in spite of himself, until daybreak, when the birds began to announce the coming of a bright new day. He got up and saw that the beast was already in front of him and was signaling him to make ready to continue on their way. After he had saddled his horse, he mounted and followed the beast, who led him into a place that was so beautiful and filled with such a good smell that it really seemed to be Paradise to him; and he followed the beast until vespers, when they came upon a ruined castle, in a very beautiful place that had been ravaged by the marshal. The beast went straight to it, making signs that it wished to sleep and rest, and the knight dismounted next to one of the most beautiful trees that anyone could see, no matter where, which had leaves and flowers of such quality as to give off the sweetest smell that ever a man could enjoy.

After he dismounted, he saw approaching him on foot a very handsome knight who was all bald and dressed in a totally white robe. The Knight of the Parrot greatly marveled at what this could mean, and went forward to meet him, greeting him in the name of the King of Heaven; and when the other returned his greeting, he said: "King of Britain, have no fear, for I am he for whom you go on the most perilous adventure that ever there was in the world, which can only be ended by a man of royal lineage who is also the most just and noble knight in the world."

"My lord," said the Knight of the Parrot, "who are you?"

"I am," said the bald knight, "the beast who has led you here."

"How is that so, my good lord?" said the Knight of the Parrot.

The other answered him: "I am King Belnain, who was killed by great felony in a tournament by one of my barons whom I shall not name, for my soul would be imperiled if I did. When I was wounded and near death, God allowed me sufficient respite to make my will, and thus I elected the marshal, as the best of all those around me, and gave over to him in trust my kingdom and my daughter, but he has betrayed this trust, as you have already learned elsewhere; yet the time is coming when he shall be duly rewarded." The Knight of the Parrot asked him then about where he was living then. "I live," said he, "in a beautiful place where I will stay until Merlin's prophecy is fulfilled, and then I shall go to another place, even more beautiful and pleasant, such as God gives His friends in reward, and where there will be a glory that no one can ever hope to describe." Then he said to him: "King of Britain, I cannot tarry longer here with you, but before I leave, I charge you to stay this night beneath this tree where you are now, and from which you will take a flower and put it away in your bosom; and I shall tell you the reason why. When nightfall arrives, you will see in this meadow before you a very great company of armed knights and barons, riding on their chargers and carrying many big and small pennants in their hands. So too you will see a beautiful court of ladies and damsels, as rich as any held by any king or emperor. After they all assemble, you will witness the most beautiful and pleasant tournament you ever saw in your whole life. The knights of the tournament will come up to you crying and saying: 'Where is the Knight of the Parrot? Why does he not come tourney-ing with us?' Then you must make sure to not go out there unless you wish to die. For if you do enter the tournament, you will be mortally wounded by a javelin, from which no doctor in all the world would be able to heal you. But if you wish to escape this and bring to conclusion what you have undertaken, you must then remain beneath the tree where you now are, for none of those in the tournament can come to you there for as long as the shade and aroma of the tree shall endure."

After he taught him all these things, that one commended him to God and went off, saying that he would never see him again. Therefore, the Knight of the Parrot stayed beneath the tree, drew his horse closer to him, and then took one of the flowers and put it to his nose, which offered him such a fine aroma that he thought surely he was in a heavenly spot. It so satisfied him that he had no thought for food or drink. When night fell, he saw coming into the meadow varlets and sergeants who began to set up tents and pavilions and lay out silken cloth. Again he looked and saw richly dressed ladies and damsels riding in with great lights, torches, and candles, to the sound of viols and a great many other instruments. Following the ladies, he saw knights and barons who were better dressed than any he had ever seen in any court in the world. Each and every one of them dismounted in front of his own pavilion.

After they had rested a while, there was begun the most pleasant tourna-ment ever to be seen. When they had jousted a piece, they went about shouting and saying: "Where is the Knight of the Parrot? Why is he not in this tournament?" Then some knights who were fleeing before the pursuit given them by some others went up very close to the precious tree where the Knight of the Parrot was to be found. They said in a loud voice: "Ha, Sir Knight of the Parrot! Noble lord and sire, mercy! Help us against our enemies, for if we are laid low within your sight, we who ask so sweetly for your mercy, you will be blamed for it as long as you live!" They said this so many times that the Knight of the Parrot took pity on them. Then, after he had put bridle and saddle to his horse and wanted to join in the fray, he heard matins sounded by a hermit who was in the hermitage very close by. As soon as the bell sounded, the tournament was dispersed in such a manner that the Knight of the Parrot could not understand what had happened, and did not see any of the tents or pavilions again.

At the crack of dawn the next morning, he mounted his horse, very heavy in thought about all he had seen the night before, and went off riding until he came upon a boulder that bore a small and very beautiful cross upon it. When he went closer to it, he looked all over the boulder and saw there were letters carved thus: "You who read me, know from me that there are three misadventures in this world. The first is about him who does not know the Good and does not wish to learn about it. The second is about him who knows the Good but does not apply it, either for himself or for anyone else. The third misadventure is about him who knows the Good and chastises others, but who does not refrain at all from doing evil." Together with this, the letters on the other side of the boulder read: "If you wish to find a marvelous adventure, ride forth, keeping to the right, and tarry here no longer."

Thus the Knight of the Parrot rode on and kept to the right of the road as the inscription had indicated to him. He rode for the whole morning and afternoon without finding any adventure, until evening, when he heard a voice that cried out loudly: "Ah, my good friend, may God have mercy on you. I cannot assist you!" He looked in front of him and saw a damsel who was coming down from a mountain as quickly as she could with great grief on her face. The Knight of the Parrot asked her what was the matter, and when she was more composed, she told him: "My good sire, I truly carry a great sorrow because a serpent has carried off a friend of mine in such rough fashion that I fear he is dead."

"Damsel, where is this serpent?" And she showed him the direction it had flown off to. The Knight of the Parrot went in this direction, but did not continue long when he saw the most horrible serpent ever seen anywhere, carrying in its mouth an armed knight who, because of his armor's protection, was still not dead. Then the Knight of the Parrot set his horse at a gallop and hastened to strike the serpent a blow on its chest with his lance, which penetrated right through its heart, so that the serpent, upon feeling the blow, let the knight fall down; then it rolled over again and again, and lashed its great winding tail, so that it seemed to be very much like a devil. It so thrashed its tail about, because of the death it felt gripping it, that, by mischance, it hit the Knight of the Parrot, striking him so hard that both he and his mount were thrown into some wide and deep water, and were it not for this lake, he would have been mortally wounded. Nonetheless, he was grievously wounded and totally poisoned by the serpent, which had stung him, and would have been in great peril, were it not for God's help.

When, with great difficulty, he finally came out of the water, he rode off in the direction he believed to be the best. He had scarcely continued for a league beyond the lake when he fainted from the effect of the poison coursing through him, and so he fell onto the ground, almost back into the water, and he was in such painful straits that he felt numb all over. When the knight whom the serpent had dropped from its mouth saw the snake dead, he went up to his damsel and asked her what had become of the knight who had killed it; she told him how she had met the other knight and how he had gladly accepted to go to his rescue. Very sorely did this knight grieve for the other one whom he thought had died. So they told one another that whoever he was, the rescuer had been truly brave and worthy; and then they set out on the road and came to a keep close by that belonged to them, which was very beautiful and strong. After they went into the hall, they ordered candles and torches to be lit, for it was past nightfall. Then they overheard a fisherman who was passing by telling his wife: "I think he is still alive. By God, what beautiful armor he had!" To which his wife answered: "God, how we would have sinned had we left it there!"

When the knight heard the fisherman, he leaned out of the window and said: "Who are you there who speaks like that?"

"My lord," answered the fisherman, "I am a friend."

"What were you saying just then?"

The fisherman, who was afraid of his lord, said: "Sire, we were talking about nothing." The knight saw that he had perhaps committed a crime, so he ordered his people to bring the villein and his wife to him. When the men went to arrest the man, they found the richest armor they had ever seen in the fisherman's skiff. The knight who had been watching them from his window cried out: "Ha, vile villein, I think you have committed a deed that will grieve me all the days of my life! Now tell me the truth about the knight to whom these arms belonged!"

The fisherman, who was very frightened, answered him: "My lord, have mercy, for God's sake! I did not kill him! Close to nightfall on the banks of this stream, I came upon a very stiff knight with a dead horse beside him; the knight was still alive, although he could not speak." Then the knight realized that it could be none other than the knight who had delivered him from the serpent. So he and his damsel hurried down, got into the skiff with the fisherman, and ordered him to take them to the place where he had found the knight; and so they found him in a poor state, quite paralyzed, and knew he would very soon die if he was not given help. But why should I make the story longer for you? They put him into the skiff and took him up to the castle. They bedded him down in a beautiful bed and covered him up, and did everything possible for him. They did so much that, before the hour of midnight, he opened his eyes and said: "Good Lord God, where am I?" The damsel, who was standing in front of him, told him the whole story. It became known then that the leaf he had plucked from the precious tree worked to his great advantage, for it had guarded him so well against the poison that this did not kill him; instead, within three days he recovered as good a state of health as he had known a month before or at any other previous time.

Then the Knight of the Castle asked him who he was and where he was going. When he learned that he was the Knight of the Parrot, who was on his way to battle against the marshal, he was filled with such joy that he told him: "My good sweet sir, you will surely reach, in the space of two short days' traveling, the dangerous castle of your enemy, which is the most perilous place in the world, for it is situated on a round mountain which, although not high, is the strongest in the world. It is surrounded by wide and deep water, so that none may cross over except by a bridge, which is the most dangerous passage in the world, since it is so narrow that it cannot be crossed on horseback. In the middle of the bridge, there is a wheel which turns by such strong magic that no knight may pass it by, and more than fifteen knights who have gone in quest of this adventure have died there;

but since you have saved me, I wish to render you as reward my service in this matter. My good lord, you are going to a place where no foreign knight has gone since the death of King Belnain. You will find in the middle of the bridge, on either end of the wheel, two marble columns of a very beautiful red color, on which is written the following: 'Ye who wish to cross over, go ye not away but come ye close to me, for the way is most perilous.' He who crosses away from it is instantly killed by the wheel, against which there is no safeguard. This is because it has been set up by magic to guard the passage for the marshal, but I shall teach you what you must do. When you have climbed on the bridge and come close to the inscription and can see the writing which asks you to pass it close by, do not believe it at all, but instead you must turn around and look at the middle of the column; there in the middle where you will find a hole; whatever you see turning inside the hole, you will completely sever with your sword, and in this way the enchantment will be undone and the wheel will no longer turn round. My good lord, only in this way, and in no other, shall you be able to cross. Now, since you wish to go there, I shall detain you no longer."

After the Knight of the Castle had pointed out the way, the Knight of the Parrot was armed, and he set out on the road. The Knight of the Castle accompanied him until they came up to a mountain, where he told the Knight of the Parrot: "My good lord, I may not go further, for I would perjure myself if I did. Here is the road that will lead you directly to the Castle Perilous." The Knight of the Parrot asked him his name, and he answered that he was called the Amorous Knight of the Savage Castle. He then turned to go back to his keep, praying God to come to his aid.

The Knight of the Parrot went along the side of the mountain where the other one had left him, and by following the road, was led onto a great heath, and while looking always in front of him, he rode all that day and the next one until prime (6 a.m.), when he came to a very narrow pathway, thick with trees and thorns, near a rather tall mountain. At that place, a savage woman, whom he did not notice until she grabbed and hugged him in her arms, jumped up behind him. Were it not for his armor, she would have killed him, but his horse started neighing and bucking violently on sensing that evil thing, which caused her to loosen her grip a little. The Knight of the Parrot threw her down on the ground and he drew out his sword and had done with her; then he mounted his charger and went galloping on his way. Indeed, he dared not sleep as long as he was in that heath out of fear of the savage woman; and so he kept riding that day until the sun went down.

About that time, the Knight of the Parrot reached the ramp of the bridge of the Castle Perilous. There was never a more horrible terror than this in all the world, for the water was deep, wide, dark, and black, more than anyone could ever describe, and the bank of the moat was in fact well over a hundred fathoms deep. The bridge itself was so narrow and made in such a way that no one could step onto it without its shaking so violently that it caused him to fall; and the wheel, made completely of iron and honed as sharp as a razor, turned so swiftly that it could not be seen by anyone. At the end of the bridge, there was a tower more than thirty fathoms tall, all of carved marble, with varicolored steps, and behind the tower there was the most beautiful and strongest keep in the whole world.

The Knight of the Parrot stared at the bridge, the tower, and the castle and thought: "My good Lord God, how shall I cross over there?" Then he remembered what the Knight of the Castle had told him. So he dismounted and tied his charger to a boulder at the head of the bridge. Then he began to go very carefully over it, but the bridge started shaking so violently that he could not hold himself up straight; so he got down on all fours to continue forward, which he did very gingerly because he feared he might fall off. He dragged himself along as best he could until he reached the wheel; and then he became even more afraid, for its swift turning created such a wind that it really would have taken very little to cast him off the bridge into the water, which seemed to him to be nothing less than Hell itself. Thus, the Knight of the Parrot found everything to be exactly according to what the knight had told him about the bridge. So when he reached the hole in the column, he drew out his sword, thrust it inside and chopped apart everything he saw moving within, which was nothing more than a metal wire that made the enchantment work.

As soon as the Knight of the Parrot cut the metal wire, the wheel stopped moving and the bridge ceased its shaking. So he went straight up to the tower which was at the end of the bridge and entered there by means of a door that was wide open. When he went inside, he found before him two great and fully armed villeins, except that they wore no iron shoes, and he was told by one of them: "Friend, you have come to your death, for you have crossed the bridge and come into our keeping."

"Ha, my good lords," said the Knight of the Parrot, "must all who cross the bridge die then? That would be too great a pity."

The villeins looked at one another, and said: "This knight seems so very brave that it would be a great wrong to kill him. Let us allow him to do battle with the marshal. If God wishes to help him, this one will be grateful to us for it. But if he should lose the battle, we shall have more than enough time to escape before he is killed." When they had agreed on this, they told him: "My good lord, your courtesy has caused you to be quit of your death. Continue now and bring your adventure to a close there above. We have killed so many knights and other people that we do not wish to kill any more."

The Knight of the Parrot was made very glad by what they told him, for he sorely feared an encounter with those two. Therefore, he went up into the hall, which was then very dark because of the coming of night. The marshal already knew about the adventure this stranger had gone through, and that his champions had allowed him to reach that far. While the Knight of the Parrot was in the middle of the hall, in deep thought, he saw a chamberdoor open, from which a damsel came forth who was dressed in a robe half-purple and half-scarlet, and who held a lighted torch in each hand; and when she came into the hall, she climbed upon a high table along the hall, and placed herself opposite the Knight of the Parrot. Hardly any time passed when he saw another come out, dressed in similar fashion, who also held two lighted torches in her hands and who proceeded to do the same thing as the first, except that she placed herself on his other side. Why should I make this story longer for you? So many of these damsels, all dressed in the same cloth, came there that they formed a circle around the hall. The light from the torches they held in their hands was so great that it seemed that bright daylight was in the hall, which caused the Knight of the Parrot to wonder greatly about the damsels and about the fact that not one of them was uttering a word.

A short while later, a knight, well appointed in new armor, all painted red, issued forth, from the same door which the damsels had used. After him came a very beautiful lady, who was his beloved and who was accompanied by some twenty girls playing an assortment of instruments. Thus the marshal entered the hall in great ceremony. When he saw the Knight of the Parrot, he gave him no greeting; instead, he put his arm into the sling of his shield and charged straight at him yelling: "You whore's son, you rogue! Unlucky are you indeed to have come here!" The Knight of the Parrot, not the least unnerved by this, drew out his sword and met the marshal's charge, just as he should have. There began there and then a perilous battle which lasted well past midnight, during which neither one was able to gain a foot of ground on the other. All this caused those who were watching to say to one another: "It may very well be that our marshal has found his match."

When the marshal saw that he could not best his opponent, he became very angry and he raised up his sword and struck the Knight of the Parrot on his helmet so hard that neither a mail hood nor an iron cap were of any use to him; it gave him such a deep head-wound that all of the damsels believed that the blow had finished the battle right there. When the Knight of the Parrot felt the blood, all hot and red, running down his forehead, he felt such shame and anger that, because of his righteous ire, he gained the strength and power to strike the marshal with so much might and force that he split him down to the jaw, and the man collapsed there at the feet of the Knight of the Parrot. When his beloved saw him lying there all quite dead, she ran up and embraced and hugged him with such great distress that she too died there beside him. Then all the damsels who were holding the torches came down to put the torches they were carrying in silver holders on the tables, and ran up to the Knight of the Parrot and hugged him and kissed him more than a hundred times, all the while joyfully singing: "May good adventure come to the best knight in all the world, who this night has delivered us from the worst and most evil lord there ever was!"

Then four damsels ascended to the highest rafter in the marble tower, where they rang a little bell that had never been rung since the time King Belnain died, and the ringing of this bell caused all who heard it to know that they were freed from their evil lord. Because of the great happiness, they caused all the bells in the district to ring in response to the little bell of the Castle Perilous, with the effect that, before the third hour [9 a.m.] had passed, there assembled well over a thousand knights, with their wives and children, who all went up to the Knight of the Parrot, to hug and kiss him and to say to him: "Sire, receive the homage of your people, whom you have delivered from the fear of our devil lord. For all who served him best always had the worst reward for their pain. So we tell you truly that there are three sorrows given to this world. The first, and by the far the worst, is very bad sickness; the second is evil living; and the third sorrow is a bad overlord. All these griefs are given to men for their torment. Thus, more than any other men in the whole world, we have been tormented by this evil overlord from whom you have delivered us, through God's mercy and your own, and for which we have come here to do anything you may command."

The Knight of the Parrot, who was feeling the greatest joy he ever knew, answered them: "I wish that you and all your people would come with me, just as you are now, to the queen and her daughter, who is your lady, both by reason and by right, and that you pay her homage and fealty, as you owe it to her." This pronouncement pleased them so well that they answered they would do this willingly. So every one of them dressed up very richly. As soon as the Knight of the Parrot rested a bit and had his battle-wounds tended to, they all set out on the road, with exceedingly good cheer and great joy. They made progress in so good a fashion that soon they all came to the Fearless Keep, where the queen and her daughter were to be found. They were met there by a great party of knights which my Lord Andois had brought for the service of his lady, as he had promised.

When they heard the news of the marshal's death, the people all felt full of the greatest joy anyone could ever know. Then the queen commanded that every man and woman mount, as she herself and her daughter did, and with a great escort of ladies and damsels, they set out to meet the Knight of the Parrot on the road. Nor did she wish to forget the parrot, who had been in prison a long time indeed, so that he might provide them with song. He had been much afraid for his lord, inasmuch as he did not know any of the adventures that had befallen him since the time he was left behind, and so the lady had him brought along with her. They rode gaily onward until they encountered the Knight of the Parrot and his party. Never was such great joy and happiness shown to anyone as that which they all showed to the Knight of the Parrot.

The parrot reached there by singing all along the way the many deeds of his lord to Flor de Mont. When he got near his lord, he began such a sweet melody that there were none present who did not stop because of the sweetness of the song. After he had finished, he fell down in his cage, and all thought him to be dead, but his lord went up to him and said: "Ha, my good parrot, I pray you, if it is at all possible, not to leave me so soon!" As soon as the parrot heard him speak, he got up and began to sing all the more gaily. After this, they took up their way and rode until they came to the Fearless Keep, where they dismounted, with great joy and happiness. There began then a feast that lasted a full eight days, during which the queen accepted the homage of all her men and women. At the end, they each took leave of the queen, and everyone went off to his land.

After spending a full fifteen days there, the Knight of the Parrot also took his leave of the queen and her daughter, and although they entreated him to prolong his stay, he would not, nor would he take anything from them, except a ship that they ordered to be made ready for him at a harbor on the sea some three leagues distant from the keep; for he wanted to return to Britain by sea. They did this most willingly, and they ordered the ship provisioned with everything he might need and for twenty knights whom they sent along as an escort. When they were all ready, they rode toward the port. Those who witnessed it would never forget the grief the queen and her daughter displayed when the Knight of the Parrot boarded the ship, for they did not wish him to leave. But after they had commended one another to God, the sailors pulled up the anchor, unfurled the sails to the fair wind that had risen up, and sailed into the open seas. Thus they went off, in great joy and high spirits, while the parrot sang them the loveliest song in all the world.

But very soon their joy was turned to grief, for one of the strongest winds rose up and carried the vessel to a wild land. This wind violently rent the sails and split the mast so that the ship was in danger of being completely wrecked. But God the Glorious, who heard the prayer of the Knight of the Parrot, swiftly brought them without further harm to the shore of that land. During the time of danger, the parrot called to his dwarf and said: "Dwarf, for God's sake, open my cage so that I may at least go out and fly to land. If the ship should sink, I shall have prayers said for the soul of my lord and for you too, and I will carry the news to the court of King Arthur."

"Indeed," said the dwarf, "I shall not do it. You will stay and suffer here with us and await the outcome of this adventure together with us."

"Oh, dwarf, do let me sway you to cover my cage or put me in a place where I will not see the waves of the sea, for they frighten me greatly."

"No indeed," said the dwarf, "I shall not do that, for I dare not move about. I will fall into the sea because of the great pitching of the ship. But I shall teach you what you, in fact, can do: if you do not wish to see, close your eyes and you will not see anything at all."

"Ha, vile dwarf, rotten and depraved, are you making fun of me?" "Yes, just as you are mocked by God and everyone." But the parrot complained about his dwarf to the Knight of the Parrot, and the knight directed the dwarf to follow the parrot's instructions. The dwarf answered: "Willingly, my lord!" But just as the dwarf was getting up to cover the parrot's cage, there arose such a gust of wind that it brought the bow of the ship aground. When the parrot saw this, he began to sing and to comfort his lord and all the others who were there with a song so beautiful that they soon forgot the grief they had just suffered.

Then the Knight of the Parrot got off the ship with the other knights, and was the first to speak: "My lords," said he, "do any of you know this land or have ever been here?" And they all answered no. "Now hear me well, my lords," said the Knight of the Parrot. "This adventure pertains entirely to me alone until such time as I have returned to court. You have come with me simply as an escort and to do my bidding; now I will tell you all what you must do. I shall go and search this land, both near and far, until I learn where we have come and can discover where we shall find food when ours is finished, for we do not have enough to put out to sea with. I have with me a horn that, should I sound it, will alert you to come to my rescue, for you should know clearly that I shall not blow it except in great need."

The knights answered: "Sire, if it pleases you, we will go along with you for your protection." But he told them to remain behind in the ship. So they said: "Since such is your pleasure, we shall do as you wish." They led out the Knight of the Parrot's charger from the ship, and, armed with all his weapons, he mounted without putting his foot to the stirrups; then he commended them all to God, spurred on his horse, and rode hard until he came to a hill. When he looked down on the other side of it, he saw a single tower set at the edge of a wood and without any other habitation anywhere near it. He was very happy about this and made his way towards it, for he thought he would find someone there who could give him some information. As he got closer to the tower, he saw that it was situated on open land without a trench around it, and it was square and high, well over sixty fathoms, but of poor masonry work and ill-made. He looked at it all over but could not find a door or a window. So he rode up a little closer to see if it had any openings at all, and saw a large hole in the roof above. He went closer to the tower and began to shout in the loudest voice he could: "You who are in the tower, speak to me, for I need you to tell me the direction I should follow!" He cried out three times in this manner, and when he looked up toward the hole, he saw a dwarf, old, bald, and humpbacked, who had stuck his head out.

When the dwarf saw the Knight of the Parrot, he was so bewildered that he began to cross himself. When the Knight of the Parrot asked him why, the dwarf told him: "I cross myself because, in all the more than sixty years I have been here, I have not seen anyone come here, either man or woman, except for you. But dead people I have seen more than I might have wished, and I shall tell you why. I was born in Nortonbellande [Northumberland], and I came here with my wife while she was pregnant with a son whom I have here with me, and who, since I have come to live here, has grown so big and strong that he carries a large, square club fashioned from an oak that was large enough to support six men as big as yourself. He carries the club in his hand when he goes out to play in the forest and elsewhere, and if he finds anything, be it man or woman, of which there are many in this forest, he kills them and then brings them to me to learn if they are good to eat. He brings me many folk, all dead, and dressed and armed as when he killed them. For this reason, I had him dig that large trench over there in which I have him throw the dead things that are not good for eating; but the good things, I clean and prepare for him to eat. You should know that, since we have no bread, my son eats so much of these things that it would be too amazing for me to tell you. You should know also, my lord, that I always beg him not to kill men or women, but instead bring them to me alive. He always grants me this, for it gives me much pleasure to have them with me. But my son is so stupid that he is always forgetting to do what I ask; and yet he tells me he will bring them to me alive, which he sometimes does remember to do. It happens that these always flee him out of fright, since he is exceedingly large, and so he runs after them and taps them with the tip of his club, which kills them instantly, for he is so strong that he does not know how to control his blows. He tells me that there are some who seek to do battle with him by striking at him with sword, ax, or lance; these he kills on the spot, for he is so strong that no one can ever hope to last against him. You should also know that he gets up in the morning and does not return until sunset, and that he always comes with some prey, either an hour sooner or an hour later. When he returns, he comes with such a hunger that it is a marvel to behold."

"And how does he enter the tower?" asked the knight.

"My lord," said the dwarf, "by those long stones that you see outside. He carries me when I wish to go out but quickly brings me back again from fear of savage beasts who might try to kill me when he is on the path ahead of me. You should know, my lord, that he fears, loves, and holds me in awe, so that there is nothing that I command him to do that he does not do whenever I am next to him. Yet it often happens, when I am not with him, that he forgets."

The Knight of the Parrot then asked him why the tower was made without a door or windows, and from where and how he had come, and who had made the tower. "My lord," said the dwarf, "I will gladly tell you. When we arrived on this island, the Knight of Foreign Isles, whose dwarf and servant I was, led both me and my wife here with him. My lord had intended to go on to the court of King Arthur, for he wished to become a member of the Round Table. When my wife began her labor, my lord caused her to lie down on the ground so that she would be delivered of the baby more quickly. But she seemed to become sicker, for she remained in labor for five days. On the third day, the wind rose up that was needed for my lord to sail away. The sailors told my lord they would tarry here no longer, and so they hoisted their sails. Then my lord came to me and asked whether I wanted to stay with my wife or go with the ship, for my wife could not board the ship because of the dangers of the sea. I answered that in no way would I leave my wife at such a dangerous time, but would rather die with her. When my lord heard this, he took great pity on me and gave me food for fifteen days. They then went back to the ship and left me and my wife on this island. On the fifth day, my wife gave birth; but a little while after the baby was born, she died. I buried her up on that hill. My son set up a large stone on the place the other day, and next to the tomb, there is a large cross of oak and a throne made from a tree on which we sit, my son and I, for we go there often to pray for her soul, that God may grant her His forgiveness.

"Now hear me well, my good lord, and I shall tell you of a great miracle and marvel that came to me; for if someone ever wanted to tell me the story about what then happened to me, in all truth, I would never believe it. Sire, after my wife was dead, I gathered my supply of food together and put it in my surcoat; then I wrapped my child up as best I could, and so went off searching, here and there through the wood, for a large tree in which I could sleep safely against the rain and the night, for I did not yet know how many wild beasts there were on this island. I found a hollow tree, the largest I ever saw, which is still in this wood, that had a hollow place within it that could easily hold six knights. I also found there some baby animals that had just recently been birthed by some wild beast. Each of the little animals had a small, sharp horn in the middle of the forehead. When I saw them, I climbed in and looked at them in amazement, and I sat myself down next to them.

"I was not looking at them too long when the mother of the animals appeared, which was a marvelously large animal, as big as a horse, and which had a horn in the middle of her forehead as sharp as any razor in the world. She also had fourteen great teats, the smallest of which was as large as the teat of a cow. When the beast saw me, she stared at me so horribly that I became very much afraid, which caused me to jump up and my child to fall down, who then began to cry loudly, and who was as beautiful and blond as any baby you could hope to see anywhere. This moved the beast to pity and she climbed in to the hollow of the tree. I, who had hid behind the tree, watched to see what the beast would do. With her muzzle, she picked up the child, lay down next to him, and acted so cleverly that he soon had a teat in his mouth. When the child felt the softness of the teat, he began to suck it and when he was satisfied, he fell asleep; but all that night I did not sleep or move about because I was afraid the beast might kill me.

"The next morning, when the beast went out to find her pasture, I felt a great hunger and so I ate some food, but when I became thirsty, I dared not look for water to drink. So I picked up the child, and while I was tying him on me, the beast, who offered me kindly signs of love, came back again, and I stayed close to her. When my son and her animals had been suckled enough, the beast, who saw that I was little, for I am a dwarf, thought I was a young child, and so she pushed me toward one of her teats that was still quite full. I, who was ever so thirsty, did what the beast wished, and so I sucked from her and discovered the best and sweetest milk I have ever tasted. My lord, such was the life I had while my foodstuffs lasted. My child was only too well nourished by that milk, as one can see.

"After my food ran out, I was very weakened by this diet of milk alone. So there came a day that a large deer passed in front of our hollow. I was very hungry, and so I said: 'My good Lord, if only I could now have a roasted shank of this deer!' While saying this, I stuck my head out, and the deer, who had heard me, turned and stared at me. The beast, who was coming on her way to care for her cubs and me, saw the deer staring at me, and became frightened for me and her babies. So she charged at the deer with great anger, before it realized what was happening, and was so swift that it was amazing to see. She struck the deer with her horn so sharply that she chopped it up into two pieces, and the deer fell down dead. I was made very happy by all this, and I came out of the hollow tree, which I had not done for three weeks. I looked all around me and saw a hollow piece of wood from a tree that had fallen, and I went to where it was lying. But for all the riches in the world, I could not move it, so I let it lie there and dug a trench beneath it. When the water gushed up from there, I made it run off, and then I washed the piece of the hollow tree, after which I filled it up with water and made a fire with my flint; then I went to get some salty sea-sand and put it in there.

"All the while the beast passed to and fro near me in order to protect me from the other beasts, so much did she love me—just as she now does, passing by once or twice a day in front of this tower. At the end of a year, when the beast no longer had any milk, she gave me and my child some flesh to eat. Since she loved me the same way a mother loves her child, I was so able to train and instruct the beast that she did everything I taught her: she killed deer, bears, and other beasts for me, which both my son and I ate. This is the kind of life I have led for well over twenty years, for I have never discovered any way, by water, that I could leave this island. When my son was twenty years old, he was so big and strong that he could easily uproot a large tree by his own strength. On this island there are so many stones and so much sand that I decided to make myself a tower, and so I had my son bring the stones and the sand and we made this tower within fifteen days; and I made it tall without a door because, when my son goes out to play, if a door were at the bottom, the wild beasts would be able to enter and eat me. Now have I told you, sire, the whole truth about me and my lodging."

"Now speak to me, dwarf," said the knight, "and counsel me. Very willingly I would like to see your son, and if we could leave this island and if you and your son wished to come along, I would be able to show you your lord, the Knight of Foreign Isles, alive."

When the dwarf heard this, he was overwhelmed with joy, and when he was able to speak again, he said: "My gentle sire, who are you and how have you come here, and how could we possibly take ship? Tell me now all about your adventure just as I have told mine." Then the Knight of the Parrot told him his whole adventure, from beginning to end, and how and why he had come there. After the dwarf heard it all, he said: "Ah, gentle King Arthur, flower of chivalry, since you can show me my lord still alive and you have a ship in which to sail, be comforted and keep yourself safe until my son arrives, for he will know how to pull the boat by means of a rope along the seashore until we come to sweet-flowing water. Once there, we shall easily cross by rowing, even if there is no one there but my son." When the king heard what the dwarf told him, he knew a joy unlike any he had known before, for he could not understand until then how he might escape from the island.

The Knight of the Parrot and the dwarf of the tower spoke this way with one another until the sun began to set. A little while later, there approached, in great haste, the son of the dwarf, who was called the Giant Without A Name, since he was not yet baptized. In one hand, he carried a bear he had killed and, in the other hand, he was clutching his club. When he spotted the king astride his charger, he became afraid of him, for he had never seen such a thing before, and he believed him and his horse to be all one animal. So he threw down his bear and took up his club in both hands; jumping forward with his club raised on high, he was so violent that the ground started to shake. When the dwarf heard him coming, he cried out as loud as he could: "Ha, my good son, Giant Without A Name, calm yourself so that I may speak with you."

The moment he heard him, his son stopped, but the dwarf noticed the king was getting ready to defend himself. So the dwarf said: "Sire, do not make ready to defend yourself, for he will kill you on the spot." Then the dwarf spoke to his son: "Now look, my good son, you shall do no harm to this one, for he is your lord and mine, who has come looking for us, and you shall also do no harm to anyone in his party; now carry him up here, for I wish to kiss him."

Then the Giant Without A Name went up to the Knight of the Parrot and said: "Sire, you are most welcome! Since you are my lord, I shall do you no harm. Yet speak to me if you know how!"

"Yes, my brother, by God's mercy!" said the knight.

"And who has given you such a cloak, and of what is it made?" asked the giant.

"Bring me up there, brother," said the knight, "and I shall tell you all that you wish to know." The king, who saw how big and strong the giant was, had great fear of him, since the giant had little reason, sense, and understanding. The king was very willing indeed to stay close to the dwarf until he could learn more about the giant's ways. The giant ran down for the bear he had left behind in order to carry it up into the tower; then he went over to the knight, who had already taken the bridle and saddle off of his mount and let him go off to pasture. As though he were a mere child, the giant easily picked the knight up, all armed as he was, and carried him up to the tower. When he was there, the dwarf fell down at his feet and showed him the greatest happiness in all the world, and told him: "Sire, you are the third man who has ever entered into this tower, for none have ever come in here but me, my son, and now you."

Then the Giant Without A Name ate half a deer and drank some water, all of which is not too amazing a feat for a man as large as he who only eats once a day and who drinks no wine at all. The king did not eat at all, while the dwarf ate very little because of the great joy he felt. After the meal, the dwarf commanded his son to kneel at King Arthur's feet and show homage so that he would no longer fear him. Thus he paid homage to the king and gave him his plighted word that from that day forward he would do all that would please him and that he would command. Then they planned what they should do, and afterwards went to bed and rested until morning. When daybreak came, the king, giant, and dwarf all got up. When the king mounted, he put the dwarf in front of him, and the giant went along on foot, with his club in his hand, with all his harness tied around his neck. While they were going this way toward the ship, they saw the unicorn who had given milk to the giant pass by the tower, as was her daily custom in order to see the giant, her son. She came willingly in the morning since she could never find him at midday; and she would follow the giant so that, should the need ever arise, she could help him, so great was her love for him.

In this manner the Knight of the Parrot started off for the ship, carrying the dwarf in front of him, and followed by the Giant Without A Name and the unicorn as well. When they reached the ship, the knights and sailors felt both joy and fear. They felt joy because they saw their lord once more, and they felt fear because of the unicorn and the giant. After the Knight of the Parrot told them how they should do it, the sailors took up the ropes, threw them over the sides, and tied them to the mast and to the ship's hull, and the giant picked up one end of a line, tied it around the unicorn's chest and then tied the other end about his own shoulders. After this, the Knight of the Parrot and the dwarf boarded the ship. Why should I make my story longer? The giant and the unicorn, with the sailors' help, pulled the ship into fresh water.

The giant then went aboard the ship and when the unicorn saw the giant board the ship, she did the same. So they rowed all together with great power on the river, which was actually some four miles long and was marvelously turbulent and deep.

After they had gone through the worst of it, they came to a very beautiful country. The Knight of the Parrot realized he had been there before, and he disembarked with all his party. They did not ride too far before coming to the Amorous City, where the Lady of the Blonde Hair lived, who received them in marvelous fashion. Without any delay, the Knight of the Parrot sent a message to the castle of Causuel, which belonged to the Merciless Lion, to inform him that King Arthur charged him to appear with all his knights, as he had promised he would, at Videsores [Windsor] on Pentecost when the king would hold court. The Merciless Lion replied that he would do this willingly. When the messenger brought back this news, they all went to bed.

The Knight of the Parrot slept that night next to the Lady of the Blonde Hair, as they had done on other occasions, and they knew great joy. Very early the next morning, he took leave with his escort. They rode off, making such good progress each day, that they soon came to Britain, to the castle of Videsores on the vigil of Pentecost. Once they were all there, King Arthur found King Lot, whom he had left to govern in his place, as well as all the knights of the Round Table. Together with his escort, Arthur was received with such great joy as was never known by any other king before, for they were all amazed by the marvels their lord had accomplished, and highly esteemed him for his courtesy and chivalry.

On the next day, the feast of Pentecost, King Arthur held such a great and joyous court that never was the same held by any other king. While they were all at table, the parrot sang so sweetly about the adventures that all there were more amazed by them than by anything else they had ever heard, for which they left off eating and drinking. After the parrot had finished his song, the Merciless Lion and all his knights entered the great hall, all richly dressed, as the king had commanded. He told the barons about his adventure and how he placed himself at the king's mercy, and they all had his party seated with them for the feast.

After the tables were cleared away, the king had the Giant Without A Name baptized and dubbed him a knight. This was also done to the dwarf, his father, and they saluted one another and felt great satisfaction and honor. After fifteen days, the court dispersed, and the king gave gold and silver to everyone, according to his wishes, so that everyone, both big and small, sang his praises. Everyone then left, happy and contented, for his own land, leaving the king even more happy. So ends this story about the Knight of the Parrot.

Tintagel Castle in Cornwall, the birthplace of King Arthur. The ruins look out over the Atlantic Ocean, and the Cave of Merlin is located below. (Courtesy of the British Tourist Authority)

chapter II
OLD NORSE

THE SAGA OF THE MANTLE

Marianne E. Kalinke

Mǫttuls saga (The Saga of the Mantle) is an anonymous Old Norse translation of the French *Lai du cort mantel* (Tale of the Short Mantle), also known as *Le Mantel mautaillié* (The Ill-cut Mantle), which was presumably composed toward the end of the twelfth or the beginning of the thirteenth century. The preface to *Mǫttuls saga* informs us that it is the account of a curious and amusing incident that took place at the court of King Arthur and that the translation was undertaken at the behest of King Hákon Hákonarson, who ruled Norway from 1217 to 1263. *Mǫttuls saga* is part of a group of Arthurian narratives that were translated for King Hákon from the French bestsellers of the day. In 1226 a certain Brother Robert translated Thomas of Britain's *Tristan* (*Tristrams saga ok Ísǫndar*) and this was followed by anonymous translations of Chrétien de Troyes's *Yvain* (*Ívens saga*) and a collection of Breton *lais* entitled in Old Norse *Strengleikar* (Stringed Instruments).

Among the Arthurian narratives *The Saga of the Mantle* is in a class by itself because of its irreverent portrayal of courtly society. The saga, like *Le Lai du cort mantel*, is a ribald tale of a chastity test conducted by means of a magic mantle at King Arthur's court. With one exception, all the ladies at court, starting with Guinevere, are ignominiously exposed as unfaithful wives and lovers.

The chastity-testing mantle is central to a number of medieval and modern Arthurian narratives. It is celebrated in French, German, English, and Icelandic literature. The mantle-test narratives constitute only a small group, however, within a larger—mostly non-Arthurian—corpus of tales, medieval as well as modern, devoted to chastity tests by means of such objects as shirts, gloves, girdles, rings, and roses. Antedating the *Lai du cort mantel*, Robert Biket wrote the *Lai du cor* (Lay of the Horn), in which cuckolded knights—and not their unfaithful ladies—are incapable of drinking from a horn without spilling its contents. The mantle-test compositions are nevertheless distinguished from other chastity-testing tales in that the trial by mantle always takes place at a social gathering; during a public event the infidelity of a woman becomes known not only to her lover or husband but also to society at large.

Like all the other Old Norse translations of foreign (primarily French) literature, *Mǫttuls saga* is written in prose, and like the other translations commissioned by King Hákon Hákonarson, the saga is characterized by amplification as an explicatory, emphatic, or anticipatory device. Although the translator adhered carefully to the content of his French source, he nonetheless augmented the narrative by employing alliteration and other collocations, both synonymous and antithetical, for emphasis and to achieve semantic, syntactic, and rhythmical euphony. Thus, despite its accuracy in transmitting the French matter, the saga may also be considered an interpretation.

Although *Mǫttuls saga* is translated into Old Norse, it is preserved only in Icelandic copies of the original Norwegian translation. There are two redactions: A, which is extant in one leaf, dated 1300 to 1350 (AM 598 Iβ 4to; the oldest manuscript containing an Arthurian text in Scandinavia) and B (represented by the fragments AM 598 Iα 4to and Stockholm 6 4to) from around 1400. The latter redaction was transcribed in Iceland in the seventeenth century when the manuscript was still complete. The present translation is based on a copy made by Jón Erlendsson, which is preserved in the manuscript AM 179 fol.

The Old Norse-Icelandic translations of continental literature are characterized by a paratactic style, like indigenous Icelandic prose, with frequent repetition of "and," "now," and "then," by changes in tense, and by ellipsis. Whenever these stylistic devices have been deemed too disturbing to the flow of narrative, they have been silently emended.

Bibliographic note: The text translated here is based on my edition: *Mǫttuls saga*, Editiones Arnamagnæanæ, Series B, Vol. 30 (Reitzel, 1988), which also contains an edition of *Le Lai du cort mantel* by Philip E. Bennett and my translation of the saga into English. Although I have based the following translation on this edition, the text presented here is a freer version. For a history of the Mantle-Tale in Europe consult the Introduction to this edition. See also Marianne E. Kalinke, *King Arthur, North-by-Northwest. The matière de Bretagne in Old Norse-Icelandic Romance*, Bibliotheca Arnamagnæana, Vol. 37 (Reitzel, 1981).

The Saga of the Mantle

Chapter I

King Arthur was the most renowned ruler with regard to every aspect of valor and all kinds of manliness and chivalry, combined with perfect compassion and most appealing mildness, so that in every respect there was no ruler more renowned or blessed with friends in his day in the world. He was the most valiant man at arms, the most generous with gifts, the gentlest in words, the cleverest in his designs, the most benevolent in mercy, the most polished in good manners, the noblest in all kingly craft, godfearing in his undertakings, gentle to the good, harsh to the wicked, merciful to the needy, hospitable to the companionable, so perfect in his entire authority that neither ill will nor malice was found in him, and no one could adequately laud the splendid magnificence and honor of his realm. This is attested by truthful accounts about him and much dependable intelligence recorded by worthy clerks about his many deeds—sometimes about various illustrious events that occurred in diverse ways at his court as well as throughout his realm, sometimes about valiant deeds of chivalry, sometimes about other curious matters.

This book tells about a curious and amusing incident that took place at the court of the illustrious and renowned King Arthur, who held all England and Brittany under his sway. And this true account, which came to me in French, I have translated into Norwegian as entertainment and diversion for you, the listeners, since the worthy King Hákon, son of King Hákon, asked me, ignorant though I be, to provide some entertainment through the following story.

Chapter II

During that festive period which the Holy Church calls Pentecost but the Norse call *Pikkisdagar*, there came to King Arthur illustrious chieftains and kings of many lands, together with dukes and other honorable men, as is attested by this saga, as well as many others that were composed about him. King Arthur was the most inquisitive of men and wanted to be apprised of all news of events that took place within his realm as well as in other lands, wherever he might learn of them. And therefore he let it be trumpeted about, in woods, on roads and crossroads, that everyone who was traveling about should come to his court and his celebration. The king's summons went on to say that any man's ladylove might accompany him, and the king would make her equally welcome. As a result there came so many that the gathering was too large to be counted. For this reason the wisest of men found it difficult to choose the most courtly woman in such a large gathering.

The queen rejoiced at their coming and allowed the maidens to stay in her chambers. The queen, who was the most beautiful of women, conversed with them and engaged in all manner of diversion and amusements in courtly fashion. She herself had costly garments and she gave each of the women splendid clothing of all kinds of colors and qualities, even the poorest of which was made of costly stuff and lined with grey and white fur. Whoever had occasion to look at the clothing carefully had much to talk about. But I do not want to detain you, and thus I will say but little about much: that no better garments existed in the world than those given away, and no merchant could have sold them or purchased them for what they were worth. The queen was laudable because of her exceedingly noble deportment and most blessed with friends because of her renowned munificence. She let precious brooches and rich belts be brought out, as well as rings with all kinds of precious stones. No man had ever seen such rare or excellent treasures as the queen bestowed of her abundant good will, for each of them was allowed to take whatever she wanted to have.

But now we must speak about King Arthur, that renowned man, who let rich garments and trusty weapons, magnificent apparel, and the best of weapons be given to his court and to the assembled chieftains and knights, and in addition, horses that had been sent to him from the West, from Spain, Lombardy, and Alemannia. There had come no knight, no matter how poor, who did not receive rich garments and trusty weapons, magnificent apparel, and a good horse, for there was no lack of things that one might want. And at no king's court were such rich gifts received and bestowed with such abundance as were given there. Moreover, the king was worthy of great praise because he never regretted giving, and therefore he was so free with them, as if all that he gave away cost nothing.

The Saturday before Pentecost the great court had assembled, and it was so well outfitted with horses and weapons and good clothing that nowhere in the world was there another court like this. Much diversion and all kinds of entertainments with abundant pastimes were provided for the many well-bred persons who had assembled there. When they had spent the whole day in such pastimes and evening came, all went to their lodgings, and the shield-bearers made the beds, and then all the people went to sleep.

Chapter III

When day came and it began to grow light, they all got dressed and all the people went to the king's palace and accompanied the king to the cathedral of the town. The queen with her maidens also came to attend the divine service, and one could see there many a courtly man and beautiful woman very well attired because the handsomest people in the world were assembled there. When the divine service was finished, all the court went to the king's palace, and the queen led her group of women into the chambers with her. The stewards in the king's palace and the servants had a most abundant supply of good provisions and the best beverages to be found in the world to provide for the king's tables in every way. They first covered the tables with the whitest of tablecloths and placed on them silver spoons and gold spoons, highly ornamented knives, and silver dishes with salt. Then the food was ready for the king and all his court. But it was King Arthur's custom not to go to table or to be truly content on any day until he had first received news about some event or other that had happened near or far and from which he might derive enjoyment and pleasure. The queen summoned Sir Valven [Walwen, Gawain], the chief of all the king's stewards, and asked how it came about that the king did not go to table, now that the food was prepared and all his court assembled and it was already mid-afternoon. He went at once to the king and spoke to him thus: "Lord, what is the reason that you are not eating, even though the tables have been set for a long time?"

The king looked at him and answered: "Steward, when have you seen me hold court at a feast when I did not receive news of some event before I went to table?"

Just as the king was saying this, a young man came up quickly on a galloping horse and headed toward the king's palace; he was riding so fast that the horse was all in a sweat under him, for he was hastening exceedingly.

Sir Valven saw him first and spoke to the courtiers: "If God wills it," he said, "we shall quickly dine, for I see a young man galloping vigorously on his horse in this direction, and he will surely bring us some news."

Thereupon the young man came to the doors of the king's hall and dismounted, and the servants led off his horse. The young man was most courtly; he immediately removed his outer garments and threw his mantle over the horse's neck. And when he was without his outer garments, he seemed most handsome. His hair was flaxen; his shoulders were broad and powerful; his arms were both long and sturdy; his hands were white and strong; by nature he was well built, as handsome as one might desire with respect to physical strength and prowess, so that no one could wish him otherwise than as God had created him. He did not lack for words, and chose them cleverly.

Chapter IV

When he had come into the king's hall, where the court was, he spoke to them with courteous words: "May that almighty God," he said, "Who created us all, help and preserve your assembly and fellowship!"

"Friend," they said, "may God bless you!"

Then Kay the steward spoke up: "Your horse is in a sweat. Tell us some news about your journey."

"No, sire," he said, "you shall first tell me where the good King Arthur is. And I swear, by my troth, I shall give the king such news that won't please all of you; nonetheless, some will derive pleasure from it."

All thought it took a long time to find out what it was that he wanted to say. Then a knight spoke to the young man: "Look, friend, there he is, sitting on the throne."

He went there immediately, while all those who were in his path made room for him. And when he came before the king, he greeted him with these words: "May God, Who created heaven and earth and all those creatures who are in the world, bless and preserve you, the crowned king who is highest among all those who have been and who ever will be." And then he said. "Now I'm pleased to have found you, for I have long sought you. A most beautiful maiden," he said, "far from your land, sent me here to find you, and she asks that you, as is your duty, grant her a boon, but if you refuse to do so, then she will not ask again. You are not to know, however, what she is asking or who she herself is before granting the boon. She is exceedingly beautiful and illustrious, so that there is no one like her in all the world. But I want you to know, since I am to ask this favor on her behalf, that I ask for nothing that will disgrace your honor or damage your kingdom."

The king granted what the young man asked for, and he thanked the king profusely. Thereupon he took out of a small, gold-embroidered pouch a mantle of silk that was so beautiful that mortal eye had never seen one that resembled it or was its equal. An elf-woman had fashioned it with such great and inconceivable skill that in that whole assembly of skillful and intelligent men gathered there, there was no one who could perceive in what manner the garment had been made. It was shot through with gold in a pattern of such beautifully embroidered leaves that never the like was seen, for no one could find either the beginning or the end. What was strangest, moreover, was that those who scrutinized it most closely could least discover how that wondrous piece of workmanship was put together. But I do not want to draw things out, for the mantle was even stranger than one might imagine: the elf-woman had woven a charm into the mantle so that the misdeed of every maiden who had been intimate with her beloved would be revealed at once when she dressed in it: it would become very long or very short in a flagrant manner so as to reveal how she had sinned. Thus it would expose all false women and maidens, so that nothing could be hidden when it was put on. Before the entire court and that great gathering of chieftains who were assembled there, the young man announced clearly and boldly in what manner the mantle was woven and what power it had to put women to the test.

Thereupon he spoke to the king. "Lord," he said, "I bid you now to have the ladies and the maidens of the court try on the mantle at once, for far from here I heard what illustrious women and maidens are assembled here; but do this speedily now so that they are not first apprised of this intelligence. This is the reason I have come: to ask this favor of you rather than any other, and for no other purpose."

The entire court and all the chieftains who had come there wondered and were curious about the mantle. Then Valven said that this favor was worth granting just as the boon was worth accepting.

Chapter V

The king now sent Sir Valven and Kay the steward and Meon the page for the queen. He bade them tell the queen to come to him at once, together with all those maidens and women who were with her, and to come one and all so that no one stayed behind, "because I certainly intend to keep the promise I made to the young man." They went now and found the queen in her chambers, ready to go to table, for she was hungry, since she had fasted for so long.

Sir Valven conveyed the king's message. "Lady," he said, "the king bids you not to delay to come at once to him, because a very handsome young man has come to him and brought him such a precious mantle that no mortal eye has ever seen another like it. The cloth is red and is a treasure the likes of which we have never yet seen, fashioned with such wondrous and extraordinary skill that it is uncertain whether another like it exists or can be found in all the world. And know for certain that the king has promised the mantle to the one whom it fits and best suits. Try your luck now, milady; do not delay, and bring along all the women who have come here, for the king wants to see their appearance and beauty. It is not known to me, however, on whom this praiseworthy gift will be bestowed."

The queen went at once to the king, accompanied by the entire large group of beautiful women and illustrious maidens, so that never before had the eye of man seen in one spot so great an assemblage of beautiful women and beautiful maidens, and there had never been better garments in the world than those with which they were adorned. For this reason every man looked at them, and many a man was captivated by them as well. Immediately the entire court went into the hall, wondering who it would be who would possess the mantle. Thereupon the king took the mantle and spread it out, showing it to the queen and saying that he would give it to her or to anyone whom it might fit. But not a whit more did he tell them about it, for if they had known what else pertained to the mantle, none of them would have dressed in it, not for all the gold in Araby, and it would have been as repulsive to them as a maggot or a serpent.

Now, however, the time had come for the mantle to tell how faithfully each had conducted herself toward her husband or how faithful she had been to her beloved. The queen took the mantle first and put it on, and it became so short on her that it did not reach her heels. As much as she wanted to own the mantle, she would never even have let it touch her body had she known what spell had been woven into it. She immediately blushed with shame and then immediately paled from anger and rage when the mantle did not fit.

Meon the page stood beside her and saw her face changing color, and so he spoke to her at once:

"Milady," he said, "it does not seem to me that the mantle is too long for you; instead, it is a good ell too short and in no way does it fit you. This maiden, however, who is standing here beside you and who is nearly the same size as you, neither taller nor shorter, she is the beloved of Aristes, son of King Artus; give her the mantle and then you will see how it fits her though it was too short for you."

Thereupon the queen took the mantle and handed it to the maiden beside her, who gladly took it and immediately put it on, but on her it was much shorter than on the queen. Then Meon the page spoke: "The mantle has now shrunk much in a short time and yet it has not been worn long."

The queen asked the nobles and all the chieftains: "Tell me, lords, was the mantle not longer than this?"

"Milady," said Valven, "it seems to me that you are somewhat more faithful than she is, and yet you are quite alike, but there is less falsehood in you than in her."

Then the queen spoke to Kay the steward. "Tell me," she said, "what is this faithfulness that you are speaking about and what power is inherent in this mantle?" And Kay told her from the beginning to the end just what the young man had said. The queen thought that if she got angry or became enraged about this in any way, that she would earn shame and disgrace for having been unfaithful to such a ruler, and thus she turned everything into entertainment and diversion, into laughter, jest, and ridicule. "Now," she said, "all maidens and women will surely try on the mantle since I put it on first."

"Milady," said Kay the steward, "today the faithfulness of all of you shall be made manifest, as well as the steadfastness of your love, which husbands or trueloves expect, when you claim that you have long preserved a firm faithfulness; because of the love that the knights have for your virginity, they hazard mortal danger and take many risks for your sakes. In the past you have all pretended to be so pure and faithful that if somebody asked any of you, or if a brave man wished to win one of you, you would immediately swear that you have never had anything to do with a man."

When they fully understood with what cunning the mantle had been woven and what power the elf-woman had embroidered and sewn into the leaves on the mantle, there was not a single woman in that large assemblage who would not have preferred to stay at home with honor rather than come there, for there was not a single one in that entire gathering who dared to put on the mantle or dress in it or hold it in her hands or come near it.

Chapter VII

When all drew back from the mantle and no one dared to put it on, the king spoke: "Now we shall return the mantle to the young man, for he cannot stay here with us on account of the maidens in our charge."

But the young man answered: "That is not right, sire, nor honorable, nor in keeping with your station; by no means do I intend to take back the mantle before I see that all the women and maidens have tried it on, for whatever a king grants and promises must never be rescinded or revoked because of anyone's demanding or inciting words."

"My young man," said the king, "you speak wisely; what you said is true and just, and no one shall prevent me from keeping to what has been spoken and giving what I have promised you. Now every single lady shall try on the mantle."

While all stood in silence, Kay the steward, in the presence of all the knights and men of the realm, called to his beloved with these words: "Beloved," he said, "come forward; you may take the mantle unafraid and fearless. There is no one your equal here in true faithfulness and other fitting, womanly accomplishments. With honor and distinction we two shall carry off the victory today."

But the maiden answered: "If it be your will, then I would like someone else to take the mantle, for I want to see how she fares; I see here more than a hundred of those who dare not come near it, and no one wants to put it on."

"Ho, ho!" said Kay; "it seems to me that you are somewhat fearful, and I don't know what that means."

"That is not so, sir," she said. "Much more excellent and prominent women than I am have already taken the mantle, and it is not that I am afraid of it; rather it is," she said, "that there is here such a gathering of prominent women who are good and faithful and from the finest families, and it will be ill received if I run forward ahead of them; I might suffer hatred and ridicule as a result."

"You must not," said Kay, "fear their anger, because no one desires to put on the mantle. Nonetheless, I know that you are safe and that it will be to your honor if you get the mantle but to your shame if you fail."

Then the maiden put on the mantle before all the assembled nobles and many other lords, and the mantle became so short for her in back that it hardly reached the hollow of her knees; in front, however, it did not even reach the knee.

Then all the nobles derided her and said: "Kay, our steward, can rejoice much in your love and practice great deeds of chivalry for your sake, for now your fidelity has been manifested, so that we may all know that no one like you can be found in the realm of the king of England."

When Kay saw how his beloved had fallen, he would have preferred that she had never come there rather than to receive such shame and disgrace. Ideus then spoke to Kay. "It is good," he said, "that derision and disgrace turn on you, since you deride everyone. What do you say? Doesn't the mantle fit your beloved well, whose faithfulness you praised so highly?"

The maiden was greatly distressed, since she could not defend herself against their words, for the whole court had seen how the mantle had fit her.

Then Kay spoke to the other knights. "Don't be too hasty," he said; "we shall see how beautifully the mantle fits your ladyloves."

Kay's beloved threw the mantle down, however, and went to her seat in shame and disgrace.

Chapter VIII

Now when the entire group of women saw how poorly this maiden had fared, they all cursed the young man who had brought the mantle there, for now that they were truly informed about it, there was no use objecting to putting on the mantle, even though they might come up with a satisfactory excuse for refusing. Then the courteous page Bodendr spoke to the king. "My lord," he said, "it seems to me that we are not following the proper order in trying on the mantle. The beloved of Sir Valven is so pleasingly beautiful that she should have tried on the mantle after the queen."

But Valven the steward was not pleased that she should try on the mantle because he suspected that she would not receive any more honor than those who had tried it on before. The king then said that Bodendr, the courteous page, should call her. She stood up at once because she dared not do otherwise. The king had the mantle brought to her and she tried it on at once as the king had asked. But as soon as she had it on, it was so long for her in back that she dragged it behind her for four and a half ells, but in front it shrank up to her knees and on the left side it rose as high up as her back. Kay the steward was glad when he saw that the mantle was so short for her, because people thought that she was probably more faithful than all other maidens and women who were at the king's court.

"By my troth," said Kay the steward, "praised be God! I shall not be the only one to be disgraced today because of my beloved, for I now deduce something from the mantle and I can easily interpret what that means: this beautiful maiden," said Kay, "has raised up her right leg but the left leg she let lie quietly while she allowed the man she liked to do what she wished him to do."

Sir Valven was annoyed that the wrongdoing of his beloved was so openly manifested, but he made no comment about it.

Then Kay spoke to her. "Come here, my lovely," he said. "I shall lead you to a seat beside my beloved because there are no women more alike than you two are."

Then the king took by the hand the daughter of King Urien, who was a most lovely maiden. The king, her father, was a powerful man who often went hunting with dogs and hawks.

"My lovely," said the gracious King Arther, "the test will rightly award you this mantle, because no one finds fault in you."

"Lord," said Geres the Little, "do not speak at length about this before you have really seen how the mantle fits her."

Now the maiden knew right away that it was no use objecting to what the king had ordered, and therefore she took the mantle at once. But as soon as she was dressed in it, it became so long for her on the right side that one and one half ells dragged on the ground, while on the left side it rose over her knee.

"Lord," said Geres the Little, "foolish is he who trusts any woman because all deceive their beloveds and not a single one is trustworthy; moreover, the least faithful are they who act and speak most virtuously, and betrayal comes from those from whom one least expects it. No woman comes off well when she is tested. All deceive their husbands and want a man who is new as soon as they have tired of the old one. They have such a desire for novelty that no one can trust their actions. And now I want to say what I think is obvious about the conduct of this maiden: the mantle is long for her on the right side to show us that she more willingly let herself fall on that side, but the left side—where the mantle is raised—shows us that she is not annoyed if someone should lift up her dress there."

Then the maiden was so overcome by anger that at first she was speechless; she took hold of the ties on the mantle and cast it far from her and cursed repeatedly the one who had brought it to the court.

Kay the steward then said. "Don't get angry, lovely maiden; you too will sit beside my beloved. The three of you are equal in this respect and none of you can blame the others."

Chapter IX

Thereupon the king ordered that the beloved of Paternas should come forward, and he spoke to her with gentle words. "You, my lovely," said the king, "will undoubtedly get the mantle because you have a true and loyal love for your beloved."

Then Gerflet, the king's fool, could not keep quiet. "Milord," he said, "for the sake of God, do not settle the matter so quickly with words before you see how things turn out, for the day is to be praised at evening, and many a thing can turn out otherwise than one expects."

The maiden took the mantle at once because she knew that it was no use objecting. But when she was about to put it on, the mantle's ties broke off and right away they fell to the ground, with the mantle following so readily that it didn't stay in place anywhere. The maiden immediately trembled all over and did not know what she should do because she was surrounded by a large group of illustrious women and handsome shield-bearers and many other powerful men. They all cursed the mantle and the one who had made it, as well as the one who had brought it to the court. They all asserted that no one would be found in that great assemblage of court-ladies whom the mantle would fit; it would rightfully fit neither wife nor maiden, and there probably was no one created, no matter how fair or beautiful, who had a figure to which the mantle would conform, no matter how much she wept or grieved. Despite all this, everyone still wanted to own the mantle.

Valven then went to his beloved and spoke: "I bring this beautiful maiden to you here so that she might join your company." There was no one among them who thanked her for her coming. But Valven made light of it and then turned back laughing. Thereupon the young man picked the mantle very quickly up from the ground and took ties out of his pouch and attached the ties at once, since he did not want his mission to fail. The king then took the mantle and spoke in great anger: "We are fasting too long," he said. "What is the matter with these women? Why do we delay in having them put on the mantle?"

But Gerflet, the king's fool, spoke: "Milord, for God's sake, you might as well acquit those who are left, or do you want to bring even greater disgrace on them? Now that they see the mantle, they all admit here to their husbands and their lords and trueloves that they have gone somewhat astray." Once more the fool spoke to him: "What else do you want to demand from all of them?"

The king wanted to leave matters as they stood. Then the young man hastened before the king and spoke so that all the court heard him: "Lord," he said, "keep your word to me and the favor that you promised me. These knights do not know what they should say concerning their ladyloves, if it should turn out that some are tested but some are not and are let off free."

Then Ideus spoke up and called to his beloved: "You, my lovely," he said, "earlier today I thought that there was no one more faithful than you at this court, and Kay the steward answered me when I reproached his beloved; but I was rash in saying that I had such great confidence in your faithfulness, and that I was quite fearless about you. Now I regret this greatly, since I see that you are afraid. Take this mantle now and put it on."

The king had the mantle taken to her at once, and she took it right away and put it on. And when she had put it on, it fit perfectly in front, so that all thought nothing but good might be revealed about her. In the back, how-ever, it was so short that it did not reach down to her loins, so that it hardly covered her belt. Gerflet the fool, who saw this first, spoke at once with a loud voice. "Noble maiden," he said, "the mantle is too short for you in the back, and it will never become so long in front that it will fit you well."

Then Kay could not keep silent any longer because Ideus had derided his beloved, and he quickly addressed Ideus with mockery and derision: "Look, Ideus, how do you think matters are going? Has your beloved not gone somewhat astray? This is what I think about her affairs, since you can deride all of us and yet we, in truth, can all see that your beloved is not properly clothed where her loins are bare. Now I will tell all of you who are listening that she is accustomed to let herself be taken shamelessly from behind, as the mantle openly manifests."

Ideus did not know what to say; he could only snatch the mantle in anger and rage and cast it at the feet of the king. Kay then took his beloved by the hand and led her where those were sitting who had tried the mantle on before, and said: "I know for certain that there will soon be a large and fine gathering here."

Chapter X

Now there was no longer anything else to do but for all those who had come there, both wives and maidens, old and young, to put on the mantle as quickly as possible, one after the other, while the beloved of each was watching. And it fit not a single one. Kay took each one of them by the hand and led her to a seat in that large circle that they made on the floor of the hall. There was no one in that large gathering of chieftains and knights who were there who did not have a beloved, and everyone who saw their faces could right away discover distress and sorrow in them. It was a consolation that no one could mock another without himself being implicated.

Then Kay the steward spoke: "Good lords," he said, "do not become enraged or angry on account of this, for we are all in the same position. Our ladyloves have been honored and exalted over and above all other court-ladies near and far, wherever they may be, and today they have earned for themselves a certain renown; their only consolation may be that not one can blame another."

Then Sir Valven responded thus: "It does not seem to me that you are considering this case correctly, because it would be improper and in every way abominable if I took consolation in their disgrace; we shall never admit that a good, valiant man is reprehensible because his beloved besmirches herself with another man; rather, she herself is as evil because of her deeds and vices as is he who consented to her follies."

At this moment the young man hastened before the king and said: "I suspect, my lord, that I shall have to take the mantle back, even though I cannot understand how in such a large group it can be that there is not a single woman who can wear it. Have your chambers searched now, wherever the ladies are accustomed to sleep or sit, to make sure that no one is hidden or concealed there. The members of your court have fame and renown above all other people in the world, but if, as matters stand, I must leave, less news will come from now on to you than before if I have to depart with my mission unaccomplished."

"By my troth," said Sir Valven, "the young man speaks the truth; have the chambers searched as quickly as possible to ascertain that no one is hiding there."

The king then ordered all the upper chambers to be searched, and when he had said this, Gerflet the fool ran very quickly into the chambers and found a noble maiden right away. She had not hidden herself, however; instead, she was not feeling well and was lying in bed. Gerflet the fool then spoke to her right away: "Noble maiden," he said, "no one has ever seen a fairer adventure than the one now taking place in the king's hall, and you will have to take part in it as all the others have already done."

"I shall gladly go there," said the maiden, "but you must wait until I am dressed suitably."

Now the maiden got up and dressed in keeping with her station, in the finest clothes that she had; these were very costly because she came from a noble family. Then she went into the hall. Although her beloved was cheerful and in good spirits before she came in, he became distressed and angry when he saw her coming because he did not want her ever to try on the mantle. He loved her so much that even though he were to find out for certain about any misdeed of hers, he did not care; on account of the great love that he had for her, he never wanted to leave her.

The young man then brought her the mantle and told her with what artifice it had been woven. But Karadin, her beloved, called out with a loud voice while all were listening: "You, sweet beloved," he said, "if you have gone astray in any way, then don't ever go near the mantle. I love you so profoundly that I certainly don't want to lose your love—not for all the gold in the world, even though I were to be aware of any misdeed of yours."

But Kay the steward responded: "Why do you speak in such a way? Anyone who loses an unfaithful beloved should be joyful and delighted."

Then the maiden answered with gentle mien: "Sir," she said, "it may in truth cause a good man lasting distress if his beloved is proven to be unfaithful to him; still, if my beloved does not take it amiss, then I will put on the mantle."

"By my troth," said the knight, "there is no way you can avoid the test or refuse to take the mantle, since all the others have tried it on."

But she still did not want to try it on before her beloved allowed her to do so. As soon as he permitted it, she took the mantle and put it on before the entire court, and it fit her so well that it was neither too short nor too long; instead, it reached the ground evenly on all sides.

Then the young man spoke: "By my troth, this maiden may fittingly and boldly ask to keep the mantle, and I think, noble maiden, that your beloved has reason to be happier than the others who are here. But now you are to know the truth: I have taken this mantle to many courts where there are many people, where more than a thousand of those considered to be maidens have been exposed by this mantle. Never before has it shown your like in the purity of your maidenhood. And now I bestow on you this precious mantle, which is so excellent that there is none like it in all the world. No man can estimate its true value, and you alone may rightfully keep it, wear it, possess it, and leave it to your heirs." Thus the young man concluded his speech. Then the king spoke and said that she alone might rightfully have the mantle since she alone was worthy of owning it.

Chapter XI

Although all the women who sat about were envious because all of them wanted to own the mantle themselves, still none of them had been able to obtain it, and no one dared to object. Then Sir Valven spoke: "You, noble maiden," he said, "I take it upon myself on your behalf to proclaim that you are not indebted to anyone for the mantle except to yourself, to the purity of your maidenhood. For that reason all men and women who see your goodness now grant it to you, although they would gladly object if they could find true grounds for reproaching you. But now the situation has undergone a change for the better, as their envy and grief become your joy, their sorrow your consolation, their disgrace your honor, and their misdeeds your praise, which will swell in every land."

Thereupon the young man took leave of the king. By no means did he want to stay there any longer and eat the food; instead, he wanted to hurry back to his lady and report to her about his mission. The king sat down at table, however, as did all his court, and it can be said in truth that many a good knight sat there distressed on account of his beloved. But King Arthur let his court be entertained at such great cost that never had there been such entertainment either offered or enjoyed.

When the court had eaten its fill, Karadin went before the king and asked permission to depart; cheerfully and in good spirits he left with his beloved. They placed the mantle in a monastery, however, for safekeeping.

Recently inquiries have been made about it, and he who has it says that he will have it taken everywhere in order to test lovely maidens and beautiful women. We expect that few will be found who will be able to own it, and thus it will remain new for a long time. He who has the mantle intends to send it to all the courts, so that all the court-ladies and court-maidens will have to try it on. I would rather not be the messenger accompanying the mantle, so as not to be ill-treated by those powerful men who are confronted by such a gift.

Now let no one say anything but good about women, because it is more fitting to conceal than to reveal something, even though one may know the true state of affairs. No matter who puts it on, the mantle will show what the one trying it on is truly like. Therefore let us praise good women according to their merits, because they have earned renown and happiness.

Now the *Saga of the Mantle* ends here; may you live happily for many years to come. Amen.

chapter III
LATIN

THE RISE OF GAWAIN, NEPHEW OF ARTHUR

Mildred Leake Day

The Rise of Gawain, Nephew of Arthur tells the story of Gawain's birth, boyhood, and early adventures. It ends with Gawain being received by King Arthur and acclaimed as the pre-eminent knight of the realm. Other Arthurian works tell of Gawain's parentage and training in Rome—Geoffrey of Monmouth's *Historia Regum Britanniae*, Wace's *Roman de Brut*, Layamon's *Brut, Enfances Gauvain, Perlesvaus*—but *De ortu Waluuanii* is the only complete source.

The Rise of Gawain is written in Medieval Latin. The single remaining manuscript is a copy made in the early fourteenth century. Its date has been debated, but it was written after Geoffrey of Monmouth (mid-twelfth century) because the plot and many specific passages are borrowed from Geoffrey. Although J. D. Bruce and R. S. Loomis propose a date of composition in the thirteenth century, several details of costume and ship construction suggest an earlier date.

The work is anonymous, but the catalog tradition as recorded by John Bale in the sixteenth century lists Robert of Torigny as author. Robert was the renowned abbot of Mont St. Michel in France from 1154 to 1186. Although no other evidence indicates that Robert was the author of this romance or of *The Story of Meriadoc (Historia Meriadoci)*, a second romance by the same hand, the two romances with their learned style must have been composed by a cleric with a similar background and range of interests.

One of the most interesting episodes in the series of adventures concerns the making of the explosive known as Greek fire. The description is a bizarre combination of folklore, literary passages about Medea's magic from Ovid's *Metamorphoses*, and a layman's description of the method of processing and projecting the petroleum mix. The method described would have produced a flame-weapon of thickened gasoline, much like a primitive napalm. This description, odd as it is, is one of the earliest documents on Greek fire from a European source.

Although most of the work is concerned with serious adventures, some passages are funny, as when Gawain forces Arthur into the River Usk. Arthur's explanation to his wife Gwendoloena (Guinevere) about why he is so cold and wet is one of the most delightful bits of humor in Arthurian literature. Equally funny is the scene on the next day when the proud Gawain presents horses to Gwendoloena and the King and meets the angry face of Arthur. Arthur opens a packet from the Emperor of Rome, but keeps the enclosed knowledge of Gawain's lineage to himself. The trick now is how Arthur can manage to save face, yet retain this remarkable kinsman in his service. So the King rebuffs Gawain until the frustrated knight makes the rash promise that if he can perform an exploit beyond the capability of Arthur's entire band of knights, then Arthur must accept him into their number. Arthur, delighted, agrees.

The theme of establishing one's identity gives *The Rise of Gawain* its structure and plot. Gawain first must learn who he is as an individual: a knight of incomparable prowess but known only as "Knight of the Surcoat." Then he must learn who he is by lineage. The reader, like the Emperor, holds the true knowledge from the beginning.

Bibliographic note: Scholarly work on *De ortu Waluuanii* has not been as extensive as that on many other Arthurian romances. James Douglas Bruce prepared two editions, the first for *PMLA*, 13 (1898), 365–455; the second as part of his volume *Historia Meriadoci* and *De ortu Waluuanii*, *Hesperia 2*, Göttingen: Dandenhoed & Ruprecht, 1913. The most recent edition is by Mildred Leake Day, *The Rise of Gawain, Nephew of Arthur* (*De ortu Waluuanii nepotis Arturi*), Garland Library of Medieval Literature, 15, Series A (Garland, 1984), which contains a full bibliography. The version that follows is slightly revised.

The Rise of Gawain, Nephew of Arthur

King Uther Pendragon, father of Arthur, subjugated the kings of all the provinces bordering Britannia to his authority; in order to insure their subjection he held their sons in his court, partly in the position of hostages, partly to be trained in nobility of conduct and military discipline. Among these hostages was Loth, nephew of King Sichelm of Norway, a young man of striking appearance, who was strong of body and manly of spirit. For these qualities Loth was held in higher esteem than others of his age by Uther and his son Arthur, and he frequently visited their private living quarters. King Uther also had a daughter named Anna, an incomparable beauty, who still lived with her mother, the queen, in her chambers.

As Loth would often tease her playfully and engage in merry words with her quite privately, they were both seized with love for one another. Yet for a long time, from shyness and shame, their mutual affections were hidden from each other. Truly, "love is like a flame, the more it is concealed the hotter it burns," and from hasty suppression it becomes intensified. Not being able to contain so great a love within themselves, they revealed to each other what possessed their hearts. With both their prayers answered, they yielded to their desires, and soon Anna conceived a child. When she was near the time to bear the child, she feigned illness and retired to a private bedchamber, with only her lady-in-waiting knowing why.

At last the time came for the delivery of the infant, and she gave birth to a male child of rare beauty. Earlier, Anna had made a contract with certain wealthy men who had come from beyond the seas seeking trade, confirming a pact with them under oath that as soon as the infant had come into the world, lest anyone should find out, they would carry the child away to their own land and bring it up with care. So with no one knowing of the child's birth, the merchants accepted the infant son along with an untold wealth of gold, silver, and rich vestments that the mother had provided. In addition, she entrusted to them an immensely valuable cloak embroidered with jewels worked in gold over its entire surface, as well as a signet ring set with an emerald that she had received in trust from the king, a ring which he himself was accustomed to wear only on feast days. She added also a document impressed with the king's seal, the text of which identified with irrefutable proofs that the child, whom she had named Gawain, was the son of the nephew of the King of Norway and of the sister of Arthur; the document explained further that he had been sent to a foreign land out of fear of the king. Thus these items—the cloak, the ring, and the document—she wanted the child to have, foreseeing that whenever he returned, if he was not recognized by his parents and they rejected him, these would display proof of his identity, and through their evidence he would attain the acknowledgment of his parents.

The merchants, accordingly, boarded ship carrying the infant committed to them for fostering. Hoisting the canvas to the winds and plowing a wake across the sea, at last on the eighth day they were sailing toward the coast of Gaul, and reaching shore, they came to land two miles from the city of Narbonne. From here, once they had heaved to, all the men, dripping salt and sea-water, hastened on foot to the city, leaving the ship in port with only a single serving-boy to look after their merchandise and the nursling in the cradle. Actually, they had steered under a steep cliff quite a distance from the city and thought that no one would come near the ship in the meantime. But after they had gone, by chance a certain fisherman from the neighboring region, who was called Viamundus (a man poor in possessions but noble by birth and bearing), came walking along the shore with his wife, as was his daily routine, searching if he might find a fish stranded on the shore by the ebb of the sea, with the price of which he could buy food. When he saw the keel drawn to the shore, abandoning his other plan, he at once set out in that direction. On boarding, he found that no one except a boy had been left to guard it and, what is more, he was asleep. Seeing an infant of great beauty and an unguarded ship filled with all riches, and considering his own poverty which, with fortune favoring, he would be able to relieve (as the proverb says, "opportunity of place and time makes the thief"), he plundered whatever seemed to him of greatest value in silver and gold and various furnishings. He handed the infant to his wife as well as the coffer placed at his head that contained the cloak, the ring, and the document. Laden with riches, they escaped quickly to their dwelling, the affair being observed by no one.

When the merchants, though, returned later to the mooring-place, they discovered the theft of their property. They were shocked by the unexpected turn of events, and overwhelmed by the great loss, they began weeping and groaning. They continued all day in deep despair, particularly for the kidnaped infant who had been entrusted to their safekeeping. In a short time they sent carefully chosen agents through the neighboring shores and fields to investigate the matter thoroughly and to find out who had inflicted such a loss on them. But since "that which lies hidden from the knowledge of all is with difficulty discovered," those who had been sent returned sadly to the ship without having discovered any trace of the infant or the treasure.

Viamundus, meanwhile, hid the stolen wealth that he had carried to his cottage, along with the infant boy. He cared for the child, exerting great concern, as if the boy were his son, since he had none of his own. He was afraid to reveal the riches which he now had in his control, lest by ostentatious display the ugly truth of the crime he had perpetrated would become known, because not only was the poverty which had burdened him up to this time quite obvious, but also the investigation of his theft was still in progress.

After a period of seven years had elapsed, he decided to make a pilgrimage to Rome, led both by repentance for his deed and by the fact that he did not doubt that he would be able to spend his wealth without fear of the law in a region where he was not known. When everything necessary for the journey had been prepared, he set out with his wife and adopted son, with his household staff accompanying him with all his possessions. By good fortune he arrived in a short time safely at the walls of Rome. When he entered, he walked around the city all day through every section and scrutinized the entire area. He shrewdly inquired about the conditions of the place, the customs of the citizens, and the names of the senators and the most distinguished men.

In fact, Rome at this period had been captured by the barbarians and sacked, ravaged almost to the point of utter destruction—walls thrown down, buildings burned, and citizens captured, driven out, or slain by various means of torture. But a new emperor had succeeded to the throne who, although grieving over the ruin of the city, was rebuilding the destroyed sections, gathering together the scattered citizens, redeeming the captives, striving with all his might to bring Rome back to her former good fortune. Viamundus perceived this and, since he was astute, saw that the situation was favorable to his own goals, and so without delay he dressed himself in an impressive style and acquired servants and as many slaves as possible from the neighboring towns, fitting them out magnificently. Escorted by a numerous train of servants, he proceeded through the center of the city to the palace, creating a spectacle for all to behold. Coming before the emperor, he was received with honor.

When at last he had the opportunity of speaking with the emperor, Viamundus stated in his petition that he came from a very noble family of Romans and had been the military leader of a region of Gaul until he heard about the destruction of the city of Rome; he had hastened there to swell the ranks of his fellow citizens, and he now begged the emperor to grant a place in the city for him and his people to live in together. The emperor, judging him to be of no minor nobility, not only from his venerable gray hair and the elegance of his many possessions, but also from his numerous followers, gave thanks because he had come to him and promised that if he remained in the city he would be endowed with many honors. He also gave him a marble residence of remarkably good design located in front of the gates of his own palace, a home that allegedly had belonged to the great Scipio Africanus. The emperor also conferred on him towns, vineyards, and fields outside the city which were to provide for his expenses.

Viamundus, having obtained these favors of good fortune beyond all estimation, conducted himself so fitly and nobly and charmingly that he earned the admiration of the emperor, senate, and people, and the much repeated story of his lavish generosity spread privately and publicly throughout the city. Daily the senators and nobles of Rome gathered about him—not only these men, but out of regard for his young son, boys wearing the toga of noble birth and a number of knights from the imperial court, all of whom Viamundus honored with many delicacies, sumptuous banquets, and rich gifts. Meanwhile, as the boy grew, he increased both in manly spirit and physical skill, and he strove hard for courtesy and prowess, emerging as the equal of his supposed father. He frequented the palace and was considered a friend to the emperor and to those under him. Truly something of excellence flourished naturally in that young man and with this he ravished the hearts of the perceptive and drew them to love him. He had a tall and noble stature, a graceful bearing, and a handsome face, and he was endowed with remarkable strength.

When the boy had reached his twelfth year, Viamundus took to his bed, stricken with a serious illness. Then because of increasing weakness, he realized that the end of his life was imminent, and he begged earnestly that the emperor and the pope—Sulpicius occupying at that time the papal throne—should come to him and hear his words. Those men, not wishing to spurn the entreaties of this great man, whom they esteemed so much because of his generous character, came, bringing with them high-ranking men of the city who gathered before him with heavy hearts. Viamundus first gave thanks to those present for the benefits they had shared with him; then consulting with them in private, he revealed his former life, how by chance he had obtained such great wealth and the boy whom he had raised as his son; and he laid bare his whole life in proper order.

He concluded: "I resolved often with a burning desire to reveal this to your highnesses, but I delayed, always waiting for the opportune moment; I put it off till the present. Now, however, since my ultimate fate is imminent, I am compelled to confess these things. Though what I ask may be summarily granted to a man of my lowly estate by you masters of the entire world, still I believe that you, remembering our friendship and fellowship, will not deny my petition. It is specifically for this reason that I summoned you: to commit to the protection of your highnesses this boy whom I have nurtured as my son and with whom all these material things fell to my lot, so that you may advance him, educating him for the order of knighthood when he comes of age. From the proof I will give you, you will learn that he is the nephew of Arthur, King of Britannia" (by this time, Uther had died and Arthur had succeeded him), "the man whose fame for great prowess flies everywhere. I do not doubt that this boy, outstanding in nobility, will show this quality without dishonor. I recommend, nevertheless, that the matter be held secret from everyone and from the boy himself; don't even let his name be revealed until he is acknowledged by his parents because the terms of the document that attests to his origin prohibit it. But when he comes to manhood, I beg you to let him be sent back with this letter offering the sure evidence of his lineage." And summoning the boy, who until that time had been called the "Boy with No Name," because it was not known by what family name he should be registered, Viamundus embraced the feet of the emperor and commended the boy to his care with humble pleas and solemn vows. Ordering the coffer which contained the proofs assembled by his mother to be brought out, he presented it to the emperor.

When the emperor had inspected it, he praised the man's generosity toward his foster-son, and he accepted the boy, throwing his arms around him and promising that he would fulfill Viamundus' desire in all respects. Thus Viamundus, having achieved to his satisfaction what he had striven for so intensely, with the emperor sitting by his bedside, died happy. With great mourning, he was buried among the tombs of the nobility in a monument of marvelous workmanship erected by the emperor.

So it was that, after the death of Viamundus, the nameless boy was conducted to the palace by order of the emperor and included among the royal children. When three years had passed—that is to say, when the boy had reached fifteen—and his prowess met the test, he was granted arms by the emperor. As a mark of favor, the emperor also granted arms to twenty other young men in military training with him. Then from the palace with the other new knights and young Romans still in training they proceeded to the Circus, where the racing of horses was customarily practiced. On this day so great was the valor with which the new knight conducted himself, and so vigorous were his exploits that the cheers of all the people served as a testimony. No one in that spectacle could withstand him, no one could match his strength; in truth, whomever he encountered in a single combat he overthrew.

Later at the festival of Equirria, the new knight, wearing the golden circlet which the emperor had promised to the victor, was led into the emperor's presence, with a cheering procession of people escorting him. The emperor, praising him in no small way for his outstanding prowess, granted him any reward he would ask for, but the young man replied, "I desire nothing of your bounty, O emperor, unless that I may take part in the first combat that you wage against your enemies."

The emperor assented and placed him in the first Order of Equestrians. On the day when he received his knighthood, before he went out to combat on horseback, he wore a crimson tunic to cover his armor. He called it a "surcoat for armor." When asked by the knights why he had put it over his armor—since no one before this time had worn a tunic while dressed in armor—he replied that he wanted a splendid attire. After that reply, everyone chanted: "New knight with a surcoat for his armor, New knight with a surcoat for his armor"; and so "Knight of the Surcoat" became his name.

This man, who was advanced by the emperor to very high honor, strove always for even higher achievements in valor and prowess. A distinguished reputation and singular daring were attributed to him in every encounter of every tournament. While this was going on in Rome, war broke out between the King of Persia and the Christians in Jerusalem. When the day came for battle, the besieging formations of both cavalry and infantry produced a spectacle of terror as they drew near to battle. While the trumpets were being sounded, the bowstrings tautened, the lances couched, and the chief centurions tensed to join in hand-to-hand combat, those more mature in age and wisdom on both sides were meeting in council. When these men considered that the clash of such multitudes could not take place without great disaster, they proceeded between the lines, restrained the first attack, and then sent officials to discuss the conditions of peace with each side. After talks between them went on for some time, all parties agreed to this: from each side one man should be chosen to duel, and victory would go to the man who won, as would the final decision on those matters over which the war had broken out. But because the Jerusalemites did not dare to agree without the assent of the emperor, they bound themselves to a truce to be granted until they could send a delegation to the emperor and ascertain his will. They swore an oath that they agreed in principle to this procedure if it was affirmed by him. Therefore, when the truce had been granted, they selected those who were to act as delegates, and without delay they sent them on their way. When instructing these men, they emphasized that if the emperor did not deny their petition, they were also to entreat him earnestly for a man capable of handling the proposed deal. The emissaries made a hurried journey to the emperor, and when they were brought into the senate, they explained in their most eloquent manner why they had come.

The emperor, after taking counsel concerning their pleas, considered agreeing to their petition but was undecided about whom he should send on their behalf. When the talk had dragged on with a diversity of opinions, the substance of it reached the ears of the Knight of the Surcoat. Without delay, he burst into the presence of the emperor, exclaiming, "O emperor, I want you to remember the honor you so graciously bestowed on me at the arming of the new knights when you promised me the first single combat that would be undertaken by you against your enemies. Now war is declared by the infidels not only against you and the Roman people, but also against the Christian faith. I beg your highness to allow me what you granted, so that I may not only receive your reward but may also avenge the honor of the Roman people and their religion."

Although it required a parting with this excellent knight in assigning him to this duel, because fulfilling his promise compelled it and because he knew no better man for such a mission, the emperor granted that it be done according to the rules of the senate. The emperor directed that the knight, along with the delegation, be well equipped, and that a hundred knights with a centurion in command escort them, so that not only would the knight go forth with honor, but also whatever dangers might confront him through the expanses of land or sea, he could thwart them with their help.

Without delay they began the journey, and reaching the Adriatic Sea they boarded ships. There were sixteen other vessels along with theirs, some of which were merchantmen, others fast ships bound for the Holy Land which had joined their convoy because of the savage pirates who roamed the wide seas. The ships formed up, left the harbor, and set sail for deep water.

For twenty-five days they were tossed on huge waves, unable either to seek haven or to steer a straight course. Beset by mounting gales and driven in great circles, they were brought to shore on an island with barbarous people. The inhabitants were so savage that they would arrange no safe conduct for anyone either for sex or for age, but would inflict punishment on all landing from outside, whether guilty or innocent. For this reason they were approached by no one seeking trade, and were branded with a reputation for such cruelty that they were shunned by all, remaining cut off from the society of all others. They were said to consume voraciously the meat of all cattle and fowl; and since they were so dominated by passions of the flesh, the fathers did not know their own sons, nor the sons their fathers. Their stature ranged to three cubits, and their life expectancy was fifty years. Rarely did anyone die before the tenth year or live beyond fifty. Accustomed to hard work, they were known for their cultivation and production of food, abounding in wealth and with many children.

The news had spread through all the pagan lands that a knight whose passage at arms no one could withstand was being sent by the emperor to undertake the duel. For that reason, to all the islands in the Aegean Sea under pagan control near which the knight would have to pass, secret orders were sent to keep a constant watch over the ports and shores and, if by chance the knight should come to land, they should overpower him, so that he would not be able to arrive on the designated day. They also directed pirates to blockade the open reaches of the sea in different areas so that if the men escaped unharmed by those on guard at the ports, they might be taken by others patrolling the seas.

Reigning at this time on that island was a man named Milocrates, an enemy of the Roman people, who had captured and abducted by force the emperor's niece, whom the emperor himself had betrothed to the King of Illyricum. Since the stratagems above had been made known to him, he fortified the cities and towns that lay near the sea so that his soldiers could attack them as they approached, or the guards could capture them if they landed.

However, the shores by which the Romans did land were lined with dense forests in every direction—not the best land for animals of the field. Because of this scarcity, the wild beasts were protected quite carefully and strictly from the local people as well as from any outsiders who might land. According to the law, no one was to have the pleasure of eating this game, except the king himself or his princes. So it happened that when the centurion mentioned earlier and the fleet under his command landed on this island, the Knight of the Surcoat disembarked with a few companions to hunt. Six stags were soon slain, and with dogs set loose, he began to pursue the seventh, when suddenly the keeper of the preserve, stationed in the interior of the forest, heard the baying of the hounds and the blasts of the horns. The keeper summoned his companions and commanded them to arm themselves. As ordered, these men went out to confront the hunters, who were already in possession of the quarry. The foresters demanded by whose authority they poached on the royal game preserve, where no one was allowed entrance even with peaceful intent. They ordered the hunters to lay down their weapons and go before the king to submit to his judgment for the rash act they had committed.

To this our knight responded, "We have come for these deer which we took because of our need, and we will not sheathe our weapons anywhere except in your guts."

> He spoke, and brandishing spears with a powerful arm,
> He hurled cold steel into the arrogant throat;
> With his powerful right arm he stopped the mouth of the
>   menacing one.

The wounded keeper of the preserve groaned, so enraged by the intensity of the pain that when he had wrenched the spear from his wound, with supreme effort he flung it back at the Knight of the Surcoat; yet because his arm shook, it went awry and struck a tree.

At once the rest of the men from both sides attacked; grappling in close conflict, hand to hand they slashed at each other, and from a distance they fought by hurling spears. Actually the Knight of the Surcoat had more men, but none of them were wearing armor, while all their adversaries were fully protected. But the Knight of the Surcoat, when he saw his own men giving way before the enemy, drew his sword, and rushing at their leader, knocked him to the ground, grabbed the noseguard of his helmet, dragged him toward his own men, and stripped him of his life and his armor together. Having equipped himself with this armor, shouting for his men, he then attacked the enemy, and although some fled, he alone slew thirteen of them.

The hunting party followed the fugitives through the forest and sent to the Underworld all they could overtake. Only one man was left as a survivor to be the messenger of this great defeat. He had hidden himself out of sight within the dense foliage until his adversaries stopped searching for him and went away. When the Romans had left, he rose up quickly and went to the king and related what had happened. King Milocrates was staying at that time in a nearby city that he had founded in a delightful setting three miles from the sea. When he learned of the landing of the enemy and the slaying of his knights, he at once dispatched messengers and ordered the princes of all the provinces to come together as quickly as possible with as many men as they could muster. They complied with the command and came with a vast army. Those arriving were lodged throughout the neighboring countryside because the king's city was not able to hold them. Then King Milocrates deliberated with his princes about what they must do.

Meanwhile, the Knight of the Surcoat, having overcome the foresters, returned to the ships. The entire contingent, rewarded with the spoils of victory, congratulated him. Then on the third day they attempted to get on with the voyage they had begun, but because the winds continued to be unfavorable, they were forced to remain where they were. The centurion, quite disturbed by the delay, assembled the leaders of the knights and sought counsel from them about what could be done toward proceeding with their mission. He assumed that the king of that island and his princes were now moving against them in retaliation for their resistance, and that they had by now mobilized to crush them in vengeance for those deaths— and would do so, unless they could quickly get under way. He contended that unless the wind abated for them, they lacked the strength to row the ships from that place, and it would not be safe to remain there, since they had too few knights to fight off the great numbers of the enemy, and their provisions of food and fodder would not last much longer. "It is necessary then," the centurion began, "for some of our men to go spy on the manpower and plans of the enemy so that when we know how he usually deploys his forces, we may see more practically what must be done."

The words of the leader were well received, and two of the men were chosen to perform the task. One of them was the Knight of the Surcoat; the other, named Odabel, was a blood relative of the centurion. They were known in uncertain situations to be careful and prudent, and in danger to be stronger and more skillful than the others. Protected with armor, they began the journey as ordered and made their way through the forest to the city. At the entrance to the king's forest an enormous boar rushed upon them, its neck covered with bristles like shafts, its gaping jaws armed with curved tusks, thunder roaring from its mouth, and saliva spewing over its forequarters. It charged at an angle to the attack. Seeing it, the Knight of the Surcoat leaped from his horse and, brandishing a flashing hunting-spear in his right hand, struck a blow before it had a chance to strike. The spearhead pierced into its foreskull between the brows; forced on through the body, it came out above the flank. Yet not only did the boar not fall immediately, but with the wound it seemed to gather fury, so that although its strength was diminished greatly by the loss of blood, with all the might it could muster, it could still attack him with its tusks. While blocking the slash, the Knight of the Surcoat took the blow on his shield, unsheathed his sword, cut off the head of the beast as it was raging at him, and left it rolling around in its own blood. The beast was lifted onto the armorbearer's horse, and the armorbearer delivered it to the centurion on their behalf.

Returning quickly to the path, the Knight was waiting for Odabel at the gates of the city by midday. When they entered the city, they proceeded to the palace and mingled with the king's men as if they belonged with them. Actually the very large number of men made it possible for them to go unnoticed as strangers, while as an additional safeguard, they had a practical knowledge of the language of that country. They scoured the city and also the rural regions in every direction, noting the strength and number of military groups. By no means had the entire army assembled. Actually, the day before, King Milocrates had sent some men to spy on the fleet of the Romans, and when they returned to the city, they had terrified him by reporting a multitude of armored men. As a result, Milocrates feared that the fleet had invaded with an overwhelming force. Through messengers he summoned his brother, Buzafarnan, who reigned over a nearby kingdom, so that he might bring him help in his great need as fast as he could. While he waited for his brother's arrival, the action of the attack was postponed. On the day that the Knight of the Surcoat came to the city, Milocrates had called an assembly of the nobility, discussing with them what steps to take in this emergency. The consensus was that when his brother Buzafarnan arrived, the army should be divided into two parts—one for ship and the other for land—so that when they engaged the enemy in battle, no route would be open for escape. The Knight of the Surcoat, who remained unrecognized among them and listened intently, noted what each man said and committed the plan to memory.

When the sun had set, King Milocrates hurried to his evening meal. The Knight of the Surcoat, placing himself in his company, entered the royal palace while his companions waited outside for his return. When the rest of the king's men had reclined to eat, the Knight slipped out unnoticed toward the bedchamber where the niece of the emperor—that is, the queen, whom Milocrates had stolen from her lawful husband—resided alone with her maidens. The rather late hour had dimmed visibility; still it was said that the chamber was unapproachable. He began to deliberate what in his judgment should be done and to plan carefully, picturing in his mind how he would have the strength to meet whatever traps he might encounter. If, for instance, he was to hide in the bedchamber and kill the king while he was asleep, as he had originally planned, he knew that if he was caught in the act of murder, he would suffer the same punishment. On the other hand, if he returned to the ship with no deed accomplished, he would be rightfully considered a slacker and a coward. While he turned such things over in his mind, a knight named Nabaor (who had been taken prisoner by the Romans but later released) came along, having been sent by the king to the queen. The Knight of the Surcoat could see him clearly, but he himself remained unnoticed by the man. (Those standing in the shadows see clearly those in the light while they themselves remain unseen by others.) While this man was being held captive earlier with other spies, the Knight of the Surcoat had struck up a strong friendship with him; for remembrance sake, he had shared with him a ring and a crimson mantle.

Recognizing him now and gambling on his friendship, the Knight of the Surcoat called Nabaor over secretly, embraced him, hinted at the reason for his coming, and by some preliminary remarks tested his feelings. When he perceived that Nabaor would protect him, forsaking all pretense, he asked the man to help him accomplish what he had in mind. Nabaor, for his part, wondered greatly about his presence there and when he learned why he had come was delighted to have found the chance to return his generosity. After leading him to a private chamber, Nabaor said: "My beloved friend, what you desire is greater than what you can accomplish, and it ought not to be undertaken by you alone. For thirty very strong men, always on watch, surround the couch of the king; no one is allowed access to him until daylight, not even his servants. Besides, you know that on the whole you have to use more care than strength, because what is longed for is often accomplished successfully by careful planning in support of strength. Strength without cunning never gets the job done. Follow this advice as you approach your venture, but with me to guide you in what order it is to be carried out. The queen is greatly attracted to you; she desires most ardently to make your acquaintance either by addressing you in person or through intermediaries. She has often inquired of me, after I returned from my duty as a spy, what form and stature you have, and I, replying that you are incomparable in both, kindled her heart with love for you, so that she is more concerned with your welfare than with the king's. Though doubt-lessly the queen of this country has been raised to the highest degree of honor and glory by King Milocrates, still because she has not forgotten that she was abducted from the marriage bed by plunder, the shame of captivity constantly torments her, and she would even now prefer to be free with a poor man than to live on here with ostentation as a captive. Hearing that you have landed here on a mission for the emperor, she yearns desperately to have a chance to speak to you. For she hopes that if she gains your attention, she can be freed from the yoke of captivity and restored to her own husband, whose marriage was approved by the emperor. You know without doubt that this venture will require effort and cunning; from her it will require commitment with sagacity, so that your strength and courage may allow you to prevail against King Milocrates. Yet because a woman's mind is always changing with random moods more quickly than the wind, one must first discreetly test in which way her disposition is inclined. If this woman has learned you are here, neither fear of the king nor shame of gossip will keep her from coming to you; she will still speak with you. I shall go to her, then—being sent to carry her the king's messages—and among other things I mention, I'll speak of you artfully and learn where her will is inclined. You, meanwhile, stay hidden here until I know the outcome."

Nabaor accordingly approached the queen. Between them, as various topics of conversation were discussed, there was talk concerning the Knight of the Surcoat. As Nabaor narrated his marvelous deeds with much praise, the queen replied, "How happy I'd be if I could tell such a worthy man my heartfelt distress! Certainly if only because of the emperor whose niece I am and whose knight he is, he would rescue me from this man's tyranny. I desire, therefore, to find someone trustworthy to send as a messenger to him, so that in one way or another he may be given the opportunity of seeing and talking with me." Nabaor was also one of those whom Milocrates had captured with her and forced into chains of servitude. Thus to this man as a fellow-conspirator of her secrets, she safely committed the confidences of her heart.

He replied to her, "My queen, there is no impediment to your wishes, nor will there be need of a messenger. Only let yourself be free from deceit; only let your wishes agree with your words, and he whom you desire will be present as you command."

When she had sworn in reply that she wanted this to be done more eagerly than she had dared to confess, Nabaor led the Knight of the Surcoat into her presence, and he laid open to her the purpose for which he had come. Moreover, as was earlier understood, he loomed handsome to her sight with a manly build that drew glances from people who were amazed at his beauty. The queen, greeting him as he entered, bade him sit down, and having contemplated him intensely for some time, finally burst into tears, brought forth a deep sigh from her breast and explained the distress by which she was burdened, adding that he could offer her, if he were willing, the remedy for her great ills.

He replied, "If my desire could be joined by equal ability, without doubt there would be no delay in obeying your will. But it is plain that the king exceeds us in the number and strength of his soldiers, and it is uncertain for that reason what conclusion awaits us. If you know anything that could help us bring this undertaking to a successful end, tell me and you will not find me either slack or slow in carrying it out."

While the queen, pausing for a moment, considered what she would say to this, Nabaor spoke: "It is by no means hidden from you, my queen, that the king is summoning the army against these men for what will be a pitched battle. In the great mass of this army I see the best opportunity for taking action. If, therefore, you are burdened with such concern, you have the means both to remove him and his comrades from the impending disaster and also to accomplish what you have longed for so intensely. The king's attention, fixed on the strategies of war, will be less concerned with other matters. Command, then, through this knight that the centurion should select forty armed men and send them here tomorrow through the forest in secret, so that the day after, when the king advances against him in battle, they will occupy the city, which you will betray to them; and when they have set it on fire, the horrible spectacle for the king and his men will provide the means of victory."

She begged him with many prayers to carry out the proposed plan. She then bestowed on the Knight of the Surcoat the king's sword and his gilded armor, on which lay the curse that the king, having been overcome, would be stripped of the royal crown by the one who first wore it other than the king himself. In addition she gave him abundant gifts of gold, silver, and gems of great value and, above all, sealed the pact with friendship. With these matters settled, the Knight of the Surcoat quickly rejoined his comrades and, leading them from the city, came upon the centurion at the first light of dawn. Displaying the gifts he had been given, he also reported what he had done, what he had seen, and what he had heard.

The centurion, exhilarated beyond all expectation by hope of victory, assigned selected knights to go to the queen. When they were chosen, he made his kinsman Odabel the ranking officer, and having urged him to lead those under him with care and foresight, he sent them off toward the vineyard close to the palace as soon as it was dusk, to wait there hidden all night. On the following day Nabaor would admit them by order of the queen.

The next day was dawning when Milocrates marched out of the city with his army to meet the centurion in battle. The larger part of his army he had committed under his brother's leadership to attack the enemy from the rear by ship, so that, having been surrounded on both sides by the fighting, they would surrender more quickly. But the centurion, knowing their plan in advance, had relocated the ships side by side around the camp, so that later if it became necessary, they would form a rampart for those retreating to them. From the camp set up in a secure place a short distance from the sea, the centurion himself led forth his band of knights. He divided the knights and their units into five squadrons. He himself was the commanding officer of the center. They were openly moving forward face to face against the king, who was surrounded in the front line by a thousand armored men. But however superior in number and strength of warriors the king might be, he held little hope of victory: the armor upon which he thought rested the protection of himself and his kingdom had been stolen. When he looked for it as he was preparing to go into battle and could not find it anywhere, all hope of success for his plan left him, even though he did not know for certain that the Knight of the Surcoat had it until finally he saw the man himself clad in it on the field as he was about to begin the battle. On seeing this he shrieked in terror. Supposing only too truly that what later did happen would happen to him, he was panic-stricken. Still, he was unable to stop what he had begun, and he realized that, to advance his own personal glory, he must either conquer courageously or die bravely.

The blare of trumpets sounded then from both sides, a call which traditionally inspires a fighting spirit and signals the attack on the enemy. The foot-soldiers had already begun to make contact when the smoke rising from the city indicated plainly what was happening there. For as planned, once the king had led his troops from the city in haste to battle, immediately those waiting in hiding had risen up and seized control, and they had set aflame the structures below the walls by throwing fire. As the flames reached skyward, the catastrophe of the city was revealed to the citizens already stationed at some distance; so also ashes carried by the south wind flew into the faces of the men fighting. The heart of the king was so aghast at the impending disaster that, disregarding the battle already engaged, he turned quickly to the aid of the city:

> You could see the lines in confusion, hands without spears,
> Men urging dispersal and flight.
> They go a thousand ways, no two together;
> Thus flees the enemy like cattle from a barking dog.
> The avengers press on, charge the enemy in flight,
> Settle accounts by slaughter of those overtaken.
> Rocks bury some, some lie vanquished;
> He who suffers neither endures the harsh chains.

The Knight of the Surcoat, seeing the formations of the enemy dissolving and suddenly turned to flight, regrouped his own men and pursued and inflicted mass destruction. Not only had the blast of flame that was consuming the buildings of the city terrified them, but the very flight they attempted made them for the most part mentally and physically helpless. Scattered throughout the declivities of the mountains, through the unfrequented places of the forests, like a flock attacked by the fury of wolves, they headed toward the city walls, and they received ceaseless vengeance from the swords of their pursuers. The knights who had set fire to the outskirts of the city, meeting the fugitives, kept them away from the walls, and driving them back into the field of battle, forced them to fall into the hands of those from whom they fled. On either hand there was the horrible slaughter, and they were impeded by the very numbers of their own men so that they had recourse neither to flight nor to skillful defense. They were shaken and without a protector, like an unarmed rabble, and no one thought it right to give help to him who sought it.

Finally King Milocrates, realizing that he was surrounded on all sides by the enemy, reckoned infamy upon himself if he died without some worthy action. He gathered his scattered men into a unit and, advancing bravely against his challengers, restrained the force of the enemy in their first encounter and even compelled them to give way before him. With his own right hand he attacked as many as possible and turned the rest to flight, until at length the Knight of the Surcoat, seeing his comrades hard pressed by that man, gave rein to his horse and bore down upon the king. Milocrates daringly met the charge of the challenger, and as they exchanged blows, each in turn unhorsed the other. But the Knight of the Surcoat, rising more quickly, drew his sword and rushed the king the moment he was struggling to get up. He would have inflicted a fatal wound, had not the king blocked the blow with his shield. No great injury resulted, but it so stunned the king's brain that he collapsed and lay for about an hour as if asleep.

At that moment, the nephew of the king, a skillful young knight, bore down upon the Knight of the Surcoat as he was about to dispatch the king with a second thrust of his sword, and with threats and blows the horseman attacked the Knight of the Surcoat from the left. The knight on foot repelled the attack with his own shield and, grasping a javelin that had by luck fallen near him, flung it back by the thong. It was not stopped by either shield boss or iron lorica, but passing through the horseman's saddlebow, it pierced deeply under the belly of that one who had made threats beyond his power.

Once he had eliminated that attacker, the Knight of the Surcoat again sought out the king, but he was received with a boldness of greater intensity than he expected. For shame and wrath had brought back to the king's memory his former dignity and prowess and given him strength as he regained his breath. He was inspired to avenge himself on the enemy, reckoning that he should not be punished like some commoner, especially since there was no hope of rescue. He was determined to expend every effort to prevent the joy of victory from falling to his enemies. First, then, he attacked the approaching Knight of the Surcoat, slashed a swordcut across his forehead where it was unprotected by the helmet, and had not the nosepiece projecting from the helmet blunted it, would have brought death from the gash. The Knight of the Surcoat, wounded, became frantic with fear that his sight would be dimmed by the flowing blood, and striving to exact revenge for the injury, he rushed the king and, swinging his sword with a sidelong blow to the nape of the neck, severed the head along with the right arm.

When he fell, those who were with him took flight, their only hope of safety. The centurion, wishing to spare the multitude, signalled the knights by trumpet not to pursue the fugitives, knowing that with their leader dead, those under him would surrender without a fight. After collecting the spoils of the enemy, they entered the city with triumphant pomp, and an arch was built in their honor. The queen, niece of the emperor, met them, led them into the palace, and with every attention refreshed those most exhausted by the fighting. She directed that the dead be buried and the wounded cared for with healing remedies, and she showed herself most bountiful to all and rewarded each man according to the prize deserved.

The centurion, staying on at the island for fifteen days, allowed the country to be plundered by the army. Prominent men and administrators, because they had collaborated with the enemy of the Roman people, he had executed and dismembered. He punished the common people by a harsh levy of reparations. Leaving some of the knights there to protect the island and choosing others to accompany the queen, he returned the niece of the emperor to her rightful husband, the King of Illyricum, from whom she had been forcibly seized.

With two hundred additional knights enlisted from that province, he boarded the refurbished fleet with his companions in order to complete the mission that they had undertaken. When he had already completed a day's journey through the waves of the sea, the brother of King Milocrates, whose kingdom he had conquered, appeared with no small fleet. For, as stated earlier, he had been sent by King Milocrates before the battle to surprise the fleet of the centurion so that, surrounded on all sides, flight for him would be cut off, whether by land or sea. Although he had reached the fleet, or rather the landing area of the centurion's ships, he found neither the ships nor the men. The centurion had hurriedly fortified the camp at some distance from the sea and set up the ships as a rampart for his people, prows pointing outward on all sides. King Egesarius (so the brother of Milocrates was called) assumed they had already escaped. Turning his ships about, he sailed back into deep water, where he was storm-tossed for three days. When he wanted to come about to seek port again, the winds blowing from every direction drove him farther off toward distant lands for a five-day voyage. Now with a lighter wind behind him, he had returned, and he was confronted by the fleet of the centurion in the midst of the sea.

By chance, however, the centurion himself was seated in the tower-like structure which he had erected in the stern as a defense, and with the Knight of the Surcoat sitting near him, he was scanning the horizons of the sea from this vantage point. At first he had given attention to figures contrived in the likeness of a cock or some such thing placed on the masts, doubtless to test by which wind the keel was being propelled. For toward whatever corner of the earth the wind of the region is inclined, these always face into it. The banners, devices carried on the masts of the approaching fleet, were tossed higher and then lower by the action of the wind.

The centurion, thinking he saw birds—kingfishers—on the horizon, shouted to the ship's captain, "Ahoy," and said, "I think a mighty storm is upon us. For as these birds direct their course, beating their wings and wheeling through the empty air, so they taste their joys almost with a knowledge of the future, with our corpses about to be food for their crops. Indeed it is said that with a storm imminent, these birds, wheeling about, now together, now separated, circle into mass flight and foretell by their behavior coming disaster."

The Knight of the Surcoat, however, standing by him at that moment and perceiving things as they really were, said, "Sir, your concept is in error. For those are not birds which you think you see, but standards mounted on mastheads. You must realize that it is without doubt the enemy fleet approaching, which was sent to pursue us some time ago by the king already subjugated by your forces. Perhaps they were driven by some storm and forced to seek a foreign harbor—the reason, it seems to me, for the delay. Now since the wind favors their plans, they have returned. Order the knights to put on their armor so that the enemy will not find us unarmed."

At the command of the centurion, those who were aboard that ship armed themselves; and to the rest of the ships (for there were thirty, fifteen of which he had led ther˄ and just as many others he had acquired later from the conquered island) the ship's trumpets gave a signal to do the same. The ships were placed in battle order: some to attack the enemy from the front, others from the left or right, and still others to remain in the rear as a trap. Moreover, five ships that had rams, in the first of which he was himself, he ordered ahead to attack the advancing enemy vessels with sudden force. Those experienced in naval battle use this particular type of ship fully rigged for piracy, the armament of which is so strong that whatever ship it strikes, it rips the planking open from top to bottom. Because all the area projecting between the prow and keel is covered with iron, the ridge armed with iron hooks, the vertex of the extension of the ram carrying iron points and armed like the crested beak of the cock, these ships are termed "rostrated." Towers are also erected on which are stationed the strongest men ready to stop the impetus of the enemy defense by hurling stones and javelins from above. The merchant ships were placed toward the rear so that if the ships carrying knights yielded, these could withdraw and might at least escape the hands of the pillagers.

When everything necessary was done, dropping anchor, they awaited the coming of the enemy. The sighting of the hostile fleet brought quick confirmation to the words of the Knight of the Surcoat. What he had reasoned had not been false. The men observed for themselves the fleet in formation and foresaw with no less astuteness the tactics required for such a battle. The Knight of the Surcoat, observing the pirates to be prepared for battle and closing in, immediately ordered the anchors raised and, as soon as the sails caught the winds, the ships to be driven forward by oars. With armed men in place on deck, he rushed the foremost galley on which the commander of the enemy fleet was sailing. The knight, smashing first with his single ship, drove home a blow by the force of its ram with such power all the way through to the mast that when the ram struck with its iron vertex, it forced the crippled vessel to seek the depths.

The other ships came up and surrounded the shattered vessel as reinforcement for the Knight of the Surcoat, and even though the enemy soldiers defended themselves vigorously, the knight's men overcame those who resisted. Some of them were thrown overboard; others were cut down by battle-axes and swords. Those remaining they restrained with chains. They slew the commander, who fought valiantly lest he fall living into the hands of his enemy. Then they seized the riches and arms and sank the ship beneath the sea.

After overthrowing these men, the Knight of the Surcoat advanced even more daringly into the remaining ships. With a battlecry these ships regrouped; he was intercepted, surrounded, cut off from his companions, and attacked fiercely from all sides. You could see the air darkened by the hurling of javelins and the surface of the sea covered with their great numbers. From one side and the other, a huge piece of stone-throwing equipment was manipulated in a circular course, the din of which produced no less horror than the danger. The contenders pressed with every kind of weapon trying to destroy the ship of the Knight of the Surcoat, but the planking, each board individually fastened with iron, did not separate from the blows. Hemmed in as he was by the formations of the enemy, he still did more damage than he received. When the enemy saw his determination, that he preferred to die rather than be conquered, and he could not be forced to submit nor lower his defense for an instant, they hurled their fire, that is to say "Greek fire," into the ship.

Fire of this kind may in fact be made in several ways. But the power of the formula that produces the fiercest fire and continues burning longest is prepared in this way. Those who possess the knowledge of preparation first make ready a brass vessel, and they collect poisonous toads of the kind called "rubetae," as many as needed, and they force-feed them with dove-meat and honey for three months. After this period has elapsed, they allow the toads to fast for two or three days; then they put the little beasts to the teats of some prolific creature, recently delivered and lactating, whose milk they suck for such a long time that they fall off from complete satiety. Swollen by poisonous fluid, they are laid upon a small vessel, and a fire hot enough to consume them like a funeral pyre is set under it. To these also are added water snakes, "chelyndri," which for ten days preceding their inclusions on the pyre are fed on a human cadaver.

There is in addition an asp (whose name escapes me), poisonous and deadly, bearing three heads upon one gullet, a venomous creature able to corrupt with incurable disease whatever it touches. At the touch of it the field loses its vegetation, the sea its fish, the trees their fruit, and so it is a very great marvel. Even if the most minute distillation infects a tree, no matter how huge, at that spot where it drops, it is absorbed inwardly, and like a chancer it will corrode, felling the tree to the earth. It has been learned that no remedy can stop the destruction; and even worse, if men or beasts are touched even slightly on the surface of the skin by this poison, it penetrates and they are slain instantly. How great its power is can be determined from the flame spewing intensely from the creature's mouth; and while it is itself burning with greatest heat, very often the forest it inhabits is set afire. From the venomous slaver that flows from its triple gaping mouths, three extracts are produced, doubtless a trace from each. The first of these, if consumed by anyone in meat or drink, will drive him mad; the second also brings death with but a taste; the juice of the third infects with the king's evil by swallowing or rubbing it. This monstrous beast, if one comes upon it when the poisons are fully developed, will destroy itself. If indeed it is captured, before it can be added to the above process, it must be fattened for a week on the proper food for these creatures.

In addition there must be included the gall bladder and testicles of a wolf that does not lack the ability to change its nature, a creature engendered by air and wind so that whatever it touches, by contact it receives that form. Also a "ligurius," obtained from the end of the earth, occupies no small place among the other ingredients, the same stone that is believed to be both endowed with virtue and to originate from the solidified urine of the wolf. For nothing interrupts the concentrated staring of the lynx; even the inner matter, which surely must be excreted, hardens while it contemplates the light. Also the head, the heart, and the liver of a crow which has measured out its ninth generation are added to increase the strength of the formula. Sulphur, also, and pitch, resin, olive oil, tartar, and petroleum are not in the least withheld from these things already mentioned; they feed the fire quickly when the flame is applied; they are set aside until later.

When these items have been collected in the order I have stated, they are enclosed in a heating vessel made of the purest bronze, and the vessel is filled to the brim with the blood of a red-haired man and a dragon. Indeed, a fiery nature is attributed to the blood of the red-haired man because of both the color of the hair and the great vigor these men usually have, a vivacity that openly attests their nature. A youth, then, whose beard and hair are red, with skin eruptions of the same color sprinkling his face, is led into a fine bedroom, and for the space of one month he is fattened sumptuously on every prepared delicacy. During this time, each day a hearth-fire is kindled before him, and he is made drunk with wine in order to increase the blood; and he is carefully kept from the embraces of women. When the month has come to an end, in the middle of the room charcoal fires of a man's length are lighted; he is exposed between these when he is full of food and drink and his clothing is removed; in the way meat is turned on the spit, he is turned before the fire. Warmed sufficiently, the veins on his entire body soon become swollen, and he is bled, that is the veins of both arms are cut transversely. In the meantime, while he loses blood, he receives wafers in wine to sustain his spirit, lest because of weakness or a trance, the desired liquid be clotted. For a long time, then, the blood is allowed to flow, until it brings on death by its deficiency and casts the soul from the body. Next, having been mixed with the blood of the dragon, it is heated separately for a long time. Finally poured over the other substances, it blends the mixture together.

If one is asked how a dragon may be caught, first stalwart men are chosen to search out the dragon's cave, the den where it lurks, and when they have found it, they sprinkle sleep-inducing drugs moistened with various spices across the rim of its entrance. When the dragon, leaving the mouth of the cave, smells these fragrances, it consumes them voraciously and is at once overcome by sleep. The men, who have been hidden in a safe place not far away, surround the beast and slaughter it. The men carry off the dragon blood, along with the dragon gem that they shake loose by smashing its brain. The gem may then be used in many sorts of undertakings.

The vessel in which these substances are placed is a tripod whose handled upper section with its lid of bronze is constructed to fit the narrow neck snugly. Closed by this, it is so tightly fitted on all sides that not even the least wisp of smoke escapes from it. When everything has been placed in this vessel, fire is immediately kindled under it, and for seven days and seven nights the flames are fed with pitch and naphtha so that it will boil intensely. There is, in addition, a copper tube, the uppermost end of which has been bent, that is attached in the manner of a valve. By means of this a small hole on top of the lid of the vessel is kept closed for the first six days. On the seventh day, when the flame in the heating vessel is ignited, a tremendous roar inside can be heard, like an earthquake, or as if at a distance you heard the rumblings of a raging sea. When the attendant has observed the familiar signs of the ignited fire, he pours into the valve on the outside some very sharp vinegar; penetrating its mass, it checks the force of the fire now striving to burst out.

Bellows are constructed of bronze, as many as suffice, by which the fire is drawn out; their connectors are screwed together so tightly that the series of connections is penetrated by the fire under the blast of air as though made of wood and leather. For they are indeed so meshed that you would more easily believe them composed of leather than bronze. Once the fire has been moderated from its intense heat by the vinegar dousing, the valve is released and the ductile pipe projecting forward in the bellows is applied to the small opening of the vessel. By the suction of the air flow of this, the fire is pumped out of the heating vessel. Immediately, lest the flames rise up, the mouth of the tube is closed by the valve. Thus the fire is received into other containers to be held for later use. A small part, it is true, is retained in the heating vessel; the heat by which it is nourished must be applied daily. Small openings with a leaf in the middle like a small shutter are provided through which fuel is fed lest the flame go out. By this routine is Greek fire prepared. If you ask what power it has, no military machine is so strong, no ship so great but that if the fire is thrown it penetrates defenses and consumes everything on every side. It has the strength to resist being extinguished by anyone until the matter that it consumes is exhausted. What is more astounding, it burns also among the waves; and if it is mingled with common fire, it will continue to hold itself in a separate fireball and will consume common fire like wood.

When the enemy discovered that the Knight of the Surcoat was unconquerable by arms, one of them seized the bellows in which the baleful fire was contained and, removing the valve from the tube, pressing down one of the boards with his left hand and raising the other with his right, he compressed them by turns with the greatest exertion. As the flaming fuel streamed forward, he sprayed the centurion's galleon amidship, consuming four oarsmen with flames. Quickly everything was enveloped in fire, and panic spread among the men on board. Surrounded by the flames aboard and the enemy outside, the Romans did not know what to do; they had no power to defend themselves nor to attack. If they wanted to consider flight, neither to the waves nor to the enemy was it safe to commit themselves. Either way, death was imminent for those remaining on the ship. The Knight of the Surcoat, considering the crisis, drove himself forward with renewed determination. Alone, he leaped onto the ship of the attackers, cutting down some of the enemy, throwing others to the waves. He transferred his companions over to the other ship, rescuing them from a threefold threat: the balls of fire, the shipwrecking waves, and the fury of the enemy. Enraged with an increasing fury, as soon as the fleet again came together, he immediately avenged himself. After having sunk every tenth ship and broken the enemy's power, he captured thirty of the pirate vessels.

When, not without grave peril, the naval battle was finally over, the Romans completed the journey with good fortune, arriving safely in Jerusalem at the appointed time. After being received with unbelievable acclaim by everyone, the men, exhausted, restored their bodies with rest and leisure. Meanwhile mighty hosts of warriors had assembled, and facilities were prepared for these men by the local and foreign commanders of the knights. They also ordered knights to be chosen throughout the entire region, which was to be put into a state of defense by the strongest men, with weapons and stores of provisions and fodder adequate for siege made ready. Prayer was offered daily to God by all the people through various relics of the saints, and devotion to prayer with fasting and almsgiving was continued so that He might confer the desired triumph to those who served Him, and so that destruction would await the adversary.

The day dawned that had been set for the duel, and when the vast army of armored Christians and, of course, pagans had been drawn up in formation on either side, the two men who were to render judgment by combat, sheathed in armor, proceeded according to the agreement to the center. Here the Knight of the Surcoat, by boldness of spirit, courage, prowess, habit of winning, and the more righteous cause, filled his allies with the hope of victory. His opponent Gormundus, because of his remarkable limbs, huge stature, glowering face, war experience, much-touted courage, and the horror and din of his weapons, seemed to promise that triumph would be accorded to him. Both of them came on foot; because of his immense height Gormundus could find no horse strong enough to bear him.

With shields opposing and right arms raised, they met boldly in attack. However much strength each had and however great the force that anger directed, each went after the other with naked blade. A thousand thrusts were returned and in a thousand ways they pressed on with their exchange of bloodletting and wounding. They strike and are stricken; they advance and are driven back. The wheel of Fortune favors them with various turns. Nothing whatever is omitted that may be summed up in courage and strength; everyone's eyes are fixed on them. If either is more prepared for dealing death or if either is braver in endurance, this is not known; between these men such frequent thrusts and severe blows are unceasingly exchanged that who gives and who receives them is hard to discern. You cannot tell which man has greater strength. The more they press the fight, the more they hunger for battle. At times they intersperse their blows with clever taunts; at times they inflame each other with witty obscenities. Now they withdraw, out of breath; now refreshed, they more eagerly rush together. With renewed strength they join in a more heated attack; and as if nothing had yet been done fiercely, their spirits rage with greater ferocity.

You could see them facing each other like two ferocious boars in mortal combat who now attack each other with curved tusks in sidelong slashes, now strike their flanks, now trample hoof under hoof; their jaws are now foaming with smoky spume, now sparking forth fire. If one presses more violently, the other, yielding, is forced back; then with the other prevailing, the first is forced to retreat. This one, as if setting a trap, strives to inflict a wound. The other, if anything lies open to the point of his sword, skillfully makes a thrust; but the first, with equal skill, mocks the other's effort and blocks it. The clash of arms echoes loudly far and wide, and the density of the armor blunts and dulls their sharp blades. From the striking of the arms sparks leap up. Because of the intense effort salty sweat pours off their limbs from top to toe. It was uncertain to whom victory would fall; everyone thought that the strength of the two was evenly matched. With remarkable courage and remarkable prowess the fight was fought; from the first hour till sunset, nothing during the fighting gave preference to one over the other. So when evening fell, they were drawn apart with no deep wounds. In the morning they would fight again, and again the struggle would begin from the beginning.

At Aurora's rising the helmeted phalanxes came together in a twofold battle-line, and the contending factions led their men to the arena. They clashed; there was a shout; each man intended to inflict death on the other. The man-to-man fight was repeated with greater rivalry because the more one made trial of the other, the more the other conducted himself with care and bravery. It was a source of shame that men who in everyone's judgment were definitely proven to be of equal strength should yield in the smallest degree. For if on that day you had watched the battle of these two, you would have sworn that they had merely played the day before. You would have been astounded, considering these repeated blows and severe buffets, how the keenness of the sword blades could have lasted without dulling, how the solidity of the armor could have remained intact, and particularly how they themselves, unwearied and uninjured, could have stood as long as they chose to. Indeed with such vigor and such bravery the swords clashed against helmets and pounded against shields that the air glowed with bursting sparks, and steel repelled clashed steel and then sprang back at the one who had wielded it.

With frequent gasps they agitate the air, throwing weapon against weapon, blow upon blow. With one mind they stand; they wage a valiant fight, and the prolonged battle produces a lust for conflict. Chest expands to chest, and they strive with every effort to attack and to resist. The boldness of one provokes the wrath of the other; and the stubbornness of that one increases a bolder intensity in this one. Each man's strength offers stimulus to the other's courage; and the vigor of one advances as it is matched by the other.

Most of the day the odds between them were considered equal until the Knight of the Surcoat contrived a particular feint: while he pretended to cut down Gormundus above the left knee and drew Gormundus to lower his bronze shield, with his right hand turned to the right of the other, the Knight's sword unexpectedly struck into the middle of Gormundus' mouth, which was unprotected, knocked out four front teeth, and broke the jawbone on the left side. The wound was not grave, and it seemed to act more powerfully as a goad to fury than as an incitement to despair, as the strength of a wounded man may seethe with more fury than that of one unharmed. Enraged by the wound inflicted, Gormundus shouted no more words; he had to conserve his strength. Like a wild beast he lunged at the Knight of the Surcoat, and with his right arm high, he slammed his sword on the shield with such force that the row of set jewels, sharply jarred, flew piecemeal in different directions, as the boss tore off, and the upper edge of the shield hit the Knight's forehead hard enough to cause an effusion of blood.

Even more enraged, the Knight of the Surcoat again drew him out, and with redoubled savagery, the contest was pressed fiercely till the duel reached a crisis. The Knight of the Surcoat, seeking a weak spot, ran with sword raised at the unprotected flank of his enemy. But since Gormundus was experienced and parried the thrust, when the Knight pressed his effort, his sword was caught by the blocking of the shield and broke down to a small shaft. Neither the density nor the resistance of Gormundus' shield was able to withstand the force of that blow, with the result that it was smashed through the middle, and splitting under the boss, flew into pieces.

At this a great shout rose from all the assembled armies, with cheers from one side, and from the other insults. The greater danger to the Knight of the Surcoat was apparent: since his sword was shattered, nothing at all was at hand by which he could defend himself or by his own effort keep the enemy at bay. For Gormundus, although his shield was smashed, his blade was intact; he was pounding his adversary with the rigid two-edged sword without a moment's pause. The Knight of the Surcoat then faced the attack and was skillfully blocking with his shield in every direction. If the setting sun had not ended the duel, he would without doubt have incurred the most severe loss. The end of the match had been decided so that at the time the shadow of the setting sun reached a determined mark, it fulfilled the agreement that the men were to be separated, without regard to advantage or disadvantage. The shadow reached the mark then, and although the pagans were unwilling and barely held themselves from revolt, the two combatants were in fact separated. Whatever remained of the fight would be postponed till the next day.

When the radiance of the sun had put to flight the darkness of the night, the lines from both sides assembled, and the seasoned warriors presented themselves strengthened and grim, with arms repaired. A bitter, almost fatal quarrel arose between the two armies over whether the sword should be conceded to the Knight of the Surcoat or the shield to Gormundus, or to both, to neither, or to one and not the other. After the dispute had continued for some time, and the main disagreements had been aired, the consensus was that the combatants should be made equal; both sides agreed that the Knight could not defend himself without a sword, nor could the other, with his shield destroyed, be strong enough to protect himself from attack.

When the multitude was assembled, the duelists—protected by loricas and crested helmets, horrible to see—once again challenged each other and attacked and assailed with powerful hands. The thunder of battle arose, the clash of arms rang out, the sound of blows increased, and the fiery shock grew fearfully hot. The air rebounded and resounded with terrible noise, and, as the bronze was struck, the hollows of the mountains re-echoed that noise. As the duel was demanding no rest was given to the weary nor breathing space allowed for the winded. They fought wholeheartedly, and wholeheartedly they struggled until one would fall and the other achieve the victory. Neither the hot summer sun nor the continuous strain hindered them, yet no decision was reached because they resisted always more boldly, each one throwing himself against his ever more unconquerable opponent. Thus the participants were inspired by ferocity and were invigorated by animosity.

When most of the day had passed, Gormundus began to waver from the heat and also from the constant harrying of his adversary. The attack was increased against him vehemently, and the whole weight of the clash fell on him. He weakened in spirit and fought less effectively. Perceptibly drawing back from the Knight of the Surcoat, he retreated, not defending himself with such courage as before; by no means was he pressing his opponent. The Knight of the Surcoat, aware of this, stood his ground more boldly and caused the anxious man's spirit more anxiety. He did not stop till he had pushed him beyond the boundary of the circle that surrounded them. The noise and murmurs, the shouts and screams of the incredulous people rose to the stars, and dismayed groups shouted: "Back, Gormundus; come back, Gormundus! What are you trying to do? Where do you think you're going, great knight? Making others run—not running yourself—has always been your style. Come back, or in the end shame will erase all the winning

you've ever done. You can't run away from here! Here you must either
conquer or be conquered!"

At these shouts, Gormundus, overcome by shame and gasping somewhat, took his stand more bravely and weathered the charge of his adversary more manfully. Brandishing his sword, he dealt a blow that felled the
Knight, whose legs folded under him. Gormundus forced him to his knees
by the force of his thrust. But his breastplate remained impenetrable. Then
the Knight of the Surcoat, wild and enraged, sprang to his feet, drew
himself up in his armor, brandished his right arm and shouted, "Here is the
blow that ends the game!" Striking with his double-edged sword on the top
of Gormundus' helmet while the armor was hot and thus less resistant, he
guided the blow, fracturing, splintering, and penetrating everything all the
way to the breastbone. (Hardly a desirable stomach remedy!) When he
drew the sword from the wound, the skull split into two parts, with the
brains oozing out. The victor kicked it away with his foot.

When they saw their champion vanquished and cruelly slaughtered, the
pagans united in the grief of death, mourning over him with interminable
wailing; and as they gathered his armor, they would have attacked the
Knight of the Surcoat in vengeance, had they not been restrained by their
inviolable laws. Once their defender had been given over to death, the
pagans yielded to the pact with the Romans according to the agreed conditions: peace confirmed, hostages given, heavy reparations imposed. The
enemy then retired in confusion to their own country.

The Knight of the Surcoat, having been awarded the trophy for his
supreme victory, while the highborn Jerusalemites then honored him with
many rewards, in the fullness of time returned to Rome. He was received by
the emperor and the Senate with a triumphal procession. The emperor,
restoring him to the company of his closest companions, resolved to raise
him to the highest honors and to grant him high rank. Once these deeds had
been accomplished, since no one was presuming to move against the Roman
Empire by sword, the Knight of the Surcoat, disdaining a peaceful life and
desiring military action, eagerly inquired what region was torn by the
tumults of war.

When the name of Arthur, the famous King of Britannia (his uncle,
though he did not know it), who was acclaimed for prowess around the
world, was brought to his attention, unmoved by all that the emperor had
given him, the Knight of the Surcoat humbly begged permission to leave
time and again. Although the emperor had already decided to promote him
to the highest position, and he had no doubt that the departure of so worthy
a man would be to his own loss, he gave assent to the petition in order that
the Knight might learn about his lineage, and also because he felt confident
that through him the Kingdom of Britannia, so long separated from the
Roman Empire, might be regained for himself. The emperor bestowed on
him rich, sumptuous, and priceless gifts, and gave him the coffer in which
the proof of his parentage remained, with orders that it must be presented to
King Arthur, adding his own letter as testimony that everything the documents stated was established and confirmed. Further, the emperor forbade
him to look inside the coffer before he entered the presence of King Arthur.
He ordered, then, that the first citizens of the Gauls, through whose lands
the Knight must pass, should receive him with honor, serve him, provide

him with necessities, and escort him safely through their territories all the way to the sea. So, farewells were spoken and the Knight departed, leaving the ruler behind.

With everyone grieving over his departure, the Knight of the Surcoat began the journey as planned. He crossed the Alps and after having made his way through Gaul, arrived safely in Britannia. Inquiring where King Arthur was in residence, he learned that he was staying at the city of Caerleon in Demetia [South Wales], where he was accustomed to spend more of his time than in his other cities. That charming place was laid out with groves, abounding in animals, rich in treasures, pleasant for its green meadows, and watered by the Usk River, and not far away the Severn River offered a dwelling place of the utmost delight. Here was the metropolitan city of the province of Demetia; here the legions of Rome used to spend the winters; here King Arthur celebrated the high feasts, wore the crown, and convened all the barons of Britannia for his assembly. As soon as the Knight found out where Arthur was residing, he made his way in that direction, traveling swiftly in high spirits, pressing on day and night without a break. When he was almost there, on the last night before he expected to reach Caerleon, he was just outside the town of Usk, six miles away, when a sudden, violent storm struck with a driving rain. Everyone with him either left the high road or was unable to continue.

That same night, King Arthur and Gwendoloena, his queen, were talking to each other about many things while resting in bed. (Because of the length of the night they had had enough sleep.) Queen Gwendoloena was indeed the most beautiful of all women, but she had been initiated into sorcery, so that often from her divinations she could read the future. Among other things, she said, "Lord, you boast and greatly extol your prowess, and you assume that no one is your equal in strength."

Arthur replied, "That's so. Doesn't your own heart feel the same about me?"

The queen answered, "Of course it does—but there is at this very hour of the night a knight from Rome who is passing through the town of Usk on his way here. Have no doubt that you will find him pre-eminent in courage and prowess. He is mounted on a steed to which no other can be compared in vigor, value, or grace. His armor is impenetrable, and no one withstands the blow of his right arm. Lest you think I declare this to you lightly, look for this sign: he will send me a gold ring and three thousand-piece coins, as well as two horses, by mid-morning."

Arthur, aware that she had never deceived him in any prediction whatever, still decided to test this information without her knowledge. For it was his custom that whenever he heard about any strong man, he would challenge him, so that by single combat he could display the greater valor. So a little later when the queen had drifted off to sleep, he got up, armed himself, mounted his horse, and took as his companion for the encounter only Kay, his seneschal.

He came upon the Knight of the Surcoat halting at a little stream flooded by the storm, looking for the ford and cursing the delay. Actually because the Knight was confused by the foul fog of the night, he had decided to cross through the deep channel of the river. Sighting him by the gleam of his armor, Arthur shouted, "Where do you come from, you who wander over this countryside in the dead of night? Are you an exile, a bandit, or a spy?"

To him the Knight replied, "I wander because I do not know the roads. No flight of an exile drives me, no pillage of a bandit tempts me, nor does any deceit cover any trickery." Arthur answered, "You rely on a quick tongue. I see your game. I know very well that you have to be one of those three I named. So without more ado, lay down your arms. Unless you give yourself up to me entirely, you will learn immediately that I am the scourge of your wickedness."

The Knight responded, "Anybody is foolish and fainthearted who starts to run before the fight, or who gives in to his enemy before he has to. If, however, you still want my arms, I swear to their power; I'll match you for them, blow for blow."

So words exchanged between them erupted into threats and abuses, and Arthur, goaded to fury, got ready to cross the river, spurred his horse to the encounter, and rushed blindly at him. The Knight of the Surcoat, waiting for him with drawn and couched lance, drove at him in the ford itself and knocked him into the middle of the river. Backing up, he caught hold of his struggling horse by the reins. Kay the Seneschal, wanting to avenge his lord, spurred his horse and met the Knight of the Surcoat, but just as before, with the first blow he was piled on top of Arthur in a single heap. The knight, using the point of his lance, pulled the horse toward him. The darkness of the night saved Arthur and Kay from being harmed. Those two who had come to this place as knights returned home as foot-soldiers with no little disgrace. Arthur, in fact, climbed back into bed. Queen Gwendolo-ena asked him, stiff as he was with cold and soaked not only by the rain but also by the river-water, where he had been for so long and why he was so wet.

Arthur replied, "I thought I heard some sort of commotion outside in the courtyard. I figured it might be some of my men fighting, so I went out. It took a while to settle, and I was drenched in the rain."

The queen answered, "Whatever you say. Truly, wherever you went and whatever took place, my messenger will tell me in the morning."

The Knight of the Surcoat, having crossed the shallowest part of the water and not realizing with whom he had done battle, turned toward the nearby village and found lodging. At the first light of day, he hurried on toward Caerleon. About two miles down the road he noticed a boy and asked who employed him. The boy told him, "I am a messenger of the queen, whose personal instructions it is my duty to carry out."

And the Knight said, "Will you do what I ask of you?"

The boy replied, "I am at your service."

The Knight said, "Take these two horses and lead them for me to the queen as my gift so that she may gladly accept the proof of my prowess in pledge for requesting friendship." Handing him the gold ring and the three pieces of gold to be carried to her as well, he told him his name and declared that he would follow him on the road. The messenger did what had been asked of him. He accepted the gold items and led the horses with him.

Meanwhile, Queen Gwendoloena, aware of what was going to happen, stood on the wall of the castle watching the road that led to the town of Usk. When she observed from a distance her messenger returning, leading two horses with all their trappings, she understood the situation and, descending quickly, met him as he entered the hall. The boy transacted the business gracefully, revealed his instructions, delivered the things sent, and announced that the Knight of the Surcoat was about to arrive. The queen, smiling at the name, accepted the gifts and thanked him. She ordered that the horses should be led into the bedroom right to the couch of the king, who was still resting, since he had spent the whole night being active. Having roused him from his sleep, she said, "Lord, lest you accuse me of fabricating what I know, see the ring and the gold which yesterday I promised would be sent to me today. Furthermore, the knight I told you about last evening has given me these two horses which, having thrown their riders into that river, he commandeered for himself."

King Arthur, recognizing his own horses and seeing disclosed what he had hoped would be kept secret, was consumed with shame. Then he went to the assembly of nobles he had ordered to come together on that day for pressing concerns. As he sat outside the hall under the shade of an ash tree with his people, the Knight of the Surcoat entered the gates on horseback. Approaching King Arthur, he greeted him along with the queen and knights sitting nearby.

Arthur, not unaware of who he was, turned a grim face toward him and responded quite bluntly. He asked about his origin, where he traveled, what he sought in these regions. The man replied that he was a Roman knight, and that, since he had heard Arthur was pressed by war and in need of knights, he had come to offer his services, and that furthermore he had brought imperial mandates. He then handed the sealed coffer and letter to the king. When Arthur had received the emperor's letter, he withdrew from the assembly and ordered it to be read. On receiving the testimony of the document along with the records of proof and the cloak and the signet ring offered in evidence, he was greatly astonished. All this he strove to regard as truth. Despite his immense joy, he simply could not believe that this man was indeed his nephew. He remained incredulous about the matter till both parents had been summoned—Loth, King of Norway, and Anna, the Queen—who, it happened, were there. He exacted the truth from them and rigorously tested the facts. They confessed that this was all true, that he was indeed their son, and their testimony was sworn by special oaths. Arthur was exhilarated with incredible joy that the man upheld in so many ways by the emperor's commendations and by a great reputation for exalted prowess was, as a final surprise, related to him by close kinship. Nevertheless, he purposely ordered that none of this should be revealed to the Knight till he had accomplished some outstanding exploit in his presence.

So returning to the assembly and calling the Knight before everyone, Arthur said, "Your help, friend, I do not need at the present time. I do not know precisely whether prowess or awkwardness is stronger in you. I have a band of knights of such incomparable prowess, endowed with such strength and courage that to include a clumsy and cowardly man among the skillful and daring is to risk weakening their spirit from its customary boldness and aggressiveness. An enormous number of knights like you serve me voluntarily without stipend, among whom, unless you first show that you deserve it, my decision stands that you should not even be enrolled."

To this the Knight of the Surcoat, goaded by his words, replied, "By offering to serve you, I have incurred from you a grave rejection and an unexpected injury—I, who up to now was deemed worthy to come to your aid, inasmuch as I was not influenced by others' entreaties nor by great wealth. I do not doubt that I will find someone whom I may serve; yet even if I do, I will not easily find your equal. Indeed, since a desire for military challenge brought me here, on the following condition you might consider me worthy to be one of your knights: if I alone can accomplish something in which your whole army has failed."

Arthur answered, "My reply is this decree: if you should accomplish what you have bargained for, I shall not only enroll you among my men but indeed set you to be loved above them all." The plan pleased the king and all his nobility as well, and he kept the Knight at his court for the present under the agreed condition.

Not twice six days had passed when an occasion of this sort compelled Arthur to send out an expedition. In the northern part of Britannia was a place called "the Castle of the Maidens," which a young woman, who was noted for her grace and nobility, governed by right of lordship. She was allied to Arthur by the deepest obligations of friendship. A certain pagan king, captivated by her graceful bearing and great beauty and having in turn been rejected by her, had besieged her in her fortified town. Since the siege machinery had been constructed and transported to the site and the mounds to support it built up, he was threatening to storm the castle and seize her. Since she knew she could not bear up under the unremitting attacks and daily assaults, she sent a messenger and begged Arthur to come to her aid. As she was barricaded in her tower and the farther wall had already been breached, she deemed it necessary to surrender very soon to the enemy unless Arthur brought up reinforcements immediately.

So Arthur, fearing the peril of the young woman in her castle, at once mustered, armed, and drew up the ranks of his knights; and fully prepared, though consumed by great dread, he began the march to the place where he had been summoned. Many times, it is true, he had encountered and fought this very king, but it had always resulted that he was repulsed and beaten. As he was approaching the siege, a second messenger arrived, running with hair loose about his cheeks, who reported that the pagan king had razed the city and had seized and carried off the lady. The messenger continued to plead for his mistress that the love King Arthur had held for her in prosperity he would now show her in adversity. Arthur pursued the enemy, which was burdened with plunder. He fell furiously upon their rear guard, where he thought them least protected, but because of an unfortunate omen, he was intercepted by them. Having been thus warned of his approach, they repulsed him. To protect themselves, they had placed their more experienced warriors in the rear guard, which would not easily be thrown into confusion by sudden attack.

Arthur's front ranks, instead, were brought to confusion by the unexpected strength of the enemy's rear guard, which, surrounding Arthur's men on all sides, contained them, pressed them, and shattered them. Here the bitterest battle was fought, and bloody slaughter was inflicted on both sides. Arthur, in the very lap of the enemy, was being pressed back, demoralized and exhausted; and unless by cutting his way out he could immediately retreat, he would be slain, and his entire army cut down. He therefore gambled on flight, guessing that it would be wiser to run to safety than to succumb to the disaster hanging over him.

At the beginning of the engagement, the Knight of the Surcoat had withdrawn to a high, remote lookout in order to see what happened to the fellowship of knights during the course of battle. When their retreat revealed the disaster to him, he met Arthur fleeing with the first wave, and laughing at him, shouted sarcastically, "Tell me, O King, are you hunting deer or perhaps rabbits as you go scattered this way along the paths?"

Arthur replied indignantly, "I see your great prowess, since you, while others are involved in battle, have removed yourself to the hiding-places of the forest!" Without further words, he rode off, with the enemy in pursuit.

The Knight of the Surcoat, taunting every one of the knights he encountered with jeers and slurs, turned to attack the pursuing enemy. He rushed raging upon the advance patrols, penetrating through the tight and strong formations into their very midst like a winter storm, injuring all those who offered him resistance. When he saw the pagan royal guard, he instantly spurred his horse forward; with lance couched, the unexpected assailant ran the gleaming point into the hollow of the pagan king's chest. Having thrown the dying man to the ground, he seized the young woman by her horse's bridle and at once set out to return the way he had come.

But the guard which surrounded the pagan king, thrown into disorder on seeing their lord struck down in their midst, with a shout cut the invader off, and, with swords drawn, they charged upon him. They rushed at him together, and he at all of them. From a distance some threw spears at him; from all sides others struck at him ceaselessly with their blades. Like a rainstorm a multitude of blows beat upon him. Still, he continued on his way, leaving them cut down. But he was greatly hampered because he had to defend not only himself but the lady. Not far distant was a broad and deep fosse marking the boundary between two provinces. It had a narrow access since its bridge allowed only one person to cross at a time. To this place, then, the Knight of the Surcoat raced, and arriving there, he sent the lady to safety within the fortifications of the fosse, ordering her to remain hidden from sight until he returned. Once more plunging into the ranks of the pursuing enemy, he turned them back and put them to flight. Roaring like a lion bereft of its cubs, he inflicted cruel slaughter on them without mercy. Not one of them bore up under the attack and none who came into contact with the massive power of his right arm went away uninjured. Wherever he turned, they were scattered, as from the blast of a tempest. The powerful one continually slashed them to death without pity. Not withdrawing until all of them had been routed, he marked them all for death: some flung themselves from the steep banks, some by choice threw themselves into the obstructing waters, and the remainder he himself cut to pieces in a massacre.

The Knight of the Surcoat, having gained victory without injury to himself, cut off the head of the pagan king with the royal diadem still in place, fastened it onto his standard and, raising it on high, returned to King Arthur with the lady by his side. Exulting, he entered the hall where King Arthur, depressed and grieving at the misfortune of war, was seated. He cried out, "Just where, O King, are your famous champions about whom you so long boasted that no one was their equal in courage? See the head of the man I alone conquered and laid low, along with the entire force of his knights! He was the king who with a handful put to fight so many thousands of your men that it is shameful! Do you consider me worthy now to be your knight?"

Arthur, joyously recognizing the head of the king who was hateful to him beyond all others and the young woman so dear to him rescued from the hands of the enemy, ran to embrace the Knight and replied, "You are truly worthy to be one of us and you must be granted special honors! Nevertheless, since till now we have been uncertain as to who you are, I ask you to explain where your native land is, from whom you trace your lineage, and what family name you bear."

The other replied, "The truth of what I have told you holds. I was born in Gaul, fathered by a Roman senator. I was educated in Rome, and 'Knight of the Surcoat' is what I happen to be called."

Arthur returned, "You are plainly mistaken. What you have thought true cannot be confirmed. In a word, you have been deceived by this information."

The knight asked, "How so?"

Arthur explained, "I shall show you your true lineage. This knowledge shall be the reward for your deeds." Then with both of his parents present (to wit, Loth, King of Norway, and Anna, the Queen) Arthur ordered the letter written by the emperor to be brought to him and, when it was brought, to be read in the hearing of the common people and the nobles. When the documents were read, amazement and incredible joy arose with the comprehension of it all, and everyone proclaimed the parents blessed for such an offspring.

Then King Arthur, gazing at him with joy, said: "I acknowledge you, dear friend, as my nephew. You are the son of my sister, to whom Fortune gave such a child not for disgrace but for honor." He added, "Indeed at an early age you were called 'Boy with No Name,' and from the time you entered knighthood till the present, 'Knight of the Surcoat.' From now on you will be known as 'Gawain,' your real name."

When Arthur announced this, three times, then four times the entire assemblage repeated and echoed, "Gawain, nephew of King Arthur."

When the son had been acknowledged by his father and the nephew by his uncle, the magnitude of joy doubled, not only for the recovery of a lost loved one, but also for this man's incomparable courage and strength. What other outstanding exploits fell to Gawain, anyone who desires to know must ask from one who knows these things. Realizing that just as it is harder to take part in a battle than to record one, it is even more difficult to compose a history in an eloquent style than to present it orally in the words of common speech.

chapter IV
MIDDLE ENGLISH

THE WEDDING OF SIR GAWAIN
AND DAME RAGNELL

James J. Wilhelm

This amusing romance, written about 1450 at the end of the Middle Ages, treats the Loathly Lady theme that medieval readers know well from Geoffrey Chaucer's *Wife of Bath's Tale.* In essence, this familiar folklore motif concerns the transformation of an ugly hag into a beautiful woman after a man has placed himself under her "sovereynté" (sovereignty, power). To this is added the theme of A Riddle Asked and Answered; both here and in Chaucer, the riddle asks what women most desire. In both cases, the answer is that very same sovereignty that transforms the harridan into a lady of beauty and grace. In Chaucer, the tale is didactic, enforcing the Wife of Bath's own selfish desires and dreams of wish fulfillment; here, without the Wife as a narrator, the tale has a whimsical charm that makes it one of the most delightful of Middle English romances.

Peculiarly enough, the story does not end on a humorous note. At line 841 the otherwise unidentified narrator suddenly steps out of his creation and informs the reader that he is "besett withe gaylours" (beset with jailers), and he ends by praying for deliverance. This is like *Le Morte Darthur*, where Malory in his ending indicates that he too is a prisoner who dreams about being liberated from his inhibiting earthly condition. Both Malory and the anonymous author here are thus like the enchanted Loathly Lady, hoping for some miracle to transform them into creatures of happiness.

The dialect of the poem is East Midland, and is easy to read with a few simple transformations. The scribe frequently uses *y* for *i* ("lyf" for "life," "wyf" for "wife") and either *y* or *i* for *e* in preterite situations: "lyvid, belovyd" for "lived, beloved." Terminal *e* is often added where it does not exist in Modern English. The scribe doubles terminal *t* throughout. In my editing, I have doubled the vowel on "thee" (meaning "you") and in a few other cases where it does not influence the pronunciation; I have also made a few normalizations.

Bibliographic note: A standard edition of the Oxford manuscript (Bodleian Library, Rawlinson C 86) was made by Laura Sumner (Smith College Studies in Modern Languages, 1924), which was reprinted by B. J. Whiting in his commentary on the *Wife of Bath's Tale* in *Sources and Analogues of Chaucer's "Canterbury Tales"*, ed. W. F. Bryan and Germaine Dempster (Humanities, 1941), pp. 223–268, which also mentions John Gower's "Tale of Florent" in *Confessio Amantis*. One modern edition is by Thomas J. Garbáty (Heath, 1984).

The Wedding of Sir Gawain and Dame Ragnell

Lythe* and listenythe* the lif of a lord riche,   *hark/listen to*
The while that he lyvid* was none hym liche,*   *lived/like*
Nether in bowre ne* in halle;   *neither in chamber nor*
In the tyme of Arthoure thys adventure betyd,*   *happened*
5   And of the greatt adventure that he hymself dyd,
That kyng curteys* and royalle.   *courteous*
Of alle kynges Arture berythe* the flowyr,   *beareth*
And of alle knyghtod he bare* away the honour   *bore*
Where-so-evere he wentt.
10 In his countrey was nothyng butt chyvalry,
And knyghtes were belovid by that doughty,*   *valiant one*
For cowardes were everemore shent.*   *disgraced*
Nowe wylle ye lyst* a whyle to my talkyng,   *if you will listen*
I shalle you telle of Arthowre the kyng,
15 Howe ones hym befelle.*   *once it befell him*
On huntyng he was in Ingleswod*   *Inglewood*
Withe alle his bold knyghtes good;
Nowe herken to my spelle.*   *tale*
The kyng was sett att his trestylle-tree*   *hunting-station*
20 Withe hys bowe to sle* the wylde venere,*   *slay/deer*
And hys lordes were sett hym besyde;
As the kyng stoode, then was he ware*   *aware*
Where a greatt hartt was and a fayre,
And forthe fast dyd he glyde.
25 The hartt was in a braken ferne,*   *fern thicket*
And heard the groundes,* and stoode fulle derne;*   *earth-sounds/very still*
Alle that sawe the kyng:
"Hold you stylle, every man,
And I wolle goo myself, yf I can,
30 Withe crafte* of stalkyng."   *the skill*
The kyng in hys hand tooke a bowe,
And wodmanly he stowpyd* lowe,   *woodmanlike he stooped*
To stalk unto that dere;*   *deer*
When that he cam the dere fulle nere,*   *near*
35 The dere lept forthe into a brere,*   *briar patch*
And evere the kyng went nere* and nere.   *nearer*
So kyng Arthure went a whyle
After the dere, I trowe,* half a myle,   *believe*

And no man withe hym went;

40 And att the last to the dere he lett flye,*   *fly [arrows]*

And smote hym sore and sewerly*—   *hard and surely*

Suche grace God hym sent.

Down the dere tumblyd so deron,*   *wounded*

And felle into a greatt brake of feron;*   *fern thicket*

45 The kyng folowyd fulle fast.

Anon* the kyng bothe ferce and felle*   *at once/savage*

Was withe the dere and dyd hym serve welle,*   *killed him*

And after the grasse he taste.*   *tasted (bit the dust)*

As the kyng was withe the dere alone,

50 Streyghte* ther cam to hym a quaynt grome,*   *straightway/strange fellow*

Armyd welle and sure:

A knyghte fulle strong and of greatt myghte,

And grymly wordes to the kyng he said:

"Well i-mett,* Kyng Arthour!   *met (welcome)*

55 Thou hast me done wrong many a yere,*   *year*

And wofully I shalle quytte* thee here;   *repay*

I hold thy lyfe-days nyghe* done;   *almost*

Thou hast gevyn* my landes in certayn*   *given/indeed*

Withe greatt wrong unto Sir Gawen.

60 Whate sayest thou, kyng alone?"

"Syr Knyghte, whate is thy name withe honour?"

"Syr Kyng," he sayd, "Gromer Somer Joure,*   *Summerday Man*

I telle thee nowe withe ryghte."

"A! Sir Gromer Somer, bethynk thee* welle: *consider*

65 To sle* me here, honour getyst thou no delle;*   *slay/part*

Bethynk thee thou artt a knyghte;

Yf thou sle me nowe in thys case,

Alle knyghtes wolle refuse thee in every place.

That shame shalle nevere thee froo;*   *go away from thee*

70 Lett be thy wylle* and folowe wytt,*   *anger/reason*

And that* is amys,* I shalle amend itt,   *what/amiss*

And thou wolt, or that* I goo."   *if you wish, before*

"Nay," sayd Sir Gromer Somer, "by hevyn* kyng!   *heaven's*

So shalt thou nott skape,* withoute lesyng;*   *escape/a lie*

75 I have thee nowe att avaylle;*   *my advantage*

Yf I shold lett thee thus goo withe mokery,*   *only banter*

Anoder* tyme thou wolt me defye;   *another*

Of that I shalle nott faylle."

Now sayd the kyng, "So God me save,

80 Save my lyfe, and whate thou wolt crave,

I shalle now graunt itt thee;

Shame thou shalt have to sle me in venere,*   *while hunting*

Thou armyd and I clothyd butt in grene, perde."*   *par Dieu, by God*

"Alle thys shalle nott help thee, sekyrly,*   *surely*

85 For I wolle nother lond ne* gold truly,   *want neither land nor*

Butt yf* thou graunt me att a certayn day   *unless*

Suche as I shalle sett, and in thys same araye."*   *attire*

"Yes," sayd the kyng, "lo! here my hand."

"Ye,* butt abyde, kyng, and here me a stound;*   *yea/while*

90 Fyrst thow shalt swere upon my sword broun,*   *burnished*

To shewe* me att thy comyng whate wemen* love   *tell/women/field*

best in feld* and town;

And thou shalt mete* me here withouten send,*   *meet/my sending for you*
Even att this day xij monethes end;
And thou shalt swere upon my swerd* good   *sword*
95 That of thy knyghtes shalle none com with
    thee, by the rood,*   *cross*
Nowther fremde* ne freynd.   *neither stranger*
And yf thou bryng nott answere withoute
    faylle,
Thyne hed thou shalt lose for thy traveylle*—   *trouble*
Thys shalle nowe be thyne othe.*   *oath*
100 Whate sayst thou, kyng? Lett see; have done."
"Syr, I graunt to thys, now lett me gone;*   *be gone*
Though itt be to me fulle lothe,*   *loathsome*
I ensure thee, as I am true kyng,
To com agayn att thys xij monethes end,
105 And bryng thee thyne answere."
"Now go thy way, Kyng Arthure;
Thy lyfe is in my hand, I am fulle sure;
Of thy sorowe thow artt nott ware.
Abyde, Kyng Arthure, a lytelle whyle;
110 Looke nott today thou me beguile,
And kepe alle thyng in close;*   *secret*
For and* I wyst,* by Mary mylde,   *if/knew*
Thou woldyst betray me in the feld,
Thy lyf fyrst sholdyst thou lose."
115 "Nay," sayd Kyng Arthure, "that may nott be;
Untrewe knyghte shalt thou nevere fynde me;
To dye yett were me lever.*   *preferable*
Farwelle, Sir Knyghte and evylle mett;
I wolle com, and I be on lyve* att the day sett,   *If I'm alive*
120 Thoughe I shold scape nevere."
The kyng his bugle gan* blowe,   *did*
That hard* every knyghte and itt gan knowe;*   *so that heard/they recognized it*
Unto hym can they rake;*   *they did hasten*
Ther they fond* the kyng and the dere   *found*
125 Withe sembland* sad and hevy chere,*   *semblance, face/spirit*
That had no lust to layk:*   *desire for sport*
"Go we home nowe to Carlylle;*   *Carlisle*
Thys huntyng lykys* me nott welle"—   *pleases*
So sayd King Arthure.
130 Alle the lordes knewe by his countenaunce
That the kyng had mett withe some
    dysturbaunce.
Unto Carlylle then the kyng cam,
Butt of his hevynesse knewe no man;
Hys hartt was wonder hevy;
135 In this hevynesse he dyd abyde,
That many of his knyghtes mervelyd that tyde,*   *wondered at that time*
Tylle att the last Sir Gawen
To the kyng he sayd then,
"Syr, me marvaylythe ryghte sore,*   *I wonder very strongly*
140 Whate thyng that thou sorowyst fore."*   *for*
Then answeryd the kyng as tyghte,*   *immediately*
"I shalle thee telle, gentylle Gawen knyghte.

In the forest as I was this daye,
Ther I mett withe a knyghte in his arraye,
145 And certeyn wordes to me he gan sayn,
And chargyd me I shold hym nott bewrayne;*   *betray*
Hys councelle must I kepe therfore,
Or els I am forswore."*   *forsworn, perjured*
"Nay, drede* you nott, lord, by Mary flower,*   *fear / the flowering Virgin*
150 I am nott that man that wold you dishonour,
Nother by evyn ne by moron."*   *evening nor morning*
"Forsoothe I was on huntyng in Ingleswod;
Thowe knowest well I slewe an hartt, by the rode,* *cross*
Alle myself alon;
155 Ther mett I withe a knyghte armyd sure;
His name he told me was Sir Gromer Somer Joure;
Therfor I make my mone.*   *moan, lament*
Ther that knyghte fast* dyd me threte,*   *much / threaten*
And wold have slayn me withe greatt heatt,*   *anger*
160 But* I spak fayre agayn;*   *except that / back well to him*
Wepyns* withe me ther had I none.   *weapons*
Alas! my worshypp* therfor is nowe gone."   *honor*
"What therof?"* sayd Gawen;   *why*
"What needys more?* I shalle nott lye,   *what more to say*
165 He wold have slayn me ther withoute mercy,
And that me* was fulle lothe;   *to me*
He made me to swere that att the xij monethes end,
That I shold mete hym ther in the same kynde;*   *way*
To that I plyghte my trowithe.*   *pledged my faith*
170 And also I shold tell hym att the same day
What wemen desyren moste, in good faye;*   *faith*
My lyf els shold I lese.*   *lose*
This othe I made unto that knyghte,
And that I shold nevere telle itt to no wighte;*   *person*
175 Of thys I myghte nott chese.*   *choose*
And also I shold com in none oder arraye,
But even as I was the same daye;
And yf I faylyd of myne answere,
I wott* I shal be slayn ryghte there.   *know*
180 Blame me nott thoughe* I be a wofulle man;   *if*
Alle thys is my drede and fere."
"Ye, Sir, make good chere;
Lett make your hors redy
To ryde into straunge contrey;
185 And evere wheras* ye mete owther* man   *everywhere / either*
        or woman, in faye,
Ask of them whate they therto saye.
And I shalle also ryde anoder waye
And enquere of every man and woman, and gett
        whatt I may
Of every man and womans answere,
190 And in a boke I shalle them wryte."
"I graunt," sayd the kyng as tyte,*   *right away*
"Ytt is welle advysed, Gawen the good,
Even by the holy rood."
Soone were they bothe redy,

195 Gawen and the kyng, wytterly.*   *indeed*
    The kyng rode on* way, and Gawen anoder,   *one*
    And evere enquyred of man, woman, and other,
    Whate wemen desyred moste dere.
    Somme* sayd they lovyd to be welle arayd,*   *some/arrayed, dressed*
200 Somme sayd they lovyd to be fayre prayed;*   *gallantly courted*
    Somme sayd they lovyd a lusty man
    That in theyr armys can clypp* them and kysse
        them than;*   *embrace/then*
    Somme sayd one; somme sayd other;
    And so had Gawen getyn* many an answere.   *gotten*
205 By that* Gawen had geten whate he maye   *by the time that*
    And come agayn by a certeyn daye,
    Syr Gawen had goten answerys so many
    That had made a boke greatt, wytterly;
    To the courte he cam agayn.
210 By that* was the kyng comyn withe hys boke,   *that time*
    And eyther on others pamplett* dyd loke.   *pamphlet*
    "Thys may nott faylle," sayd Gawen.
    "By God," sayd the kyng, "I dred me sore;*   *I'm much afraid*
    I cast me* to seke a lytelle more   *intend*
215 In Yngleswod Forest;
    I have butt a monethe to* my day sett;   *till*
    I may happen on somme good tydynges to
        hitt—
    Thys thinkythe me* nowe best."   *seems to me*
    "Do as ye lyst,"* then Gawen sayd;   *please*
220 "What-so-evere ye do, I hold me* payd;   *consider myself*
    Itt is good to be spyrryng;*   *inquiring*
    Doute* you nott, lord, ye shalle welle spede;*   *doubt/succeed*
    Some of your sawes* shalle help att nede;   *answers*
    Els itt were ylle lykyng."*   *otherwise it would be bad luck*
225 Kyng Arthoure rode forthe on the other* day,   *next*
    Into Yngleswod as hys gate* laye,   *way*
    And ther he mett withe a lady;
    She was as ungoodly* a creature   *unattractive*
    As evere man sawe, withoute mesure.*   *exceedingly so*
230 Kyng Arthure mervaylyd securly.*   *indeed*
    Her face was red, her nose snotyd withalle,*   *snotty also*
    Her mowithe* wyde, her teethe yalowe over alle,   *mouth*
    Withe bleryd eyen* gretter then a balle;   *bleary eyes*
    Her mowithe was nott to lak;*   *mouth lacked nothing (was huge)*
235 Her tethe hung over her lyppes;
    Her cheekys syde* as wemens hyppes;   *broad*
    A lute she bare upon her bak.
    Her nek long and therto greatt,
    Her here cloteryd on an hepe;*   *hair clustered in a heap*
240 In the sholders she was a yard brode;*   *broad*
    Hangyng pappys* to be an hors lode;*   *paps big enough to/horse's load*
    And lyke a barrelle she was made;
    And to reherse the foulnesse of that lady,
    Ther is no tung* may telle, securly: *tongue*
245 Of lothynesse inowghe* she had.   *loathliness enough*
    She satt on a palfrey was gay begon,*   *that was gaily decorated*

Withe gold besett and many a precious stone;
Ther was an unseemely syghte;
So foulle a creature withoute mesure
250 To ryde so gayly, I you ensure,
Ytt was no reason ne ryghte.
She rode to Arthoure, and thus she sayd:
"God spede, Sir Kyng, I am welle payd*   *very pleased*
That I have withe thee mett;
255 Speke withe me, I rede or* thou go,   *I advise before*
For thy lyfe is in my hand, I warn thee so;
That shalt thou fynde, and I itt nott lett."*   *if I don't prevent it (your death)*
"Why, whatt wold ye, lady, nowe withe me?"
"Syr, I wold fayn nowe speke withe thee,
260 And telle thee tydynges good;
For alle the answerys that thou canst yelpe,*   *boast of*
None of them alle shalle thee helpe—
That shalt thou knowe, by the rood.
Thou wenyst* I knowe nott thy councelle,*   *thinkest/secret*
265 Butt I warn thee I knowe itt every dealle.*   *bit*
Yf I help thee nott, thou art butt dead.
Graunt me, Sir Kyng, butt one thyng,
And for thy lyfe, I make warrauntyng,*   *I'll give a guarantee*
Or elles thou shalt lose thy hed."
270 "Whate mean you, lady, telle me tyghte,*   *quickly*
For of thy wordes I have great despyte;
To* you I have no nede.*   *of/need*
Whate is your desyre, fayre lady?
Lett me wete* shortly;   *know it*
275 Whate is your meanyng,
And why my lyfe is in your hand,
Telle me, and I shalle you warraunt*   *guarantee*
Alle your own askyng."
"Forsoothe," sayd the lady, "I am no qued;*   *villain*
280 Thou must graunt me a knyghte to wed;
His name is Sir Gawen;
And suche covenaunt I wolle make thee,
Butt thorowe* myne answere thy lyf savyd be;   *if through*
Elles* lett my desyre be in vayne.   *otherwise*
285 And yf myne answere save thy lyf,
Graunt me to be Gawens wyf.
Advyse thee nowe, Sir Kyng;
For itt must be so, or thou artt butt dead;
Choose nowe, for thou mayste soone lose thyne
    hed.
290 Telle me nowe in hying."*   *haste*
"Mary,"* sayd the kyng, "I maye nott graunt
    thee   *by Mary!*
To make warraunt Sir Gawen to wed thee;
Alle lyethe in hym alon.
Butt and* itt be so, I wolle do my labour   *so that*
295 In savyng of my lyfe to make itt secour;*   *secure*
To Gawen wolle I make my mone."*   *lament*
"Welle," sayd she, "nowe go home agayn,
And fayre wordes speke to Sir Gawen,

For thy lyf I may save;
300 Thoughe I be foulle, yett am I gaye;*   *lusty*
Thourghe* me thy lyfe save he maye,   *through*
Or sewer* thy dethe to have."   *allow*
"Alas!" he sayd, "nowe wo is me,
That I shold cause Gawen to wed thee,
305 For he wol be lothe to saye naye.
So foulle a lady as ye ar nowe one
Sawe I nevere in my lyfe on ground gone;*   *to go*
I nott* whate I do may."   *know not*
"No force,* Sir Kyng, thoughe I be foulle;   *matter*
310 Choyce for a make* hathe an owlle;   *mate has (even an ugly) owl*
Thou getest of me no more;
When thou comyst agayn to* thyne answere,   *for*
Ryghte in this place I shalle meete thee here,
Or elles I wott* thou artt lore."*   *know/lost*
315 "Now farewelle," sayd the kyng, "lady."
"Ye, Sir," she sayd; "ther is a byrd men calle an owlle,
And yett a lady I am."
"Whate is your name, I pray you telle me?"
"Syr Kyng, I highte* Dame Ragnelle, truly,   *am called*
320 That nevere yett begylyd* man."   *beguiled a*
"Dame Ragnelle, now have good daye."
"Syr Kyng, God spede thee on thy way;   *prosper*
Ryghte here I shalle thee meete."
Thus they departyd fayre and welle.
325 The kyng fulle soone com to Carlylle,
And his hartt hevy and greatt.
The fyrst man he mett was Sir Gawen,
That unto the kyng thus gan sayn,*   *did say*
"Syr, howe have ye sped?"*   *fared*
330 "Forsoothe," sayd the kyng, "nevere so ille.
Alas! I am in* poynt myself to spylle,*   *at the/kill*
For nedely* I must be ded."   *of necessity*
"Nay," sayd Gawen, "that may nott be;
I had lever* myself be dead, so mott I the;*   *rather/may I thrive!*
335 Thys is ille tydand."*   *bad news*
"Gawen, I mett today withe the fowlyst lady
That evere I sawe certenly;
She sayd to me my lyfe she wold save,
Butt fyrst she wold thee to husbond have;
340 Wherfor I am wo-begon;
Thus in my hartt I make my mone."
"Ys this alle?" then sayd Gawen.
"I shalle wed her and wed her agayn,
Thoughe she were a fend;*   *fiend*
345 Thoughe she were as foulle as Belsabub,*   *Beelzebub*
Her shalle I wed, by the rood;
Or elles were nott I your frende,
For ye ar my kyng withe honour,
And have worshypt* me in many a stowre;*   *honored/time*
350 Therfor shalle I nott lett;*   *hesitate*
To save your lyfe, lorde, itt were my parte,*   *would be my duty*
Or were I false and a greatt coward;

And my worshypp is the bett."*   *better*
"Iwys,* Gawen, I mett her in Inglyswod.   *indeed*
355 She told me her name, by the roode,
    That itt was Dame Ragnelle;
    She told me butt* I had of her answere,*   *unless/an answer from her*
    Elles alle my laboure is nevere the nere;*   *nearer (to a solution)*
    Thus she gan me telle.
360 And butt yf* her answere help me welle,   *unless*
    Elles lett her have her desyre no dele*—   *not a bit*
    This was her covenaunt;
    And yf her answere help me, and none other,
    Then wold she have you; here is alle togeder;*   *that's the whole story*
365 That made she warraunt."
    "As for this," sayd Gawen, "it shalle nott lett.*   *hinder (me)*
    I wolle wed her att whate tyme ye wolle sett;
    I pray you make no care;*   *don't worry*
    For and* she were the moste fowlyst wyghte*   *if/person*
370 That evere men myghte see withe syghte,
    For your love I wolle nott spare."
    "Garamercy,* Gawen," then sayd Kyng Arthor;   *many thanks*
    "Of alle knyghtes thou berest the flowre,
    That evere yett I fond;*   *found*
375 My worshypp and my lyf thou savyst forevere;
    Therefore my love shalle nott from thee dyssevyr,*   *be severed*
    As I am kyng in lond."
    Then within v or vj days,
    The kyng must needys* go his ways   *of necessity*
380 To bere his answere.
    The kyng and Sir Gawen rode oute of toun,
    No man withe them, butt they alone,
    Neder ferre ne nere.
    When the kyng was within the forest:
385 "Syr Gawen, farewell, I must go west,
    Thou shalt no furder* goo."   *further*
    "My lord, God spede you on your jorney.
    I wold* I shold* nowe ryde your way,   *wish/should (could)*
    For to departe I am ryghte wo."*   *woeful, sorry*
390 The kyng had rydden butt a while,
    Lytelle more then the space of a myle,
    Or* he mett Dame Ragnelle.   *ere, before*
    "A, Sir Kyng, ye are nowe welcum here;
    I wott* ye ryde to bere your answere   *know*
395 That wolle avaylle you no dele."*   *not a bit*
    "Nowe," sayd the kyng, "sithe* itt wolle none other be,   *since*
    Telle me your answere nowe, and my lyfe save me:
    Gawen shalle you wed;
    So he hathe promysed me my lyf to save,
400 And your desyre nowe shalle ye have,
    Bothe in bowre* and in bed.   *chamber*
    Therfor telle me nowe alle in hast,
    Whate wolle help now att last—
    Have done; I may nott tary."*   *tarry*
405 "Syr," quod* Dame Ragnelle, "nowe shalt thou knowe   *said*
    Whate wemen desyren moste of highe and lowe;

From this I wolle nott varaye.*	*vary, deviate*
Somme* men sayn* we desyre to be fayre;	*some/say*
Also we desyre to have repayre*	*the company*
410 Of* diverse straunge men;	*with*
Also we love to have lust* in bed,	*pleasure*
And often we desyre to wed;	
Thus ye men nott ken.*	*don't understand*
Yett we desyre anoder manner* thyng:	*kind (of)*
415 To be holden* nott old, butt fresshe and yong,	*considered*
Withe flattryng and glosyng* and quaynt gyn;*	*complimenting/clever ploys*
So ye men may us wemen evere wyn,	
Of* whate ye wolle crave.	*for*
Ye goo fulle nyse,* I wolle nott lye;	*very foolishly*
420 Butt there is one thyng is alle oure fantasye,	
And that nowe shalle ye knowe:	
We desyren of men, above alle manner thyng,	
To have the sovereynte,* withoute lesyng,*	*sovereignty/lying*
Of alle, bothe hyghe and lowe.	
425 For where we have sovereynte alle is ourys,*	*ours*
Thoughe a knyghte be nevere so ferys,*	*fierce*
And evere the mastry wynne;*	*mastery we gain*
Of the moste manlyest is oure desyre;	
To have the sovereynte of* suche a syre,	*over*
430 Suche is oure crafte and gynne.*	*conniving*
Therefore wend, Sir Kyng, on thy way,	
And telle that knyghte, as I thee saye,	
That* itt is as* we desyren moste;	*what/that*
He wol be wrothe* and unsoughte,*	*angry/harsh*
435 And curse her fast that itt thee taughte,	
For his laboure is lost.	
Go forthe, Sir Kyng, and hold promyse	
For thy lyfe is sure nowe in alle wyse*—	*ways*
That dare I well undertake."*	*vouch for*
440 The kyng rode forthe a greatt shake*	*distance*
As fast as he myghte gate*	*go*
Thorowe mire, moore, and fenne,*	*bog*
Whereas* the place was sygnyd* and sett then,	*where/assigned*
Evyn there* withe Sir Gromer he mett.	*right there where*
445 And stern wordes to the kyng he spak withe that:*	*spoke then*
"Com off, Sir Kyng, nowe lett see	
Of thyne answere whate itt shal be,	
For I am redy grathyd."*	*all prepared*
The kyng pullyd oute bokes twayne:*	*two books*
450 "Syr, ther is myne answer, I dare sayn,	
For somme wolle help att neede."	
Syr Gromer lookyd on them everychon;*	*every one*
"Nay, nay, Sir Kyng, thou artt butt a dead man;	
Therfor nowe shalt thou bleede."	
455 "Abyde, Sir Gromer," sayd Kyng Arthoure;	
"I have one answere shalle make alle sure."	
"Lett se," then sayd Sir Gromer,	
"Or els so God me help, as I thee say,	
Thy dethe thou shalt have with large paye;*	*violently*
460 I tell thee nowe ensure."*	*for sure*

"Now," sayd the kyng, "I see, as I gesse,
In thee is butt a lytelle gentilnesse,
By God, that ay is helpand.*   *ever is helping*
Here is oure answere, and that is alle,
465 That* wemen desyren moste specialle,   *to what*
Bothe of fre and bond.*   *from freemen and bondsmen*
I saye no more, butt above al thyng,
Wemen desyre sovereynte, for that is theyr lykyng,
And that is theyr moste desyre:
470 To have the rewlle of* the manlyest men,   *rule over*
And then ar they welle;* thus they me dyd ken:*   *happy/teach*
To rule thee, Gromer Syre."
"And she that told thee nowe, Sir Arthoure,
I pray to God, I maye see her bren* on a fyre,   *burn*
475 For that was my syster, Dame Ragnelle;
That old scott,* God geve* her shame;   *hag/give*
Elles* had I made thee fulle tame;   *otherwise*
Nowe have I lost muche travaylle.
Go where thou wolt, Kyng Arthoure,
480 For of me thou mayste be evere sure;
Alas! that I evere se* this day;   *saw*
Nowe, welle I wott,* myne enime* thou wolt be,   *know/enemy*
And att suche a pryk* shalle I nevere gett thee;   *on such a note*
My song may be welle-away!"*   *alas*
485 "No," sayd the kyng, "that make I warraunt;
Some harnys* I wolle have to make me defendaunt,*   *armor/defensible*
That make I God avowe;*   *I swear to God*
In suche a plyghte shalt thou nevere me fynde,
And yf thou do, lett me bete and bynde,*   *be beaten and bound*
490 As is for thy best prouf."*   *advantage*
"Nowe have good day," sayd Sir Gromer.
"Farewell," sayd Sir Arthoure, "so mott I the,*   *may I thrive*
I am glad I have so sped."
Kyng Arthoure turnyd hys hors into the playn,
495 And soone he mett withe Dame Ragnelle agayn,
In the same place and stede.*   *spot*
"Syr Kyng, I am glad ye have sped welle;
I told howe itt wold be every delle;
Nowe hold that* ye have hyghte.*   *keep what/promised*
500 Syn* I have savyd your lyf, and none other,   *since*
Gawen must me wed, Sir Arthoure,
That* is a fulle gentille knyghte."   *who*
"No, lady; that* I you hyghte* I shalle nott faylle;   *what/promised*
So* ye wol be rulyd by my councelle,*   *if/advice (for secret wedding)*
505 Your wille then shalle ye have."
"Nay, Sir Kyng, nowe wolle I nott so;
Openly I wol be weddyd, or* I parte thee fro;*   *before/from*
Elles shame wolle I have.
Ryde before, and I wolle com after
510 Unto thy courte, Syr Kyng Arthoure;
Of* no man I wolle* shame;   *from/want*
Bethynk you* howe I have savyd your lyf.   *consider*
Therfor withe me nowe shalle ye nott stryfe,*   *quarrel*
For and* ye do, ye be to blame."   *if*

⁵¹⁵ The kyng of her had greatt shame;
Butt forthe she rood,* thoughe he were grevyd,*   *rode/grieved*
Tylle they cam to Karlyle forth they mevyd.*   *moved*
Into the courte she rode hym by,*   *by his side*
For no man wold she spare, securly—
⁵²⁰ Itt likyd* the kyng fulle ylle.   *pleased*
Alle the contraye* had wonder greatt,   *country, people*
Fro whens she com, that foule unswete;*   *ugly thing*
They sawe nevere of so fowlle a thyng;
Into the halle she went, in certen:
⁵²⁵ "Arthoure, kyng, lett fetche me Sir Gaweyn
Before the knyghtes, alle in hying,*   *haste*
That I may nowe be made sekyr;*   *secure, sure*
In welle* and wo trowithe plyghte us* togeder   *happiness/woe our troth pledge*
Before alle thy chyvalry.
⁵³⁰ This is your graunt; lett se, have done;
Sett forth Sir Gawen, my love, anon,*   *right away*
For lenger tarying kepe* nott I."   *care*
Then cam forth Sir Gawen the knyghte:
"Syr, I am ready of that I you hyghte,*   *pledged*
⁵³⁵ Alle forwardes* to fulfylle."   *promises*
"God have mercy," sayd Dame Ragnelle then;
"For thy sake I wold* I were a fayre woman,   *wish*
For thou art of so good wylle."
Then Sir Gawen to her his trowthe plyghte,*   *pledged his troth*
⁵⁴⁰ In welle and in wo, as he was a true knyghte.
Then was Dame Ragnelle fayn.*   *pleased*
"Alas!" then sayd Dame Gaynour;*   *Guinevere*
So sayd alle the ladyes in her bower,
And wept for Sir Gawen.
⁵⁴⁵ "Alas!" then sayd bothe kyng and knyghte,
"That evere he shold wed such a wyghte!"*   *creature*
She was so fowlle and horyble.
She had two teethe on every syde,
As borys* tuskes, I wolle nott hyde,   *like a boar's*
⁵⁵⁰ Of lengthe a large handfulle;
The one tusk went up, and the other down;
A mouthe fulle wyde, and fowlle i-grown*   *grown*
With grey herys many on;*   *hairs many a one*
Her lyppes laye lumpryd* on her chyn;   *lumped*
⁵⁵⁵ Nek forsoothe on her was none i-seen—
She was a lothly on!*   *loathly one*
She wold nott be weddyd in no maner
Butt* there were made a crye in all the shyre,   *unless*
Bothe in town and in borowe.*   *borough*
⁵⁶⁰ Alle the ladyes nowe of the lond,
She lett cry to com to hand,
To kepe that brydalle thorowe.*   *proper*
So itt befelle after on a daye
That marryed shold be that fowlle lady,
⁵⁶⁵ Unto Sir Gawen.
The daye was comyn* the day shold be;   *came when*
Therof the ladyes had greatt pity;
"Alas!" then gan they sayn.

The queen prayd Dame Ragnelle sekerly*   *earnestly*
570 To be maryed in the mornyng erly,
"As pryvaly* as we may."   *privately*
"Nay," she sayd, "by Hevyn Kyng,
That wolle I nevere for no-thyng,
For oughte* that ye can saye;   *aught, anything*
575 I wol be weddyd alle openly,
For with the kyng suche covenaunt made I;
I putt you oute of dowte,*   *doubt*
I wolle nott to churche tylle highe masse-tyme,
And in the open halle I wolle dyne,
580 In myddys* of alle the rowte."*   *the midst/company*
"I am greed,"* sayd Dame Gaynour,   *agreed*
"Butt me wold thynk more honour,   *I'd think (the other) more honorable*
And your worshypp moste."*   *and to your benefit*
"Ye, as for that, lady, God you save;
585 This daye my worshypp wolle I have;
I telle you withoute boste."*   *boast*
She made her redy to churche to fare,
And alle the states* that there ware,*   *ranking people/were*
Syrs, without lesyng.*   *a lie*
590 She was arrayd in the richest maner,
More fressher than Dame Gaynour;
Her arayment was worthe iij mlle. mark,*   *three thousand marks (huge sum)*
Of good red nobles styff and stark,*   *gold coins sturdy and strong*
So rychely she was begon.*   *adorned*
595 For* alle her rayment she bare the belle*   *despite/bore the (highest) prize*
Of* fowlnesse that evere I heard telle;   *for*
So fowlle a sow sawe nevere man,
For to make a shortt conclusion.
When she was weddyd, they hied them home;
600 To mete* alle they went.   *meat, dinner*
This fowlle lady bygan* the highe dese;*   *sat at the head of/dais*
She was fulle foulle and nott courteys,
So sayd they all verament.*   *truly*
When the servyce* cam her before,   *servings*
605 She ete* as muche as vj that ther wore,*   *ate/were*
That mervaylyd* many a man;   *so that marveled*
Her nayles were long ynchys iij;
Therwithe she breke her mete ungoodly;*   *broke (cut) her food uncouthly*
Therfore she ete alone.
610 She ete iij capons and also curlues* iij,   *curlews (large wading-birds)*
And greatt bake-metes she ete up, perde;*   *by God*
All men therof had mervaylle;
Ther was no mete cam her before
Butt she ete itt up lesse and more,
615 That praty,* fowlle dameselle.   *odious*
Alle men then that evere her sawe
Bade the deville her bonys* gnawe,   *bones*
Bothe knyghte and squyre;
So she ete tylle mete was done,
620 Tylle they drewe clothes* and had wasshen,*   *took towels/washed themselves*
As is the gyse* and maner.   *custom*
Many men wold speke of diverse service;*   *various meats*

I trowe* ye may wete inowghe* ther was,   *believe/know enough*
Bothe of tame and wylde;
625 In King Arthours courte ther was no wontt
That* myghte be gotten withe mannys* hond,   *of what/man's*
Noder in forest ne in feld.
There were mynstralles of diverse contry.

[*About 70 lines are lacking here.*]

"A, Sir Gawen! syn* I have you wed,   *since*
630 Shewe me your cortesy in bed;
Withe ryghte itt may nott be denyed.
I-wyse,* Sir Gawen," that lady sayd,   *indeed*
"And* I were fayre, ye wold do anoder brayd,*   *if/act a different way*
Butt of wedlok ye take no hed,*   *heed*
635 Yett for Arthours sake kysse me att the leste;*   *least*
I pray you do this att my request;
Lett se howe ye can spede."*   *manage*
Sir Gawen sayd, "I wolle do more   *will*
Than for to kysse, and God before!"
640 He turnyd hym her untille.*   *toward her*
He sawe her the fayrest creature
That ever he sawe without mesure.
She sayd, "Whatt is your wylle?"
"A, Jhesu!" he sayd, "what ar ye?"
645 "Sir, I am your wyf, securly;
Why ar ye so unkynde?"
"A, lady! I am to blame;
I cry you mercy, my fayre madame—
Itt was nott in my mynde.
650 A lady ye are fayre in my syghte,
And today ye were the foulyst wyghte
That ever I sawe withe myne ie.*   *eye*
Wele is me,* my lady, I have you thus";   *happy am I*
And brasyd* her in his armys, and gan her kysse,   *he embraced*
655 And made greatt joye, securly.
"Syr," she sayd, "thus shalle ye me have;
Chese of* the one, so God me save   *choose*
(My beauty wolle nott hold):
Wheder ye wolle have me fayre on nyghtes,*   *at night*
660 And as foulle on days to alle men sightes,
Or els to have me fayre on days,
And on nyghtes on the fowlyst wyfe;*   *one of the foulest women*
The one ye must needes have;
Chese* the one or the oder,*   *choose/other*
665 Chese one, Sir Knyghte, whiche you is levere,*   *to you is dearer*
Your worshypp for to save."
"Alas!" sayd Gawen, "the choyce is hard;
To chese the best, itt is froward;*   *difficult*
Wheder* choyse that I chese—   *whichever*
670 To have you fayre on nyghtes and no more—
That wold greve my hartt ryghte sore,
And my worshypp shold I lese.
And yf I desyre on days to have you fayre,

Then on nyghtes I shold have a symple repayre.*   *lean time*
675 Now fayn* wold I choose the best;   *gladly*
    I ne wott* in this world whatt I shalle saye,   *do not know*
    Butt do as ye lyst* nowe, my lady gaye: *please*
    The choyse I putt in your fist.
    Even as ye wolle, I putt itt in your hand;
680 Loose* me when ye lyst, for I am bond;*   *relieve/bound*
    I putt the choyse in you;
    Bothe body and goodes, hartt, and every dele*   *part*
    Ys alle your own, for to buy and selle—
    That make I God avowe!"
685 "Garamercy, corteys knyghte," sayd the lady;
    "Of alle erthly knyghtes blyssyd mott* thou be,   *blessed may*
    For now am I worshyppyd;
    Thou shalle have me fayre bothe day and nyghte,
    And evere whyle I lyve as fayre and bryghte;
690 Therfore be nott grevyd.*   *grieved*
    For I was shapen by nygramancy,*   *transformed by magic*
    Withe my stepdame,* God have on her mercy,   *by my stepmother*
    And by enchauntement,*   *enchantment*
    And shold have beene oderwyse understond,*   *taken differently*
695 Evyn tylle the best of Englond
    Had weddyd me verament.*   *truly*
    And also* he shold geve me the sovereynte   *so that*
    Of alle his body and goodes, securly,
    Thus was I disformyd;   *misshapen*
700 And thou, Sir Knyghte, curteys Gawen,
    Has gevyn me the sovereynte certeyn,
    That wolle nott wrothe* thee erly ne late.   *disturb*
    Kysse me, Sir Knyghte, evyn now here;
    I pray thee: be glad and make good cheere,
705 For welle is me begon."*   *all turned out well for me*
    Ther they made joye oute of mynde,
    So was itt reason and cours of kynde,*   *reasonable and nature's way*
    They two themself alone.
    She thankyd God and Mary mylde,
710 She was recovered of that that she was defoylyd;*   *what she was defiled of*
    So dyd Sir Gawen;
    He made myrthe alle in her boure,*   *bower, chamber*
    And thankyd of alle oure Savioure,
    I telle you, in certeyn.
715 Withe joye and myrthe they wakyd tylle daye,
    And then wold ryse that fayre maye.*   *maid*
    "Ye shalle nott," Sir Gawen sayd;
    "We wolle lye and slepe tylle pryme,*   *late morning*
    And then lett the kyng calle us to dyne."
720 "I am greed,"* then sayd the mayd.   *agreed*
    Thus itt passyd forth tylle mid-daye.
    "Syrs," quod* the kyng, "lett us go and asaye*   *said/find out*
    Yf Sir Gawen be on lyve;*   *alive*
    I am fulle ferd of* Sir Gawen,   *afraid for*
725 Nowe lest the fende* have hym slayn;   *fiend*
    Nowe wold I fayn preve.*   *gladly find out*
    Go we nowe," sayd Arthoure the Kyng;

"We wolle go see theyr uprisyng,
Howe welle that he hath sped."
730 They cam to the chambre, alle in certeyn.
"Aryse," sayd the kyng to Sir Gawen;
"Why slepyst thou so long in bed?"
"Mary," quod Gawen, "Sir Kyng, sicurly,
I wold be glad and* ye wold lett me be,   *if*
735 For I am fulle welle att ease;
Abyde, ye shalle see the dore undone;*   *unlocked*
I trowe* that ye wolle say I am welle goon;*   *believe/in good shape*
I am fulle loathe to ryse."
Syr Gawen rose, and in his hand he toke
740 His fayr lady, and to the dore he shoke,*   *hurried*
And openyd the dore fulle fayre;
She stod in her smok alle* by that fyre;   *smock right*
Her her* was to her knees as red as gold wyre: *hair*
"Lo! this is my repayre,*   *refuge, pleasure*
745 Lo!" sayd Gawen, Arthoure untille,*   *unto*
"Syr, this is my wyfe, Dame Ragnelle,
That savyd onys* your lyfe."   *once*
He told the kyng and the queen hem beforn*   *before them*
Howe soddenly from her shap she dyd torne:*   *turn*
750 "My lord, nowe be your leve."   *by your leave*
And whate was the cause she forshapen* was,   *transformed*
Syr Gawen told the kyng both more and lesse.
"I thank God," sayd the queen;
"I wenyd,* Sir Gawen, she wold thee have myscaryed;*   *thought/harmed*
755 Therfore in my hartt I was sore agrevyd;
Butt the contrary is here seen."
Ther was game, revelle, and playe,
And every man to other gan saye:
"She is a fayre wyghte."
760 Then the kyng them alle gan telle
How did held hym att* neede Dame Ragnelle,   *save him at the time of*
"Or my dethe had beene dyghte."*   *prepared*
Ther the kyng told the queen, by the rood,
Howe he was bestad* in Ingleswod   *beset*
765 Withe Sir Gromer Somer Joure;
And what othe* the knyghte made hym swere,   *oath*
"Or elles he had slayn me ryghte there
Without mercy or mesure.
This same lady, Dame Ragnelle,
770 From my dethe she dyd help me ryght welle,
Alle for the love of Gawen."
Then Gawen told the kyng alle togeder
Howe forshapen she was withe* her stepmother   *by*
Tylle a knyghte had holpen her agayn;
775 Ther she told the kyng fayre and welle
Howe Gawen gave her the sovereynte every delle,
And what choyse she gave to hym;
"God thank hym of* his curtesye;   *for*
He savid me from chaunce and villony
780 That was fulle foulle and grym.
Therfore, curteys knyghte and hend* Gawen,   *gracious*

Shalle I nevere wrathe* thee, serteyn;   *upset*
That promyse nowe here I make—
Whiles that I lyve, I shal be obeysaunt;
785 To God above, I shalle itt warraunt,
And nevere withe you to debate."
"Garamercy, lady," then sayd Gawen;
"With you I hold me fulle welle content,
And that I trust to fynde."
790 He sayd, "My love shalle she have;
Therafter* neede she nevere more crave,   *for it*
For she hathe bene to me so kynde."
The queen sayd, and the ladyes alle,
"She is the fayrest nowe in this halle.
795 I swere by Seynt John!
My love, lady, ye shalle have evere
For that ye savid my lord Arthoure,
As I am a gentilwoman."
Syr Gawen gatt* on her Gyngolyn,*   *begot/Guinglain, Gingelein*
800 That was a good knyghte of strengthe and kynn,*   *nobility*
And of the Table Round.
Att every greatt fest* that lady shold be,   *festival where*
Of fayrnesse she bare away the bewtye,*   *beauty-prize*
Wher she yed* on the ground.   *walked*
805 Gawen lovyd that lady Dame Ragnelle;
In alle his lyfe he lovyd none so welle,
I telle you withoute lesyng;
As a coward* he lay by her bothe day and nyghte: *lazy lover*
Nevere wold he haunt justyng* aryghte;   *engage in jousting*
810 Ther-att mervayled Arthoure the kyng.
She prayd the kyng for his gentilness,
"To be good lord to Sir Gromer, i-wysse,*   *indeed*
Of that to you* he hathe offendyd";   *about that (in which) you*
"Yes, lady, that shalle I nowe for your sake,
815 For I wott* welle he may nott amendes make;   *know*
He dyd* to me fulle unhend."*   *acted/ungraciously*
Now for to make you a short conclusyon,
I cast me* for to make an end fulle soone,   *intend*
Of this gentylle lady.
820 She livyd with Sir Gawen butt yerys v;*   *only five years*
That grevyd Gawen alle his lyfe,
I telle you securly;
In her lyfe she grevyd hym nevere;
Therfor was nevere woman to hym lever;*   *dearer*
825 Thus leves* my talkyng;   *ends*
She was the fayrest lady of alle Englond
When she was on lyve, I understand,
So sayd Arthoure the kyng.
Thus endyth the adventure of Kyng Arthoure,
830 That oft in his days was grevyd sore,
And of the weddyng of Gawen.
Gawen was weddyd oft in his days,
Butt so welle he nevere lovyd woman always,
As I have heard men sayn.
835 This adventure befelle in Ingleswod,

As good Kyng Arthoure on huntyng yod,*   *went*
Thus have I hard men telle.
Nowe God, as thou were in Bethleme born,
Suffer nevere her* soules be forlorne   *their*
840 In the brynnyng* fyre of Helle!   *burning*
And, Jhesu, as thou were borne of a virgyn,
Help hym oute of sorowe that this tale dyd devyne,*   *compose*
And that nowe in alle hast,   *haste*
For he is besett withe gaylours* many   *jailers*
845 That kepen* hym fulle sewerly,*   *hold/very securely*
Withe wyles wrong and wraste.*   *hard*
Nowe God, as thou art veray* kyng royalle,   *true*
Help hym oute of daunger that made this tale,
For therin he hathe bene long;
850 And of greatt pity help thy servaunt,
For body and soulle I yeld* into thyne   *yield*
    hand,
For paynes he hathe strong.

Here endythe the weddyng of
Syr Gawen and Dame Ragnelle
For helpyng of Kyng Arthoure.

chapter V
RUSSIAN

THE BYELORUSSIAN TRISTAN

Zora Kipel

The beautiful love story of Tristan and Isolde, which originated as a Celtic legend and was adapted by French and German poets in the twelfth and thirteenth centuries, eventually found its way to Russia. The sixteenth-century *Povest o Trishchane* was written by an anonymous author who based his work on the French *Prose Tristan*. Composed in Byelorussian, this is the only Slavic version stemming from this source. It exists in a single manuscript written about 1580. The work is a curious mixture of a French romance in terms of content and Slavic folk-tale or legend in terms of style and composition.

The *Byelorussian Tristan* can be divided into two parts: the first follows very closely the standard *Prose Tristan* texts. It includes Tristan's ancestry, birth, childhood, and youth; his sojourn at King Marko's court, his sword fight with Amurat (Morholt), his poisoned wound, and his journey to seek a cure; Izhota's (Isolde's) healing the wound and their first, innocent love; Tristan's return to King Mark(o) and his subsequent quest for Izhota on behalf of his uncle Marko; the drinking of the love potion and Tristan and Izhota's irresistible love, followed by the substitution of Braginia (Brangain) for Izhota in the marriage bed and Marko's suspicion of the lovers.

In the second part, which begins with King Marko's allegorical dream, the Byelorussian translator allowed himself many liberties, remaking his text into what amounts to a new version of considerable interest for comparative study. It is characterized by various knightly adventures, often very violent. Many Arthurian personages are introduced and treated in a surprising way—depicted as being lesser in importance, power, bravery, and beauty than in most other versions. Tristan's own character undergoes a transformation: he loves amusement and splendor, and is fickle, mischievous, and at times even cruel. His love for Izhota, however, is still strong, but his is the protective love of a knight for his queen rather than that of a passionate lover. There is no idyllic love in a forest, and there is no Love Cave or Hall of Statues, as are found in other West European versions.

Instead there are some new elements: Marko's allegorical dream; the episode of The Lady Who Castrates; the Old Knight and his beautiful wife; and the Bereaved Maiden episode. The main characters in the *Byelorussian Tristan* are realistic, almost devoid of romantic traits. There is very little fantasy, except for Merlin's presence at the beginning of the story and Tristan's extraordinary strength and agility. There are some symbolism and allegory but chiefly used as a folkloric device and not with religious or metaphysical import. Slavic folkloric elements prevail, as in the ambiguous, almost fairy-tale ending of the story, where the lovers do not die. Instead their happy reunion is intimated.

Bibliographic note: The translation that follows is based on the 16th-century manuscript 94 located in the Raczynski Public Library in Poznan, Poland. The manuscript was first edited and published in St. Petersburg (1888) by A. Veselovskii, *Belorusskie povesti o Tristane . . .* in his *Iz istorii romana i povesti*. Other editions and translations include: Irene Grickat, *Povest o Tristanu i Izoti* (Belgrad, 1966); A. Mikhailov, *Povest o Trishchane* in his *Legenda o Tristane i Izol'de* (Moscow, 1976); Emanuela Sgambati, *Il Tristano Biancorusso* (Florence, 1983). A detailed bibliography is provided in Z. Kipel's *Byelorussian Tristan* (Garland, 1988).

The Birth of Tristan

[After a brief recounting of the early history of Kornovalia or Cornwall:]
Then the Kornovalian kingdom came into the hands of King Pelish; he had a son by the name of Marko [Mark], for he had been born in the month of March, and another son, Perla [Pernehan]. When the king was near death, he crowned his son Marko as the king over Kornovalia. King Marko gave his sister Eliobela in marriage to King Meliadush, who was the king of nearby Elionos [Lyonesse]. Queen Eliobela was very beautiful, and they lived with great love for each other. Thus, it was strange that the queen, who lived with him for many years, had no children; but later she carried their child in her womb. The entire kingdom of Elionos was rejoicing, for the people wanted to have an heir.

The king went on a hunt with many of his knights and came to a body of water where a knight had died. There also came a maiden who had loved the king very much for many years, more than she loved herself, and because of this love she was able to find him. She said to him, "Many say how good you are. I wish to know this goodness: I want to take you to a place where you will see at night a marvelous thing which you have not seen for a long time." The king being a very good knight wanted to see this thing. She said, "I will guide you there." The king mounted his horse and said to the maiden, "Mount, and I will follow you." She rode along the road through the evening, until night fell, and soon they saw a very fine castle set high on a rock. When they approached the place, the people there rejoiced. Many came out and gladly took the king's horse and armor from him. This was the maiden's town; she led the king into a very beautiful chamber, and when he was in the bedroom his heart and his thoughts changed, and neither his queen nor his kingdom of Elionos was on his mind, nor his people— only the maiden who had carried him off to this castle—since he had become enchanted.

The king's knights, seeing that the king had not returned for several days, rode searching for him but could not find him or hear any tidings of him. Then the queen, taking one handmaiden with her, went herself in search of King Meliadush so that she might have some news about him. They rode through a big forest and wandered far and wide, searching for the king in every direction until they encountered Merlin the prophet. Merlin greeted the queen and she responded respectfully, "Good man, if you should have any news of my lord, King Meliadush, who vanished without a trace, for God's sake, tell me whether he is alive." Merlin said, "Milady, truly, I will tell you that he is alive and healthy and very joyful, more than he ever was before: but you will not see him with your eyes again." Having said this, he vanished from her.

She was very sad and began to grieve and cry, cursing the day of her birth and the hour in which she had been born. If someone had seen this, he could not have remained hardhearted, but would have cried watching her. The queen's grief so increased that she could not ride further, and she dismounted. And because of this grief the time of giving birth arrived; she began to pray to God, saying, "My Lord, my God, set my body free and keep my soul in grace." And her maiden said to her, "Milady, how are you feeling?" The queen said, "Here is my end now; if only God would grace me with the delivery so that I can give birth, and may His holy mercy be over me." And the handmaiden said, "Milady, please mount the horse; I will help you, so that we may ride to a place where we can have a fire." Said the queen to her maiden, "This cannot be; here is my end; pray to God for me." The handmaiden began to cry bitterly and in her sorrow did not know what to do.

In the morning at dawn the queen gave birth to a fine knight, but she was near death. She said to the handmaiden, who was holding the child, "Give me my child." The handmaiden gave it to her. The queen, looking at the most wonderful child that she had ever seen, said, "My son, I wished so to see you, but when I behold you, by God's grace, the most wonderful child I have ever seen born of woman anywhere, your beauty will not do me any good—only my death from the torment that I have had with your birth. I came to this place sorrowfully, and with sorrow I gave birth to you; my sorrow changed into joy when I gave you birth, yet this is my end. You were born in sorrow, and so let your name be Sorrow [Tristan]. May the Lord God change your life into a joyful and a happy one and guide it." Having said that, she handed the child to the handmaiden and gave her soul to God. At this hour was born the valorous knight Trishchan [Tristan], whose marvelous deeds and great chivalry I wish to recount to you, as well as how a maiden took hold of him.

When the handmaiden saw her lady dead, she began to scratch her face and cry so that she was heard from afar. Two knights, who were close relatives of King Meliadush, approached the cries of this handmaiden. When they saw the handmaiden and the child covered with the queen's mantle and the queen dead, they said, "Since King Meliadush is missing and the queen is dead, let us kill this child so that we will be the lords of Elionos." Having heard that, the handmaiden approached them and said, "Knights, do not take a sin upon your soul and your mind before God; do not kill this child! I swear on my faith and my soul I will take him to another country, where nothing will be known about him."

The knights gave the child to the handmaiden and took the deceased queen and carried her to the town. And the people began to say: "The queen was pregnant; where did the child disappear?" The knights denied that they knew of the child, yet could not disavow it. Then Merlin the prophet came and told them, "You found the queen and her child and wanted to kill the child, yet the maid pleaded for him; you contrived this so that this land would be left to you." And Merlin said further, "My lords, I will inform you of your king, Meliadush, who forgot himself and his kingdom and all of you, his people." They began asking Merlin, "We beg of you, for God's sake, tell us about our lord, King Meliadush." Merlin said, "In three days you will see him."

Then Merlin noticed one youth, who was from the kingdom of Gaul. His name was Govornar [Governal]; he had run away from home, fearing his father and brother; he was very brave and wise. Merlin said, "Master Govornar, take the king's son and guard him and teach him wisdom and chivalry, for he will come to much greatness and to knighthood; even if you do not want to, you must care for him." And the youth responded, "I don't know you; nevertheless, I will willingly take him under my instruction and my care; I want to keep him and care for him as best I can." Merlin said, "I am entrusting him to you."

Then they rode off together and the next day came to a stream by the name of Brykinia. If a woman drank from this stream, she would not be able to carry a child to term. By this stream there was a stone column, and on this column words had been carved long ago which said, "By this water three great knights will gather." Merlin reading the inscription asked, "What is this?" Said Govornar, "I can read the words but do not know who the knights are." Merlin said, "These are to be the greatest knights in the world: Galets, Antsolot [Galahad, Lancelot], and Tristan, who will be so magnanimous and chivalrous that the world will have high praise for them and much goodness because of them, and one of them will be the prince of all this kingdom. But be vigilant so that he does not perish under your guardianship." Govornar said, "He will not perish under my guard, so long as I am able."

They departed from there and rode to the handmaiden, who had sheltered the child and already had christened him, giving him the name that the queen had chosen. Merlin said to the girl, "Take the child to the town, for it is not proper to keep him here, and he can find his father there." The girl took him to Elionos.

Then Merlin went with the lords to the place of the lady who had enchanted King Meliadush, and they seized her and said to her, "We will kill you if you don't release King Meliadush to us." She used much cunning in order not to give him up, for she loved him much more than she loved herself; they pressed her fiercely and she said, "Come, I'll give you your lord, King Meliadush." And they were very happy and joyfully came to

Elionos and there, together with all the people, made a big feast. Then the maid came to Elionos with the child and handed him to his father, the king. The king, who was very sad about the queen, rejoiced when he saw the child, since he had assumed that he had perished with her.

When the lords saw Tristan they said, "We are all happy today." And they said about Merlin, "This prophet did you much good." Merlin said, "The good that I rendered you, I did more for the others than for you. And I am telling you now, take care of this child, since he will create great goodness for humankind and for the glory of this world."

The king, hearing this, marveled greatly, and, taking Merlin aside, begged him to reveal who he was. Merlin said, "I may reveal this to you, but you should not reveal me to anyone." The king promised him this; he said, "I am Merlin the prophet: I came to deliver you from the captivity in which the maiden held you enchanted; I did this for the love of your son." The king said, "Sir Merlin, tell me, what do you foresee for my son?" Said Merlin, "He shall be the best knight of the three knights, of great fortitude, and he will be needed by many; do not entrust him to anyone's care but to Govornar from Gaul, who is a very good and trustworthy man who will guard him well." The king said, "Let it be as you command." Then Merlin departed; he did not want to yield to any pleas. And then the king went to the handmaiden and asked, "Has the child been christened yet?" The maid said, "He has been." The king asked, "What is his name?" The maid replied, "Sir, his name is Tristan, which his mother gave him as she was dying." Afterward the king called Govornar and said to him, "Take my son under your instruction and care for him and guard him faithfully and wisely, so that you will not be disgraced; assign to him a wet nurse, as is proper for a prince."

Let us now talk about Marko, the Kornovalian king. Marko had a younger brother by the name of Perla, a good knight. At the time Tristan was born, envoys from Orlendea [Ireland] came to Kornovalia to demand tribute which had been due for seven years. When this was reported to King Marko, he became very sad. His brother Perla saw that the king was frightened. There were many people in the hall, and so he said, "Come closer, everyone, and hear me." He added, "Do not be frightened, King Marko. Do not pay the tribute. But get out of it with your sword on the field, for if you die by the sword, you will die honorably." The king said, "We have paid the tribute previously. I cannot disengage myself from it now." Perla said, "If others acted foolishly earlier, should you also?"

The king knew his brother was a valorous knight, brave and well-liked by all good people. Marko planned to kill him, so that the other would not take his kingdom away from him; and he acted promptly. They both went on a hunt and, becoming weary, came to a river. The king quenched his thirst and when Perla bent down to drink, the king took his sword and struck his brother Perla on the head very hard, and Perla died instantly. Immediately Merlin made everything known to Antsolot, the valorous knight; thereupon Antsolot accused him to his face, "You've treacherously killed a valorous knight, your brother."

But let us leave this and return to Tristan, whom Govornar took under his care from King Meliadush. Meliadush remained unmarried for a long time after Queen Eliobela died. Then he took a queen from the Little Land

[Brittany] in marriage, who was quite beautiful. When she came, Tristan was then seven years old. He was so extraordinary that in the whole world there was no equal to him, except Antsolot. His stepmother had a son, and when she watched Tristan growing up, she being afraid that he might take the kingdom away from her son, who was one year old, said, "Even if I have to die, I must put Tristan to death." She could not do this any other way except with poison.

Thereafter she prepared a poisoned drink in a silver flagon and put it at the head of Tristan's bed. The handmaiden who carried around the queen's son came into the chamber. The child began to cry, and the maid seeing the clear wine in the flagon, took it and gave it to him to drink; when the child drank it, he died instantly.

The girl uttered a loud cry, and many people ran over, saw the dead child, and said to the maid, "You deserve death, for you have killed the prince." When the queen came in and saw her son dead, she fell to the ground and fainted. When she came to herself, she said to the handmaiden, "What wrong have I done that you should kill my son?" The girl objected, "I did not kill him; the one who placed this poison here did."

They seized the girl and took her before the king, who said to her, "You are guilty." She said, "The one who prepared this poison is guilty." The king said, "Let her go; she did not prepare this poison, but some vicious one who hated this child did."

Govornar, who was very wise, said, "My lord, be advised that the poison was intended for you or for your son; now be watchful and know how to protect yourself. Tristan, who is in my care—leave him to me: God knows, he will be well guarded." The king, who understood well that the poison was prepared for one of them, had a privy council with his lords to find out who had done this. They advised him, "You and Tristan must be cautious."

The queen was very sorrowful for causing her son's death by her own recklessness; she wished herself dead and thought in her heart: "I only caused the death of my son, and what I have planned I did not accomplish." And she began to plot anew every day.

Govornar, who was very wise, saw her craftiness and her glances and began to realize that she was planning Tristan's death, and that she had prepared the poison. He told the boy, "If you associate with your step-mother, you may encounter death; honor her, but beware of eating or drinking anything from her hands; only what I give you should you eat and drink." And Tristan said, "I shall not disregard any of your instructions."

One summer day the king was sitting alone in his chamber, and he was thirsty. Tristan came to him and the king said, "My son, bring me something to drink." The boy opened an armoire where fine drinks were kept, picked up a goblet of pure poison and took it to the king. The queen came in at that moment, saw the goblet, and shouted: "My lord, for God's sake, do not drink this beverage!" The king said, "Lady, what is this?" She did not dare tell him that it was poison and said, "It is not good for you to drink this." The king said, "Why are you saving this?" She kept silent, and the king had a revelation and felt great wrath.

Tristan came and bowed at the king's knees with great reverence, asking him for a favor. The king loved him more than he loved himself and did not suspect that he might plead for the queen. The king said, "Do not ask, but take what you want freely; nothing is forbidden to you from me."

Tristan thanked his father very gratefully and said: "My lord, you gave me the queen's life; I beg you to calm the anger you feel for her. I do not wish to see my stepmother die in this manner." The king did not see the treachery from anyone but her, and he was not willing to pardon her. He said, "My son, who advised you of this?" Tristan said, "God knows, I did not confer with anyone, but justice and decency guided me; it would not please me for my lady to perish if I can save her life."

The king said to the queen: "Drink from this cup." She said: "I will not." The king said, "You have to die, since you wanted to poison Tristan or myself. Tell us quickly: for whom did you prepare this poison?" She said, "Not for you." The king said, "For whom, then? You ought to perish!" The queen began to cry: "My king, for God's sake, be merciful to me." He said, "Tell us quickly." He took his sword and said, "Tell us or you will die now." When she saw herself near death, she said: "I contrived this for Tristan." The king said, "On my faith, you contrived your own death, for Tristan did not offend you in any way."

He ordered her conducted to prison and assembled his lords, presented the case before them, and said to them: "On my faith, if you do not judge truthfully, death will be yours." They said, "It is proper that she should die; it cannot be otherwise, because she wanted to murder your son." The king said, "Your judgment is not going to be changed." When the lords knew this, they began to lament and carry on with great grief, but they did not say anything.

The king said, "My son, Tristan, you faithfully wished her good, but she wished you evil and treachery and wanted to murder you; but the outcome was worse than she deserved. As you desire, let her be freed by you." Tristan thanked his father respectfully for this and saved his stepmother from death. All the good people of Elionos said, "When he comes of age he will not lack great goodness." The queen remained in peace by the king, but the king had no love for her; he hated her with all his heart.

The Youth of Tristan in France

Then, after a short time, the king went on a hunt with his retinue and with him went Tristan and Govornar, so the boy could learn hunting. As they rode through the forest two knights arrived in full armor and inquired, "Who is the noble here?" They said, "This is our king with his son." Govornar said: "What are you saying? His son is not here; he left him at home." These knights approached and said to the king, "You have done us no harm, but someone from your house intends to destroy us and now we intend to slay him if we can."

They took out their swords and no one could protect the king from being wounded by a fatal blow to the head. Both attackers, however, were killed instantly. They both were from the tribe of the Prince of Norot, which was the largest tribe of Kornovalia. One soothsayer had predicted thus: "You will perish by King Meliadush's house." And in this they had taken the advice of the Kornovalian King Marko, for he was afraid that when Tristan came of age, he would dethrone him as the soothsayer had predicted. And so when Tristan did come of age, he went with his companions and killed the Prince of Norot with his own hands and destroyed that town, so that there was no stone left upon stone.

When the barons saw their ruler dead, they did not know what to do and reflected among themselves, "No lord was ever so badly guarded by his people as our king by us." They cried and Tristan joined them. They hitched a litter to two horses and carried off the body of the king. When they were near the town, the people made a great lament for him; they buried him with honors, as is proper for such a lord.

When King Marko saw this, he began to reflect deeply about it. Then a youth came to him who knew more than other people except for Merlin about all that might happen; the king liked him much for this. He said to the king, "Your nephew Tristan is going to cause you much sorrow." The king asked, "How can Tristan achieve such valor?" The youth said: "In the whole world there will be no knight superior to him." The king became silent.

Govornar, seeing that the stepmother coveted the kingdom and still hated Tristan, took him aside and said, "My good friend, your stepmother hates you very much and plots to murder you. Let us go secretly to France to King Peremont [Pharamont]. There you will learn bravery and you will be a distinguished person, and when they discover your worth, you will reach knighthood; then you can return to Elionos, your fatherland; no one will dare to say anything disrespectful to you." Tristan replied, "Master, wherever you order me, I will go, since I have found no one with more good will than you." Govornar said, "Let us get ready and leave tomorrow at dawn."

They equipped themselves with what was needed, taking enough gold and silver with them, and departed that day to France. Govornar warned Tristan not to disclose who he was and where he was from. Tristan said, "I will listen to you gladly." When they came to Peremont, the king received Tristan graciously and ordered fine quarters to be given him.

Tristan began to develop and improve himself, so that they all began to be amazed. He played chess and checkers better than the others, and no one sat on a horse as handsomely as he. And when he was twelve years old, he showed great virtue and wisdom in all things. Ladies and maidens and every man who saw him marveled; every lady and maiden would have been happy if Tristan were to fancy her. Tristan, indeed, served King Peremont courteously and honorably, and the king considered no other youths from his court a match for him; and yet no one knew who he was or where he had come from.

The king had a daughter, a very beautiful princess; she fell in love with Tristan, and said, "Human eyes have not seen such a marvelous youth as Tristan." Whenever she saw him, her eyes and her thoughts were nowhere but with him. She loved him as she loved herself and could not imagine how she could obtain his grace and his love and how to satisfy her desire for him. She thought: "If I let him know, he might not consent—he is too young; he will not be tempted to such love. But if he promised to love me, I would wait for him until his time; I would rather wait for him than to be the greatest queen of the greatest kingdom. But I am afraid that he would not be willing because of his youth and he would not dare to do anything because of my father."

One day when she was sitting alone in her room, she ordered Govornar to be called, and said to him, "Sir Govornar, I love your Tristan more than I love myself; I beg you to persuade him to love me. If he does not want to do this, I will cause him great shame." Govornar became sad. He did not know what to do about it, and thought for a long while: "If Tristan would do this, and the king learned of it, he would punish him dishonorably." So he said to her, "My gracious princess, for your grace I'll tell him that he should fulfill your will; but he is young; if it does not happen promptly, do not be angry with him." She thanked him very gratefully. Then Govornar went to his quarters and was very sad and began reflecting, "If Tristan does this, it will be bad, but not doing it is also not good."

He asked Tristan, "What do you think you will do? The princess likes you enormously; if you do not want to love her, she wants to kill herself." Tristan answered him, "If she loves me with an excessive love, I will not love her; let the excess be with her: I do not want to be a traitor to my lord, for all his kindness and honor he bestows on me, not even knowing who I am and where I came from." When Govornar heard that from Tristan, he was very surprised that for such a young age he was exhibiting such honor, for Tristan was only thirteen years old at this time. Govornar said to him, "Why don't you want to love such a beautiful princess?" Tristan said: "Her beauty can only bring me to treason; if I had agreed to what you suggested, you should have dissuaded me from it."

The next morning the princess called in Govornar and said to him: "Did you find out anything from Tristan?" He said, "Tristan loves you with a refined love; yet he does not want to do anything that would be treacherous to your father." Said the princess: "Is Tristan rejecting me altogether?" She departed very sadly, damning the day she was born; she went to her bedchamber and cried very bitterly.

[*The jealous princess accuses Tristan of raping her, but he vindicates himself and prepares to go with Govornar to his uncle Marko's court in Cornwall.*]

The next day Tristan came before the king, bowed low, and said: "I wish to go to my land." And he thanked the king and the good people for their kindness; the king thanked him for his loyal service and promised his friendship.

When the princess saw that Tristan was going away, she became extremely sad and sent him an ambler and a hunting-hound with a servant. Tristan promised a gift to this servant of whatever he might ask. He said, "My lord, when you become a knight I want to be knighted by you." Later the princess sent a message to him, asking, "My lord, give me your sword for me to cherish." Tristan sent her his sword, and she said, "I prefer to die by Tristan's sword than to be the greatest queen." And she pierced herself to death then and there.

The Duel with Amurat

Tristan departed with Govornar from France to Kornovalia to the court of King Marko, where Govornar said: "Gracious king, this is a lord who came to serve you, so that you may knight him with your hand." The king gladly received Tristan and promised to knight him later, without recognizing him. Tristan served Marko courteously and nobly, and everyone who saw him all wondered who he was. Later on Tristan wished to be knighted. The king ordered what was needed for a knight to be prepared and they arranged everything with great dignity. Tristan went to church, and the next day the king knighted him; everyone who saw him said, "We have not seen a better knight."

While he was at this celebration, four knights from Orlendea came to King Marko, and began to talk without any bowing: "King, good King Amurat [Morold, Morholt] from Orlendea sent us to you, saying: 'Give me the tribute which your Kornovalian ancestors have always given to my Orlendean ancestors; let it be ready in ten days. If you give it, we will promise peace, but if you do not give it, be aware that in a few days there will not be an inch of land left unspoiled.'" Hearing this, King Marko was extremely frightened and did not know how to respond. Tristan came forward, stood before the king and said to the messengers, "Come here, you who brought this boastful message; tell your lord: even if our ancestors by their foolishness gave tribute to your kingdom, you will not take any more; if your king wants to have it, let him come with a sword on the battlefield—he cannot have the tribute any other way than by my own hand."

The messengers said to King Marko, "Is it you who says this?" The king said, "If my liege wants to fight for the Kornovalian freedom, I am saying so too." The messengers said to Tristan: "Who are you?" And he said: "I am a guest here; my name is Tristan." They said, "Pardon us. Amurat is not going to fight with you if you are not a man of great parentage." Tristan said, "The fight will not be prevented for this reason: I am a son of King Meliadush of Elionos and a nephew of King Marko. I was concealing myself before but now I cannot conceal myself any longer."

The messengers rode away quickly and related to King Amurat what Tristan had replied. The king asked, "Who is he that took on this fight?" They said, "He is the son of King Meliadush, and a nephew of King Marko; he is a newly dubbed knight; we have not seen such a marvelous knight, for he challenged us all by himself without urging." Amurat said, "He will be sorry. A new knight wants a new death. Did you arrange where this fight should be?" They said, "No." He ordered, "Go again and arrange it; I do not want to delay this." His friend Garnot said, "I will keep you company. I would like to see this knight whom they praise so."

They traveled by sea and by land and came to Kornovalia to King Marko and reported King Amurat's words. King Marko said, "Better if this fight takes place on Samson Island; they will come in their boats and each will be his own navigator." They arranged the fight to take place in two weeks.

The messengers came to Amurat and reported to him that they had arranged the fight on Samson Island. Said Amurat, "This is pleasing to me." And he asked Garnot, "Did you see this knight?" He replied, "I saw him; and if you want to hear my advice, you should forgo this fight and make peace, because if the two of you battle, it will not be without great sorrow; if something happens to you, there will be great damage in Orlendea; and if something happens to him, great damage will be done to the entire world. In my days I have not seen a better knight; when he comes of age, he will be of great valor." Amurat said to him, "There can be no peace if the tribute is not delivered," and he began to prepare himself.

King Marko and Tristan and all the knights, the king's maidens and ladies went to church and prayed to God to deliver them from Amurat. The next morning Tristan heard mass and went to the hall in full armor and with arms. All the lords came toward him, and King Marko said, "My dear son, why did you hide from me? If I had known about you, even if all Kornovalia was enslaved, I would not have allowed you to fight; for if something happens to you, I will never have any joy." Tristan said, "My lord, do not fret, for God in His mercy will not forget us; I hope that God will give us honor and help."

Then came the message that Amurat was already on Samson Island. Tristan said, "Hand me my helmet." And so they gave him a good helmet, and the king himself strapped him and adjusted the arms, and checked and approved them; they also brought him a fine horse. Tristan went to his boat and soon was on the island.

Amurat wondered how this knight dared to fight against him and, as he came ashore, asked him, "Why did you push away your boat?" Tristan said: "One of us will depart in your boat; the other will remain here." Amurat took this answer for courage and wished he had not asked him; he said, "Abandon this fight; I would not be glad to destroy you; I would rather have you for my companion and love you like my brother." Tristan said, "I will abandon the fight if you will waive the Kornovalian tribute; but if you will not, you must fight." Said Amurat, "Then be prepared to fight." And Tristan said, "I have come for this."

They both mounted their horses and struck so hard that if their good armor had not sustained them, they would have been dead; the poles broke and both men fell with their horses to the ground, but immediately both, though wounded, leaped to their feet. Tristan was wounded in his thigh with a poisoned spearhead; Amurat was wounded by one without poison. They took their swords and began to slash very hard for a long time, hitting and wounding each other in many places; and they both recognized that they were very good knights. Amurat imagined that he was the greatest fighter in the world, but when he saw Tristan, he got a scare; they both got so weary that there was no alternative but for one to remain; therefore each one fought for victory; and all who saw them witnessed a great wonder. While fighting, they separated from each other and leaned on their shields. Amurat said, "If Tristan comes at me again with such force, I will not be able to withstand him." While they rested, Tristan began to slash on high with his sword, and began to cover himself with his shield and his sword. Amurat could not stand any more. Tristan saw this and got angry and hit him hard on the top of his helmet, slashing his head to the brain, so that a piece of the sword remained in his head. Amurat felt himself fatally wounded and, leaving his shield and his sword, ran to the boat and headed for the larger vessel, which was waiting for him. The servants received him very sadly and put him into the vessel. They began to sail away, crying. The Kornovalians who watched this began to shout: "Bad journey to you! There is your tribute!"

Said King Marko and the other Kornovalians: "God and the valor of Tristan gave us this honor." Seeing him alone on the island, many people hurried to him; they found Tristan badly wounded and very weak from bleeding, for he had lost much blood and could not stand on his feet; none of the wounds bothered him as much as the one on his thigh, where he was wounded by a poisoned tip. When they brought him to the shore, the king came over and took Tristan and began kissing and embracing him, and asked, "How are you feeling?" Tristan said, "I am badly wounded, but with God's will I'll be well." The King escorted him to church to give praise to God, then conducted him to the palace with great joy and fanfare, for they had been delivered from slavery.

Then Tristan came to his chambers and became so ill from his poisoned wound that he could hardly stand; the physicians came and applied the best ointments so that he soon was cured from all his wounds except the one that was poisoned; they could not cure that: whatever they applied to this wound, nothing helped. One night Tristan said to Govornar: "Call King Marko to me." The king came and asked, "My son, why did you call me?" Tristan said, "I ask you, sir, to give me one thing that should not overburden you much." King Marko said, "Even if it costs much, I would act according to your wishes; there is nothing that I would not do for you." Tristan thanked him humbly for this: "I, my lord, cannot find a healer in this land; I suffered greatly and now I see clearly that my death is nearing. I want to go to some other country in the world; prepare a good vessel for me and equip it with what I will need, with food and drink and one sail so light that one person can take it down; and cover the boat with a good cloth against rain and wind. I want to sail into the sea, where fortune will take me; maybe I will find a healer for the wound I am dying from; but if I do not find him, then I am dead." The king said, "Son, how can you depart, being so weak?" Tristan said, "If it is God's will, perhaps the sea and wind will drift me to my fortune. When the vessel is ready, put me in it and give me my harp and also my lute and from time to time I will play to myself to ease my grief and my pain."

Hearing this, King Marko began to weep very sadly and could not respond to him for a long time through his tears. When he composed himself, he said, "My son, Tristan, do you want to leave me altogether?" Tristan replied, "My lord, it cannot be otherwise now, but if I find a healer and when I am healed, I promise to return to Kornovalia." And when the king saw that it could not be any other way, he prepared the vessel as Tristan himself commanded and put in it all that was necessary. When it was ready, he ordered him to be brought, very weak, to the vessel. And seeing this, the Kornovalians began to cry very bitterly; and the king and all his lords cried without ceasing. When Tristan saw this, he was greatly moved; he pushed away from the shore hurriedly and raised sail. The wind was favorable and he sailed swiftly but did not know where he was going.

The Healer Isolde in Ireland

And so he sailed two days and good fortune drove him to a town in Orlendea where King Lenviz ruled. He had a wife, the sister of King Amurat, whom Tristan had killed, and he had a daughter by the name of Izhota [Isolde]. This young lady knew a lot about healing wounds; there was no wound that she was not able to heal. When Tristan was near the shore, he took his harp, tuned it, and began to play the best way he could.

King Lenviz saw this from the palace, and listened a long time; it seemed to him wondrous that Tristan played so marvelously and sadly. He called the queen, and she saw the vessel and heard the harp and marveled a great deal. She said to the king, "I beg you, let us go to see this marvel." Both of them went down to the sea and listened. When Tristan stopped playing, he began to weep and cry from the pain he had. The king and the queen approached the vessel, saw Tristan, and greeted him. Tristan returned the greeting and asked the king, not knowing that he was the king, "I beg you, sir, what is this country that I've landed on?" Said the king, "You are in Orlendea." When Tristan heard this, he felt more faint from his wound than before, since he was afraid that if recognized, he would perish because of Amurat.

The king asked him, "I beg you, knight, tell me, where are you from?" Tristan said, "My lord, I am from Elionos. I came here ill from a wound for which I could not find a healer. I have suffered such torture and pain that if it had been up to my will, I would have rather died long ago, but if the Lord God does not want this, I must endure."

When the king heard Tristan saying this, he had mercy on him and believed that he was telling the truth. The king asked, "Are you a knight?" Tristan said, "I am." The king said, "Do not worry, knight. You came to such a place where, God willing, you will be cured. I have a daughter who understands every wound better than any doctor; I know she will be happy to care for you, for God and for courtesy." Tristan thanked him very courteously and humbly.

The king and the queen returned to the palace and prepared him quarters in one of the bedchambers and ordered him to be brought up to the room where a place for him was arranged. Then the king sent for his daughter Izhota and said to her, "My dear daughter, come with me to look at a knight, our guest, who is very sick from a wound, and care for him for God's sake and mine, so that he will get well soon." She said, "My lord, I will be happy to fulfill your command and will labor the best I can."

And so she went to Tristan. When she saw the wound, she applied an herb that was suitable. Then Tristan sighed from the pain he had. The princess, who did not notice or suspect that the wound was poisoned, began to calm him and said, "Don't be afraid, knight; with God's help, I will make you well very soon." Tristan said, "O my God, I could not ask for any more."

For ten days the princess applied herbs she knew, but he still became worse. Izhota began to curse herself and said, "I do not know what to do; what is needed for this wound?" She started to examine the wound, and it occurred to her that it was poisoned. She said to herself, "If the wound is not poisoned, I must leave him alone, since I cannot help him." She ordered Tristan to be brought out to the sun and began to examine the wound with greater scrutiny. The wound started to pus, and Izhota said: "Sir, I see well what aggravated your wound and why you were unable to find the medicine: the iron you were wounded with was poisoned; and nobody realized this, but now that I've discovered this, with God's help you will be cured." Tristan was happy about this. The maiden started to draw out the poison from the wound, and began again to apply medicine to it. In a short time Tristan felt improvement, yet he was no more than skin and bones. But in two months he was cured and was as beautiful and agile as he had been before. Then the thought came to him that he should go to Kornovalia as soon as possible, since he was afraid of being recognized; and he was reflecting about this.

Arthur's Knights at the Irish Tourney

At this time came three knights of King Artiush's Round Table by the names of Garnot, Kazhyn, and Bandemagul [Gaheriet, Kay, Bademagus]. These three knights had great valor and fame. Kazhyn was of lesser chivalry than the other two, but he was proud and outspoken; they had come to Orlendea for a maiden who wanted to be married and who had ordered a tournament called for this purpose. Many good knights arrived, and whatever knight showed the most bravery at this tournament would receive her; if he did not want to receive her, she would have to give him a gift big enough for a dozen knights. This is why those three knights came to Orlendea. King Lenviz knew them and was happy to receive them at table. When they saw Tristan, no one recognized him. Garnot had seen him before, but Tristan had changed from his sickness, and because of this he was not recognized, despite his splendid looks. Tristan, however, recognized Garnot, who had come to Kornovalia with King Amurat's messengers; he was thus ever more afraid of being recognized. The three knights were looking at Tristan very attentively because he seemed like a guest, and asked the king about him. The king explained that Tristan had come from Elionos: "There is no man in the world who, seeing him so afflicted, would not have pitied him; but by God's grace and by the labor of my daughter Izhota, he is well." And they talked and looked at him attentively.

Garnot came over to Tristan and, taking him aside, asked, "I beg of you, knight, tell me, if you please, who you are and where you are from." Tristan said, "I am a guest; you will not find out any more from me; I beg of you, don't hold this as evil against me." And Garnot left him at this.

Then the king said, "I want to go to the upcoming tournament, but I don't want to be recognized; I ask you not to disclose me if someone should inquire." Then the king asked Tristan, "Knight, how do you feel?" Tristan said, "Good, by God's mercy. Why do you ask me?" The king said, "If you need arms and a horse, I will give them to you, and young men to serve you." Tristan replied, "My lord, I have not recovered my strength: I don't dare to labor much, but if you want to go, I will help you for all your kindness; and we will carry arms, for a man never knows what might happen to him and where." The king said, "Be it as you wish, but I want very much for you to ride with me." Tristan promised him.

The next morning they went to the tournament and met Gavaon [Gawain], the nephew of King Artiush, and following him there was a youth who carried his shield and his lance; it was the boy who had presented Tristan with an ambler horse and a hunting-hound from the daughter of King Peremont. He saw Tristan, ran to him, and began to kiss his feet. Tristan, afraid that the youth might reveal him, told him, "I want to pass by; don't tell a living soul about me."

The boy said, "Lord, do not worry; but I beg of you to grant me a boon, by your grace." Tristan said, "I am willing if the thing is givable." Said the youth, "Lord, many thanks; you remember what you had promised me; give me this." Tristan said, "I do not recall." "You promised to knight me when I presented you with the ambler horse and the hound from King Peremont's daughter. So, my lord, I want you to dub me tomorrow." Said Tristan, "Let it be as I promised to you." Then Tristan inquired, "Who is this knight whose arms you are carrying?" Said the youth, "This is Sir Gavaon, the nephew of King Artiush; he promised to knight me when I wish; but after seeing your grace, I would rather be knighted by your hand." Tristan said, "As you wish; now go back to Sir Gavaon and carry his spears and arms, as you should." The youth said, "Let it be, my lord, as you advise." And he took Gavaon's arms and rode after him. Gavaon asked, "Who was that knight whom you greeted so touchingly?" Said the youth, "He is a guest, and a very brave one." Asked Gavaon, "What is his name?" The youth said, "My lord, you cannot know that yet." Gavaon let this matter be.

The king rode with a small retinue and no one recognized him, including Gavaon. King Lenviz asked Tristan, "Do you know who this knight is who rides alone?" Said Tristan, "That is Gavaon, the nephew of King Artiush." The king said, "I have heard of him; he is courteous to ladies and maidens." But the king did not disclose himself to Gavaon. When evening was nearing, they met a knight carrying a black shield without insignia, and with him there were two squires. The knight rode in a very elegant, stately way and carried two swords. When they came nearer, Gavaon said, "Do you see that great knight?" The king said to him, "How do you know that he is great?" Gavaon said, "No good knight would dare to carry two swords unless he fought with two knights at once; only a good knight carries two swords." The king said, "On my faith, this knight acts very boldly, but I beg you, if there happens to be a knight who defeats him, what will he do about it?" Gavaon said, "My lord, if it happens to be a single knight who is not from Londresh [Logres], the Black Knight will not carry either weapon during the entire year for his dishonor; but if a knight from Londresh defeats him, he will throw away one sword and carry only one, since the knights from Londresh are the greatest." When the king heard this, he said, "Now I would not for anything at all miss seeing this tournament and this great knight." They stayed that night in a castle ten miles from the tournament.

The next morning Tristan made the youth a knight and he became afterward a companion of the Round Table. Later Tristan, by misadventure, killed him by his own hand, because the youth followed Palamidezh [Palamedes], who loved the marvelous Izhota very much. The young knight was named Berbesh.

Early the next morning the king and Tristan went to the tournament, which was widely attended by many people. There came two kings: King Ianish from Lokva and King Artiush from Londresh, who had with him a hundred knights. When the two sides met and presented lances to each other, the fighting was very dense and heavy, and the knights were falling from their horses to the ground. There were ten knights of the Round Table, who performed very marvelously as they held one side against King Ianish from Lokva. They were Garnot and Ivan, son of King Urian, and Gavaon, Geesh and King Bandemagul, Dondiel, Sogremor, Gviresh

[Gaheriet, Yvain son of Urien, Gawain, Gaheris, Bademagus, Dodinel, Sagremor, Guivret]. When they dashed into this tournament, they accomplished great wonders in no time, and all the others would have been defeated if the knight with two swords and a black shield had not been there. As he struck from the other side of the field, he began marvelously and unbelievably to take off the helmets of the knights and to throw them off their horses to the ground. All who saw him said that he won this tournament, and because of his knightly skills all were frightened of him and could not stand against him. Gavaon was injured with two wounds, Garnot had three wounds, as did Ivan; others also had wounds and were thrown off their horses.

When Artiush of the Hundred Knights saw himself defeated, he was sad, almost crazed, for he loved beautiful Izhota with all his heart and worried lest she find out about this; and he began to plan revenge. Thus he had proclaimed in all places that there would be a second tournament in ten days, for he planned to arrive more prepared and better equipped than at the first. When the tournament was proclaimed and every one heard it, all departed, and King Lenviz too, to get ready for the second tournament.

When Ianish from Lokva saw that the knight with a black shield had won this tournament, he took a great liking to him. Palamidezh [Palamedes], the Black Knight, had come to Orlendea to claim this tournament in Izhota's honor. Tristan thought deeply about what to do to get even with this knight with the black shield and two swords at the second tournament. He became belligerent against Palamidezh, looking at him with angry eyes, because it seemed to him that he had caused great shame to the other knights. Tristan had an angry heart against him and wished him evil because he saw that he was such a handsome knight and worthy of great valor. It seemed to him that Palamidezh wanted to have Izhota, and that she loved Palamidezh with all her heart.

The Battle of Tristan and Palamedes

Tristan and Palamidezh thus began to be hostile. Izhota, however, did not know about this and was unaware that they both loved her. She had a handmaiden by the name of Braginia [Brangain], who was beautiful and wise, who realized that they both loved Izhota. And one day Braginia said to Izhota in jest, "My lady, just for fun, if these two knights loved you, which one of them would you want to love: Palamidezh or our knight, for they both love you?" Izhota laughingly replied, "I cannot forbid their love, even if my heart does not turn to them; but if it came to this, I would prefer to join Palamidezh, since he is the better knight. If ours was such a good knight and of such noble birth as he looks, he would be the more valorous of the two." Palamidezh and Tristan heard this talk while they were sitting in a room. When they left, Tristan went for a walk in the meadow and began to think, because his love for Izhota tormented him. He said to himself, "I will not win the favor of the beautiful Izhota if I don't destroy Palamidezh's loftiness; and I cannot do this without a good horse and good armor, and without great difficulty and labor, since Palamidezh is a great knight." With that heavy heart Tristan remained until the second tournament.

Then King Lenviz asked Tristan, "Do you want to ride to the tournament in our company?" And he told him, "Sir, I still am not feeling up to my strength." The king believed him and left it at that; but Tristan had responded thus because he wished to go to the tournament without being recognized. In three days the king went to the tournament with a small retinue; and Tristan remained very mournful, since he did not know how to accomplish what he intended.

While he was deep in thought, Braginia, who liked him very much, came to him and said, "My lord, what are you thinking of?" Tristan replied, "My maiden, if I knew that you might help me in my intentions, I would tell you." She promised him: "I'll do whatever I can." He said, "Maiden, I would go to this tournament if I only had a horse and armor." She found him a good horse and armor without an insignia and gave him her two brothers for his service. Tristan asked Braginia not to disclose him to anyone and departed secretly, encountering many knights from many lands at the tournament.

When they saw Tristan there, all those who were knowledgeable praised him, for he sat on the horse in so stately a manner. He stood on one side, watching what was going to happen. Then came Palamidezh in the same armor and with the same elaborate insignia as before. When Gavaon saw him, having looked at the good knights, he said, "Now you have something to watch; see what the great knight will do; be on guard for his strike." Garnot said, "We have not yet seen an equal to him in the world." Palamidezh began to perform such marvels that there was no knight at the tournament who was not afraid of him; he defeated many knights on the left and right, and there was no knight to be found who would dare to face him. King Lenviz and the King of a Hundred Knights and all the great knights who had been holding the field very well finally had to abandon it. Palamidezh sat up proudly at this time, and all began to shout: "He with the black shield and two swords has won the tournament for the second time!"

When Tristan saw the insignia, he said, "That is Palamidezh. Hand me a helmet; I want to meet with the good knight on the field." All the others ran to him, each one offering his helmet. When Tristan put a helmet on, he took a lance and stood up against Palamidezh. When they faced each other, Tristan said, "Knight, I have some business with you." The other headed toward him and said, "Come here and we'll see."

And so they charged at each other and struck very fiercely. Palamidezh broke his lance, and Tristan hit him so hard that he fell to the ground with his horse. After this blow he became very much confused and did not know what to do; he mounted his horse and wanted to go to the camp without casting his eyes here or there. Tristan angrily saw him running away and rode after him and overtook him; he wished to bring him to such a point that he would never dare to appear before Izhota's eyes again. He shouted, "Knight, turn around and we will see which of us is more worthy and which of us is more deserving to love the marvelous Izhota." When Palamidezh heard this speech, he realized that it was Tristan and was very distressed because he had not believed that he was so brave. So he turned to him and took his sword, realizing that he would not leave without an injury.

Tristan approached very swiftly, and they began to hit hard. Tristan struck him with a hard blow on the helmet. Palamidezh could not stay on his horse but fell to the ground defeated. He lay there a long while, not knowing day from night. When Tristan saw this, he was joyous that things had befallen him well: he saw that he had accomplished the aim that he wished for the most. When he had defeated Palamidezh, he left the tournament for home.

Tristan rode swiftly and came to Izhota's and Braginia's quarters at night, in hiding. Braginia met him, happy to know the result of the tournament. She asked: "My good and honorable lord, how did your affair go? Tell me about the tournament; who received honors from it?" Said Tristan, "My dear maiden, I cannot tell you this now." Said Braginia, "Sir, tell me about Palamidezh. Is it he who won the tournament?" Said Tristan, "I cannot tell you about him, but know this well: he is one of the greatest knights in the world, but it has so happened that he did not receive the honors at this tournament." She said smiling, "And did you?" Tristan said, "I achieved my purpose, and I beg you not to ask me more." She left him at this, since she gathered that he did not want to talk about his defeat or accomplishment. She gave him good bedding and he went to sleep, for he was extremely weary and very swollen from blows. After he had rested to his contentment, the next day his face was black and blue from so many blows. When people began to talk about the knight in white armor, Tristan was modest, since he would not have been happy if he were recognized.

The Recognition of Tristan

On the third day King Lenviz came back with his retinue to his court and with him the knights Garnot, Bandemagul, and Ivan. They did not talk about anything but the White Knight and Palamidezh; and they were amazed that the White Knight had left without a word. Bandemagul said to Garnot, "It looks to me as if this is the knight who conquered the Dolorous Guard [Lancelot], who always concealed himself." The king said, "I beg you, who is the knight you are talking about?" Said Garnot, "My lord, we are talking about the one whom my father King Artiush knighted recently; he accomplished more chivalry by his hand than anyone ever saw, but there is no man who knows his name." The king said, "If he won the fight but hides his name, he is very valorous." And all these words Tristan took to himself.

Braginia was very wise and attentive, and she wondered: "Maybe it could be the knight to whom I gave the horse and armor and shield?" She began to ask one and another about the White Knight and discovered that, indeed, Tristan had been honored in the tournament. She was very joyous about this and wondered how she could find out his name and where he was from. One evening she went to King Lenviz and said, "Lord king, I want to inform you about the White Knight who won the tournament." He said, "Maiden, I wish this very much, since I saw with my eyes his great valor." Braginia said, "Do not despair. I will put you on the right path." The king said, "If you are telling the truth, I will be very grateful."

The next day Braginia said to the king, "Come with me to my quarters." He went there and she showed him the armor and the shield and said, "Could you recognize whether you saw this in the tournament?" Said the king, "Indeed, this armor and this shield were on the knight who won the tournament. By God, maiden, tell me if you know anything about him." Said Braginia, "My lord, be happy, for I am not going to hide it from you: this was the knight who is now in your court, whom you took in injured and sick, whom your daughter cured."

The king was very surprised and could not believe that this knight was so great and began to question: "What do you know about him?" She told him everything: how she gave him a horse and arms and how he returned to her. The king called in a few people who were with him at the tournament, and said to them, "Could you recognize this armor and shield?" They said, "Indeed these arms won the tournament." And the king was happy about this.

He came to Tristan and said to him, "My honorable knight, I am sorely disappointed that you were hiding your honor from me. If it pleases you, tell me your name." When Tristan heard this, he was very frightened that he would be recognized, for he knew that here they wished him the worst evil, and he responded to the king, "My lord, you did a lot for me, and I do not owe as much to anybody as to you; as long as I live, I will return it to you with my services, wherever there will be a need for me." Said the king, "I don't ask anything now but for you to tell me your name." Tristan said, "My lord, I cannot tell you my name now." Said the king, "Tell me then if you were wearing the white armor that Braginia gave you at this tournament?" Tristan said, "I was wearing this armor; and I am sorry you know this." Said the king, "Knight, you should not be sorry, for you did me a great honor, since a knight from my court won the tournament. For your chivalry and your friendship and your valor I grant you my friendship." Tristan thanked him very humbly.

Thereafter Tristan's great deeds became known throughout Orlendea, and he was greatly honored by the king and by all good people; and there was no lady or maiden in all of the king's court who would not have been happy to love him with her whole heart. They suspected that Izhota loved him secretly, but she had a modest heart. The king was agreeable that she should love him, and he her, and that the youth should marry her, since the king knew that she could not marry a better knight than he, but he was very sorry that he did not know Tristan's name, and did not dare to bother him or inquire further.

One day Tristan was bathing in a tub in one of the bedchambers, and Izhota and many other maidens were serving him; each considered it a great privilege to wait on him. One man by the name of Kushyn approached Tristan's bed and picked up his sword, and began to look at it. It seemed to him so fine and sharp that he could not get enough of it, and admiringly he brought it to the queen. She began to examine it and noticed a dent in it, and said to Kushyn, "Tell me, whose sword is it?" He told her. She said, "Carry it for me." He carried it and stepped into her chamber after her; she took from a chest a chip from a sword, matched it with the sword, and it fit. She saw that it was the sword that killed her brother Amurat. She slapped her face and said, "O my God, my foe is in our house, the one who killed my brother, the good knight! It is Tristan—that is why he concealed himself; and this is the sword that made all of us sad and debased, and demeaned all of Orlendea."

Suddenly she became very angry and, taking the sword, rushed at Tristan, and raised the sword to strike him. Tristan cowered in the tub. She said, "Tristan, you will be killed here by the sword with which you killed my brother, King Amurat; now you will be killed by my hand." Tristan was frightened, but a squire intervened and said, "My lady, beware; do not kill this knight by your hand: it is not worthy for a royal lady to stain her hands with the blood of a knight. If he is guilty, leave this revenge to the king: he will do what is just to him, and he will avenge your sorrow suitably." The queen, however, did not quiet down, and advanced to strike Tristan, but the squire held her by the hand and prevented the stroke. Izhota, putting shame aside, since her love for Tristan impelled her, shielded him with her hand very magnanimously. And the queen said, "Izhota, my daughter, what are you doing? This is Tristan, who killed your uncle Amurat."

The king approached and heard this clamor and said, "My lady, why are you so angry?" She said, "How could I not be angry? I found my greatest foe, Tristan, who killed my brother Amurat; that is why he was concealing himself in our court; either you kill him or I will. This is the sword with which he killed Amurat; let him die by the same sword!" The king, hearing this, reflected, for he was very wise, and he said, "Calm, my lady, leave this revenge for me: I will act as is lawful, and you will not be sorry." He took the sword from her and said, "Now, go outside." And she left. The king questioned Tristan, saying, "My dear friend, did you kill Amurat?" Said Tristan, "I cannot conceal myself any longer, I did kill him. But no one should blame me, because I had to kill him, or he would have killed me; it could not have been otherwise." Said the king, "You are dead." And then he told him, "Dress yourself and come to me at the great hall." He left three squires to assist him.

Tristan dressed elegantly and with distinction and went to the main hall in great sadness, mostly because his sword was not with him. The place was full of good men and ladies and maidens; and when they saw him, they looked at him very attentively because of his beauty, valor, and chivalry; and they admired his great beauty and his marvelous deeds, his accomplishments and his courtliness. And maidens were telling Izhota: "If Tristan, who is the most marvelous man in the world, meets his death, all people will be sorry for him."

And all good men and knights were saying: "God knows, there is no such knight in the world; and it would be a great sin to kill him for one who cannot return." Then the queen came and began to annoy the king with her tears, saying, "My lord, he is my enemy; take revenge upon him, while it is in your power, for if you let him go he will not be at your disposal."

The king loved his queen and did not know what he should do. He kept silent for a long while, and finally spoke for everyone to hear: "Tristan, you are very guilty in connection with me, but even if all the people hold it as evil against me, I want to let you go in peace, to deliver you from the death that you were supposed to have. First of all, I took you into my house, injured and sick, and restored your health; secondly, you are such a great knight that I do not know an equal to you in the world; thirdly, you have killed my brother-in-law Amurat, not treacherously, but in a knightly manner. For these three reasons I release you from death, but you have to do as I say: as it happens, you should as speedily as possible flee from my land; do not linger anywhere, for if I find you, I will surely have to kill you if I can."

Hearing this, Tristan very humbly thanked first God and then the king, and took his leave. The king sent him off honorably, giving him a horse and armor. Braginia gave him her two brothers to serve him; she was very sad, but did not want to show it before the queen, since the queen was angry because the king had commuted his death. Izhota and the other maidens said, "It is better that Tristan is acquitted of the death of one who can never come back." Tristan rode with his retinue to the harbor, and people were talking and admiring his valor and courtliness.

Return to Cornwall

While they sailed on the vessel, a good wind moved them toward Kornovalia swiftly. Tristan was very happy about this and rendered praise to God with all his heart. He rested there one day, asking about King Marko and other lords, and the next day rode to where King Marko was said to be.

When he arrived at King Marko's court, the king greeted him very gratefully, and there was a great merriment made by the king and the lords, as if the Father had come to them. The king asked Tristan what had happened to him and Tristan recounted how fortune had taken him to Orlendea, where the king took him into his court and was kind to him, and how he had entrusted him to his daughter Izhota, who knew more about wounds than any doctors. He also recounted her beauty, and how he was recognized by his sword, and how the king acquitted him from death, and let him go honorably away. But he did not tell Marko how he defeated Palamidezh and won the tournament. Tristan was now honored in Kornovalia by the people as much as King Marko himself was. The entire Kornovalian kingdom was now liberated by him, and many countries were afraid of it.

At this time there was a lady, the daughter of a duke, the most wonderful lady in all Kornovalia. Recently one knight from Londresh by the name of Seguradezh had married her for her beauty, for she was as a flower, like a rose. King Marko was so enamored of her that there was nothing on earth he would not have done for her if only he could have her at his will. She often visited the king's court for entertainment. One day she came to the court for a festivity and the king was very pleased with her arrival. When Tristan saw her, he began to look at her often, since she seemed to him the most wonderful being after Izhota; her heart attracted him, and he eyed her stealthily so that no one noticed it. When she saw Tristan, the most wonderful and the greatest knight, it came to her mind that if he wanted to love her, she would not want more, since she knew his valor; and all her thoughts were on him and how she could love him without dishonoring herself; her eye was nowhere but upon Tristan. She forgot all the other people because of Tristan, and Tristan forgot Izhota; they looked at each other very tenderly and one knew what was on the mind of the other.

When evening came, the lady took leave of the king and approached Tristan very obligingly and said smartly, "Lord, I am yours, if you want me." Said Tristan, "Many thanks, my lady. I take you very gratefully as your knight." Having said only this to each other, the lady left for home, carrying Tristan in her heart; when she got home, she sent a servant, whom she trusted very much, to Tristan, saying, "Go discreetly to Tristan and tell him secretly that he can come to me at dusk to talk with me; let him come dressed in full armor, since one never knows what might happen to him and where; both of you come to the meadow near the sea." The servant said, "My lady, I am ready to fulfill your wish." He went to Tristan and took him aside and relayed to him his lady's message. Tristan said, "I will be happy to act according to her wishes; and you, do not go anywhere from the court: we will depart together." He called a squire and said, "Keep a horse saddled and arms ready at twilight, and do not tell anyone."

King Marko, seeing Tristan talking alone with the servant, departed from his lords to a room and ordered everybody to leave. He said to the servant, "What were you discussing with Tristan, my nephew?" The servant Magush said, "My Lord, I cannot tell you this, but I can let you know that your nephew is neither cold nor warm." Said the king, "I want you to tell me, even against your wish." Said the youth, "It is not proper for me to reveal secrets, lest I become a traitor." Said the king, "You must tell, or you will die now." The youth became very frightened and said, "Master, I will tell you, only, for God's sake, do not tell anybody." The king promised him, and he recounted everything: how his lady had sent for Tristan and how he had ridden to see her.

The king heard this and was very sad about it, because he wanted to have her himself and she had resisted him, not allowing it in any manner. As he sat there thinking hard, he said to himself, "Look at this: she refused me, a great lord; I could have done evil and good for her, but she gave herself to a man who cannot do anything for her, and he is not as good a knight as I am; really, she is a foolish woman, and she will have great sorrow for this." But he did not let Magush know his thoughts; he said to the youth, "I am surprised that your lady is so quickly enamored of Tristan, who is still a child; I know a better knight than Tristan; he is a great lord like myself, who wants to love her very much, but she has refused him."

Said Magush, "Sire, don't you know what often happens between men and women? One man will choose for himself someone lesser, just as a young woman might not prefer a good knight or a great lord." The king said, "I sought her myself, but she refused me; and for her foolishness I want to kill her and to destroy her house." When Magush heard this, he became frightened, because he knew the king to be a most treacherous man; he gathered that the king would go instead of Tristan to have her for his desire. It would be better for his lady to perish than to do this, for then Tristan would be plotting something evil against the king. The king said to Magush, "What are you thinking?" And he told him the whole truth.

When the king realized that Magush wanted his lady for him rather than for Tristan, he was very glad about it: "You could do me much good, since I have your lady on my mind; for if she would have me once, then she will have me again." Said Magush, "My lord, I will gladly do what I can, but what are you thinking about Tristan? I promised to go with him; if I lie to him, it will turn out badly for me." "Don't worry about this; I will go with one armed squire and will wait for you by the well as you pass; there I want to deal with Tristan, so that he will forget your lady's love. When I overcome him, I will then go with you and you will escort me instead of Tristan; and good will come to you because of this." Magush said, "I will gladly do it, but, by God, tell me how you plan to undo Tristan, that valorous and strong knight. For God's sake, do not set out on such an adventure foolishly because he is planning to ride armed." The king said to Magush, "It looks as if you consider Tristan to be stronger than I am? Do not fret. I want to disgrace him." And the king stepped out of the room with Magush. Tristan, seeing him, said, "I am ready to go." Said Magush, "Let's be quick."

The king called a squire: "Prepare for me a horse and armor at dusk, and do not tell anybody." He put his armor on, mounted his horse, and rode with his squire to some water, where the king dismounted and said, "We have to wait here for the one we have invited." While waiting, they saw Tristan riding up with one squire and Magush. The king mounted his horse and said to the squire, "Hand me my shield and my lance." The squire said, "My lord, what do you wish to do?" The king said, "The one that I hate is coming; I won't be happy until I shorten his life." The squire said, "My lord, forgive me, but it does not look good to me, for if he is in your house, you should not avenge him treacherously; if he wronged you, do not engage in such an adventure." The king said, "You just watch and see." When Tristan was near, the king shouted: "Knight Tristan, on guard!" Tristan was surprised and took his shield and his lance.

They fought hard. The king broke his lance in many pieces; Tristan struck him in his chest, and the king fell to the ground severely beaten. Then Tristan rode past him. When the king saw himself defeated, he was very distraught and wished himself dead rather than alive. The squire jumped off his horse and asked, "Sire, will you live?" The king said, "What is my life if I remain dishonored until my death? Give me my horse and we will go home discreetly. Where did Tristan go?" The squire said, "I do not know; he rushed by." "It would be even worse if he recognized me." The youth said, "How could he recognize you? You are in full armor and the night is dark." The king rode on and said to himself, "O my God! if my armor had not sustained me, I would be dead." When Magush saw what had happened, he was glad on the one hand, and on the other hand sad.

[*Tristan commits other deeds of valor, such as defeating the Arthurian knights Sagremor and Dodinel.*]

The king did not disclose his thoughts to anyone; he began to fear Tristan and there was nothing on earth that he would rather do than somehow to destroy Tristan cunningly, so as not to be found out. He began to ponder how it could be done: "I cannot please him in everything, and if I fail, I am dead; but if he was no longer in this world, I would not fear anything at any time." Finally an idea came to his mind by which he could destroy Tristan.

One day there were some seneschals with him and they told him: "Gracious king, you are not acting wisely in not having a wife." And

Tristan said, "My lord, it is very right for you to marry: all Kornovalia would be better regarded by the surrounding neighbors." The king said, "My nephew, since you care so much, I will take a wife: no one else can help me marry but you; if you please, find me a beautiful and good wife whom I can love." Said Tristan, "If it depends on me, you will have her, even if I should lose my life." He pointed his hand toward a church which he saw nearby and said, "May God help me; I want to do all in my power." The king said, "Already I feel as if I have her. I'll relate to you the kind I want to have. You know that you described one maiden to me and praised her, saying that her beauty has no equal in the world—let this one be my wife, and no other—she is the Orlendean princess, the beautiful Izhota. Do not linger. Go bring her to me, and take what you need—as many lords and everything else that is necessary for you."

When Tristan heard this, he knew that his uncle hated him and was sending him to his death in Orlendea. But even though it might be unfortunate for him, he consented. The king said, "My dear nephew, promise me that you will carry it through with an upright heart." And Tristan said, "My lord, even if I were to die, you will have her." The king thanked him and said, "Be ready and prepare yourself ceremoniously, so that you conduct this matter honorably; yet my heart will not rest until you return and Izhota is in my house."

The Quest for Isolde and Duel with Blanor

Tristan would have been glad to refuse this journey, for he knew that he was being sent to his worst enemies because of Amurat, but he did not refuse. He chose forty young lords to go with him who were very sorrowful since they could not expect more disgrace from even their greatest foes; but even though they did not want to, they had to prepare for the journey. Soon the vessel and they were ready. Govornar was weeping and said to Tristan, "You can see how your uncle hates you; he plotted it more for your death than for Izhota." Said Tristan, "Master, do not fret; even if he thinks evil, if I accommodate him in this and that, he will have to think and act well toward me." Said Govornar, "God keep you well."

Lord Tristan departed to sea in his vessel with his retinue, with abundance and riches. While sailing, they played and jested among themselves, as is common among knights and young people; but when they remembered where they were heading, they did not know what to say. Tristan comforted them and turned distress into laughter, and they enjoyed themselves and trusted Tristan's chivalry and said, "With Tristan we will not get into trouble."

They encountered a strong wind, and the mariners got scared and fought it, but could not advance; they let the vessel go where the wind took it, and they began to pray to God for mercy to save them from death. This ordeal lasted a day and a night, and the next day, with the wind quieted down and the sea calmed, they found themselves near a town called Damolot [Camelot], the capital of King Artiush. Since it was luxurious and rich, it had been chosen over all other towns, and it was by the sea. But King Artiush was not there; he was in Karduel with a small retinue. Tristan asked his mariners, "Where are we?" They said, "We are in the Great Land." Said Tristan, "Then we need have no fear. Let us give praise to God that we are on land; we will take a rest here and solace, praising God that He conducted us safely to land." They did so: they put up six large tents, and took out their shields and armor, led out their horses, and camped in that place with games and enjoyment.

At this time two errant knights rode out who had met each other on the road, not having known each other before—one named Iashchor [Hector], Antsolot's brother, the other Marganor. Iashchor had been dubbed a knight some four weeks before, but he did not stay at the court a week: he went to seek his fortune, and much goodness came to him, since he was a good lancer and very big-hearted. Marganor was older in years and had never been defeated, but he did not have as big a heart as Iashchor. When they came near Tristan's tents and saw the shields and helmets, they said, "Here are some errant knights sitting in the cool; they put up their shields in the Londresh manner, so that those riding by could compete with them. And those who pass them by without a bold challenge will be shamed." Said Marganor, "We will joust, as they are waiting for us or for others; if we do not joust with them, we will be in disgrace." And Iashchor said, "In God's name, then!" And they prepared themselves as necessary.

There was a knight with Tristan who knew this custom since he had traveled through King Artiush's land; he said, "Tristan, see these two knights preparing themselves for a joust: they cannot ride by without a fight, seeing our shields by the tents." Said Tristan, "Is that their custom?" He said, "It is." Said Tristan, "God bless those who established this custom; give me my armor." The others asked, "Why?" Said Tristan, "Do you see those two knights who would like to fight with us?" They said, "And if we do not want to?" Said Tristan, "If we are afraid of these two knights, then we will not get Izhota from Orlendea, since we cannot obtain her otherwise."

Tristan mounted his horse and rode a bit away from the tents. Said Marganor, "The knight is ready; if you will, let us ride up to him." Iashchor, being the younger, did not want to go ahead of him; so Marganor rode and struck Tristan very hard on his shield. His lance went to pieces, but Tristan did not budge a bit and struck Marganor very hard, who fell on one side, while his horse fell on the other and he was very bruised from the fall.

Tristan then rode toward the other, and Iashchor toward him; he struck Tristan, so that his lance went to pieces. With this strike he pierced Tristan's shield and armor and slightly wounded him on his left side. Tristan, however, struck him so hard that Iashchor fell to the ground. Seeing himself stricken, he rose up, drew his sword, and said, "Knight, you distinguished yourself with your lance. Fight now with your sword until one defeats the other." Said Tristan, "I do not want this. We were jousting because of the custom, but I do not want to fight." Said Iashchor, "Let us fight a bit." Tristan said, "I do not want to." Iashchor was very sad, and said, "God help you, who are you that you are so afraid of a sword-stroke?" Said Tristan, "I am from Kornovalia." Iashchor asked, "Are you King Marko's knight?" Said Tristan, "I am, and so are all those you see." Iashchor said, "Your arrival has brought an evil hour to this land, for I am now dishonored." Said Tristan, "Why so?" He replied, "Whoever hears that I was beaten by you will consider me a bad knight; I am unworthy to carry weapons." And he threw away his shield and his sword and began to lament and curse himself. Said Tristan, "What are you doing, I beg you?" Iashchor said, "I do not want to carry these weapons, nor to ride the horse on which I received such a disgrace from a knight; it suits me to go afoot." And he let his horse go free to the field. At this Tristan laughed and said, "Knight, it is shameful for me to let you go afoot; if you do not want this horse and these arms, take my arms and my horses." Said Iashchor, "God forbid, I would be even more dishonored if I dressed in Kornovalian armor." And he went afoot, leaving his horse and arms in the field; with him rode a very sorrowful Marganor. Tristan returned to his company and recounted Iashchor's deeds, and they began to marvel.

The next day while they were stationed there, they saw a big vessel coming toward them into the haven. On this vessel was the Orlendean king, Lenviz himself. They landed a shot away from Tristan's vessel, disembarked, put up a tent, and led out horses; the king mounted and rode toward Tristan's tents, where he asked, "Where is this company from?" They said, "From Kornovalia." Said the king, "What brought you here?" They said, "An evil hour." The king inquired if Tristan was there. They said, "He is; there he is resting in the tent. But where are you from, that you are asking about Tristan?" The king said, "I am a knight from Orlendea; I am very happy to see him. I suspect he will be happy to see me too." They said, "What is your name, so we know what to tell him?" He said, "My name is Lenviz."

When Tristan heard Lenviz's name, he jumped up and said, "Where is he?" They said, "There. He is waiting for you." Tristan ran to him very joyously and they embraced very tenderly; and they were asking each other what had happened from the time they parted. Said the king, "I am very glad that I found you." Said Tristan, "My lord, what is your need for me? I had many honors at your court; then you recently delivered me from death, and I promised you that there was not a thing in the world that I would not do for you, unless it caused my disgrace."

The king said, "I will tell you what I came here for. There have been in Orlendea frequent tournaments after you left. To one came four knights, kinsmen and blood relatives of King Ban of Banak, and they won that tournament. I invited them to stay in my house, and they came to the town where you had stayed. While they were there, something sinful occurred— which I was not aware of—one of them was killed in my house, which I cannot deny. But God knows that I am innocent of it. I was very sorry about it, so help me God. I would rather have lost my castle than to have this evil happen in my house. Seeing this, these three knights who were with him were angry with me but could do nothing to me; then one of them, by the name of Blanor, said, 'King Lenviz, we came into your home as friends, but you acted like a foe and treacherously killed our brother. Here, we cannot start anything with you, but you will answer to me with a fight at King Artiush's court.' Having said this, he departed; and the other knights who were there said the same, since all were distraught about it. Not long ago letters from King Artiush were delivered to me, summoning me and giving me a time to stand up before them and fight to refute the falsehood which Blanor accused me of because of the death of his relative. He let me know that if I do not appear, I must perish as a traitor. I must respond to this summons since King Artiush is so powerful that he can destroy me; but among all my people there is no one who can fight with Blanor, neither do I feel as if I could exonerate myself from his slander, since he is one of the knights who are world-famous. For this reason I am in great distress and do not know what to do. For the kindness which you enjoyed in my home, I dare to ask you to fight for me with Blanor, and I am hoping for your compassion."

When Tristan heard this, he was very joyous and said to himself, "Now I will get Izhota, for whom I came." He responded: "My lord, you did a lot for me, and I am ready to do this for you. But let us agree: if, God willing, I accomplish this, give me a boon that I will ask of you." The king promised him very gladly. Govornar and all Kornovalian and Orlendean lords began to talk, so that both parties standing there could hear: "Tristan is ready to fight with Blanor for the truth. The king promised Tristan a boon that he will ask if he accomplishes this task." And they said, "Is this so?" And Tristan said, "It is." From both sides they struck the tambourines and sounded the trumpets, and there was great merriment, because the Orlendeans knew Tristan to be a very valorous knight, and they said, "Blanor is surely dead if we have found Tristan for this cause." The Kornovalians were saying, "And we have what we wanted." Tristan said to one and another, "If you leave me, do not say where I came from or that I will take on this fight." They said, "My lord, be it as you wish." And both Orlendeans and Kornovalians joined ranks together.

Tristan said to Lenviz one day, "Let us go to Artiush's court." Then having prepared themselves nobly, they went to Damolot, to the king's court, where many good people were sitting. Tristan was riding with his party in lordly fashion with his helmet on, for he did not want to be recognized; one knight carried his lance, another his shield. At that time there were at the court many good knights, blood relatives of King Ban of Banak, and there were the two kings whom the absent King Artiush had left to oversee the fight. When these clans saw the Orlendean king, who came arrayed to be vindicated of the treachery that Blanor had accused him of, and when they saw that a youth was ready and outfitted, they began inquiring about him, but could not find out anything. King Lenviz approached the two kings and said, "My lords, I am ready, in the name of truth, to be vindicated of the falsehood that was thrown at me by another." The clan of King Ban came forward and said, "We want to teach you something, since you treacherously murdered our nephew in your court." Said Blanor, who was one of their best knights, "I want to teach you with a sword, if God will let me." And he dropped his glove as a sign of battle.

Tristan came forth to the two kings and said, "My lords, I am taking over for the Orlendean king, since he is not guilty in the death of the one who was killed in his house." And he took the glove. Said the kings, "Then go without delay, and so be the end of this matter." Blanor went to dress himself in the best of armor; they checked him over and gave him a big, fine horse, which belonged to Galiot [Galehaut] the King. His brother Bleryzh [Blioberis] carried his shield, and another knight, his lance. Then they rode outside of the town with a great retinue, but not one of them was armed, only Blanor. When they were in the field, King Lenviz led Tristan out and said, weeping, "I beg you, for God's sake, keep yourself together and do not be afraid." Said Tristan, "If God, Who is truth, is willing, I want to deliver you from Blanor." He took his shield and his lance and stood courageously in the field. Said Bleryzh to Blanor, "There is the knight whom you will fight: one can see that he is valorous by the way he sits mounted and carries his armor. Think of this, that not one knight of our lineage was so bad that he did not receive honors; now, guard yourself, lest we be disgraced by you. My brothers, do not despair."

The opponents rode through the field until they saw each other, then rushed toward each other and struck; both broke thir lances and fell with their horses to the ground; both were wounded and beaten. But they rose bravely and began to strike each other very hard over the helmets, not giving in to each other; all who were there marveled at their deeds. In a short while their armor weakened and the handles of their shields fell off, and they were wounded in many places. Tristan marveled about Blanor, and Blanor also said, "No man has seen such a wonder." Both were afraid of death or disgrace. Tristan recognized Blanor as a valorous knight, the likes of whom he had not seen in his days; he saw that he was striving with all his might, and that he could not endure much further. Tristan began to gain ground; the fighting became fierce, and all were saying, "These are valorous knights." Bleryzh said to his kinsmen, "I see that this other knight has no equal in the world, not even Antsolot—I know this by his blows; watch Blanor, who will not be able to withstand him to the end." The Orlendean king, seeing Blanor's bravery against Tristan, had great fear. After much slashing, their strikes weakened. Tristan said, "I wish to see how long you can bear it." Then there was a need for them to rest.

Blanor was no longer able to fight; he put down his shield and his sword and lay down on the ground; he was afraid of death, as was Tristan. When they had rested a good while, Blanor, who saw himself in danger, thought, "If he does not tire a second time, I will not be able to withstand him." He said, "Knight, I know that you are the greatest knight in the world; for this reason I wish to know your name. I do not want to do you any good, only the greatest evil; yet let me know from whose hand I will perish or whom I will defeat." Said Tristan, "If you wish me evil, I will know it by the strikes of your sword, and will praise you; but you are not thinking of yourself, for you cannot gain anything but death—so know by whom you will die: I am Tristan, the nephew of Kornovalian King Marko."

When Blanor heard this, he was very joyous and said, "I have heard your great fame through the world, so if you beat me, my relatives will not know shame, and if, God willing, I beat you, I will have great honor." He took his shield and his sword and said, "You see, you came here for your disgrace, if my right hand is well." Tristan responded, "You will not be able to brag about my disgrace: you will find out with whom you have shared the ring." He dashed at him and a very fierce fight ensued, and all began to say: "If we had not seen this, we would not have believed it." And so they went, taking the field from each other and striking a great while. Blanor could no longer lift his sword; seeing this, Tristan said, "Protect yourself; you need it; or think about yourself." Blanor could not respond. Tristan, seeing that he was abashed, struck him on his helmet so hard that he could not stand on his feet. Blanor fell to the ground and could not move his hand or his foot, and he said to Tristan, "Take my head off, I beg you; let it be the end of my shame." Tristan saw that he had a great heart and would rather die than to say, "I am defeated." He thought: "If I let him go, and he does not hand me his sword, my fight is not won; but if I kill him, I will commit evil by killing such a knight." He went to the kings and said, "My lords, we fought, as you have seen yourselves, but one of us does not want to hand the sword and does not want to say 'I am defeated'; he would rather die than say it with his tongue. Where is the shame if fortune did not serve him rightly at this time? If you see fit, make peace between us; let the Orlendean king be free from slander, for if there is to be a fight, it will be even worse, since one of us will have to give up his life."

The kings understood that Blanor would die rather than give in, and they saw Tristan's valor: that he was not willing to kill Blanor, even though he had him in his power and could do to him whatever he wanted; they conferred about what they might do. It seemed to them that the fight should stop, and Blanor should not die, if such was Tristan's will. They said to Tristan, "We thank you for your courtliness, that you forgo Blanor's death. You may disarm now if you wish. We decided that the Orlendean king is vindicated from Blanor's slander." Tristan thanked them. The Orlendean king said, "May we go freely where we want, completely vindicated?" They said, "You may go where you wish."

Tristan put his sword in the sheath and his shield on his shoulders, went to his horse, and mounted as lightly as if he was not wounded. All marveled how he could sit on a horse, since Tristan jumped up so bravely. Blanor's kinsmen, seeing him down, went to him, thinking that he was dead. King Lenviz saw Tristan departing, and said to the two officiating kings, "My lords, let me go after my knight, so that he does not ride off, so that I do not lose him." They said, "Tell us the name of this knight; then go with God." He said, "I cannot tell you without fault, but I want to go, so as not to lose him: this is Tristan, the nephew of the Kornovalian King Marko, the greatest knight in the world." Having said so, he mounted his horse and dashed promptly after Tristan with his seneschals. And so was the chivalry of Tristan known for the first time in the Londresh kingdom at the court of King Artiush. When they reported to King Artiush how Tristan spared Blanor after defeating him—and how Blanor did not want to hand in his sword—the king said, "This is the greatest knightly deed that I have seen anywhere; the whole world should praise him for this. It cannot be that he will not come to great glory, if at this young age, he was able to show such valor."

When Tristan rejoined his company on the shore, they ran toward him with great joy and asked him what had happened. He said, "With God's mercy, I delivered the king from Blanor and from sorrow." They praised God and said to him, "My lord, are you wounded much?" Said Tristan, "I am not without wounds, but I do not care about this; when we are not disgraced, we should be joyous, since we have gotten what we wanted." King Lenviz came with his retinue and, having dismounted, went to Tristan and began to embrace him, saying: "Tristan, you saved me by the sword. I am yours and all I have; but I want to know if you are wounded much?" Said Tristan, "If there is a good healer, I do not fear death from my wounds." Said the king, "We will get a healer, now that we are freed from misery." The king called the healers, who examined his wounds and did what was needed. Said Tristan, "My king, do you know our agreement?" Said the king, "I know; I have to give you whatever you want." Tristan thanked him very humbly and said, "I seek your daughter Izhota for my uncle, King Marko." Then he asked him, "My lord, where do we go from here?" Said the king, "I do not want to leave here until I see you well; then we will go to Orlendea, as promptly as we can. But I am asking you, by your courtesy: let us go together." There was great merriment among the Orlendeans and Kornovalians, who before bore great enmity toward one another.

Tristan labored all that night, and the king slept little. The next morning, the king called a wise man and told him a dream he had. The sage said, "My lord, I would advise you: do not give your daughter to Tristan, because if she goes to Kornovalia, she will suffer very painful things that no maiden has ever suffered." The king said, "I cannot do this: I promised her to Tristan, who did much for me; if I did not give her, I would be a traitor, for I made this agreement when I needed him. I love my daughter very much, but it is not right for me to lose my honor for her. So, in God's name, I cannot hold on to her."

The Drinking of the Potion

Lord Tristan rested and ordered his mariners to prepare the boat and they sailed for Orlendea. At the king's court there were honor and merriment; here were many knights, ladies, and maidens, who admired Lord Tristan, who had delivered them from Blanor's villainy. And so, after the merriment, the Kornovalians departed from the king and the queen with great joy, taking with them beautiful Izhota and with her many fine ladies. The king was crying from joy, as were the queen and all good people. The queen called Govornar and Braginia aside and said to them, "Take this silver flask full of potion and save it: when King Marko and Izhota are in bed, give them this potion to drink—first for the king, then to Izhota; and after they both drink, pour out the rest, for if someone else drinks this potion, much evil might happen, since it is called the love potion. After they both drink it, they will be very much in love: as long as they live, no one will be able to interfere maliciously between them." They promised to do so, and then took leave of the king and the queen, spread the sails, and sailed off with great joy; Izhota was near Tristan, but neither of them had ignoble thoughts about anything—only upright, good, and honorable thoughts.

On the sea on the third day, Tristan played chess with Izhota. Tristan was wearing a brocaded tunic and vestment, and Izhota a green velvet skirt with bodice, yet it was summer and very sultry. Said Tristan, "We need to have a drink." Govornar went and poured a cup from the flask of love potion—by accident, since there were many other vessels in the cabin—and gave it to Tristan; he gave another cup to Izhota. As soon as they drank the first part of the potion, they fell deeply in love with each other; as long as they lived, one would not leave the other. They began to look at each other and were not thinking of anyone else. They sat there as if mesmerized. Tristan was thinking about Izhota, and Izhota about him, forgetting King Marko. Tristan thought, "I wonder how this came over me so quickly? I did not feel it before." They thought about each other and said to themselves. "Our thoughts are not loyal." But they were overcome by the drink. Tristan thought, "If I love Izhota, it is no wonder: she is the loveliest thing in the world. I could not find a better lady; and I picked her out—she was given to me—besides, our love can be concealed." Izhota thought, "If I love Tristan, it is no wonder: he is my equal, of the same high lineage as I am, and there is no greater knight in the world." They realized in their thoughts that they loved each other with all their hearts. Izhota rejoiced in this and said, "If the greatest knight loves me, why do I need anything finer?" And Tristan said, "I have the great fortune that the most marvelous maiden loves me, though I do not deserve it."

When Govornar realized that he had given them the love drink, he became frightened and stood there shocked; he began to wish himself dead, because Tristan loved Izhota, and Izhota him. He said to Braginia, "We are culpable, for we unknowingly let them drink the potion." Said Braginia, "We fell on evil ways and we are lost; we have destroyed Tristan and Izhota too." He pointed to the flask and said, "Do you know what was in here?" She said, "This is the love potion." He said, "Badly did we oversee what was entrusted to us; we gave this to Tristan and Izhota to drink; now they are in love." Braginia began to cry and said, "We did a great wrong; it can only be that because of this much evil will develop; now we need to be very wise, even if we are sad about it."

But their sorrow was well hidden, so that the others would not know. Tristan and Izhota could not bear it; said Tristan to Izhota, "I love you with all my heart." She was very happy about this and said to Tristan, "I do not love any other thing in this world but you, as long as I live, God willing." Seeing that Izhota had the same mind as he, without further delay he led her to the cabin and consummated their desire. From then on their love did not abate, and because of this love they had great suffering. There was no knight who could endure such suffering because of love—only Tristan.

Said Govornar to Braginia, "How does it look to you? It looks to me as if Tristan took Izhota's virginity: I saw them together." She said to Govornar, "We are lost if King Marko does not find her a virgin: he will destroy us all." Said Govornar, "Do not despair; since this happened because of our transgression, we ought to worry now that someone should find out about this matter." Said Braginia, "What can we do?" Said Govornar, "Leave this to me; I will resolve it." She said, "That would be great, if God is willing!" Tristan and Izhota, however, perceived nothing that the others knew about them; since Tristan did not think of anything but Izhota, and Izhota of Tristan, they had nothing else on their minds—they were as if in Paradise, loving each other more than themselves. So deeply rooted was their love that they did not know how to abstain from each other as they headed for Kornovalia without delay.

The Adventure of Tearful Town

Then a great adversity happened to them: one day the weather changed—the sea swelled, the wind increased and took them violently where they did not want to go; the next morning they found themselves at a

large, well-fortified town that was on an island in the sea; near it were many
islands called the Lower Islands, where there were plenty of fine people and
all kinds of goods. The lord was Sir Galiot [Galehaut], whose homeland
this was. Said Tristan, "Mariners, do you know if this is the Tearful
Town?" They said, "We do not know that but this is Sir Galiot's town."
Said Tristan, "I would not willingly find myself in it, since they have told
me that it has an evil law." As they were talking thus, six armed men
approached. When these saw that the others could not move anywhere with
their boat, they said to them, "Where are you from, who put into our
harbor without our permission?" Said Tristan, "We are from Kornovalia,
the messengers of King Marko; we are coming from Orlendea; an evil hour
drove us here, and we are not guilty of doing you any harm." They said,
"Wherever you are from, you are our prisoners. Disembark, however many
of you there are, and go into town and you will learn our law." Tristan said
to his company. "What do we want to do? If we listen to them, we will be
in their hands: they can do us evil." The others said, "We do not know
what they intend—better to defend ourselves here as we can, even if we
have to fight. Our defense is of no help, since we are in their hands; they can
sink us with a vessel, or shell us with stones from the town; better we
surrender to their hands."

Said Tristan, "My lords, beware: this town has such an evil law that even
if we put ourselves into their hands, they might destroy us or throw us into
a dungeon. There our good will shall not be acknowledged by them, and
their kindness of no use to us. I would say: let us defend ourselves as we
can—better for us to die than to be at their mercy, since their mercy will not
be beneficial to us."

Said Tristan to Izhota, "What do you think of this?" She was overcome
by fear and said, weeping, "O, Tristan, I don't know what to say about it. I
was put into your hands and your care; you took me out of my land, and if
disgrace or death comes to us, it will be because of you." When Tristan
heard this, he began to curse the day he was born and said, "Milady, do you
want to remain on this vessel until they kill me, or shall we go up to their
castle and surrender ourselves into their hands?" She said, "Let it be as you
wish." Said Tristan, "Let us go up to them and endure what shall come to
us from them." To this everyone consented.

They disembarked and went up to the castle, where they were conducted
into a large building that had many cells, and in them were prisoners who
had been captured. The court was enclosed by a very strong wall, so that no
prisoner could escape. Having led the foreigners inside, they locked the
gates. Said Tristan, "My lords, we are prisoners; we are lost, since these
people have an evil custom and are so unfaithful that we will not get away
from them without being killed unless God delivers us." They all began to
weep and grieve very deeply, but silently, since they did not want the
others to hear. So Tristan with his company was in prison that day and
night, and no one attended them.

The next day six unarmed men came to them and said, "How are you?"
Said Tristan, "Well as could be in such an adventure, but I beg you, my
lords, so help you God, are we going to stay in this prison? Tell us." Said
one knight, "This is the wretchedness from which no victim departs; it
awaits all who are put here and who will spend all their days in tears; for this

reason it's called Tearful Town." Said Tristan, "O, my dear God, can it be the truth that no one survives who comes here?" And the other said, "Indeed, no one, from the time this law was established; but if a knight of very great heart and chivalry is to be found, and a lady more beautiful than our ladyship, and they both came together—they would become our rulers, and these we are serving now would have to die."

When Tristan heard this, he rejoiced very much and said, "If we are justly judged, we will be freed from this prison, since Izhota is the most wonderful lady in the world, and as for the knight—be it as God allows." And he said to the knight, "I beg you, tell me if there happens to be a knight who is greater than your knight, and a lady more beautiful than your lady, could we get free of this bondage?" The other said, "This cannot happen, since our knight has no second in the world." Said Tristan, "But if there should be a greater knight in the world than Antsolot?" "We will find an equal for that one too." "But if he conquers your knight, will we be freed?" The other said, "You will be if a lady comes together with him." Said Tristan, "Bring forth your lady and your knight and give us fair judgment: if our lady is better and our knight is better, let us go free; but if not, cut my head off!" Said the knight, "Enough said. I shall go and report where I should." And so he left.

The knight went to Lord Brunor and to his lady and said, "My lord, we have captured some young Kornovalian people and told them the custom of this town; a knight from their company claims to be better than you and a lady better than our ladyship; for this reason we came to let you know, since we cannot dismiss customs established by our ancestors: tell us what you will do." Said Brunor, "I did not establish the custom, nor can I dismiss it; call the ones who will judge which lady is more beautiful; she will hold the power, and the other must die. Prepare the fight—I am ready." His men said, "It cannot be otherwise" and went to Tristan and said to him, "If you are a champion knight, as you said, it might go well for you; get ready, for tomorrow you will fight." They freed the prisoners that day and night and gave to Tristan what was necessary; many knights came by, asking his name, but could not learn it. They were looking at Izhota, though she was concealing herself, but she was not able to hide, and the ones who saw her were saying among themselves, "We have lost our mistress, since this one is superior."

The next morning Tristan was dressed. They were giving him a different sword, but he said, "Give me my sword." And they gave it to him. He mounted a very fine horse while Govornar carried a shield and a lance for him. Izhota was dressed in very rich clothes and mounted an ambler; Braginia and other handmaidens were with her. They went to the tents where they saw the ones who were going to judge their beauty; the tents were full of good people who had come to see this contest. Tristan came with his retinue and, having dismounted, they sat down, since Brunor had not arrived yet. Then a man sounded a horn which could be heard from afar; Brunor mounted his horse and came out of the town armed and with him came a few other knights and his lady, who was Galiot's mother. When Brunor approached the tents, he said, "Where is this woman who is equal in beauty to our lady?" They pointed out Izhota to him and when he saw her, he said, "In all my days I have not seen a better woman. I am afraid to lose the thing most dear to me because of the beauty of this lady." Galiot's mother, who was of great beauty, came and when she saw Izhota she was alarmed that she might die because Izhota seemed to her the most wonderful woman in the world.

Tristan came forward to the judges and began to say, "My lords and ladies who are going to judge the beauty of these ladies, look: there they are standing together—judge fairly." All were silent, since they saw that Izhota was far more marvelous than the other lady. Tristan said, "I beg you, judge me rightly by your law." They responded sadly, "We have to do so, though we are very sorrowful." Addressing themselves to Izhota, they said, "My lady, you are superior; your beauty has saved your life; and we want to make you our mistress, but if someone better than you comes along, be aware that you must die like the one who was so long among us, but now is sentenced to death. We are very sorry about this, but it cannot be otherwise, since we pledged to uphold this law. Cursed be the one who established this law in the first place!" When they announced this, all uttered a great outcry, weeping with such sorrow that there was not a man who could see it without feeling pity.

Said Tristan, "My lords, great is your kindness; where is the one whom I am to fight?" They said, "There he is," and they indicated Brunor. Tristan said, "Take guard, for I do not want to postpone fate." He took his shield and his lance and charged at Brunor, and the other at him; they struck each other so hard and so fiercely that the weapons and shields fell from their hands, and they both were wounded and fell off their horses. Tristan was slashed slightly on his side, and Brunor was very deeply wounded in his chest. Having broken their lances, they took out their swords and began to strike very hard. Brunor recognized that Tristan was one of the world's best knights, and began to strive harder; each slashed the other very fiercely and very often; they slashed with both hands, since for both the issue was life. Brunor realized that Tristan was the greater knight, and thus began to shield himself with his sword, so that Tristan would tire—but this did not happen—then he tried to hit Tristan in an unprotected spot, but Tristan was too expert; he knew how to safeguard himself.

They fought a long time and both were wounded and exhausted, so that there was a need for them to rest; thus they recoiled from each other and stopped, leaning on their shields and swords, observing each other, and they remained so for a long while. Said Tristan, "My lord Brunor, I consider you a very valorous knight and very skillful one—for this, God knows, I sympathize with you—I would not be glad if you had to perish; but I beg you, if you can, relinquish this fight with honor and with freedom for my company, and I will gladly agree that you do not die." Said Brunor, "We are at the point where either you will kill me, or I you, or we both will be dead—it cannot be otherwise." Said Tristan, "Where there is hate, there is no love, and if this is so, be on guard!" They began to slash, and everyone marveled at them. Finally Brunor could not bear it any more, dropped his shield and sword, and fell to the ground. Said Tristan, "Are you not able to fight any longer?" Brunor said, "Knight, I relinquish this fight to you—do not hold it badly against me, since I am not doing it of my own volition." Said Tristan, "I want to pardon you. Give me your sword and say: 'I am defeated.'" Said Brunor, "I would be a wicked man if I were to say this—

that would be my disgrace; God forbid it to my death, which is near me!"
Said Tristan, "Do you feel that you want to live?" Said Brunor, "Your
sword did not give me any more time; my end is near now; if you do not
believe me, you will see for yourself." And having said this, he gave up his
soul.

Tristan saw that Brunor had died, took the helmet off his head, and
threw it far away from him. He called the men who had accompanied him
and said, "My lords, did I do enough for my company's liberation?" They
said, "Indeed! You conquered this town and the entire island, and you are
our master; and the lady whom you brought is our mistress. But you have
to undertake one more thing." Said Tristan, "What?" They said, "You
have to cut off the head of our lady Brunorovitsa with your sword."
Tristan looked at her crying very bitterly. He felt great pity for her and
said, "How could I kill a woman?" They said, "It cannot be otherwise."
Tristan was angry and began to think hard. Said Tristan, "Cursed is the
person who established such a law, and the ones who maintain this custom;
if I have to do such a deed, I will never be happy for as long as I can
remember it." Yet he went and cut her head off and said to them, "You
forced me into disgrace!" They said, "This is not your disgrace, but a
disgrace for those who established this law. Let us go up to the town, and
there you will pledge to maintain the law of this land as did the ones who
were here before you." Lord Tristan was not happy about this lordship,
but it could not be otherwise—and so he made the pledge. They directed
him to stay with Izhota at the palace where Brunor had stayed with his
lady. They lived here in the midst of great love: Tristan had nothing on his
mind but Izhota, and Izhota nothing but Tristan.

[*Urged by his sister to avenge the deaths of their father and mother, Galiot or
Galehaut returns disguised to face Tristan.*]

The inhabitants of the castle came over to him and said, "You are
captured." Galiot replied, "Though we have landed on your shores, it is
not proper for you to hold us; furthermore, I am willing to uphold your
law." They said, "Then you have to fight with Tristan, who is the greatest
knight in the world." Said Galiot, "Even if he were greater than he is, I did
not come for anything else but to fight with him." They said, "Come on
then." They disembarked and the townspeople took the mariners to the
dungeons. Said Galiot, "Leave me these two youths and the knight; let
them keep me company up to the place where the fight will be." They
asked him, "What is your name?" Said Galiot, "You cannot know my
name yet; tell me where we are to fight." They said, "Do not worry about
this—the fight will be soon." And they mounted their horses, all fifteen,
and Galiot with his retinue rode to the place where the fight would be.

Tristan had stayed in the high castle in great joy with Izhota and
Govornar and Braginia. Here Tristan was not conscious of anything but
Izhota, and Izhota of nothing but Tristan. That misfortune was very sweet
to them, and they lived as with God; they did not think about King Marko
nor about Kornovalia—they had lived there in joy for two months. At the
end of the third month a knight came before Tristan and said, "My lord,
you can rejoice with Izhota today, but tomorrow you have to fight with a
knight who came from King Artiush's court; we left him at the place where
you will fight." Said Tristan, "Do you know who this knight is by name?"

He said, "We don't know—he did not want to talk about himself." Tristan thought that it might be Antsolot and said, "I know which knight it is; did you prepare the fight? If he came for this, he will have it; even if he came for my harm, greet him for me, for I understand he is a great knight." With this, the knight left him and went to Galiot and said, "Tomorrow you will fight; and Tristan greets you." Said Galiot, "Tristan greets me as an adversary, and I also greet him as an adversary." Tristan's men discussed who he was, but could not recognize him. Govornar, listening as the knight was talking about the fight, said, "This is definitely Antsolot, who came from the court of King Artiush, seeking different and ferocious adventures." Govornar was very fearful of him, and he approached Tristan and said, "Tomorrow you are to fight." Said Tristan, "Do you know with whom?" He said, "I do not know, but I suspect that Antsolot came purposely to fight with you; he is the greatest knight in the world." "I am glad to joust with him, but if it comes to blows, may God favor me, or make us equal. I would not wish greater honor; but if he kills me, I would rather be defeated by him than by five other men." Govornar was frightened even more and said, "It is as you say, but there are great fear and great danger." Said Tristan, "One should not fear death; you yourself know, master, that we are always near it."

Hearing this, Izhota began to cry and grieve, saying, "Heavy is my heart; this is an evil adventure; in an evil hour was I born to this world. I have not had three months of fortune and joy, and already my suffering and the shortening of my life are here, so that if a serious wound or death happened to me, it would be sweeter and better for me." Tristan consoled her, saying, "On my faith, he is not going to pull anything over me." Said Izhota, "I ask only that you will be safe for me and not shamed by this battle, since I do not fear any other knight but Antsolot." And so they remained in this anxiety, but Galiot knew nothing of it.

At dawn, Tristan dressed in his great armor and, having heard mass, rode out of town, and with him Izhota, Govornar and Braginia, and four squires. When he was near the tents, Galiot was already on his horse and, seeing Tristan nearing, took up his lance and his shield. Tristan saw that he was ready and said to Govornar, "Go to this knight and find out whether he is Antsolot—I want to establish friendship with him." Govornar went and greeted Galiot, and he returned his greeting. Govornar said, "Knight, this is Tristan with whom you are about to fight, but he is asking you, for your courtesy, tell him who you are. You know already with whom you will fight; let him also know with whom he is going to fight." Said Galiot, "If he is Tristan, I am his mortal enemy, and rightly so, since he killed my father and my mother: I came to take revenge on him with all my might if I only can; my name is Galiot from the Lower Islands—far and wide my name is heard." When Govornar head this from Galiot, he became frightened, knowing that Galiot was the greatest lord in the world, and he told this to Tristan. Tristan said, "God be praised that the greatest lord and knight in the world is taking on a fight against me on the field; he, who is the flower of valor and bravery, lord over lords, came to fight with me, though being capable of sending on the field a hundred thousand soldiers armed with lances. Let us end this matter."

They charged toward one another as fast as their horses could gallop, and struck each other so hard that their lances broke; and they thrust so hard that both fell with their horses to the ground, and were wounded from this blow, but both bounced back, like men of great valor and high spirit, seized their swords, and began to slash. Tristan was afraid; they both were great men and were fighting so fiercely that no man, seeing this, could not have fear. Tristan acknowledged his adversary; and Galiot said, "This is the greatest knight known to the world: here I will receive death or become a valorous man." They both struggled, showing each other their knightliness. Izhota dreaded the end of the one whom she loved more than herself; when he received such fierce strokes she was pale and would have given the whole world if he were only sound and free from this fight; when Galiot hit Tristan and he fell to his knees, Izhota felt the strokes in her heart and paled like a ghost, but when Tristan struck Galiot and gained the field, Izhota was joyous and her face became pink. They fought, and Izhota took the strokes in her heart, but was sure that Tristan was putting up a good fight, for he chased Galiot all over the field at will. Galiot was wounded much and losing blood. Tristan was not much wounded. Galiot struggled against Tristan as hard as he could and thought, "Let me see how long I can hold out against him." Galiot, being thus quite spent, whispered, "I cannot avoid death from Tristan."

Then the King of a Hundred Knights came with his armed men in aid of Galiot; they came up swiftly, since the king saw that Tristan was defeating Galiot. When Galiot recognized their banner, he said, "Tristan, you are dead; you can see these are my people; since you have killed my father and my mother, if I do not take revenge upon you, all the world will hold me at fault." Said Tristan, "My lord, it cannot be that you would threaten me with your men; I know you as a valorous man; you would not have come to me if you had wanted to take revenge upon me through others. I do not have fear, nor do I guard myself from anyone but you; and, God knows, I am not guilty against you in the death of your father and mother; you know it well yourself; but I am giving you this fight as won. Let me go free with my company. I acted badly when I drew my sword against you, the greatest knight known, and, God knows, I am not saying this in fear, or as if I am afraid of death." Then he came forth and handed him his sword. Galiot took the sword and said, "You have done such things to me that I should hate you with all my heart, but I am not acting that way because of your valor: you are the greatest knight in the world. It is not right to destroy you—I promise you my friendship." Tristan knelt and thanked him courteously for his kindness. Galiot lifted him by the arms and said, "This is not right: even though I am a great lord, you are also a great man of good birth, and you are an even greater knight than I—there is no equal to you in the world."

The King of a Hundred Knights was advancing toward them with his lances aimed at Tristan. Galiot shouted at him as loudly as he could, "Stop! Retreat from Tristan if you value your life!" The king, hearing this, stopped and recalled his army, rode alone to Galiot and inquired of him, "My lord, what happened to you?" Said Galiot, "Good luck, with God's grace, but not entirely." Said the king, "I told you so before." Galiot said, "But I am alive; besides, I very much wanted to fight with him, and I am glad that I encountered him; if it could happen, I would like to have him together with Antsolot, since these knights are as courageous as they are courtly and full of virtues." Said the king, "What do you think now?" Galiot said, "Let us all go to Tristan's home with him—there I will rest until I am well." Galiot, Tristan, Izhota, and all their retinue mounted very promptly, and when they came to the castle, which was called Orash, they examined Galiot's and Tristan's wounds. Galiot had deep wounds and he had lost blood; the healers applied herbs to the wounds and marveled that he was alive; he could not move his body for an entire month. Tristan rested for fifteen days; his dungeon companions were with him, and they all gathered around Tristan. Tristan's men joined with King Artiush and his hundred knights; they entered the Tearful Town, freed the prisoners, and burned the town, because the citizens were fighting with them about the cruel laws which they had maintained for many years.

Galiot ordered, however, that no one should harm Tristan's people or the guests; and he would not let Tristan leave his side until both were healed. Galiot said to Tristan, "I came to this island for your death, to avenge the death of my father and my mother, but I know that you killed against your will; because of your chivalry, I forgive you. You have told me that you were taking this maiden to your uncle, as you have promised him; I will let you go with her, but I am very sorry that you cannot come with me, for I do not envision any more precious thing than seeing you together with Lord Antsolot. You can take leave of your uncle and come to me in the Soreilonean Kingdom or wherever I might be; remember the courtesy you had from me and the abatement of my anger; come to me as quickly as you can; and I, as a knight, for I am not a king, promise you and Antsolot all the lands that I have amassed; if I had a friendship with you two and you with me, I could not wish for greater wealth." Said Tristan, "My lord, your grace is great; you did so much for me that I cannot return the service to you; if God gives me life, I want to see you soon wherever you are. I am telling you this before my company." When the sea was calm, Galiot accompanied him to his ship and implored him to act as he had promised. But then, a bit later, the news came to him that Galiot had expired; Tristan was very sorrowful about it.

Tristan and Isolde in Cornwall

When Lord Tristan came with Izhota and his retinue to King Marko in Kornovalia, there was great rejoicing; old and young made merry and amused themselves. When the king came to the festivities and it was time for Izhota to go to the wedding bed with him, Izhota was in great distress, since she could not forget the man she loved. She said to herself, "I would rather be on Orash Island, where I had Tristan to myself." With this thought she lay in bed. Because she had already lost her virginity, she talked Braginia into sleeping with the king in the wedding bed this first night.

King Marko, having lingered a while, came to her in the chamber where there was no one but Tristan, Govornar, and Braginia. As soon as the king undressed, Tristan blew out the candles, and the king said, "Why did you do this?" Said Tristan, "There is a custom in Orlendea that when a great lord lies with a maiden on the first night, the candles are extinguished so that the maiden will not be bashful. Her mother asked me, and I promised her

this." Said the king, "You did rightly." Afterward Tristan, Izhota, and
Govornar left the chamber, and Braginia lay in the bed instead of Izhota,
who had appeared before the king for a while until Braginia came to replace
her. The king, having consummated the marriage with Braginia, did not
recognize that she was not Izhota. Soon after they had slept together,
Braginia left, and Izhota, coming in, lay down with the king.

When morning came, Marko said to Tristan. "O Tristan, my obliging
adopted son, you brought me pure gold." Tristan was very happy about
this. In his happiness King Marko commanded the knights to fill their hearts
with joy, and said, "Tristan brought me pure gold." He ordered various
instruments to be brought—pipes, tambourines, trumpets, chess and
checkers, and lutes and organs; he prolonged this merriment to make the
knights feel brave. The maidens, seeing this revelry, performed a circular
dance in Tristan's honor, saying, "Lord Tristan gave us the reason to sing
and dance for the rest of our days." The blonde Izhota looked with her
bright eyes at the person of Lord Tristan, and Tristan also was glancing at
Izhota. None of the knights and ladies and maidens knew about this—only
Tristan and Izhota, Govornar and Braginia. And King Marko abided in
conviviality with his knights.

Some time later, a knight of King Marko came and said to him, "Gracious king, keep secret what I am about to tell you." The king looked at the
knight and said, "Tell me what you want." Said the knight, "You are a
mighty lord, and your dishonor is not gratifying to me; I will tell you:
Tristan has loved Izhota carnally." The king said, "Can you prove this?"
The other said, "My lord, indeed, I heard that they are to meet in the
garden, behind the portico at the first night-watch." King Marko, wanting
to investigate this, said to his knights, "We have to go away." Said Tristan:
"Whom do you want with you?" He said, "O honorable Knight Tristan,
do not go with me now—wait for me here tomorrow." The king rode out
far from his court, turned the knights away from him, and returned to the
court; he entered the garden and climbed up into the apple tree. The moon
shone brightly that night, and because of this, he could not hide his shadow.

As Lord Tristan had arranged with Izhota, she stepped out into the
garden; she stood near the apple tree, very joyous because of Tristan's love.
As Tristan came near her, he saw a man's shadow on the apple tree; he
looked up, kneeled on one knee and said to Izhota; "O my noble lady, the
crown of all ladyship, I asked you to come out in the garden to tell you my
thoughts. I am contemplating going to sea, for I heard that King Marko
said, 'Tristan looks at Izhota in an amorous manner.' So, for God's sake,
recount to the king my service: how I fought for him with fiery Blanor, the
great knight, so as to get you for him; the king should not be angry with
me." Izhota, who was very wise in every way, understood that Tristan had
noticed something; she looked around the garden and noticed the man's
shadow on the ground and said without looking up the tree: "O my noble
knight, the crown of all knighthood, who respects King Marko's lordship,
the king knows your great service, that you freed all of Kornovalia, young
and old; and all our neighbors have been moved by your great chivalry. It
would be a wonder if the king should forget your valor and trust some
other knight; I will speak to the king about you; be assured that the king
will trust me, his wedded wife. And if you are contemplating going to sea,

linger a while until King Marko returns." Lord Tristan praised the glory of God, thanked the fair Izhota for everything, bowed and went to the main palace, and Izhota to her chamber.

King Marko climbed down from the tree and said to himself, "Tristan is without fault; if this is the truth, it will be different from now on." It came to his mind that the informer had borne anger against Tristan since he had gone with Tristan after Izhota; and when they landed by the castle of Damolot in the Londresh kingdom, and two knights had confronted them, Tristan wanted to measure up to them, but the knight had restrained him, saying, "Tristan, we did not come to fight with these knights but to carry Izhota to King Marko." Then Tristan had said to him, "If you are afraid to joust in Londresh, do not go with us to Orlendea, since there we will find many good knights who will not give up Izhota to us without a fierce battle." Because of this, the knight was angry at Tristan; and this animosity came to the king's mind now, and he doubted the knight.

King Marko returned to the palace, and Izhota came to him and said, "My noble lord, I will tell you one thing. When you departed with your knights to the other court and left Tristan here, he decided to go into the world. I asked him: 'Why are you going?' He told me: 'I recognize that the king looks at me with angry eyes.' I detained him until I heard from you. I beg you, my lord, for your consideration: you know yourself how Kornovalia was belittled until Tristan freed it; he killed Amurat on Samson Island and freed Kornovalia, from old to young. He did so that you might rule. He also conquered the great knight Blanor; he did this for you, obtaining me for you. And furthermore, if some knight came to your court from anywhere seeking an equal, and if he knew that Tristan was with us, he would not fight with him, but if he did, you would be elevated through Tristan; for when the knights came to my father's court, not one was to be found who could withstand Palamidezh, but when he fought with Tristan, Tristan threw him off his horse. For all this, my lord, do not let him go away from you." King Marko listened to her marvelous words and said to her, "Bad things were reported to me about Tristan, but I myself know him to be faithful to me and I love him with my heart, as I love myself."

Then King Marko said to fair Izhota: "I had a dream: there was a very fine kingdom and within it grew a very pretty rose bush, with very beautiful flowers on it; some knights were saying: 'This is a good country for this beautiful rose.' And the lord of this kingdom was saying: 'The kingdom is mine, but the rose is not mine; whoever picks the rose flower will have the bush.' Many knights came to this kingdom, and every knight wanted a flower from this rose, but no one could take it; then one knight came and extended his hand to this bush and took away one rose-bloom. And the knights all said, 'This is a wonder: for so long no one could take a flower from that bush, but this knight took it.' This knight was very happy about the rose, but when he wanted more flowers, he was not able to pluck them. At this time I woke up from my dream."

Izhota said, "My lord, it seems to me that knight who took the rose will own the bush." The king thought that no one would comprehend this, but Izhota was very wise and understood why the king was saying this; she thought that Braginia had recounted to him her and Tristan's lovemaking. Izhota was very angry with Braginia and thought that she should not be alive.

Tristan went into a leafy virgin forest to seek a joust, since for several days he had longed for it. Izhota said to Braginia, "Lord Tristan went to seek a joust, and is bound to have some wounds there; the plants that heal wounds are scarce, and so you or I should go and gather some herbs." Said Braginia, "O honorable lady, it is not suitable for you to go instead of me. Even if I have to travel far over sea and over land, I will go—and not only to the virgin forest but even further—to bring the herbs for Lord Tristan. But I beg you: send two knights with me so that no misadventure befalls me." Izhota ordered two servants called and told them to put on armor. When they had dressed themselves, she said to them, "Go with that maiden and put her to death, and I will plead to the king for you so that he makes you knights."

When they came to the virgin forest, the men thought much, saying: "This maiden served Lord Tristan a great deal in Orlendea; she is wise and smart—let us tell her why we are going; maybe she will be able to do something so that we will be cleared from punishment and she from death." They said, "Maiden, do you know that you will receive death from us?" She said, "I cannot talk with you about anything until I see your faces." They took their helmets off and showed her their faces. Braginia recognized that they had come to kill her and said, "Do not dare to do anything but what was ordered, but if you want, you can be free from sin to act by Our Lord's commandments." They said, "O, good maiden, we have told you this so that we might be free from sin, and you from death." The maiden said, "Lead me to the crossroads of the virgin forest; there is one very beautiful tree where there are always many wild animals. Tie me to that tree and let me die from the animals."

She spoke thus because it was seldom that there were no knights by that tree. The servants tied her to the tree and were looking in all directions where the wild animals might come from, and they suddenly saw the handsome Palamidezh Anuplitich riding by with his servants following him. Braginia's heart was full of joy, since she recognized him. Palamidezh, seeing her, said to his companions, "It is not happening according to my thoughts. I have come here so that I might die from Tristan's hand, but he has met his death already, for if Lord Tristan was alive, this would not have happened to Braginia." He said to her, "God have mercy on you, maiden; by what death has Lord Tristan perished? For if he were alive, this calamity would not have happened to you." She said, "Knight, I know that you are the brave Palamidezh, son of King Anuplit, the greatest enemy of Lord Tristan. Let me die from wild animals. I never saw Lord Tristan more joyful than he was yesterday when he went into the virgin forest seeking to joust with some good knights." Said Palamidezh, "What is your transgression against the fair Izhota that has put you in such suffering?"

She said, "It happened this way to me: I went with my mistress from one kingdom to another. She was carrying her virgin flower, and I was carrying my own. While going by sea, my lady drowned her flower, but I did not drown mine. Then she placed my flower where her flower should have had its place; because of that, this evil happened to me." Palamidezh said, "Does Lord Tristan know this?" She said, "He does not know." He said, "O my good maiden, you have served Lord Tristan well, and transgressed much against me, but when I free you from your death, serve me too." She said,

"It is befitting for every knight to wish honor for other knights and maidens." Palamidezh said, "Go with us to Kornovalia and tell me about the customs of your lord King Marko." She said, "There is one good custom of our lord: when King Marko is informed that knights have come from another country to seek a joust, the king must send each of them a horse and armor if their own horses are tired, so that they may compete on the fresh ones." Palamidezh said, "How was this custom established, for it is a custom of King Artiush, who is the crown of all the kings at all four corners of the world?" She said, "This custom was established when Lord Tristan came from Orlendea to Kornovalia." Palamidezh rode to Kornovalia and said, "Maiden, I don't want them to know anything about me for a while: who I am and from where." When they came to the knights' quarters, the local knights led up a horse and brought out armor. Then the handsome Palamidezh, with two swords and a black shield, came to the palace of King Marko and bowed. The king greeted him very courteously, then said, "If someone might know by what death maiden Braginia perished, I will reward him very greatly, yet if he declares her alive, anything that his hand might reach for will not be denied him."

Palamidezh began to tell him about King Artiush, and Marko's heart was filled with joy; he commanded that chess be brought in and asked Palamidezh to play with him. When they sat down to play, the king said to Palamidezh, "I am telling you, knight, that no one can compete with me in playing chess." Said Palamidezh, "I know, my king, that you are shrewd. Do you want to play for these stakes: whichever of us wins, anything that his hand grasps, let him take." They both agreed to this. Palamidezh then won and said, "King Marko of Kornovalia, you said: 'Whoever tells me about the maiden Braginia being alive may take anything that his hand might reach for'—and, furthermore, you said, 'Whoever wins in chess, anything that his hand grasps, let him take.' And a king's faith is a greater thing than even his kingdom. Please give me fair Izhota and I will give you the maiden Braginia." The king said, "Where is she?" He said, "At my quarters." Palamidezh said to his vassal: "Bring Braginia." The vassal led her in. When King Marko saw her, he was very joyous and said to a maiden, "Go and tell Izhota: 'Get arrayed, you must go with Palamidezh.'" The fair Izhota was dressing very slowly, waiting for Lord Tristan to hurry back; then Palamidezh would not dare to claim her. But finally the marvelous Izhota came before the king, and Marko said, "Knight, here is the lady for you."

Palamidezh's heart was filled with joy; he gave praise to God and thanked King Marko for Izhota. The beautiful Izhota said, "Knight, my transgressions led me to be given to King Marko of Kornovalia, and he commanded that I be given to you; you know yourself, when you had served for three years at my father's court, that you could not earn me, but you have obtained me quickly from King Marko; let us go to church and swear to God not to leave each other until death." Palamidezh was very happy about this and said, "Let us go, lady." They rode to the church, and Izhota dismounted and entered ahead of Palamidezh. In this church there was a rope ladder. Izhota climbed up this ladder to a high window, and when she was at the window, she pulled the ladder up to herself. Then Palamidezh Anuplitich entered the church very joyfully. When he saw his

Izhota in the church window, he became very sad and said, "O, honorable lady, why are you acting like this? Come down and we will swear to each other by God not to leave each other until death; you said so yourself, milady. I am telling you on my knightly faith: if King Marko gave you to me, I do not want to go without you." Said Izhota to the knight, "Go with God; there are knights of King Marko who went on a hunt, and if they find you in their church, you will have a fierce fight." Palamidezh said, "O, honorable lady, I am not afraid of any knight, since King Marko gave you to me."

Then Izhota looked in the direction where the knights had ridden off and saw that Lord Tristan was riding toward the church, for Tristan had the custom when returning to the court of always entering this church. Izhota said to Palamidezh, "Go with God; a knight is coming at you!" Palamidezh said, "Milady, why are you threatening me with a knight? If there is not one, let there be two! Come down, milady; you should go with me." Izhota said, "Go with God; a knight is coming toward the church in a knightly manner; guard yourself from his blows!" Palamidezh said, "If not one, let there be three! Milady, come down, and let us renew our pledge." Said Izhota, "Knight, ride away from this church, for you will be shamed by the strokes of another knight, since my knight is near the church already, and he is riding at you." Palamidezh said, "If not one, let them be ten! I pledge on my knightly faith to wait for you three days and three nights; I will not go away without you!" Said Izhota to Palamidezh, "Not three, not two, but one Tristan is coming!" Palamidezh jumped on his horse and rode away as fast as he could, since he knew that Tristan was skilled with his lance on horseback.

Tristan saw that the knight was running away from the church, and, recognizing him by his insignia, galloped after him as fast as he could, but could not catch up with him, for his horse was tired from the hunt, and he turned back. When Lord Tristan came to the church and saw the beautiful Izhota, he became very angry and did not want to ask about Palamidezh, but said only, "Milady, mount the horse; let us go to King Marko." Izhota said, "It is not right for me to go to the king, since he gave me to Palamidezh." Tristan said, "O my honorable lady, how is it possible that he gave you to Palamidezh, for King Marko likes many pleasures?" Izhota said, "Tristan, if pleasure was dear to him, why did he give me to an errant knight indeed?"

The Lovers at Camelot

After these words Tristan rode away from the church with Izhota into the world. They rode from Kornovalia to Damolot, where they met a maiden who said, "Knight, I do not know who you are, but I see you are a good one; I fear your dishonor; however, if you take that road, you will avoid disgrace." Lord Tristan said, "Maiden, blessed be you by all knights for kindly forewarning me to prevent disgrace; I beg you, maiden, why are you restraining me from this road?" She said, "My good knight, ahead of you lives King Artiush with his Queen Zhenibra [Guinevere] and many valorous knights, since every good knight worships King Artiush's lordship; so these knights, when they see this beautiful lady with you, will want to take her away from you with a fierce fight. Knight, there will be not one or two, but many valorous knights to break lances: you will have to give her up." Lord Tristan said, "Maiden, praised be you by all the knights and maidens for gladly drawing away a knight from his disgrace, but please know that no one can divert me from this road." Then Tristan parted from the maiden.

When he saw King Artiush's tents, he was expecting an encounter there. And so Lord Tristan said to fair Izhota, "Honorable lady, do you see the tent of King Artiush, which is pitched so close to the road? I know that there are many valorous knights there; if we ride straight toward his tent, I will face a hard fight, yet if we ride around King Artiush, I also expect a fight. They will say, 'There goes a fearful knight leading a most beautiful maiden.' Because of this, milady, I must go straight toward the tent of Artiush. And I am telling you on my knightly faith, if you look anywhere but between my shoulders or between the ears of your horse, I will be very angry with you." Said Izhota, "O my honorable knight Tristan, if I traveled over sea and land, I would not see any greater knight than you; and as to the knights from the court of King Artiush, I saw them all at the court of my father in Orlendea."

And so Tristan rode to King Artiush's tent, which was pitched so close to the road that the cords were reaching across it. Tristan rode through the cords and touched them so that the entire tent shook. At that time the king was sitting at the table with Queen Zhenibra and his knights. Seeing this, the knights jumped over the tables, saying, "Who is so arrogant toward King Artiush, the crown of all kings?" The fair Izhota and Tristan, hearing the sound of falling vessels in the tent—for the knights while jumping over the tables had broken some—became very frightened, fearing disgrace. When Artiush's men came out of the tent, they saw Tristan, the great knight, and the lady with him. There was Antsolot [Lancelot], Tristan's dearest friend, but he did not recognize Tristan in his armor. He said, "I have traveled at sea and on land very much, but I never saw a knight who could sit on a horse so solidly, or who could keep his feet in the stirrups so handsomely, except for one, and I never saw a lady as marvelous, except for one."

There was a cupbearer of King Artiush named Geush [Kay], a recently dubbed knight, who had great courage but little might. This cupbearer saw the wonderful Lady Izhota, and his heart filled with joy; he gave praise to God, went into King Artiush's tent and knelt, saying, "O mighty king, if I saw the most marvelous maiden in the world, you would give her to me. Now, my lord, if I traveled many years by sea and by land, I could not find a fairer maiden than the one with the knight who passed by your tent and did not bow before you. Let me take the maiden from him, and I shall bring him to you." The king said, "If you bring me this knight, you can take not only the maiden but anything you want." The cupbearer thanked him very boldly, as if he had her in his hands already, and began very hurriedly to dress in his armor and rush after Izhota. Antsolot said to him: "Geush, do not be too eager to ride after this knight, for I see how he sits on his horse and how he holds his feet in the stirrups. Your horse may step on its bridle before you bring him in. I am telling you truly: a fearful knight could not take such a wonderful maiden because someone else would have taken her away from him before us."

Geush said, "It is not becoming for any knight to detract honor from another knight, and I am telling you, on my faith, that when we join in combat, I intend to exhibit only a little of my mastery with him." And so the cupbearer rode after Tristan as fast as he could, with great assurance.

When Izhota and Govornar saw him, Izhota said to Tristan, "A knight is riding after you as fast as his horse can take him." Said Tristan, "This is a newly dubbed one who thinks he will display his mastery over me, and so do I with him." Then Geush, the cupbearer, called out in a loud voice, "Knight who is leading that marvelous maiden, wait for me; let us see which one of us is more worthy to love her." Lord Tristan put his spear under his armpit before turning around and said, "Ride up and see."

When their spears joined together, Geush fell to one side and his horse to the other. Lord Tristan jumped off his horse and took Geush's helmet off his head and wanted to deliver him of his soul, but Geush began to pray for his life. Lord Tristan said to him, "Do as I order you, and I will release you from a brutal death." Geush said, "O, my lord, you may send me far over sea and over land if only you will spare my life." Said Tristan, "Knight, take off your armor and present your arms to the lord who sent you." The knight was content with this, and went away on foot, carrying his armor.

King Artiush was walking with his knights and Queen Zhenibra with her handmaidens, when they saw a horse coming, stepping on its reins, and a bent knight following; the friends of the cupbearer said to King Artiush, "Milord, how brave your cupbearer is, our friend Geush; we believe that he killed the knight with the maiden and is carrying his armor." Lord Antsolot said, "O my God, how inaccurately you are informing Artiush, for if our knight defeated that one, why would he abandon his horse? I am telling you, on my faith, our knight is carrying his own armor." After these words, the cupbearer approached the king and said, "My lord, accept me alive, rather than dead. I preferred to act thus rather than to lose my head. I will tell you, though, that there is no knight who could withstand him." The king, very sad that disgrace had befallen his knight, called Queen Zhenibra and said, "My lady, go ask Antsolot to bring this knight in, since Antsolot is the greatest knight among us." The queen asked Antsolot, saying: "Antsolot, for God's sake, take the crown of thorns from King Artiush and bring this knight to us, and the maiden will be yours." Antsolot said, "Honorable lady, why are you sending me after this knight, for my loathsome death? But if you command me, I must go." Then he dressed in his armor, mounted his horse, and rode after Tristan at a slow pace—for he knew that he would overtake him—reflecting: "The knight who is conducting such a marvelous maiden is not going to run."

When Antsolot was near, Izhota and Govornar saw him, and Izhota said, "Lord Tristan, a knight is riding after you in a bold manner." Lord Tristan said, "My lady, how is this knight riding?" She said, "At a slow pace." Tristan looked far ahead of him and saw a very magnificent church, and before it a beautiful portico; said Tristan, "Let us go to that church by the portico." And they rode over there. He said to Izhota, "My lady, this is a knight of old, and I do not know whether you will be his or mine." After this, they came to the church and sat down by the portico in the coolness; he took his helmet off, for he was perspiring. Antsolot saw him and jumped off his horse very swiftly, for he recognized that it was Lord Tristan, and was very joyous in this recognition. Seeing him, Lord Tristan put his helmet on, jumped on his horse, and was ready. When Lord Antsolot saw him on his horse, he cast off his helmet; Tristan recognized him and jumped off his horse; they greeted each other very cordially, and asked each other, "Knight, what adventures have you had since the time we parted?"

Lord Tristan bragged to him, saying, "Whichever knights are riding seeking their equals, no one has resisted my strokes." Lord Antsolot said: "Of the knights who worship King Artiush, I am the crown of all." Then he told Lord Tristan, "Command that your horse be prepared; let us go your way, since I am not returning to King Artiush." Said Tristan, "Why do you not want to go back to the king?" He said, "Because I will be killed by him; only by you will I remain alive." Tristan said, "How could that be, knight?" And he said, "I was sent after you, to bring you back, since no other knight could ever do it." Said Tristan, "Let us go to King Artiush, and I will tell him that you are a greater knight than I." Antsolot said, "What God is not willing to do, no man can do; I am not a greater knight than you—you are the crown of knighthood." Then they said, "We will do as Izhota shall advise." The blonde Izhota said, "You are both valorous knights; God knows which one of you is greater; but since you ask me to speak up, then let us go to King Artiush. Many knights have said that Queen Zhenibra is more beautiful than I, though I know myself that I am more beautiful; still we want to see the beauty of other ladies and the valor of other knights."

After this, Lord Tristan rode with his dearest friend, Antsolot, to King Artiush's tent, where the knights were very joyous, thinking that Antsolot was bringing this knight in; but when they were near the tent, it was clear that these knights liked each other wonderfully well. And so they came into King Artiush's tent, where Tristan fell on one knee and said, "My lord, let your kingdom know that Antsolot is the greater knight: he led me like a deer by the neck before Your Majesty." Having said this, he stood up. Then Antsolot fell on his knee and gave praise to God and said to the king and queen, "My lords, thank Tristan for my life, since he did not want to destroy me, but led me like a child with a whip to King Artiush's camp. Please know that Tristan is the crown of knights in all four corners of the world on sea and land." All the knights said, "You both are valorous; God have mercy on you, as you marvelously carried out your vows; your chivalry has no equal near or far. We have seen your valor; let us now see the beauty of your lady."

Both Queen Zhenibra and Izhota arrayed themselves as best they could. The knights and judges of King Artiush came forth, beholding their beauty, and one of the judges said, "We are appointed to judge fairly for both sides, but it seems to me, as gold is better than silver, the lady of this knight is more beautiful than our queen. How does it seem to you?" They said, "As you have judged, so it seems to us, that there is no knight equal in valor to Lord Tristan, and there is no lady who can compare to Lady Izhota." Queen Zhenibra was very angry with the judges because of this, but could do nothing about it, and so she was thinking how she could disgrace Tristan. She asked Gavaon [Gawain], the nephew of King Artiush: "Knight, compete with Tristan; if you conquer him, you will have great honor, since you will defeat the greatest knight, but even if he conquers you, there will be no disgrace, for you will be defeated by the world's greatest knight." Gavaon said to Tristan, "Knight, prepare your horse; let us try each other out." Tristan said, "Good knight, you have spoken well: for a few days I have wished to tempt my fortune." And so Gavaon rode forth in full armor.

[*Tristan easily defeats Gawain and is welcomed at Camelot, which fearfully awaits the arrival of King Samsizh of Black Island.*]

Soon after, King Samsizh came and said, "I know, O king, that you are the crown of all kings. I came because I know you have the greatest knights; and you, knights, who worship King Artiush's lordship, if I overcome any of you—I shall have my will over him, but if any of you conquers me, let his will be over me." The knights were very eager for this and dressed themselves in their armor and every one of them wished to fight with Samsizh first to please King Artiush.

After this, King Samsizh armed himself, mounted his horse, and fought with the king's knights; whoever came by Samsizh found himself off his horse. King Samsizh defeated eleven knights, and then Antsolot wanted to go against him. When they met, their poles broke in many pieces, and they butted with their shoulders, so that their horses fell under both of them. Antsolot fell off his horse, but King Samsizh hung on to his and did not lose him. The knights of King Artiush said, "The fight was not lost by our knight, since they both fell off their horses." King Artiush said, "We cannot put a fight that was overthrown back on its feet; that knight who did not lose his horse has won the fight." King Artiush was dear to his knights and said, "I would gladly go with you to the Black Island to King Samsizh's prison, rather than remain here." King Artiush armed himself, mounted his horse, and said to King Samsizh, "Guard yourself from my strokes!"

The kings met, and for King Samsizh the fight with Artiush was easier than with even the lesser of his other knights. King Artiush fell hard from his horse, and so King Samsizh led him off with the defeated knights. They were all pale from sadness. Antsolot said to the king, "My lord, let us think how to get free from Samsizh's hand; if we are not liberated by Tristan, we will not be liberated by any other knight." They called Queen Zhenibra and Antsolot said, "Milady, go find Tristan and tell him what has happened to us, and tell him from me: 'Antsolot, your dearest friend, begs you: if we are not liberated by you from the Black Island prison of King Samsizh, we are going to die in his dungeon.'"

The queen left very hurriedly; she met a girl and said to her, "Maiden, can you tell me anything about Lord Tristan?" The maiden said, "Do you see that harbor with many vessels over there? First you will notice the ship of Lord Tristan decorated with pearls and precious stones; if he is not on this vessel, you should ask for him in that camp, where you will see much splendor and merriment, because he likes this."

Queen Zhenibra left this maiden joyously and soon she saw the harbor, recognized the ship of Lord Tristan by the maiden's description, and she was very happy. Near the vessel there were many knightly stations. The lady saw a girl at the camp, went over to her, and said, "I beg you, maiden, where is Tristan's lodging?" And the maiden said, "You are standing in front of the place you are seeking." The queen entered the lodging without announcement and hurriedly began to tell Lord Tristan how King Samsizh had led off King Artiush and his knights. And then she said, "Knight, your dearest friend Antsolot tells you: 'If we are not delivered from King Samsizh's dungeon by you, then we must die there.'" At that time Lord Tristan was resting, since the day before he had been fighting with great warriors and had defeated twelve knights and received slight wounds, and because of this he was still confined to bed. When he heard the queen's words, he took his sword from near the head of his bed, but moved so quickly that his wounds bled. Seeing this, Izhota said, "Milady, you are a crowned queen; why did you come to the greatest knight with sad words? You should have come quietly and opened your soft lips with gentle discourse, so that the knight's heart would change to courage." The queen said, "Lady Izhota, how our thoughts are different! You are the most splendid lady in the world, and you have your lord near you, in whom you have your trust; you can make him sound in no more than ten days, but I saw my Artiush and his knights being led off." Lord Tristan looked up angrily at Izhota because of Queen Zhenibra's words.

Izhota, knowing that merriment was dear to Tristan, grasped the queen's hand and began to frolic in a round dance very nimbly and Tristan's heart began to change to courage; he said to Govornar, "Give me my lute." And he began to play marvelously; hearing the lute the hearts of both ladies and Lord Tristan filled with joy. Then Lord Tristan said to Izhota, "Prepare my vessel and put bread and wine in it for me; I pledge to you on my knightly faith: either I will liberate King Artiush and his knights, or I will remain with King Artiush in Samsizh's dungeon." Izhota said, "My lord, you can go when you are well." Said Tristan, "I can heal while traveling the same as lying down, since the wounds that are underneath the armor do not require a healer." Izhota, seeing that she could not restrain him, said, "My lord, your vessel is equipped and ready, and one can outfit it easily with food and wine." Then Tristan stepped into the vessel along with Izhota, Govornar, and Queen Zhenibra; when they pushed away from the shore, the wind rose and the sea swelled; they did not know where they would land. Zhenibra begged Izhota, saying, "My lady, I never learned to travel by sea: ask Lord Tristan to give the command to seek a harbor, so that we can give praise to God, Who will deliver us from death at sea." Tristan, seeing how the sea waves were, took out his lute and began to play, and when he had played awhile, not one lady cared about a haven—it was so pleasurable for them to listen. Then Tristan said to the mariners, "Lead us to harbor so that we can give praise to the Lord God for delivering us from death at sea."

The Affair with the Cruel Princess

The mariners landed near a castle where there was a good harbor, but an evil custom. Here, the inhabitants received Tristan politely and asked him, "Knight, who are those two ladies?" And he said, "They are my sisters." He pointed to Zhenibra and said, "This is my older sister"—and to Izhota—"and this is my younger." They said, "God have mercy on us, but we have not seen such a resemblance among kin anywhere!" Lord Tristan said, "Knights, do not take as evil what I am going to ask of you, for if I knew, I would not ask." They said, "Knight, ask what you want." Said Tristan, "I see you are all handsome persons, but why are you so pale?" They said to him, "Do you not know the local custom? In this castle the ruler is a lady who has not known any man and practices this custom: whoever lands in this harbor cannot show her homage unless he is castrated; but if you are castrated, go and bow low before her." Said Tristan: "I have traveled over sea and by land, but have not seen such an evil custom; it must be hard for you to suffer it; as for us, let it be as God wills. Give me a horse and my armor; I shall go where we came from." They said, "Knight, other knights would have done that too if going back were possible." Then they captured Tristan and threw him into a dungeon. There were twelve knights who had been in this dungeon for seven years, who now agreed, "Let us be castrated! It is better to die outside than here." One of them said, "O, my God, Lord Tristan is among us!" Another knight said, "Why are you glad about the disgrace of the greatest knight and our own death?" The first one said, "I am not glad because of his disgrace, but because of our freedom and his honor, since I know what Lord Tristan is able to do with his sword."

The ruling lady had two brothers: one older than she, the other younger; the younger one, when he wished, could always talk to his sister, but the elder did not dare. The younger brother said, "Princess, let me claim the older sister of that knight for my brother, and the younger for myself." She said to him, "If you talk to me about this any more, I will separate you from your soul." He went out and saw Zhenibra and Izhota standing there very nicely dressed and said from his passionate heart, "If the younger one wants to marry me, I could talk to my sister." He approached them and said to Izhota, "Maiden, if I persuade my sister, will you marry me, and then we could let your brother go free?" Izhota said, "Prince, there is nothing dearer to us than our brother, who is in your dungeon." Izhota, all this time, had been carrying Tristan's sword under her dress. The prince said, "I can let you see your brother, but reply to what I proposed to you." Izhota said, "Yes, ask your sister." At this time, Izhota managed to throw the sword into the dungeon and Tristan took it in his hand and walked to the prison gates, while his fellow knights walked after him out of the dungeon. When the local knights spied them, they rushed toward them in the streets, grabbing lances and helmets, trying to confine them again. One attacker, a very brave man, ran toward Tristan ahead of the rest, trying to chase him back into the dungeon. This knight had his head lopped off far from his body. Lord Tristan began to wield fierce strokes, and when he saw a lance in somebody's hand or a helmet on his head, he killed all of them.

The princess had the custom of not budging from her place for any knight who would bow before her. When she was told about Tristan, she was sprawling on golden cushions like a snake on a mound; but when she saw Lord Tristan at the door of her palace, she leaped up very quickly and met him in the middle of her hall, with water running down her legs, and she knelt before him. Lord Tristan grabbed her by the top of her head, which he cut off and threw far away saying, "Let evil customs not be held on this island any further." Tristan looked around the palace to see if there were any knights, but there were none—only a prince who had not yet been dubbed a knight. When he saw him, he said, "Is this not the princess's brother, who wanted to take Izhota?" He went outside with him and said to Zhenibra and Izhota, "Ladies, does this prince deserve to lose his head?" Izhota said, "My lord, we are not happy about any death; however, this prince was pursuing me." Tristan cut his head off. Zhenibra said, "Milady, why did you say that?" Said Izhota, "Honorable lady, I see now Lord Tristan's nature: if I had not told him the truth, I do not know what might have happened to us."

Then the knights gathered in the great hall and Lord Tristan ordered that all the horses and arms of the princess be brought to him, and he granted a horse and armor to each of those knights that he had met in the dungeon. And then he said, "Knights, for several years you waited to get out in the light; now let each one take what he wants." These knights thanked Lord Tristan very humbly and said to him, "O knight, since you have delivered us from death, we want to go with you and serve you." Tristan said, "Knights, thanks be to you that you honor me, but do not worry about me; go to your homes; but if any of you want to call himself Lord Antsolot's vassal, given by me, Tristan, I would like to make him the lord of this castle and this harbor." One of the knights, called Amodor, said, "My lord, I want to be Lord Antsolot's vassal, given by you, Lord Tristan." Thus Tristan gave him the castle and the harbor as a vassal of his dearest friend. And the knight said, "Dear God, how much Lord Tristan thinks of Antsolot's distinction! God have mercy on him!" Then Tristan launched himself to sea to seek King Samsizh. [*After an adventure in which Tristan kills a lawless crusader who murders guests on his island, he and the two ladies arrive at Black Island, with Tristan dressed as a Latin merchant.*]

The knights of King Samsizh, coming out, approached him hurriedly, since Samsizh had this custom: whenever a ship might come, his knights would take what they wanted, and however high a merchant would appraise what was taken, the king would pay for his knights. Tristan said to the mariners, "Push away from the shore, for I know King Samsizh's custom; if someone took Zhenibra or Izhota from me, the king would have nothing to pay me; I have enough gold and silver." Then Govornar called out, "Here comes a merchant who wants to sell his wares; let there be no violence." The others said, "O merchant, the king and all the knights pledge that if it is not in accordance with your wishes, there will be no violation of your safety." Then Lord Tristan disembarked, pitched his tent, and spread many different wares in front of it.

One knight came up to Tristan, saying, "Good knight, why did you disguise yourself as a Latin?" Said Tristan, "Many people resemble knights: I would be glad to be this knight you mention, but I am a Latin merchant; buy if you need something. I have some to sell to you." The other said, "Knight, I know you; you are the knight who just killed three nephews of King Ban of Banak at the court of King Lenviz in Orlendea; your valor has no equal near or far." Said Tristan, "Nothing belies so much as the human face: if you put on some armor, I might presume that you are a knight, but I see that you are a buffoon who wants a handout from me." The knight was very ashamed and said, "I saw no one so much resembling that good knight as this merchant."

The other knights asked him, "Latin man, what are these ladies to you?" Tristan said, "They are my sisters: one is my elder, the other is younger." They told King Samsizh: "Milord, the merchant who asked for a pledge of safety has with him two maiden sisters: if you crossed the world, you could not find any more wonderful; the younger is as white as paper and as beautiful as a rose. If you want to, you can buy them." King Samsizh went himself to look them over; he came to Tristan's tent and said, "Be well, Sir Latin." Tristan hastened toward him and greeted him. The king's knights marveled at how gracefully the Latin merchant bowed to the king: "Not one of us could have done this." The king entered the tent and found the ladies playing chess with figures of very beautiful crystal.

The king asked, "Sir Latin, what are these ladies to you?" Said Tristan, "They are my sisters." The king said, "Sell me this chess set." He said, "You cannot pay me enough." The king said, "If you want, I will give you an errant knight for every pawn and King Artiush for a king." Tristan said, "Whatever is not for sale, you cannot buy." The king said, "Sell me your younger sister; for her I will give you three times her weight in gold and as much silver as you wish." He said, "Milord, you said to me that if I did not wish to sell anything, there would be no coercion; if I wanted to sell my sister, I could have gotten a higher price in the very first harbor." The king said, "Let us play chess for her and for a third of my kingdom." Tristan said, "You told me that for whatever was against my will, there would be no violation done: I do not know how to play chess; I would put a bishop in the highest place, but where would one put the rest of the figures?" The king said, "He is a true Latin; the bishop is the most important piece with them." And then said the king, "Latin, let us scuffle then for this lady and for half of my kingdom." Tristan said, "You told me that for whatever was against my will, there would be no violence; I do not know how to mount a horse or how to dress in armor." The other said, "Let us fight for her and for the whole of my kingdom: pick out what you wish, and if you do not want anything, I will take her away for nothing." Tristan said, "If the first thing I asked for cannot be won, neither could the last, for I have not seen a bigger fight than when our children began to fight with wooden swords running down the streets; are we going to do the same?" The king said, "Indeed, Sir Latin, only we will fight with iron swords; you did well to bring me this wonderful maiden."

The next morning they brought Tristan armor from the king, saying, "Dress up, Sir Latin." Tristan began to put the left sleeve on the right arm, and the right on the left, and the right greave on the left, and the left on the right and said, "Take this armor to your lord, since it could not fit the Latin." They took the armor back, saying, "Gracious king, he does not know how to dress; our lady is laughing watching him, thus cheering herself, not minding her brother's death." Meanwhile Tristan said to Zhenibra and Izhota, "Prepare the ointments for wounds, since I am going against the greatest knight in the world; and array yourselves with your best garments."

Tristan came out in full armor and on his helmet was a crown of very beautiful flowers; both ladies followed him. King Samsizh was already standing with his knights; when he saw Tristan, he was not happy to fight with him, and when he saw Izhota so beautifully arrayed, he would have taken her without any fight, so beautiful did she seem to him. The king said, "Latin man, why have you picked a fight against me? For my kingdom?" Tristan said, "My king, I did not want this; though I see my death near, I must take on this fight with you. I have traveled much on sea and on land, and if I have to die, I wish more would see my death. I have heard that there are many good people in your dungeon; order them out—let them witness my death." The king said, "What will it help if King Artiush with his knights should see your death? Order them taken out of the dungeon."

When King Artiush exited, his knights and Lord Antsolot began to laugh, except for Palamidezh, the greatest enemy of Tristan. King Artiush said, "Why are you laughing? I am not wondering about the others, but I am surprised at Antsolot, who laughs at the death of the greatest knight and his dearest friend, as well as at our and his own destruction." Palamidezh said, "If we are going to be delivered by Tristan, better for us to die in the dungeon on Black Island." Antsolot said, "I am not laughing at his death, but because our freedom is pleasurable to me—I know this: when Queen Zhenibra and Izhota are here, Tristan will exhibit his mastery."

King Samsizh approached and said to Tristan, "Fight, Sir Latin." Tristan said, "Milord, teach me." The king took his sword out and began to rattle it over Tristan's armor, saying, "This way you pierce, and this way you shield yourself." And then he said, "Latin, do you want to forget this fight and give the maiden to me?" Said Tristan, "My king, as a great lord, you taught me well, but if I am able to protect myself from your sword, may I dare to strike?" Samsizh said, "Cover yourself if you can, but you will not be able to." Said Tristan, "But if I could strike, do I dare?" The king said, "Do strike." Tristan said, "My king, you taught me; now take guard!"

They began to chase each other around the field like lions, attacking like knights who have no equal near or far. Samsizh overpowered Tristan, who protected himself with his sword and his shield, and fell to his knees under Samsizh's mighty strokes; but when Tristan overpowered Samsizh, the other protected himself with his sword and shield and fell to his knees under Tristan's mighty strokes. The knights of King Samsizh said, "Great marvels! Not one knight has been found who could withstand our lord, but this Latin is leaping like a lion." Samsizh sprang over and began to strike as hard as he could on Tristan's armor; if their armor had not held, both would have been dead. Toward the end of the fight, Lord Tristan noticed that Izhota had lost the color in her face; and so Tristan cast his shield away, seized his sword with both hands, and began to deliver ferocious blows without cease, striking King Samsizh on both his hands; the hands dropped to the ground together with his sword. Said Tristan, "My king, collect yourself, lest I make your hands bleed; I do not know how to do more than this." He seized his sword by the tip and took it to Samsizh, saying, "Why did you drop your sword? If it is too heavy, give it to me and have my sword." King Samsizh looked at Tristan in a furious manner. Said Tristan, "Why are you looking at me so angrily? I defeated you cleverly and masterfully; I could not handle you any other way than this." The king said, "Honorable Knight Tristan, I recognized you from your fencing, and I was praying to God not to die a brutal death from your ferocious blows and from your sharp sword. I am telling you on my knightly faith, if someone had told me about you, I would have delivered King Artiush and his knights to you, for I see now that death has come to me because of them."

King Artiush with his knights saw this and came to Tristan, filled with joy; they began to greet Tristan very affectionately; they gave praise to God and thanked Lord Tristan: "Most exalted knight, praised be you by all knights, for you delivered us from Samsizh's dungeon." And everyone said, "God bless Tristan, for he labored so much for King Artiush and his knights by his own good will." Lord Tristan ordered that amusements be brought with which Samsizh entertained himself: trumpets, pipes, lutes, harps, organs, chess and checkers—everything very marvelously decorated in lordly fashion, and they began to make merry. When Tristan himself took a lute and began to play very melodiously, the hearts of King Artiush and his knights filled with joy; none of the knights could have enough of listening. Then Izhota grabbed Queen Zhenibra and presented her to King Artiush: "Milord, Tristan presents you with this lady: if ever some distress has happened between you, let it be honorably corrected." She also presented each knight with a horse and armor and said to these knights, "Whatever one's hand grasps will not be refused him." To Antsolot Izhota said, "Knight, Tristan offers you whatever he acquired from the possessions of the treacherous crusader, and also presents to you knight Amodor with the castle of that princess who established the base custom in her harbor." King Artiush gave praise to God and thanked Tristan, saying, "O most exalted knight Tristan, let your great chivalry be praised by all people in all four corners of the world! Your valor has no equal on earth, near or far!"

Palamedes and Lancelot in the Lair of Smerdodug

[*Tristan and his party are trapped in the castle of Smerdodug the infidel.*] Smerdodug's knights rushed into the palace and captured Tristan, asking: "By what death should we destroy him?" Smerdodug the infidel said, "Take him and decapitate him." That same day the brave knight Palamidezh Anuplitich with two swords and a black shield—the greatest foe of Tristan—came from the court of King Artiush. He said, "It is not right to cut off the head of such a valorous knight without a fight: defeat him in a combat in a knightly manner. I have seen one knight cutting the head off another, but in a courtly manner; I never have seen it done as you intend." They responded to him, "We have seen that one thief defends another thief."

Palamidezh, seeing that both of them were defamed, leaped forth and handed a sword to Tristan; the other was left for himself. Tristan charged like a wild one and began to slash mightily right and left: whomever he saw with a lance in hand and helmet on his head he smashed. He went to the palace to kill the infidel, and saw him running very fast. Tristan caught up with him, but the infidel darted into his church, where it was not proper for a knight to enter with a sword. Tristan said, "Come outside, traitor, and defend yourself in a fight." The other said, "Know for sure that as long as you are there, I will not come out of here."

Tristan went away from that church, since he knew the rule that it was not proper for him to remain there with a bare sword. He went to Smerdodug's palace and gave thanks to Lord God for deliverance from a violent death. He said to Palamidezh, "Knight, praised be you by knights and ladies that you did not let me perish." Palamidezh said to Tristan, "Knight, for all the service that I rendered you, give me one thing which I will ask of you." Tristan said, "Whatever you ask, I will give you, except Izhota." Palamidezh said, "Be my greatest enemy, as you were before." Tristan said, "Let us leave this, knight; you have done me a great honor, and I also want to think of your honor." Palamidezh said, "I do not want anything else but this." When Tristan saw that he must fight with Palamidezh, he said, "Knight, if I have to fight, I prefer my sword rather than this sword." They brought Lord Tristan his sword and the two knights put on their armor.

They charged at each other very bravely and began to chase each other like two lions. They were striking so hard that if their armor had not withstood it, both would have died. Palamidezh was overpowering Tristan, who protected himself with his sword and his shield, retreating under Palamidezh's strikes; then Tristan cast off his shield and took his sword in both hands and began to strike without protecting himself. Palamidezh waved his sword and his shield, falling on both knees, expecting death from Tristan's mighty strokes. The knights of that town said, "This man defeated many knights, and now he is conquering the handsome Palamidezh." Tristan struck Palamidezh over his helmet, split the helmet, and gave him a deep head wound. Tristan said, "Knight, if you defeat me, other knights will not praise you, for you saw the fight I had with them; let us abandon this fight and set ourselves a term; wherever either of us might be, let him present himself at that time by the church where the knights gather." They set the term of fifteen days. Tristan did so because his sharp sword longed to cause Palamidezh's violent death. They then parted from each other.

Palamidezh went to King Artiush's court and recounted this adventure, saying, "O, knights of good King Artiush, remember Tristan's valor, how he bestowed honor on many knights, but now he cannot do any good for himself." King Artiush and his knights said, "Why so?" He said, "Smerdodug the infidel tricked him, lured him treacherously into his town and chained him; I fought with the infidel for him and was wounded in the head; because of this I could not fight any more. We have set a term of fifteen days to meet by that church—he named it; if I am able, I will fight for him, but if my wound does not heal by that time, then you should vindicate him." King Artiush and his knights were very saddened. Antsolot said, "How could this disgrace happen to my friend?" But then he became jovial with the king: "Smerdodug will come out and he shall exhibit little of his mastery with me."

When the term arrived, Lord Tristan came to that church, and with him Izhota and Govornar. Over the door was a sign with these words: "There is going to be a fight between a lion and a dragon this day." Tristan said, "If I am a lion, Palamidezh is no dragon, and if I am a dragon, then Palamidezh is not a lion; I might be one of these, but Palamidezh will not be either." Then Lord Antsolot came in armor and thought it was Smerdodug the infidel waiting for him. And Tristan was of the belief that Palamidezh had come there. Antsolot charged swiftly and boldly, and Tristan was waiting for him fearlessly and skillfully.

When they struck, their lances splintered and they smashed together shoulder to shoulder and shield to shield; and the horses fell under both of them. Tristan fell off his horse, drew his sword, and said, "No one is superior with his lance on horseback, and no one with a sword on the ground." They leaped and began to chase each other like two lions, pouncing on each other like men who have no equal near or far. Antsolot was overpowering Tristan, who was covering himself with his shield and his sword, retreating under Antsolot's strokes; but when Lord Tristan began to smash very fiercely, Antsolot was covering himself with his sword and his shield, falling on his knees under Tristan's mighty blows. Tristan's Govornar said, "What a marvel! Not one knight up to now has been found among the great knights of the court of King Artiush or from the Banak clan of King Ban who could thus withstand my lord Tristan—only his dearest friend Antsolot." And Antsolot's mentor said, "I have traveled much over sea and land, but never have I seen any knight of King Artiush or from other far lands who could stand with his sword against my lord Antsolot—only Lord Tristan." Izhota, having heard these words, said: "O good knights, disarm yourselves, lest you become sorry about this." They took their helmets off and recognized each other, and began to embrace very tenderly; one was asking another what adventures had befallen him since they parted. Tristan was bragging and said, "As many as there were who were valorous knights, seeking their equals while traveling, from the clan of King Ban of Banak and from the French King Peremont, no one has been able to withstand me." Antsolot said, "Of all who honor our lord King Artiush, I am the crown."

Thereafter said Antsolot, "Knight, put your helmet on your head and let us strike; we are only wounded now; if one cannot be superior to another in any fight, better let one be killed by the other." Tristan said, "God have mercy on you, knight, who wants to fight! There is no knight in the world with whom I would rather have a fight than with you, for if you defeat me, I will be conquered by the greatest knight and my dearest friend, but if I defeat you, then I will be conquering the crown of all knights, the greatest knight and my dearest friend. But, knight, I wish I did not know you—I would then fight with you more gladly than I do knowing you." Izhota said, "Stay well, knights; you can be in good health in fifteen days, but leave this fight in peace." After Izhota reproached them, they departed, their wounds burning under their armor.

On the way they met with a man-at-arms with black insignia with followers, who were carrying a dead knight on a cart; the man-at-arms said to Lord Tristan, "Knight, my lord Palamidezh agreed with you on his knightly word: in whatever state, wherever one might be, one ought to be present at that church at the given time. He would have preferred to be alive, but let him, even dead, uphold his word." Tristan said, "Because of this agreement, my dearest friend and I were almost killed by each other."

King Peremont's Tourney in France

Lord Tristan and Antsolot then met a maiden who was carrying a letter to Lord Tristan; she gave the letter to Tristan and he, having read it, laughed out loud. Antsolot said, "Why are you laughing?" He answered, "Because the maiden is announcing: 'For seven years a tournament has been called for at the court of the French King Peremont; whoever wants to make his sister or his daughter a queen should come without delay'; and we cannot go there, since we are badly wounded." Antsolot said, "Knight, we could still go there to see what country's knight will win the tournament, to be able later to take a lance against that man." They came then to a village that was full of knights and maidens, and not one knight would offer them lodging. They left the village and saw ahead of them some good dwellings, but they were rundown; in front of them stood a maiden with a very small retinue. Tristan said, "Maiden, is there any way to stay with you?" She said, "There might be." She seized Tristan with one hand and Antsolot with the other and led them into a palace that was wonderfully decorated; then she went to another palace, and this one was decorated also in a lordly manner. Said the maiden. "Good knights, this is the lodging for you, and the other for your horses." Tristan said, "As good as our lodging is, so is the one for our horses." She brought them two birds to eat and some wine and bread; and their horses were also given something to eat. She said to them, "Knights, feast, for you have to think about me and about yourselves." She was soon urging them to make her a queen.

Thereafter Lord Tristan said, "Maiden, do not regard as odd what I will ask you." She said, "Knight, such is the custom here that there is no surprise in what a knight might ask." Tristan said, "This is a good custom; pray tell me, what are these birds?" She said, "These are two sparrow hawks. I am the daughter of a king who fought against King Peremont, who defeated him, took his land and chased all his servants away, leaving him only me and these hawks. I have fed my father as best I could; what I would kill for lunch was also for supper, and what was for supper would be for breakfast too." Lord Tristan said, "Maiden, you took a heavy toll in killing for our sake what was supposed to nourish your father." She said, "Knights, I am not sorry that I killed two hawks for two falcons; I see you as valorous individuals and marvelous persons. Knights, you should think about me and about yourselves."

The next morning they rode off, not talking to each other. Antsolot said, "Knight, what are you thinking about, since you are not talking to me?" Tristan said, "And what are you thinking about?" He said to Tristan, "No, you are older; it is proper for me to ask you." Tristan said, "I am thinking of how we could install this maiden as a queen." Antsolot said, "O good Tristan, God reward you, for you are thinking of this maiden's honor because of her courtesy! We both have the same thought." They returned to the maiden and Lord Tristan said, "Maiden, get ready and array yourself as best you can; God willing, you might be queen today." She said, "Knight, so help me God, I have no better vestments, only what is on me and a crown of marvelous cypress flowers brought from King Artiush's court." She took the crown and put it on her head, and they said, "This crown suits you well."

Thereafter they rode off with the maiden to the tournament, overtaking a knight riding in full armor and following him a maiden dressed in very rich clothes, riding in a carriage. Tristan asked the servants who they were. They said: "This is Knight Amodor, a servant of Lord Antsolot, given by the glorious Knight Tristan." Tristan said to him, "Tristan and Antsolot happen to be right here." When Amodor heard this, he jumped off his horse, took the helmet off his head, kneeled before them, and said, "My lords, where are you going?" Tristan said, "We are going to the tournament of your lord, King Peremont, so that we may install our sister as queen." He said to them, "By God, turn back so that I can install my sister as queen; I know you do not have a sister." Tristan said, "Knight, if you cannot make us turn back with a lance, you cannot stop us with a request." Amodor said, "I know what Lord Tristan can accomplish with just a sword on the ground, let alone with a pole on horseback; I must turn back." Tristan said, "Amodor, it would be pleasing to us if you would come with us, but if you are turning back, our maiden has no good clothes; lend us your maiden's garments." Amodor said, "My lord, take whatever you need." Lord Tristan took the clothes in which Amodor's sister was planning to become a queen and said to his maiden, "Dress yourself in these." When they saw her in these garments, they liked her so much that if she had been their sister, they would not have been shamed by her. Antsolot said to Tristan, "Knight, give me a boon that I will ask of you." Tristan said, "You are free to take anything except the fair Izhota." Antsolot said, "Be my master today, and I will be your man-at-arms." Tristan said, "No, knight, you are an older and greater knight than I— you be my lord, and I will be your man-at-arms." Antsolot said, "This cannot be."

The French tournament obeyed these rules: whichever knight came late had to seat his maiden in a lower place. When they came to the tournament gate, where the turnstile was closed, the knights were already competing. Antsolot jumped over the turnstile and opened it, and Tristan with the maiden rode in. The ladies were sitting in two rows from the arena's gate up to the judges; Tristan sat his maiden in the highest place. When the son of King Peremont saw Tristan, he said, "I wish that this knight's maiden would become queen." When the king's daughter saw this maiden, she did not wish for her knight to win the tournament. Having marveled, they said, "This knight is willful; he came to the tournament late but sat his maiden higher than all the rest." Tristan said to his maiden, "Hand me your crown." She rose, took off her crown, and with her white hands put it on his bright helmet, saying, "Good knight, carry it honorably through the tournament, and having defended it, return it to me." The other maidens were laughing at her, saying, "O foolish maiden, how could he return this marvelous crown without winning! When he mounts his horse, our knights will mix his fair face and his bright helmet with the dust." In other words, he was better liked by the maidens than by other knights.

Divdan [Dinadan] heard this, who was more pleasing to the maidens than to the other knights, and he wanted to meet with Tristan. Lord Tristan mounted his horse, which Antsolot was holding by the stirrups. Divdan said, "Knight, beware of my stroke!" Tristan said, "When you wish, let us have it."

When they struck, Divdan fell to one side and his horse to the other. The maidens were watching what was transpiring between them, but they could not discern that Tristan's feet moved in the stirrups, let alone that he moved in his saddle. Antsolot grabbed Divdan and threw him outside the arena and said, "I am telling every knight: my lord is riding freely through the tournament!" The heart of their maiden, who saw this, was filled with joy, and she began to look confidently among the other maidens. The knights of the tournament, seeing that Tristan was riding bravely, were afraid of him, and he executed fierce blows right and left; whatever knight he came across, he put behind his horse, and Antsolot, grabbing them, would throw them across the arena, saying in a loud voice, "Knights, my lord is riding freely through the tournament!" The judge said, "The knight with the valorous man-at-arms is winning the tournament."

There was a king of many years who said, "The knight who now rides freely through the tournament is winning." At this time Iashchor Made-rym, son of Domolot, was riding freely through the tournament. Tristan's maiden said, "Where there is might, there is reason." The judges said, "The knight with the good man-at-arms is winning; it is no wonder that the knight is performing chivalrous deeds, but it is wonderful that his man-at-arms is displaying great chivalry, throwing the armed knights across the arena." But the king said to himself that Iashchor, who was then riding freely through the tournament, was winning. Tristan's maiden said, "O my God, we have a fine custom in our country! Good people will not allow a buffoon to talk with them, but will give him a pipe to let him amuse them." When Lord Tristan saw what the judges were talking about, and heard his maiden's bold speech, he said "Knight, you who are riding freely through the tournament, on guard!" Iashchor said, "Let us see!"

When they clashed, Iashchor fell to one side, and his horse to the other side. Tristan said, "O brother of my dearest friend, I did not wish it to happen to you, but you are not defeated by any lesser knight—only by Tristan and Lord Antsolot." Iashchor jumped on his horse, joined them, and the three knights, Tristan, Antsolot, and Iashchor, rode across the tournament, while another adversary was not to be found. Whatever knight saw these three, he would cast the lance from his hands and the helmet from his head, not wanting to compete with them.

Tristan said, "We, Tristan and Antsolot, pledge on our knightly word not to dismount until one horse falls—lest some knight is coming from afar and has not arrived; I will await him." Antsolot saw a gardener, who was carrying some herbs, and said, "Knight, here comes a knight in a chivalrous manner; his horse's hooves clatter, and your horse is tired." He then turned around so quickly that his horse fell; Antsolot did this so that Tristan's word might be kept.

Said Tristan to his maiden, "O fair maiden, the ladies were laughing at us, but now you are the queen over all of them; you are free to send anyone wherever you wish." Here Lord Tristan called out for everyone at the tournament to hear: "Maiden, take a hawk on your arm, approach and sit on the gilded throne." And she sat and became the crowned queen. King Pere-mont, who had taken his estate from the father of this maiden, thus returned everything to him down to the last item, and took this maiden to wed his son.

Last Encounters

Having performed this act of chivalry, the two knights, Lord Tristan and Lord Antsolot, rode off to the virgin woods and came to a very big and rich town which was inhabited by three brothers, great knights who in times past were the strongest knights in the world: their names were

Librun, Igrun, and Marko; two of them had died, but Librun was alive and had control of this town of Kesaryia, which was very ancient. This knight Librun, because of his advanced age, forty years ago had dismissed his horse and hung up his armor and his lance, so that it had become covered with moss. He had a very beautiful wife whose name was Tsvytazhia.

Tristan and Antsolot halted before the town and sent for this lady, saying, "Come out of the castle; one of us will make love with you." The lady, very distressed about this, came to Librun and said, "Sadness and disgrace await us: two knights have come and are standing at the gates; they sent for me, saying, 'Come out of the town; one of us will make love with you.'" Knight Librun sent word to them, saying, "Knights, go with God." But they would not restrain themselves and sent again for the lady, ordering, "Come out of the castle." Librun sent word to them again, saying, "Knights, go with God." They again sent for the lady. Knight Librun said, "Give me my armor, my lance, and my horse." When he took his lance, it was covered with moss, so that they had to wrap it with hand-towels. He armed himself, mounted his horse, and came at them in the meadow, saying, "Thrust, knights!" They discussed among themselves who wanted to go first, and Antsolot desired this. Said Librun, "On my pledge, I do not want to fight one, but both of you together, since I am the first knight among knights."

They both charged at him and struck him equally, so that their lances broke into many pieces. Librun grabbed them from their horses, one with one hand, the other with the other hand, and sent them in opposite directions athwart his horse in front of him and patted each one on the jaw with his hand and said, "Go with God; you are both good knights." They left on the one hand very saddened, and on the other hand, laughing.

They then rode through a leafy forest and met a knight who was riding very magnificently. They said to him, "Knight, do not leave without fighting with us." He said, "I do not know how to fight." They said, "We will take away your horse then." He said, "I really do not know how." When they took away his horse and arms, he said, "If it cannot be otherwise, give me my horse and I shall fight."

Antsolot rode against the knight, and he defeated Antsolot. Tristan, feeling very sorry, charged against the knight promptly. When they struck together the straps on Tristan's saddle broke and he fell to the ground; while falling, he snatched his sword from the sheath and jumped on his feet as if immovable. The knight recognized Tristan and angrily shouted. "I am Galets Antsolotovich" [Galahad, son of Lancelot]. Tristan and Antsolot were very joyous about this, but Galets was very sorry that he had defeated his father and Tristan. With great sorrow, he soon took the monastic vow, and later there was no news to be heard whether he was alive or dead.

Tristan and Antsolot rode on to King Artiush's court, and when they arrived, the king received them with great joy. Thereafter Lord Tristan took leave of King Artiush with many gifts. All the lords and people sent him off with greetings and courtesy.

Tristan and Izhota returned to Kornovalia to King Marko. When they arrived, Tristan presented Izhota to Marko and said, "King, you should thank me for her, for I conquered her for you with my sword for a second time." King Marko thanked him, saying, "My dear nephew Tristan, you did much good; I am yours and all that I have is yours to do with as you wish." Tristan knelt and thanked King Marko very humbly. Thus, the whole of Kornovalia was together, and there was no one, old or young, who did not rejoice. They were as happy as if God Himself had come to them, even more joyful than when Tristan first brought Izhota from Orlendea. When Izhota found out Braginia's loyalty and truthfulness, she bestowed on her kindnesses even greater than before. The king was very joyful, as well as all his court; he gave the keys of his kingdom to Tristan and said, "Nephew, you are free to govern my kingdom since you have upheld loyalty and truthfulness." Tristan was honored here by King Marko and by all good people as if he were the king himself. Kornovalia came to be feared by all lands and all kingdoms because of Lord Tristan.

The End of the Story

At a later time, it was heard that a tournament was being assembled in the Pozaransk Land by the town of Barokh, called by a maiden named Izhota of the White Hands, daughter of a king; so Lord Tristan departed there. When he came to the tournament, there were many knights from many lands; one of whom took one side of the tournament and Lord Tristan the other. Then Tristan shouted to the knight with the insignia of a lion that had canine teeth: "Come and meet me."

They struck so ferociously that Klimberko broke his lance into many pieces. Tristan hit him with all the might he had in him. Klimberko fell off the horse to the ground and Tristan charged at him. Klimberko cried out, "Knight, you have won this fight." Tristan remounted his horse and rode through the tournament performing great marvels right and left; no one dared to face him openly, for he defeated fifteen dubbed knights and eighteen vassals. Tristan called out, "If someone is still willing, let him get ready to fight." One knight named Erdin [Caerdin], the brother of Izhota of the White Hands, who was very valorous, responded by calling out, "Knight, wait for me!" Tristan awaited him.

When they clashed, they broke their lances and rammed with their shields and shoulders, and fell down with their horses, but rose up and began lashing like two lions. Tristan was very skillful and though his wounds opened from the many blows, he did not care about it, and to the end struck Erdin with all his might, until Erdin fell dead.

Having accomplished this knightly deed, Lord Tristan went to the church abbey. At that time a letter from the fair Izhota came to him, saying, "My lord, just as a fish cannot live without water, I cannot live without you." From great sadness and from his wounds, Tristan fainted; it was altogether wondrous how he could endure such wounds, for he was bleeding very much. So he sent this note to King Marko: "My lord uncle, I cannot ride or endure to be driven; since I have served you well and you might have need of me, send me Queen Izhota to heal me, for she knows a good cure. I am lying in the Pozaransk Land at the Barokh Town."

King Marko graciously let Izhota go, and she left with a very joyful heart. After arriving, she began healing him as best she could. I do not know whether he recovered from those wounds or died. This is all that is written about him.

chapter VI
ITALIAN

CANTARE ON THE DEATH
OF TRISTAN

James J. Wilhelm

Although Italy has not bequeathed us the wealth of Arthurian literature that one can find in France and Germany, it has left us several jewels, such as the lengthy fourteenth-century *La Tavola Ritonda* (The Round Table), an elaborate retelling of the Tristan and Isolde love story in prose. Also, from about 1250 to 1500, there flourished a popular form of art known as the *cantare* or folk-ballad. These were narrative poems sung in the city squares about Arthurian and other themes. The compositions, whose music has not survived, were divided into 8-line stanzas (*ottava rima*) and were frequently rhymed *abababcc*.

Tristan was always one of the most popular heroes in this tradition. His love affair with Isolde, especially their tragic ending, held a grasp on Italian audiences that Arthur himself could not equal. This version of their death probably derives from Thomas of Britain's *Tristan* (see *Romance of Arthur II*, pp. 203–12) and the lengthy French *Prose Tristan*, the predecessor also to the Byelorussian version of Chapter V.

Although most folk-ballads are rather primitive in their diction and handling of plot and character, this one, despite some lapses in geographic and temporal continuity, conveys the tragic ending of the lovers in a way that is far more moving than most other versions. But it lacks two features that we otherwise associate with the love-death or *Liebestod*, as Richard Wagner called it: Tristan mistakes the color of the sails bringing Isolde to cure him (usually through the lies of his wife, Isolde of the White Hands), and two plants spring up over the double graves (usually a rose or hazel tree and a honeysuckle vine).

Like most *cantari*, this one exists in multiple versions. I have selected the more archaic one, which was printed by Giulio Bertoni in his edition of the *Cantari di Tristano* (Modenese, 1937). Very often this is joined with another *cantare* called *Le Ultime Imprese di Tristano* (The Last Deeds of Tristan), which is referred to below in stanza 2. I have omitted this earlier tale because it is not directly fused to the death scene and lacks the dramatic power of the ending.

Although Bertoni's version is archaic in its diction, I have not tried to duplicate this in my translation; nor have I attempted to follow the standard rhyme scheme. The names of the major characters in the original Italian are: Tristano, Isotta-Ixolta, Marco-Marcho, Arturo-Artuxe (from French Artus), Lancilotto-Lanziloto, and Zenevra-Ginevra.

Bibliographic note: Besides Bertoni, one should consult the modernized and normalized version of this *cantare* by Armando Balduino, *Cantari del Trecento* (Marzorati, 1970). See the articles on "Italian Arthurian Literature" by Christopher Kleinhenz and "Cantari" by Susan J. Noakes in the *Arthurian Encyclopedia*, edited by Norris J. Lacy et al. (Garland, 1986).

Cantare on the Death of Tristan

---

1. At the time when flower and fruit flourish
   And every lover makes a beautiful expression
   Of fervent love for his chosen lady
   And desires with charming and gracious ploys
   To achieve the object of his will,
   I have come here to relate to you
   How Tristan through his beautiful love affair
   Underwent death with great remorse.

2. As you know from another *cantare*,
   Tristan had left the company of good Astor [Estor,
      Hector de Maris]
   And he wanted to travel all by himself
   Until he arrived at the shore of England.
   Then he found Sagramor, without a doubt,
   And they left for Castle Dinas in their own land
   And were received there with hospitality;
   At this point Tristan felt the need for repose.

3. When he and Sagramor had finally arrived
   At the fort of Dinas in Cornwall,
   And when Tristan had sufficiently relaxed,
   He was gripped again by love in a feverish way,
   Since he had languished alone for a long, long time
   Without his Isolde—may Christ lend me aid!—
   And he could not suffer the longing any further.
   He sent the queen a note, desiring to speak with her.

4. As soon as Queen Isolde realized
   That Tristan was in this sorry state,
   She sent him back a message that said clearly
   That he should come to see her without delay.
   Tristan immediately took himself to the road
   And traveled without a pause to the waiting queen,
   But in such a way that nobody heard or knew
   A thing about it—only his fair-faced love.

5. It was nighttime when he arrived there,
   And Sir Tristan stole immediately to the queen.
   He propped his lance up outside her chamber—
   Showing very little good sense in doing this.
   As soon as Queen Isolde saw him again,
   Overwhelmed with joy, she clasped him tightly,
   Since she had not seen him for a long, long time,
   Although the current hour was hardly propitious.

6. When Sir Tristan came to this rendezvous,
   He was not wearing any protective armor
   Except for a bright sword and the discarded lance,
   Which had been given to him by Morgan the Fay—
   A lance that could kill anyone without a doubt
   Because it had been charmed with an enchantment.
   And so as Tristan went to meet the queen,
   He carried along the tool that would cost his life.

7. Innumerable were the joys and the delights
   That Tristan felt at the side of the noble queen,
   As they constantly held each other in their arms
   All that first night through until the morning.
   No third person offered them any hindrance.
   They basked for eight whole days in this blessed joy
   Without King Mark's hearing or knowing that
   Sir Tristan was dallying with his lovely wife.

8. Finally there came a day when noble Tristan
   Was amusing himself along with Isolde the queen:
   He was strumming a harp, but very softly,
   While she was dancing to the musical sounds.
   Outside her room there passed one of her cousins
   Who heard this music and attached himself to the door;
   Peering through the keyhole, he saw Sir Tristan
   And then dashed off to King Mark and said these words:

9. "O noble sire, you simply have to know
   That Tristan is in Milady Isolde's boudoir,
   And they are pleasuring each other in love,
   Without showing any respect for your majesty."
   The king, on hearing this, changed his color,

Feeling the sudden terrible weight of sorrow
And saying: "My God! My life—how grim!
Now I see clearly that he doesn't respect me!"

10. From that point on, King Mark enjoyed no rest;
    He strode to the boudoir that held Sir Tristan
    And grabbed the lance and stuck it through a window
    With frenzy, dealing his nephew a deadly blow.
    Tristan felt the stroke upon his right side,
    Which made him wobble and then—fall down.
    When the king saw that he had pierced his nephew,
    Without a pause, he quickly ran away.

11. When Tristan knew that he was badly wounded,
    He said at once to the loving queen:
    "Dear lady, I've been dealt a very bad hand;
    I'm afraid that very soon I'll have to leave you."
    The queen did not have a courageous enough heart
    To doctor him, since she saw that he was failing,
    And so he decided to leave her at once.
    And off he went to neighboring castle Dinas.

12. When he arrived at Dinas, he threw
    Himself on a bed and began at once to cry:
    "O cursed and unfortunate, unhappy me!
    I'm truly dead; I can no longer live.
    King Mark has wounded me so severely
    That no one except God can help me now!"
    Sirs Dinas [Dinadan] and Sagramor, full of grief,
    Poured out tears from their eyes and their hearts.

13. Dinas and Sagramor then had called
    Many fine doctors to the bed of Tristan,
    But the wound began to fester and show pus,
    And nobody could make a promise to heal it.
    Then it began to smell so putridly
    That everyone abandoned Tristan indeed,
    Except for his friends Dinas and Sagramor,
    Who never left his side—I'm telling the truth.

14. When King Mark received the report
    That Tristan was lying on the verge of death,
    He went to his queen and said these words:
    "From now on, I'll be safe in my own court,
    And won't have to bear any more evil gossip!"
    He chided her always with very probing words:
    "Queen, now separate yourself from Tristan,
    Who has held your love too long in his hands."

15. The queen did not deign to reply to this talk
But kept on weeping welling tears.
King Mark did not commiserate with her,
But kept on rebuking her continually.
The queen, who truly wanted to die herself,
Said, "King Mark, if dear Tristan should perish,
Those subjects who now honor you with love
Will show you dishonor once he is dead."

16. And then the queen kept weeping on,
Revealing to Mark her profound sorrow.
Finally the king began to feel remorse
For what he'd done, and from the heart
He confessed: "Our royal majesty now
Has lowered itself, Isolde, in value.
Tristan may die—I can do nothing more!"
And then he began to cry along with her.

17. Tristan, who kept failing and clearly saw
That he could never escape from this woe,
Said to Sir Dinas: "O my brave companion,
Go at once to Mark, my royal lord,
And tell him to come and see this poor sick soul,
Since every sense I own is weakening;
Before I make my exit from this life,
He should come, by God, to witness my end!"

18. Those grieving friends, Sagramor and Dinas,
Traveled together to see King Mark
And told him that he should visit poor Tristan.
King Mark came, along with many courtiers,
Arriving at the castle with funeral pace.
All of the people then reproached the monarch,
Shouting: "If Tristan dies, everyone here
Will offer indignities against your crown!"

19. The king, after dismounting in the stable,
Rushed up to the chamber where Tristan lay
And there he issued a sorrowful sigh
And began to beat his body with his hands;
And then he began to pray to Christ
That He would make his nephew whole again.
When the king saw Tristan, he greeted him,
And Tristan at once returned the salutation.

20. When Tristan saw that Mark had arrived,
He tried to lift himself up from his bed,
But he lacked the strength and the power,
And could do nothing but fall back.
With lowered voice, he began to say:

"Mighty King Mark, please feel welcomed!
My death, which you have coveted so long,
Has finally been dealt me as you planned!"

21. King Mark was weeping then with all abandon
And said: "O my son, please pardon me!
I have given you an egregious offense
That will always be a cause for misery!"
As soon as he let loose these words,
Tears sprang forth out of his eyes
So fervently that everyone around him
Also wept bitterly for Sir Tristan too.

22. Sir Tristan said to Mark: "Please don't cry.
Indeed I beg you: please pardon me.
And furthermore, I beg, if you can will it,
That you should offer me one last great gift:
Please send to me your queen, Isolde,
Whom you hold as your own beloved spouse,
So that she may see me before my life is over."
Said the king: "I shall see it's done."

23. Then the king had summoned Isolde the queen,
Telling her to come and see her Tristan.
Isolde, whose weeping now was without pause,
Did exactly what the messenger asked.
And on the way she said: "Alas, poor me!
If God only willed that I could die with you!
If I died now, my sorrow would be single,
But if I live, I'll live in constant grief."

24. When Isolde arrived at Castle Dinas,
She was crying so passionately
In the midst of all the women-servants
That they began crying with her too.
Queen Isolde, bent over with grief,
Went weeping as she made her way
Until she found Tristan, who was suffering
From a pain now approaching the final end.

25. When Tristan saw his lover coming toward him,
He said: "My queen, bright star of the sky,
My lady, I soon shall have to part from you.
There is little life left for me in this world."
Hearing these words, the queen then threw
Herself with abandon upon his chest,
So that Tristan, in the midst of his pain,
Now lost even more strength and force.

26. Noble Tristan was veering on death's edge
    In the arms of his beloved Lady Isolde,
    While King Mark, with his great royal power,
    Was not uttering a word all this time.
    During the rest of that day, Tristan was silent,
    But at last he issued a cry that startled all
    As he said: "I'm going now to my death!
    Prepare for me my shield and also my sword."

27. With great lamentation, the sword was brought
    Along with the shield, and everyone wept;
    Milord Tristan took his sword in hand
    And with tearful words entrusted it
    To the others: "O sword, how I have loved you!
    For a very long time I showed you my love!
    But now I'm dying and you'll stay here;
    You'll never strike anyone again in my name!"

28. Then the shield was laid upon his breast
    As he was fast losing his last breath:
    "O shield of mine, I want to thank you,
    For you have spared me plenty of pain and death!
    Now I have no more power even to hold you,
    For my every vein is drained of strength."
    Then he lowered his helmet onto his head,
    Causing the viewers to vent more grief.

29. Then he said to Sagramor: "My dear friend,
    When I have passed beyond this age,
    Please go to Camelot with your sad tale
    Before the court of Arthur the King
    And give my long-proved, trusted weapons
    To him, and have it bruited all around
    About my death to all his barons—
    And especially tell Milord Lancelot."

30. The queen then began to utter some words,
    Saying: "Tristan, heart of my life,
    If you die now, whatever shall I do?
    I want to beg you, for the love of God,
    Not to abandon me here behind you,
    Since my heart will always suffer grief
    And pain and deep-felt sorrow
    If I have to live without my beloved lord."

31. Sir Tristan answered this way to the queen:
    "Milady, I am truly dying now!"
    Isolde, who had never stopped her weeping,
    Hurled herself directly on his form
    As Milord Tristan was dipping now toward death,

Clutching lovely Isolde to him fiercely
So that the hearts of both truly burst apart,
And thus, in a last embrace, they perished in love.

32. King Mark, who was witnessing all this—
How his queen and nephew Tristan had expired—
Said mournfully to his surrounding men:
"This bitter act has cost me much too much!"
All of them then voiced a loud lament
With heartfelt wailing and copious tears.
It seemed as if the air and earth were issuing
Floods of sorrow for this loving pair.

33. The grief and torment felt for poor Isolde
And charming Tristan grew and grew
Until both were finally laid to rest
With noble honors in a single monument,
With an inscription engraved in silver and gold
That could be read by any viewer:
HERE LIE ISOLDE AND POOR TRISTAN
WHO THROUGH LOVE TOGETHER PASSED AWAY.

34. After Tristan and Isolde were interred,
Dinas and Sagramor, abounding with grief
And both stricken to the heart with sorrow,
Carried the sword of Tristan and his helmet
Polished bright, along with his precious shield,
And crossed the sea when the weather was fine,
Arriving at Castle Camelot in Britain,
Where King Arthur lived with all his court.

35. Here there were wailings and woeful tears
When the people heard about Tristan's death;
Everyone was denuded of every joy
As good King Arthur led the lamentations.
Seeing his people in such misery,
The king began to rend his royal vestments;
And above all others, those who wept
The most were Guinevere and Lancelot.

36. Many there were who swore that they
Would wreak a vengeance upon King Mark.
Queen Guinevere said with bitter grief:
"Lovely Isolde, you've left me alone!"
And Lancelot said, "Our dearest lord,
Sir Tristan, unless Death rushes on me,
I'll show King Mark a very grievous end."
Milords, this *cantare* ends in your honor!

[*Another cantare tells how Lancelot avenged Tristan's death by killing Mark.*]

chapter *VII*
MIDDLE HIGH GERMAN

DER STRICKER:
DANIEL OF THE
BLOSSOMING VALLEY

Michael Resler

The earliest Arthurian romance composed in the literary language of Germany during the high Middle Ages was Hartmann von Aue's *Erec* (ca. 1185). A free adaptation of Chrétien de Troyes' *Erec et Enide*, Hartmann's tale found much resonance with a German audience eager to hear such tales of knightly adventure. Hartmann, in reworking an already existent story, set the tone for future Arthurian poets in Germany, who for some time were to rely on French models for the basic outlines of their own works as the stories of King Arthur and the knights of the Round Table enjoyed considerable popularity.

While the German poets generally allowed themselves broad latitude in refashioning and recasting the stories which came to them from France, it was not until the second or third decade of the thirteenth century that a German poet, der Stricker, made a clean break with the by then well-established convention of working from a French source. With his *Daniel of the Blossoming Valley (Daniel von dem blühenden Tal)*, der Stricker produced the first freely invented Arthurian romance in the German tradition. Although der Stricker makes specific reference in his prologue to Alberich of Besançon, who, he claims, has brought to his attention this story written in French, scholars have long doubted the veracity of that claim. For one thing, there is no evidence that Alberich, who is known chiefly for his romance *Alexander*, ever composed a *Daniel*. Moreover, der Stricker appears to have lifted the passage in which he refers to Alberich almost verbatim from the German *Alexanderlied* of Pfaffe Lamprecht. One explanation for this lies in the fact that, by this point in the development of the courtly romance in Germany, the appeal to a source had become virtually canonical among poets. Hence der Stricker's claim in this passage can probably be viewed simply as a formulaic necessity. Seen from a broader perspective, of course, the careful appeal to authority is characteristic of medieval composition. In a sense, then, part of the literary significance of der Stricker's *Daniel* lies in the simple fact that it was freely invented and not based upon a French model.

This is not to say that der Stricker was unaware of either contemporary or earlier literary traditions, both inside and outside of Germany. On the contrary, in composing *Daniel* he drew freely and broadly from works of his own age—for instance, from Hartmann von Aue's *Erec* and *Iwein*, to name but two of the most significant influences. In addition, der Stricker betrays a close acquaintance with various legends of antiquity. In this regard, such motifs from *Daniel* come to mind as the blinding of the giant (a reminiscence of the Polyphemus saga), the lethal head carried about by one of Daniel's opponents (an apparent reference to the head of Medusa), and the healing quality of bathing in human blood (a motif central to the legend of Silvester). Hence, while *Daniel* marks a certain break with compositional tradition, it is clearly not a work which arose in a literary vacuum.

In keeping with established Arthurian convention, the hero is endowed with all of the requisite virtues of strength, courage, and prowess. Yet in addition to these common knightly attributes, Daniel also possesses—and makes frequent use of—a trait which is much less frequently seen in the protagonists of classical Arthurian romance: cunning. Time and again, in the face of peril, Daniel resorts to trickery in order to defeat his opponents. And at several such junctures in the story, der Stricker—through his narrator—lends a word of approbation to Daniel's application of mental, rather than purely physical, agility.

Der Stricker's *Daniel* sets itself apart in further respects from many of the other Arthurian romances of its age. For instance, the mass battles waged by King Arthur's men against the armies of Cluse stand in sharp contrast to the one-on-one duels which more commonly typify Arthurian combat. Indeed, such large-scale warfare is much more reminiscent of the style of fighting popular in the older Germanic heroic epics such as the *Nibelungenlied*. Moreover, the figure of King Arthur himself, who in *Daniel* actively takes part in battle, is markedly different from the older, more passive king of the classical romances.

In constructing a biography of der Stricker, we possess relatively few hard facts. Although various theories have been put forth, it appears most likely that der Stricker was a *nom de plume* meaning "the ropemaker" or "the weaver"—a probable allusion to the role of the poet as a weaver of stories. Several references to places and events in Austria make it appear likely that der Stricker spent at least part of his life in that area of the German-speaking world. Analysis of his language, however, points to the strong possibility that he was born elsewhere, most probably somewhere in present-day Franconia.

In addition to *Daniel*, der Stricker composed one other long work: the epic *Karl*, which is a reworking of the German *Rolandslied*. His real fame as a poet, however, is rooted not in either of these two works, but rather in the shorter didactic verse narratives (such as the "Frauenehre" and the numerous *tierbîspel*, or animal fables) which occupied his attention in later years.

Bibliographic note: The following excerpts from *Daniel* are based upon my own critical edition of the text: *Daniel von dem blühenden Tal von dem Stricker*, Altdeutsche Textbibliothek, 92 (Tübingen: Niemeyer, 1983). Among the passages omitted from the present translation are, in particular, the more extended battle scenes, some of the didactic passages, and the recapitulative sections. A full and complete version of this translation is in the Garland Library of Medieval Literature.

Chief among the relatively limited English-language secondary sources on *Daniel* are the following contributions: Thomas Elwood Hart's "'Werkstruktur' in Stricker's *Daniel*? A Critique by Counterexample" in *Colloquia Germanica*, 13 (1980), pp. 106–41, and his "An Afterword in Response" in *Colloquia Germanica*, 13 (1980), pp. 156–59; Ingeborg Henderson's "Stricker's *Daniel* in the Recently Found *Ms. Germ.* 1340" in *Journal of English and Germanic Philology*, 86 (July 1987), pp. 348–57; and Stephen L. Wailes's "Stricker and the Virtue *Prudentia*. A Critical Review" in *Seminar*, 13 (1977), pp. 136–53.

Daniel of the Blossoming Valley

King Arthur

He who gladly hears sung those things which are proper for men of virtue will be always mindful of such songs and their teachings when he himself performs deeds of virtue. He, however, who is averse to literature is slow to carry out noble deeds. Master Alberich of Besançon has brought me a story from the French which I have mastered so that it might be heard in German for the proper entertainment of all present. Let no one criticize me: for only if Alberich has lied to me, do I pass falsehood on to you. Thus begins this tale in which der Stricker wishes to display his art with words and would have you listen decorously and not interrupt with talking. Good breeding is a noble virtue: it does honor to both young and old.

"He who wishes to pursue praise and honor should have no fear, should he be lacking in material goods. For if people see in him a certain zeal, they will speak of him in the same way as of one who possesses this zeal and who also performs virtuous deeds. He who lacks zeal never finds praise from others, no matter how much material good he boastingly gives away to them." These are the words of King Arthur. Never has there lived a king comparable to him. For he loved in great measure both generosity and honor as well as virtuous teachings, and he never was guilty of dishonor or disgrace. Hence his praise and his name live on and remain untarnished. Whoever desires to live a true courtly life should covet King Arthur's good breeding, for this is a bountiful fruit and a praiseworthy possession. From such virtue one can indeed become a worthy man.

King Arthur was a knight of complete integrity. All knowledge which we have of kings throughout the ages was as naught compared to him. Except that I greatly wish to avoid conflict with others, I could very well tell of all that he did in his youth. I am well aware, however, that, should I conjure up his youth in words, people would say that I was a madman or a liar. Therefore I shall say nothing of this, and yet shall not keep it wholly a secret. Hear now of the greatness of his worthiness. He was so fully truthful that he never once spoke a word less steadfast than a jewel which endures for all eternity.

Hear now about other things he did. All of his vassals he considered comrades. Hence, the best knights from all lands came to be with him. They became comrades of his at his court and, once having left his court, were held in higher renown in their own lands. This is why they did so: he is much more esteemed who keeps company with a brave man. When King Arthur had seen the praise which all bestowed upon him, he was greatly pleased and vowed, for the sake of the world's good name, that he would every day refrain from food until he should either hear of or see a new tale of some deed worth telling. This he did only in order that his men should more actively pursue knightly deeds and not fall into sluggishness. Thus he brought about their honor in many ways which in turn led to his gaining the highest prize.

All that he possessed was held in common, and his court was never so devoid of courtiers that a festival could not be held. His praise was rightly heard both far and wide, and his retinue was countless. There stood a table in his throneroom which had the peculiar quality of refusing a seat to any man unworthy of becoming a comrade to the king. Whoever had at any time been guilty of crude behavior thereby lost the table's favor, and it scorned him, so that he never dared come near it. In such a way were chosen those men who were worthy of being King Arthur's comrades and of rightly being called men of the Round Table. There was to be found here a superabundance of whatever men engaged in with respect to entertainment and games.

There was a custom adhered to there which was seldom if ever disregarded: whomever ignominy had befallen was required to tell of it openly, and whomever honor had blessed was to hold it secret. Thus they had to report their disgrace and conceal their gallantry; he who was desirous of esteem had to guard himself from ignominy so that he might be the more highly cherished. Hence it was commonly held as blameworthy to tell of another's disgrace or to boast of one's own valor.

For every man who rode out in pursuit of adventure, there was a new shield held in readiness. As soon as he accepted it, he dared not return until it was hacked to pieces, as proof of what he had been doing during his absence. No cause for which they would ride out from King Arthur's court was so insignificant that it was left unaccomplished; for this reason King Arthur was extolled in all lands. Hence his honor multiplied farther and farther with every day. Because of this reputation, all of the most excellent knights from all lands journeyed to King Arthur's court.

Daniel's Arrival at the Court

King Arthur had in his household, amazingly enough, the most deceitful man ever to gain the title of knight. Keii [Kay] was his name, and he was at the same time the very boldest man who had ever joined the court. He one day rode arrogantly onto the fields in search of adventure and to see what else he could find. He was a calumniator who would hear nothing base said about himself. Had he slain one man, he would have claimed there were three. At this moment Sir Keii spied a knight riding toward him, and he headed in his direction. Daniel was this knight's name, and the Blossoming Valley was his land; he had heard that no matter how brave a knight might be, if he sought out King Arthur, he would find a more worthy knight at his court. Bravely he began riding faster toward Sir Keii in order to test the truthfulness of what he had heard. As they approached one another, Daniel inquired whether Keii would joust with him. Keii replied forthwith: "Indeed, but you could acquire greater fame elsewhere, for I have turned into cowards all who have ever done battle with me. No one has attacked me whom I have failed to unhorse. For this reason all who have known me avoid me. Those, however, who have nonetheless done battle with me have suffered the same fate as now must befall you. I shall show you right now a custom which I have learned."

They then rode toward one another, their spears lowered at the other's chest. Each intensely desired to unseat the other. With resounding power they came together. Sir Keii lost his knightly demeanor there and was, to his surprise, struck with such might that he fell easily a spear's length from his horse. Sir Daniel wished to do nothing further to him after this, save to catch his horse and address him courteously: "Sir knight, if this is the custom which you have learned, then take my advice and forget such a custom and remain seated on your horse the next time. Is this the sort of unhorsing you have given all of your opponents? Such a custom is indeed without honor, and you would do well to boast of it no longer."

Keii made no reply, but remained lying on the ground, for he had by no means taken a gentle fall. Then spoke Sir Daniel: "Take your horse if you want it, on the condition that you give up this custom and not fall again unless you truly must." Sir Keii did what he commanded and took back his horse. He was to fall often in the future in a like manner, and this was again to be a source of distress to him. Keii then mounted his steed and rode to the court at Karidol [Carduel], where King Arthur inquired of him as to what had transpired. Keii would reveal nothing, save to say angrily: "What happened to me happened to me." They knew his ways and asked nothing more of him. Then they cried out, one after another: "Bring out the armor and the horses!" For all of them wished to see what had happened to Keii. No one could count up how many of them tarried no longer and rode out onto the field in search of fame. On the field they spotted Daniel of the Blossoming Valley and began trotting in his direction. The first to do battle with him was Troiman du Gereit, whom Daniel unseated with dispatch. Then came Sir Gressamant, whom he cast down onto the very same spot. Gengemor and Linval, Alom and Schaitis, Pribandron and Belamis—what good would it do for me to name them all? They fell at Daniel's hand, a fate which they were helpless to prevent.

Finally Sir Gawein [Gawain] and Sir Iwein [Yvain] came riding up to the assembled knights. The sun never shone, I think, on two finer knights than they. Sir Gawein then spoke: "What is happening here?" His comrades all replied: "Many a man among us has been unhorsed here. We, too, have fared in a like manner." Then spoke Sir Gawein: "Sir knight, will you joust with the two of us to prove your courtliness?" Sir Daniel was indeed eager to do so, and once they had agreed upon this, Daniel and Sir Gawein rode out individually. The horses wheeled, were given rein and made to charge one another fiercely. With fury the game was pursued. Each thrust his spear through the other's shield with such valiant desire that it broke up and flew apart. Neither's esteem suffered on that battlefield; both remained seated, as they wished and as excellent knights should. Thereupon Sir Iwein challenged Daniel, and these two displayed such riding and jousting that they both were able only with great difficulty to avoid falling. And yet Daniel remained seated before them all, without a taint of disgrace. At the very last, Sir Parzival [Perceval] came up, anxious for the joust. This meant the end for their two spears, which at once flew apart in splinters; yet each man remained firmly seated on his horse.

The honor which fell to the stranger from these three knights (since none was able to unhorse him) caused the other knights to rejoice: they thought their own excellence much enhanced, since Daniel had remained mounted even in combat with these three. Why is it that men act so? He who has experienced adversity himself gladly sees and hears of others with a similar fate, for thereby his own adversity seems lessened. Daniel, who had remained on his horse and avoided the disgrace of being thrown off, whereby his excellence was made evident to all, was desired as a guest at court by those spotless knights Sir Gawein, Sir Iwein, and the noble knight Parzival. This wish was soon expressed, for all three of them rode forward to him and said: "Welcome! We have seen and heard that you are an excellent knight; this we readily concede. Now you shall do us the honor of telling us your business and your name. There is certainly no need for you to feel reticent toward us, for we all stand ready to serve you, as you have shown yourself worthy of this."

Daniel replied: "It is not necessary that you stand in my service. Were I so excellent and esteemed that I could perform such a service as would be fitting for you, I should not be afraid to do so. I shall be the one to serve you, and I shall tell you whatever you wish to know, for I have found here what I have sought. Often I have heard tell of the excellence and great power of King Arthur's fellowship. This is what I wished to see. I shall speak the truth: I have come for no other purpose than to gain your favor. Daniel is my name, and the Blossoming Valley is my land, which my father, King Mandogran, bequeathed to me."

The lords were all pleased at this and indeed accepted Daniel into their fellowship, which was knit together so tightly that no peril, save death itself, could separate them. Merrily they rode off, for they had found a man who did honor to the court and enlarged the number of their company. In great joy they came back to the court, where King Arthur inquired as to what had happened.

His nephew Sir Gawein told him the news: "Here is one of the most excellent knights of whom we have ever heard tell. A lucky hunt it was which we pursued this day, for God has provided us well. With this man we tested our knightly games, yet little benefit did we gain, for despite our strong determination, he thrust us all onto the grass. I, too, am one of those whom he unseated. Not a one of us can accuse the other without himself having also to confess to having been unhorsed." Sir Gawein related all of this, and, had he been able to honor Daniel even more, this too he would have gladly done. Gawein, noble knight that he was, wished no greater praise for himself than for his comrades, for he had no desire to paint himself more worthy than any of the others.

When this information had been passed on, King Arthur received Daniel with all the kindness befitting the reception of a good friend who is to be shown warm hospitality. King Arthur rejoiced that Daniel wished to remain at the court, and ordered him enrolled forthwith in his fellowship. Great was the power of King Arthur's excellence; he was praiseworthy and versed in all good qualities. His hospitality was endless, which in turn reinforced his esteem.

King Matur's Challenge

One day not long after this, as the men of the Round Table were pursuing the amusements which were always to be found there (merriment was a constant guest at the court), it occurred that they would gladly partake of food. No new and unknown story, however, had yet reached Arthur's ears. Thus he spent his time in patient expectation of such tidings.

After all had waited till nearly mid-afternoon, there came riding into the court a giant who was bare of weapons and wore neither helmet nor armor. His cloak was the most wondrous object ever sewn of silk and gold. In his hand he held a club greater than a roof-beam. Whoever might see this creature in a dream would be gripped indeed by fear, and as they saw him coming, many a brave hero became frightened. So terribly enormous was he that they all began to quake with fear. He did not even carry with him a shield, but rode barehanded atop a large camel, which was barely able to carry him. He cleared a broad swath as he rode through the courtiers. His skin was far from soft, but instead was harder than horn. Had he really become angry, he could have easily slain all of those present.

The giant dismounted and had such things to tell the king that they all became deeply distressed. The giant said to King Arthur: "King Matur of Cluse has sent me here to find out certain things about you. Many a noble story has he heard of your excellence. You are so perfect in all things that the world deems desirable that he considers you worthy of giving him your land; you shall, without resistance, surrender yourself as a vassal to him and hold your land from that time forth as a fief granted by him. Such an honor he has seldom offered to another king as he does now to you. This you can well believe: my lord is so powerful that any man can count himself forever fortunate whom he seeks out and deigns to choose as a vassal.

"This would not have come about, save that he has heard tell of your excellence. A great many powerful kings there are whom he does not deign to count among his men, though they themselves wish it. Not one of them seems worthy to my lord even of being allowed into his land. Now he has dispatched me here to you to invite you to visit his land, if you are willing to accept him as your lord and receive from him this honor. Do not tarry now; tell me forthwith what you think of this."

Then said King Arthur: "Never before has a stranger story been told at my court. If he knew that I am as valiant as you have said, then he could well have anticipated that I would not agree to this. It would do me greater honor, I believe, to be a freeman than to hold it as a fief from another man. I shall beg no man for this. Should I have need of any defense, a powerful army will carry out my request and my command. Tell me, in God's name, my friend, about your lord, as well as about the land and the people. You should tell me everything, since I am always pleased to hear such reports. If everyone in your land is as large as you, then I will indeed speak differently than I have thus far."

Then said the giant knave: "No king has ever been crowned who lived as admirably as my lord. His land is well protected, so that your military campaign will do him no harm. This is insured by a mountain range which surrounds his land. Nothing living has ever been known to cross it, save for birds which might fly over it. There is a road which leads through the mountain at the point where I came out. Whenever it is desired to close off the road, a huge boulder is lowered in front of it. This entrance is such that I can lift it alone, but you with all your men would fail to budge it. Since I rode out through it, the road is now open until I return again.

"The land is large and broad and is verdant in all seasons. Of the women I shall tell you nothing; you shall see them there yourself. Such is their breeding that neither I nor any man could ever fully describe their beauty. One thing is to be perceived there: even the least beautiful woman in that land is as lovely as a rose. So joyous and so beautiful are the women there that any man who dares observe them, be he young or old, is crowned by the power of Good Fortune. For they are lacking in nothing: they embody both inward and outward perfection. Women never before have reached such a pinnacle; they are far beyond mere beauty.

"There is a bird in this land called the Babian; the women have a great many of them, as well as whoever else might wish one. This bird has such a wondrous plumage that I hear the women speak of seeing themselves in it, as in a mirror, perhaps even more clearly. Moreover, they also use these birds when they go outside—regardless of what time of day—for the birds hover above them and are able to shield them well from the sun. At night, when all are in bed, they are so provided that one is able to see from the light emanating from them, as if from a burning candle, at whatever spot in the chamber the Babians may be. And both night and day they sing beautifully, with so sweet a sound that people long to hear it.

"My lord is distinguished in many ways: wherever he journeys, no matter how far he may ride in a day's time, his entire household accompanies him. No other king has the reputation that his household follows him about. This seems to you perhaps amazing, for you have never witnessed such a thing. It is accomplished without great cleverness, and I shall tell you precisely how: there is an animal called the elephant—probably unknown to you—whose strength is so enduring that it would not be harmed, nor even become fatigued, if a mountain of furnishings could be set upon its back. However much were loaded on it, it would not so much as bend its legs. It is one of the most massive creatures which the earth has ever carried. From its hoof to its shoulder joint is twelve double arm's lengths and more, and it senses no pain regardless of its burden. It remains standing day and night, and can be driven wherever one wishes. So great is its strength that it survives any sort of adversity, even if one purposely attempts to kill it.

"Now there are masters in this land who have two of these elephants brought together, but in a way that they do not come in contact. Then they order a forest felled, from which they fashion a great many sturdy beams, which in turn are attached to the elephants between the torso and the haunches. This holds permanently, regardless of how many beams they put on top of each other, for the beams hold together so tightly that they could never give way under any burden (this custom is the most extraordinary in that land). Then they place on this fortresses made of marble and of ivory, on which are inlaid marvelous artifices, and beneath them along the sides are a great many precious edgings of gold. Never was such wondrous work crafted and engraved with birds and animals, battles and tournaments, dancing and flirting and courting of the ladies, all of which is engraved there and explained in letters. My lord has many such movable palaces, as many of which follow him around as he pleases.

"There never was so powerful a king who exercised his might so joyously. He enjoys manifold pastimes, for there is a continuous festival in progress there. The land is great and wide, and he was so bold as to clear the empire of those who had previously occupied this land, unless they were willing to serve him in fear and fall down at his feet. Fiefs he then granted them, so that they might serve him well.

"His entire kingdom he has apportioned to seven armies, one of which is required each day to journey to the court and take part in a tournament. Many a gleaming knight one can see galloping there, whose bearing and riding skills are marked by great artfulness, and who, with knightly etiquette, fight as though obsessed for the sake of praise. The din of clanking swords and the sight of heroes pressing for worldly acclaim are to be found there. They have no outward beauty unaccompanied by a corresponding measure of inner merit; there is for them no surfeit of such games. All of this is witnessed by five hundred maidens who must sit nearby on a green meadow, and whose presence emboldens the knights. Above each of the ladies, sitting or standing, there hovers a Babian, which casts on them a refreshing shade. Well suited to joy is this place, and great with bliss for all in attendance.

"After such knightly games have gone on for a time, there follow various amusements without spear or sword. With haste the knights dismount and doff their weapons, and a great many hurry off to don their court-dress and then go off joyfully to court the ladies. The sight of joy offers itself, of singing and of dancing, and of a festival blissful in many ways. Joy alone is the object of all the competition. Each man finds there whatever pastime he can.

"Then a short time afterwards, the riding, the jousting, and the tilting once again commence. Shafts are broken in honor of the ladies, and fighting is done with great eagerness for the sake of their favors. When the riding is over, they take up whatever pastime the knight chooses. Thrice in the course of the day they ride and play courtly games. Glory is the reward for success, for their hearts are filled with joy. With the advent of evening, the knightly company takes its leave, but with the following day an army every bit as glorious arrives with great strength and passes the day with the very same clangor. Thus they come to court every week, each day a different troop. Then the first assembly returns, bringing with it handsome helmet plumes, both birds and animals crafted of gold and precious stones.

"There is a commandment in effect in all the land that, at the risk of life and property, no maiden may be seen in the protection of her father, who must send her to the court once she turns eight years old, so that she may help to complement the blissful existence there. For in such matters my lord takes great interest. He desires to give to each of these maidens in marriage that man to whom she is drawn and who, of all the men, is most pleasing to her.

"My lord has great dominion; his excellence and his strength are rare among all other kings. Every man who has ever ridden into that land in search of adventure, and who has done battle with my lord, has had death bestowed upon him. A finger of land is to be found there, on which grows a magnificent limetree. Beneath this tree stands an object of gold, in the image of a fierce beast, which has, strangely enough, a banner in its mouth. Through this animal flows water, which is brought there through artful construction by the power of the wind. Great skill and mastery are to be discerned in this. The beast is devised so as to possess the power of imperiling the life of any man who is so blind as to remove the banner. For in that very instant the animal raises such a din and wails fiercely and with so thundering a voice that any man will fall from his horse, so overwhelming is the sound.

"Thereupon my lord rides up, so fiercely angered that such a man is lost, even if he be greater in size than a mountain. The craftsman who wrought this beast likewise made me as huge as I am, as well as a brother of mine, for we are both his offspring. Because of the bond which ties him to us, he employed his craft to endow us both with an impenetrable skin, so that neither of us has ever suffered a wound. He has told me himself that he is close to one hundred years old, but nonetheless he is still so agile that no creature has ever lived in flesh or fur on this earth who could outrun or escape him. Indeed, I have seen myself that he is highly artful and far stronger than I, however old and small he may be in contrast to me. And this is evident in his offspring, for neither I nor my brother—though we often engage in combat—has ever been cut by spear-thrusts or sword-blows.

"You claim to be able to dispatch a great multitude of knights across the sea; I, however, desire no defense other than my bare hands. Even if your army were so immense that you could not look out over them all at the same time, they should still have to suffer death at my hand. Therefore, make an end to your threats. You can rejoice that you must associate with my lord. If, however, you do not do so willingly, then your honor will be lost entirely: I shall capture you and lead you off and pass immediate judgment on you and give your land to whomever my lord desires. Now, I have held back nothing and have told you everything, both the good and the bad. Now tell me forthwith your resolve. I shall not leave you until you accompany me to my land."

Thereupon King Arthur brought his wisest knights to court and entered into council with them. Not yet having been even asked for their advice, the inexperienced youths among them said: "However we may bring it about, this monstrous devil shall never live to tell in his land of standing before you today and cajoling and talking so aggressively. This must be avenged here and now, and his tale shall not follow him home."

Then spoke Sir Gawein: "Such talk and such advice as you have proffered cannot do us honor. You have all heard well that no one can defeat him, with sword or with spear, with shots or with missiles. In truth, we have need here of sound advice. I counsel, therefore, that my lord act as though he were pleased at this affair, yet at the same time weigh the means by which we might avenge this injury. My lord should declare his willingness to journey to that land, but should request that the giant first tarry here, for no more than a week and until such time as my lord has stated that he is prepared to depart; then let us all ask him that he not refuse us this, since my lord has a very faithful company of followers which he must summon to take up this venture with him. All of these followers, we shall tell the giant, have taken an oath to stand together, whether our king has been provoked to anger or wishes to defend his honor, or whatever else. These men, we shall say, King Arthur shall take along on this journey, for the honor which falls to him in Cluse shall likewise be their honor. Should we slay a messenger, we would have only disgrace to live with. Even if we could manage to take his life, I should argue against it. In truth, if he were at this moment slain, I would forever lament this to God, for then there would be no one to show us the way into his land. I advise that, once we are in this land, we take aim at his eyes, even if we cannot kill him with the sharp edge of a weapon. Thus we shall end his knowledge of light and day, whether it be a sword or a spear that hits the target. If we cannot fully take his life, we shall flee from him. Without his eyesight, he can do us no great harm. Then let us not fail to take ourselves to the limetree and cause the beast to wail, so that when the giant's comrade comes, we shall aim our weapons in search of his eyes too. With both giants deprived of their sight, the king will be deprived of his right hand."

Gawein's advice seemed to the king and to the people to be knightly and sound. All were determined to win glory there, or else die an honorable death. King Arthur, seated on his throne, spoke to the messenger: "Your words please me more than any others which I have ever heard. Wait with us here for but a week; my comrades and I are noted for our loyalty to one another, and—to prove my loyalty in this matter—I must assemble them here so that whatever glory I myself may attain in your land shall likewise fall to them. They shall all witness the moment when I cede my land to the hand of your lord, so that they too may become his vassals.

"I ask you now, good knight, to remain here for seven nights. For you can well understand that it would be quite mad of me to break the oath which I have sworn to my comrades. What good would I then be as a vassal to your lord if I were to abandon my comrades? If he were to see me arrive in such disgrace, I should have to live with eternal shame—since he has heard so much of me. Insofar as he holds me in high esteem, I should now like to journey to his land in such a manner that he might concede the truth of my reputation. Since I myself am to be so highly honored there, I wish to ride to his land in a way that will also do him honor. It is ill-fitting that I pass this Whitsuntide without a festival. Your lord, however, with his great glory, shall replace this festival, which, although it has always been my custom, I shall forgo for him. Gladly will I journey to his land, for I am greatly pleased by this matter."

The knights then all requested that the giant delay there for seven nights, whereupon they would begin the journey with him. So persistent were they

in their request that he finally agreed to their will and spoke as I shall tell
you: "Seven days I shall tarry here, since it is so important to you.
However many knights you are able to assemble in that same period you
may take with you when you leave. This is an easy game for my lord, and
you will never acquire so many knights that they can avoid surrendering or
losing their lives; this they cannot change. You should not imagine that any
defenses will ever save you from my lord. Should he become at all ill-
tempered, you are lost, each and every one."

When the giant had made his promise to delay a week, the king ordered
epistles written, which were sent with dispatch throughout his land. Requests and commands went out, saying that King Arthur was seeking his
friends and was in need of assistance and of a strong combat force. Whoever
had pledged friendship to him should renew that pledge now. Their loyalty
he wished to examine and test, for a situation had befallen him in which he
had need of a stout defensive force.

Thus King Arthur assembled an army such as no king had ever before
acquired, yet he thought it a misfortune that some of his comrades were
elsewhere in pursuit of adventure. Gladly would he have awaited their
return, but they had set out on too many diverse and unknown ways:
Lanzelet and Erec, as well as a number of those who were bent upon
winning acclaim.

The Adventure of the Dark Mountain

Now since King Arthur was about to have this huge giant at his court for
a week before his journey would begin, one of his comrades (being spurred
on by his bold valor) felt so urgently pressed to launch the campaign that
the week's wait seemed too long. This was the knight Daniel of the
Blossoming Valley. Out he slipped from the court and onto the fortress
gate, where he picked up the trail from the hoofprints of the giant's camel.
In his heart he thought: "Once at the lime tree, I shall not fail to remove the
banner and loose the wailing of the animal. Should King Matur then come,
he shall have to deal with me, regardless of whether this brings success or
failure upon me. I shall suffer at his hand either injury or good fortune, for I
desire to determine once and for all whether he is worthy to rule his land.
And so I shall seek to find out for my lord whether he ought to endure such
haughtiness."

In the evening, as night approached and he no longer could see the tracks,
it became necessary for him to seek out a resting place. He endured such rest
unwillingly, and there was no other night which seemed to him so long.
Very early in the morning he rode back toward the track and followed the
hoofprints. He made haste in his journey until night once again fell. Thus he
had to delay his journey again until the third morning. A great trial was
about to befall him. At daybreak he rode toward a mountain both craggy
and high, and save for the fact that the road went through it, no one would
ever be aware of what sort of land lay beyond it. Now he glanced here and
there and quickly perceived that he should have to go through the mountain
if he wished to enter the land in which the beast was said to be. It was a
stroke of good fortune for him that the land was so close at hand. Eagerly he

hastened onward toward the opening in the mountain, fearing no manner of affliction.

He spotted a creature seated there of which he could well stand in awe: a monstrous giant. His thoughts turned then to the other giant who had, in King Arthur's presence, claimed to have a brother invulnerable to every kind of arms. "If I avoid the completion of my journey," he thought, "and do battle here with this giant, I shall lose nothing more than my fame and the effort which I have thus far expended. If, on the other hand, I must eventually confess to having shrunk back in fear and to not having dared to determine whether this giant can be defeated—if I am unable to report on this, then I shall be held a coward. However, should I ride up to him now in order to determine the facts of the matter, and should my sword fail to pierce him, then I must suffer both disgrace and death at his hand. I am indeed in need of sound advice."

Thus Daniel weighed the dilemma in his mind, as the unfortunate circumstances forced him to do. Then, however, he seized the courage of a lion. "There is no good in my being frightened like a mere woman. I am more readily willing to lose my life valiantly than to live on in endless shame; never could I risk my life for greater stakes than these, for I find twofold comfort in the teachings of my heart: if I am victorious, the victory will always bring me acclaim; yet there is no disgrace for me in the event that the giant should defeat me. However great my injury may be, I shall gladly take the risk! I should gladly be seen injured with my reputation intact before I would turn away without battle or injury and, what is worse, laden with disgrace. Either I shall fall or I shall fell him! Even if my comrades had arrived in full force, I should still wish to be the first to take up battle if I could arrange it so. If I should be successful at this battle, then I shall have the same determination and the same physical strength left for the ensuing battles. If, on the other hand, I do not gain the victory here and if the giant departs from me unharmed, then indeed all of King Arthur's army could not inflict any harm upon him. I am anxious to see how he defends himself." Daniel dismounted, tightened the saddle girth of his steed, and, once again seated, assumed the air of a man about to take on the whole world.

All of this was observed by a lady standing nearby who took good note of Daniel's actions. Standing by a tree, she tied her horse's reins to a branch. She quickly hastened then toward Daniel and gave him her greeting; when she had said this, she fell down at his feet. "What is the meaning of such a salutation?" spoke the splendid knight, for it was grievous for him that she had cast herself at his feet. Daniel dismounted onto the turf and was about to help her up, when he perceived that she was in grief. She had the hue of death all over, so that she could neither see nor speak; and she lay in such a way that Daniel did not expect her to live much longer, but rather he supposed that she had already given up her life. It rent his heart that she was unable to speak.

He had just been about to ride off eagerly into battle against the giant, against whom he had greatly desired to prove his ability. His thoughts were filled with anger toward this giant, and he pondered to himself: "With great shame shall I depart hence if I cannot determine whether this lady wishes to relate to me her lamentation, or what it is that troubles her, since she has humbled herself so astonishingly before me. I can well see from her appearance that she possesses both great power and manifold suffering. This she has demonstrated here. I do not know, however, what it is that she wishes. Even if I knew full well, I would be unable to come to her aid if I lose my life to the giant, with whom I am now to do battle. First of all, I shall determine my fate with him. If he then lies dead before me and I remain alive, I shall ride back here and hear what she desires. For if I were to ride off from her for good, without hearing of her distress, I should be the lowliest man ever to bear the title of knight, since a lady has demonstrated in so miserable a manner her need of my help. My reputation, however, will still be meager if I am incapable of granting her what she desires."

Thus he bent down to the ground with the intention of finding out what afflicted the lady. He had abandoned his timorous demeanor and, taking the lady's head, he laid it onto his lap. Her misery remained great until he had sat there for a while, and then she gradually began to fare somewhat better. She sat up and spoke: "May God preserve your reputation and your life, my lord, for this comfort. Never has a poor woman been so wholly divested of favor, and yet now I have been granted your kind help. There is no way in which you could better increase your hope for good fortune and your esteem than by aiding me, for I am completely bereft of all favor." Daniel spoke: "This grieves me, my lady, and I tell you in truth that I, too, have endured much hardship. If I, however, can comfort you, I shall not fail to do so, as long as I am able to move a muscle."

She thanked him profusely and said: "My worry and my affliction are so great as to be incalculable, except that I realized your intention to undertake a journey from which no one could rescue you; for death would of necessity fall to your lot. If you lose your life on account of me—since you had already given it up—then I shall not be as sinful a woman for having caused this. You cannot escape alive, for the giant's skin is so hard that it has never been broken the least bit, regardless of what was ever shot, struck, or thrust at it. No matter how vicious an attempt one makes on him, no man who attacks him is so skillful as to come away alive.

"Hear now, in God's name, good sir, what it is that afflicts me and how great my misfortune is. I am the daughter of the Duke of the Dark Mountain, and I have incurred such distress from a certain dwarf that death would be a thousand times dearer to me than life. God would do well to grant me death, good sir, since I am doomed to suffer this adversity. The dwarf wished to possess me; this my father refused him and resisted angrily, for he had no other offspring and desired to give me to someone my equal, whereby I fittingly could have entered into a praiseworthy way of life. This opportunity is no longer open to me. After the dwarf had made a great many requests—all in vain—then his threats became violent to the point of being burdensome to my father, who aired his vexation to his men and proved himself not to be a coward. He did battle on the green with this dwarf, who then—my lament to God shall be unending!—slew my father!

"All who have endeavored to avenge him there, as they rightly should, have likewise met with death. When my mother saw this dire event from the battlements, her heart broke with misery and she died of grief. Thus I have lost them both. Because the dwarf has inflicted this great distress upon me and continued to woo me, my heart shall never again know gladness, since I did not likewise die of grief. In anger I sent word throughout the land: whoever should be so fortunate as to slay the dwarf and should bear his head before me, that man would be chosen as lord over me and over my land, regardless of how low he may be in birth.

"When this was heard, there came many a valiant man, for all who had the desire for glory and heard my proclamation made the journey. There occurred a procession of such proportions that I cannot describe it to you. All, however, were slain, without exception, so that not a one came away with his life who had been bold enough in strength and in skill to do battle with the dwarf. Death has been the lot of them all. For the dwarf possesses a sword whose blows no man can survive. Even if a man were protected by twelve suits of armor, he could not withstand a single blow from the dwarf, whose name is Juran.

"Now I have come here for this reason: I have often heard tell that no man comes to this place without finding death, and I seek such a man who might slightly prefer to die in my land at the hand of the dwarf than here at the hand of the giant. God has always come to the aid of a just man, and since I am without blame in this matter, such a man may profit from this attempt. For whoever wins victory in my land will receive a sword with which to slay these monstrous giants who shun all weapons, but have never been wounded themselves. Never was there a rock so hard that, being struck by this sword, it could resist being cut to pieces like mere wood.

"For this reason the dwarf is so haughty as to maintain that, with his will prevailing, I must become his wife. Since I am unwilling, he will force me, so that I must eventually fall at his feet. If he drives me to that, he claims, then he will keep me as his wife only for two or three nights. My fortress and everything in it I shall lose and then must depart from it naked. The dwarf has furthermore sworn an oath that, if I take leave in such a manner, I can be certain that he will set upon me with birch twigs until I begin to bleed. Wherever there is skin on my body, he will flog it all off. Oh, wretched woman that I am, how shall I endure this? He also plans to cut off my nose and my lips and disfigure me to the point where no man will wish to rest his glance on me. Unless something is done to him in a short time that will console me, I would rather take my own life than endure such misery."

When Sir Daniel had heard this horrifying tale, he thought to himself: "A blessing it would be to me if I knew now of a good solution. A full measure of adventure has, it seems, come my way. I have heard both alternatives, and I can neither do battle here, nor ride off with the lady. It shall be a great salvation indeed if I even come away alive from these monsters who deal out death in such a way that no man can engage in battle with them without suffering death as a result. I have set out too early! Oh woe, would that I were still at home! Never have I become entangled in a more miserable situation—of that God the Allpowerful is well aware! Now my mind is filled with misguided thoughts. For no matter how long I might lie quietly at home enjoying my comfort, I could never accomplish anything for which people would ascribe to me any sort of valor. What if I am now enduring such hardship? It may be of value to me later! Should that, however, be impossible, then it is better (as now seems my fate) that I soon give up my life valiantly than that I live forever in disgrace." All concern for his life he dismissed from his mind and said: "My lady, your misery and your distress trouble me. In all certainty I shall either lie dead for the sake of your innocence, or I shall defeat the dwarf. Ride forth and show me the way. He is not so frightening that I dare not take him on, since he has caused you such distress." The lady again gave him her thanks and was most joyful for this consolation. Yet she wept out of anguish and for fear that she should see happen to him what had befallen all whom the dwarf had ever slain. Thus she had ample sorrow to endure!

They tarried no longer, but mounted their horses and rode off. The lady was oppressed by grief, so that she rode along in great sorrow; this distressed Daniel, who wished to console her and said: "Trust in God, my lady, that I, with His command, shall overcome the dwarf. For God so loves righteous deeds that you can be assured that we shall survive any ordeal with this dwarf unscathed." The lady found comfort in this and showed somewhat more cheer than was really present in her mind. Yet heavy was her heart, so greatly did the possibility of Daniel's death grieve her. He too felt pity for her in her distress. Thus neither was disposed toward joy of any sort, but both made every effort to be happy.

All day long they rode until nightfall, when they arrived at their destination, the lady's homeland. Here they were both received most graciously, since well-nigh sixty maidens came out to meet them. Wondrous things one could see there: numerous knights and squires received both the lady and her guest in a manner befitting their rank. Except for the fact that joy was lacking, all manner of glory ever witnessed elsewhere was to be found at this court. Now, however, the sorrow of all the courtiers deepened more than before, and their hearts began to ache as they saw this knight whose death—should he fall in battle—they said they should never cease to lament. Hence their anguish was so great that no man equal to Daniel in position had ever been more deeply mourned—although he was still alive! Greatly did they fear for his life.

The lady's dearest handmaidens, who were permitted to offer her advice, fervently entreated her to absolve Daniel (since he was so fine a knight) of losing his life to the dwarf. They advised her furthermore to take him as her lord (since he would easily be worthy of her) and not to let him leave the lodgings. For they were confident that the fortress itself could always be defended against the dwarf, and they would allow whatever damage he might cause outside of the fortress. The lady then ceased to bewail her sorrow, since she had Daniel safely in the fortress with her. With a glad heart she said: "I would gladly accept this advice, and I should be ever pleased with the outcome if we could convince him of it. Now, however, the battle so occupies his mind that he will unfortunately refuse to do so."

When the time arrived for dining, an act of courteous service was performed which was most pleasing to Daniel: all kinds of food were brought forth in lavish quantity. I can assure you that they were lacking in nothing there, and that they held their guest so dear that he luxuriated in their ministrations that evening. They showed him their zeal and such good works that he soon decided—should he live to see the next day—to defend the fortress, or else die at the hand of the dwarf. During the night he slept in comfortable lodgings until wakened by the glow of dawn. He heard an early mass and prepared himself for the duel with the dwarf and for the chance to perform knightly deeds. To the Lady of the Dark Mountain he said: "Send word to the dwarf to come here; tell him that you wish to see him. Whatever you then hear me say to him, you must be prepared to do. A man can often accomplish with wisdom many a thing which he could not do relying on strength alone."

The dwarf was sent for, and Daniel proceeded with the lady to the battlements; he wished to determine whether he could, through any sort of cunning, save his life. He then spotted Juran approaching the fortress gate, where he inquired as to what his lady desired, and whether he should ever win her favor. "Yes," said Sir Daniel from atop the battlements, "my lady and her land are yours if you are willing to display whatever valor you possess. She is ready to give you her love if you demonstrate your bravery to her; she is willing to accept you as her lord."

The dwarf answered him thus: "I should be most pleased if I could deservedly earn her favor. Whatever task she can set for me, that I shall perform both willingly and well." Daniel replied: "My lady has promised to put an end to her anger so that you might demonstrate whether you are worthy of such an honor. Lay down your sword and take up the best sword which you can find here and then do battle with the very weakest man whom my lady can offer. Should you be able to defeat him, my lady will drop the quarrel and do all that you desire. It is your sword alone which is given credit for all the slaughter which you have perpetrated, for no man has been able to withstand that weapon. Now show my lady and her retinue whether or not you are capable of inflicting death on any man without the aid of that sword. Whatever you then desire will be fulfilled."

Then the dwarf Juran said: "Will I then possess her favor if I attain victory over that man?" Cheerfully the lady answered: "Indeed. If you win your life from him, then you may take dominion over all that I possess." Then said Juran: "If this is so, I shall gladly do combat with your most excellent hero. Death must befall whomever you have chosen for this battle. I shall demonstrate to you that none of my prowess is dependent upon the sword, but rather that it emanates from my body. Even if you command me to put down the sword and take up a club, I would not become afraid; on the contrary, I would trust my strength and indeed be the victor. Even if my opponent were stronger than Samson, I would take him on for such a reward."

Sir Juran surrendered himself to Lady Love's command. It seemed to him that our Lord God Himself could have no angel as full of beauty as the lady whom he saw there before him. Laughingly he said: "I shall gladly do what you wish." He removed his sword and laid it on the ground. "Now I wish to see," said he, "who it is who dares to do battle with me." The killing of his opponent as the price for her promise of favor appeared to him an easy task indeed. He went forth to the fortress gate, before which he made a circle where they should fight when they came together.

The gates opened and Juran watched Daniel of the Blossoming Valley approach him. Daniel offered Juran the choice of two swords. He took the one which he preferred, and Daniel took the other. Both men stepped into the ring. A promise was made that the fortress gate was to be closed and no one allowed outside except Daniel and the dwarf. The two of them then began to perform manly deeds. So fierce were their blows that they were in little time stripped of their shields. Then there arose such a fight that all who heard and saw it swore that neither opponent could come away alive. Angrily they struggled in the ring. Each strove fiercely for the other's death. Flashing red fire could be seen sparking from their helmets as the swords which they held in their hands resounded and struck against their helmets and armor.

The spectators were unanimous in their hope that the dwarf would be defeated, and they courteously asked of God, for the sake of the Holy Trinity, that He stand by the righteous man and that He bring about a just outcome to the duel. The dwarf Juran then spoke: "May this blow be dealt, my lady, in your honor"; then he struck Daniel on his helmet so hard that his sword burst in two. At that moment Daniel dealt him so fearsome a blow that he fell to the ground, yet Daniel's sword failed to pierce his skin, a fact which vexed Daniel greatly. Just as Juran recovered from the blow and was about to raise himself, Daniel struck him again so that he fell back to his knees. In quick succession Daniel then dealt him four powerful blows, and yet—amazing to recount!—no matter how much he battered the dwarf, he was able to pierce neither his helmet nor his armor.

Once again the dwarf jumped up and, forgetting his good breeding, took flight in the direction of his sword, for his life was most dear to him. Daniel, realizing his intentions, quickly ran in the same direction. Both combatants were in full sprint. Their resolve was identical, but favorable circumstances smiled on the one, whereas the other, who fought without this advantage, was but the shadow of a man. No matter how he strained, Juran was unable to prevent the advantage which fell to Daniel. For the latter's legs were so long that he outstripped the dwarf and took possession of the sword.

Having gained this advantage, he wasted no time, but drew the sword and said: "Should you desire to live any longer, then you must surrender as a captive to my lady's rule." Now the dwarf was so bold as to have no fear of death; in his vexation he wholly lost his senses out of his desire for the sword. He thought himself so manly that he intended, relying solely on his strength, to seize the sword from Daniel, who, however, kept him at a distance, drawing back from him thrice, informing him repeatedly that he would kill the dwarf should he refuse the surrender. The dwarf paid heed to none of this and, giving Daniel no reply, kept running at him. When Daniel had sufficient evidence that the dwarf no longer desired to live, he set about giving him a blow with the sword, so that his head came off and he never again uttered a word.

When the lady had seen this, she bowed deeply to God and gave thanks to Him for His commandment, both with her heart and her words. The gates were then opened and the lady assembled her court—a glorious multitude it was—and went up to Daniel, whom she graciously welcomed. Her heart was set free, for she had overcome both her worry and her distress. Great and ample was the praise which they heaped upon Daniel; clearly evident was the proof of the lady's and the court's indebtedness to him as he carried forth Juran's head. All those present placed themselves at his command and rendered thanks to Daniel and to God for the victory that had befallen them there. Had he set his mind on any sort of reward, had he desired their service or their gifts, you could have readily heard and seen— had you been there—that all of this would have been a joy for them to fulfill. They showed themselves willing to carry out his every request. If the lady had owned all the world, she would have deemed him worthy of receiving it. And had he desired her hand, as the story has it, they would not have refused him.

Now, however, he wished only to take his leave. They tried to dissuade him from this and said that they should always regret it if he were to ride off unrewarded for his trouble. The lady asked him to remain at least until he had rested from the battle. But every request and command which she made of him went unfulfilled. That he had won the sword from the dwarf pleased him greatly, and he intended to determine once and for all whether it would pierce the giant's skin. Thus, without fail he mounted his steed and rode off, which brought great sorrow to the lady and all her retinue.

The Adventure of the Bright Fountain

After Daniel of the Blossoming Valley had saved the Lady of the Dark Mountain from the dwarf and had taken his leave, he made haste from the place. But just as his horse was trotting along away from the fortress, he spotted before him perhaps forty young maidens, who, having caught sight of him, dismounted onto the turf. Making haste toward Daniel, they all followed their mistress, all the while lamenting and weeping. He saw that they intended to approach him, and he dismounted onto the sand and led his steed by hand until he came close enough to hear their greetings.

They then fell one and all at his feet. He immediately showed his friendly intentions and quickly had them rise, asking what was troubling them. Their mistress spoke: "It is, my lord, a heartache for me which I am forced to endure and which is an overflow of all suffering. Once I was a powerful countess and held full dominion in the land of the Bright Fountain. Now this and all my glory have been taken from me, and I shall never again find joy or comfort unless you can rescue me from my affliction. I had been filled with despair as to whether any man could help me. Since you, however, have just relieved this lady of the great worry which she suffered, now I know in truth that, if I am to encounter any sort of salvation, it will have to come from God through you. For God has taken from this world so many hundreds of men whom you have defeated that my consolation depends on you. For I wish through your help—should I be so blessed—to replace with joy the affliction which has fallen to my lot and which is soon to overcome me. If only I should find this at your hand! I swear upon my oath the truthfulness of this: that if you do not save me, I shall never receive consolation."

Daniel spoke: "This causes much grief to me, my lady. For I have gone to great trouble and have expended much courage in a certain matter which I have not yet completed and with which I must now occupy myself. If I do not carry out what I have undertaken, then I shall forfeit all my reputation."

The lady wrung her hands and said: "Never mind this. I take it upon my soul that you could never augment you reputation more than by coming to my aid. You have never been in a situation, nor will you ever be, where your favor is more needed than here. In doing so, you can acquire God's grace as well as worldly acclaim. Your good name will multiply ever more and in all respects. For God and for the sake of your courtliness, have mercy on me, my lord, and harm will never inflict itself upon you or your reputation. Help me—poor woman that I am!—from my heartache; God will always help you in return."

"Tell me, my lady," said Daniel, "what it is that you lament, and I shall right whatever wrong you have incurred if I am able." She fell at his feet and thanked him, for great distress forced her to do this; she wept profusely and said: "May God repay you for this, my lord. I am suffering shame and scorn from a devilish creature to whom no bodily harm can be done. He is truly the devil's comrade; so great is his head alone that two men could barely lift it. He wears no clothing and is covered all over with hair. Furthermore, he is wholly without a belly or a lap, so that his legs and arms grow directly onto his head. Believe me, my lord, his chin truly reaches down to his knees. Two larger eyes were never seen than those which grow on his head, and his mouth is wider than a yard. One could search forever and not find a creature more monstrous. I doubt not a whit that the hateful devil himself dispatched him straight from Hell. Whenever this creature wishes to kill, he picks up in his hand a head, and no matter how many men look this head in the eye, not one of them comes away alive. All of them fall dead instantly. This is the direst torment: as soon as he kills off the men, he will turn to the women and children.

"He leads a frightful army, all of whose members are like him and who come from the sea. They always do battle without weapons, of which they have no need, since immediate death comes to anyone who beholds the head. These creatures suck warm blood from the bodies of their victims, and after retaining it in their mouths for a short time, spit it back out. This is the way they all live; there is no other nourishment which they take. In this same manner the creature has laid waste to my land without resorting to pillaging or burning, or sword or spear.

"And yet the injury which I have incurred from this was as naught in comparison to the loss of my six fine children who perished because of him. And yet even this distress I overcame. Until yesterday morning I still possessed my castle and a large retinue, along with a knightly spouse by whom I bore my children. Then yesterday at dinner as we sat in sorrow over the losses which we have suffered, the devil came up suddenly and killed all who were present. I was barely able to escape myself by stealing off like a mouse out of the rear of the palace—only I and my remaining ladies are still alive here. My lord was overcome by anger and fled into a lofty tower into which he locked himself. I am at a loss as to how I shall get him back. If he should lose his life, then I shall return there in order to view the head so that I too may find death and follow after my lord. I shall overcome all sense of loss and consider myself most exalted if you can fully carry out what I request. If, however, my lord is dead, then I shall be freed from all affliction and shall surrender myself willingly to death."

"Now ride forth along the road," said Daniel to the lady, "until we spy the palace. Let me then ride up to it, and you shall soon see whether I can aid you. I shall win back your husband or else lose my own life in the attempt." The lady and her women thanked him profusely. They tarried no longer, but rode off quickly for four long miles until they came close enough to see the palace.

Daniel then addressed her: "Await me here, my lady, until I can determine whether God is willing to bestow His grace upon you. It is now up to God whether I shall ever see you again. No matter how wretched the nightmare that I may witness, I would gladly endure it, being spurred on by the commandment of your fear. How I shall accomplish this without the aid of my eyes (since they would bring harm upon me), I do not, in God's name, know. Have you any sort of mirror here?" The lady spoke forthwith: "Indeed, there are many; which do you wish?" "Bring me one of them!" he replied. As soon as he had spoken, she said to her women: "Bring all of the mirrors, and let him choose himself which one pleases him!"

This was accomplished in quick measure; mirrors were shown to him one after the other until he said: "Enough." Then Daniel took the one which suited him best of all and thrust it into his bosom. He promised the lady to bring back good news unless he was prevented from doing so by dire adversity. He made great haste to set out, and the ladies—to the extent that they were able—wished him well as he left. Many a tear streamed down from the eyes of the lady and all her followers.

He hastened toward the fortress, where he saw the frightful intruders locked in. Unflaggingly he rode on and dismounted at the fortress gate. There he rapped with the knocker and demanded very loudly that he be let in. Angrily the bellyless devil answered: "Who is out there before the gate?" Daniel said: "It is I." The monster thought it strange that Daniel had avoided giving his name, so as not to be recognized. Wrathfully he said: "You are heading for a precipitate downfall if you continue to strive after it in this fashion. I shall kill you on the spot unless you tell me your business immediately, as well as your name and, if your life is dear to you, your family."

Such talk was a mockery to Daniel, who said in reply: "I far prefer to follow your command in these matters than to lose my life. Listen and I shall tell you my name, for I shall never be ashamed of it: I am called by the name which the priest gave me when he baptized me. My family I can certainly reveal to you too: my father was my mother's husband, and I am their son. This is how you shall know me." Then spoke the bellyless demon: "Never have I heard such reckless talk as what I hear you saying. This I shall myself avenge; you cannot think yourself so manly that you will still be there when I come out. Even if you possessed all the valor in the world, I would not allow you to come away alive. Of this you should be assured: you face certain and unavoidable death." This vexation moved him to jump up angrily and, taking the head in his hand, to make his way threateningly toward the gate. Daniel, standing before the gate, heard these ominous words and reacted as would any man of wisdom. He first tied his steed to a limetree standing in a field a short distance from the fortress. He then undertook an act of cunning and took out the mirror, whereupon, guided by his wisdom, he turned his back to the fortress gate, which opened shortly afterwards.

Carrying the deadly head in his hand, the creature, who was able to slay men without the aid of weapons, then emerged. Daniel saw him in the mirror as he came out and made his way towards him, with the head held out before him. The creature would have perished himself had he beheld it from straight on. Now he carried it before him with the intention of inflicting death upon the courageous hero. Daniel watched all of this in the mirror, yet his heart was filled with joy at what he saw, for it seemed to him to be his salvation; Daniel took quick steps backward until he came close enough that he thought he could reach the monster, to whom death was soon dealt. For Daniel drew the sword which he had so bravely seized from the dwarf in the land of the Dark Mountain, and swung it behind his back and served the creature a gift he would not soon forget: a blow beneath the chin which cut his legs in two.

At this, the creature sank to the ground, his hideous voice shrieking in great wrath. He cried out to his men that he had been dealt a lethal blow, so that they might hasten over and take the head. As soon as he had spoken these words, Daniel saw in the mirror exactly where he lay on the ground in his agony, and proceeded to cut off the hand wherein he held the head, which he then quickly snatched up. He lifted it from the front, but was careful to look at it only from behind. A happy man was he that he had acquired this head, and he spoke to the creature lying there: "For a long time now you have beheld this head only from behind. Now you shall find out how it is when one looks into its eyes; this you shall not be allowed to forgo." Daniel then held out the head until the creature caught sight of it, whereupon he immediately fell dead to the ground.

The bellyless intruders, meanwhile, all kept their eyes shut as they pressed hurriedly out of the fortress, for they were well aware that a look at the head from straight on meant certain death. It was a stroke of good fortune for Daniel that he, however, dared to keep his eyes open, for the others ran about blindly in search of the head. As soon as the first one found his master's body, he felt in his hand for the head. But the hand had been cut off, and he reported this to all of his comrades. Afterwards they explored the entire expanse of grass around them, as fast as they possibly could, but were able to find nothing. Then they all agreed to open their eyes. This was to be their downfall. For Daniel was standing before them and held out the head until they had all beheld it, whereupon each and every one of them fell to the ground dead, never to rise again.

When Daniel saw this, he said to himself: "Who could offer me any resistance, now that I am in possession of this head? The giants, whom no man can slay, will have to behold this thing, which will assuredly bring about their death, and with which I can be the victor in the land of Cluse and can assist King Arthur in his fight against King Matur. I shall show the head to all who wish to clash with us, and it will be for them a bitter antidote. On the other hand, however, if I were to cause mass death in Cluse, I would fall into disgrace and would acquire a notorious reputation. Everyone would know that even a mere woman could easily massacre all the world by carrying around this lethal head and killing people with it. People would call me a devil and a coward and say that I carried it around out of despair, because I dared not do battle with anyone. I would be vilified and shunned by all. Indeed, it seems unavoidable that I would eventually incur misfortune from this head, misfortune which could even come in the form of my own death from having beheld its face. You have meant death for so many men; the devil has sent you; now let him have dominion over you: I do not desire to keep you." Whereupon he cast it into the water and spoke: "Never again shall any upright man have knowledge of you," and he let it sink all the way to the bottom.

Having done this, Daniel made haste toward the fortress, at whose tower he—well-born knight that he was—called up to the count in order to determine whether he was still alive; Daniel told him to be of good cheer, for his suffering was at an end. The count heard this and spoke: "Would that God had desired to bring about such an outcome!" "Come, I shall show you that this has indeed transpired," spoke Daniel of the Blossoming Valley; "their threats are over. The devilish head, which they carried around for so long, has slain them."

The count then unlocked the door and came out with great trepidation. Since he had still not heard how all of this had come about, he welcomed Daniel and asked him in the name of our Lord to relate how he had survived the creature and for what reason he had ventured into this place. Daniel told him that his wife and her ladies were all still alive, and that he had come there at her request, which she had made as if from the depths of misery. Daniel related to him, furthermore, how he had killed both the creature that carried around the head, as well as all of his comrades.

Both men made haste through the fortress gate, where the count saw all of their bodies lying there as proof of Daniel's story. "Oh woe, where is that lethal head?" spoke the lord of the house; "I have never suffered more agony than has befallen me from it. I would be forever content if the devil had taken it away." Daniel then replied: "Be not concerned about this, for I have hidden it so that it can harm neither you nor any other man." The count then spoke: "May God grant you a just recompense for this!" He placed at Daniel's disposal both himself and all that was his, and said: "Tell me, where is my wife? You have done so much for me, never has any man treated me so well; if I am to live, I shall serve you for this, as well I should."

Both men mounted their steeds and rode across the field, coming in a short time to where they found the ladies. The countess, having spotted them, said happily: "God welcome you both!" Her sorrow and her tribulation she quickly forgot, and she was overcome with gladness. Her lord was likewise happy that his lady was still alive, and he hastened to tell her that their enemies all lay dead at the hand of the lord riding with him, who had freed them from all distress. Moreover, he informed her that the head would no longer harm her, since it had been cast into the water. The lady then told him forthwith how Daniel had rescued both the lady of the Dark Mountain and her land from the dwarf, and how Daniel, with his valor and wisdom, had acquired great renown.

Although their losses had been vast, they thought themselves fortunate to have even survived. Most earnestly the count said to Daniel: "Onward, noble knight; you shall come with us to our court and decide upon whatever reward you may desire, and it shall be fulfilled. For I proclaim to God on this day that I have received from you the greatest succor which has ever fallen to my lot." Daniel, however, countered by saying: "In God's name, my lord, it is my wish and my command that you not pursue such talk. What reward could I deserve simply because your enemies lay slain? For they were as much a threat to me as to you and your people. Had the monster killed you today, he would have killed me tomorrow. Now we are mercifully spared such anguish, and it is God who has saved us all. Thus you should give thanks to Him. Now I must take up a trail which I have followed far; it is a source of vexation to me that I have been off it for so long."

The Count of the Bright Fountain, however, said in answer: "Both my court and my life you have won back for me, as well as my honor and my wife. Now it is fitting that I, in exchange, should evermore be your knight and your vassal. Whoever it is that you have been hunting, whether far or near, I shall help you undauntedly. If you wish to tarry here no longer, then I shall set out with you. Wherever you intend to journey, I shall assist you gladly, for you have rendered me great assistance."

The countess then hastened to add: "He should be assured that if I could come to his aid, I would relieve his distress, of whatever sort, in the same manner in which he has allayed my heartache." Both men then took their leave. With joy and yet with sorrow the lady and her lord parted. Two thoughts occupied her mind. She pondered to herself: "This knight is so courageous, I fear that he may, being driven on by his boldness, become entangled in a situation from which great sorrow might befall me, through the death of my lord. Oh, how could I ever live without him?" Then, however, her thoughts jumped to the opposite consideration: "Since the knight has overcome this devilish creature, he can easily vanquish whatever he desires. His guile is not to be underestimated." The lady rode back to court and decided, along with those others who were still alive, that they should all be of good cheer since they still had what God wanted them to have; they were of one accord that the lady should be content with whatever God should ordain for them. They wished nothing other than God's destiny for themselves.

Daniel Slays the Giant's Brother

Daniel and his companion whom he had rescued from the tower rode onward and came, a bit after noontime, upon a forest. There they followed hoofprints until the daylight ended and so dark a night fell that neither of them could see the other. Each of them now rode that much faster in anticipation of a resting-place; a heavy weariness beset them, and they probably should have arrived already at the stopping-over place. The count sensed this. Now it came to pass (this was caused by their haste and by the fact that they were unable to see in the darkness) that they had lost the path to the castle and had taken up another path, which they had pursued all through the night, as well as their strength allowed. The result was, however, that they found nothing but more forest.

Thus the valiant heroes rode on until the first rays of dawn hit them. Then Daniel spotted the mountain at the foot of which he had previously seen the giant; whereupon he exclaimed to the count: "Our undertaking is faring well. Here is the mountain which I seek." Even after catching sight of that mountain, they still had two long miles to ride before reaching it. In a short while, however, they came upon a field in which there was a tent pitched on the grass at the foot of the mountain. This was the most magnificent glade to be found anywhere. From atop a green limetree came the melodies of birds warbling harmoniously, and beneath the tree a lovely spring issued forth, clear and pure. A trough, made of marble and most splendidly embellished, stood underneath it, brimming with water. As they came close enough to see all of this, Daniel said to the count: "This is a suitable place and an opportune time for the horses to rest. I wish also to ascertain what is in the tent."

He dismounted forthwith and tied his horse to the limetree, walking straightway into the tent, in which he found neither man nor woman, but a lone table heaped with all manner of food and drink. Sir Daniel looked about: the tent was so marvelously embellished and decorated with letters that he would gladly have stayed there until he had eaten. But he felt a twinge of fear that something further might transpire to divert him from his journey, as had happened before. He also feared that if King Arthur had arrived in the land of Cluse before him and should enter into battle against the giants without Daniel's aid, he might lose his life. For Daniel intended to bestow death, by means of his sword, on the giants, as well as on whatever others might engage in battle with him. Thus he felt a twofold distress: he would gladly have dined on the food there, if he could only have been certain that he dared to tarry any longer.

At this moment the count spied a knight riding across the field. Immediately he cried out into the tent, saying to Daniel: "I discern a knight galloping fiercely in this direction; he is beginning to come quite near, and I don't know what he wants." Just as his comrade Daniel came out of the tent, the knight galloped up before them; he had with him a prisoner who must have been most uncomfortable, for he lay thrown across the horse like a sack in front of the knight. Sir Daniel greeted him, but the stranger merely looked ahead and rode on.

Both men were vexed that the knight remained mute and neither spoke nor nodded. The Count of the Bright Fountain spoke angrily: "In truth, I shall find out what causes this knight to refuse us his greeting." He put the spurs to his horse and wrathfully gave chase. A road, not even as wide as two men, led into the mountain, and the knight bore down upon it. The count chased him with drawn sword, but the stranger fled like a coward. Daniel, having mounted his steed, rode after the count as fast as he could, for he had no intention of remaining behind. But the knight was still ahead of them both and rode on to the gate, which was a massive boulder, forbidding entrance to the mountain. At this point the stranger turned around, but failed to let the boulder back down. But as soon as the count had ridden through, the strange knight let the rock, which was immense and bulky, drop. Thus the knight Sir Daniel remained completely cut off outside the mountain in front of the boulder. He was pained and vexed at this, and was unable to do anything to help his comrade.

Now you shall hear an amazing tale of how Daniel barely escaped with his life, so closely did death brush him: as the rock shot downward into place, one could see a stream of water gushing forth from the rock, a stream so overwhelming that all of the surrounding terrain that was of low elevation became flooded with water. For a lake had been dug in the mountain, and whenever the boulder was raised, the water flowed into the lake. Never had Daniel heard tell of a more wondrous thing. The boulder was thus placed there for two purposes: whenever it was lifted, the water was cut off. As soon as it was lowered, it blocked the road and the water came forth. In this manner the passageway could be closed off.

Now we can well believe, in all justice to Daniel, that his heart was tormented with anger because such an ordeal had never before beset him, and never had anyone seen him flee, no matter how great the danger. Had he been able to die an honorable death, he would have sooner suffered such a fate rather than take to flight. But if he had failed to retreat, because of excessive stubbornness and waited for death to overcome him, that would have been considered more foolhardiness than valor. The flood waters rushing over him alarmed him greatly, and he very much feared for his life. In great distress, however, he turned his steed around, but was unable, no matter how he tried, to traverse the raging water. Nevertheless he was able to remain mounted and did not fall from the saddle, while his horse stayed afloat and finally swam to the safety of the meadow. From here he had only to ride back to the limetree. Tying his horse to it, he thus managed to rest from his trial. He took off his clothing and spread it out in the sun, and, having drunk of the water from the fountain, he entered the tent in order to partake of the food there.

No man could reproach him for this, for he had journeyed without once eating since doing battle with the dwarf, whom he had slain with the dwarf's own sword. Now he found an abundance of food on the table inside the tent, yet he was unable to savor it fully because of the count, whom he had lost there: Daniel was wholly bereft of joy on account of the loss of his comrade. Had he been able to reach him, he would have won him back or else would have given his own life in the attempt. After eating and drinking, and as he sat there disheartened at his misfortune, Daniel said to himself: "I would have been far better off had I never set eyes on this knight. Even as he lay in his tower, still alive, deep lines of despair were evident on his lady's face—so much so, in fact, that if she should have to hear word of his death, her anguish and grief would be far more excruciating than before. Oh woe! She has been robbed of her joy on my account. I have compensated her with sorrow for the good which I had accorded her before. This shall be for me an unending heartache. I have encountered such ill-fatedness here that I shall not yet depart, but remain a while longer. If any of them should by chance emerge again, then they will be forced to let me see what is inside the mountain; and they will hand over my comrade, if God is gracious enough to allow me to find them. If, however, they have already taken his life, I shall never rest until I avenge him in a way that men will tell of it evermore."

Thus Daniel kept watch all day long, until night began to fall, at which time he spotted four young men approaching the tent. They brought with them meat, bread, and wine, and every imaginable delicacy which a king might ever desire, should he happen to dine here—of all of this they brought a great profusion. Daniel did not know whether good or ill was approaching as he watched them on their way. He went to his horse and, quickly slipping on the harness, rode to a safer position. As soon as they came within hearing distance, he offered all four of them his greeting, which they quickly returned in a decorous manner, proceeding then on foot into the tent. Once inside, they removed all of the food from the table and replaced it with that which they had brought with them. They took away the original food and were about to set out in the same direction in which they had come when Daniel asked them to stop. "What is your business here?" he asked.

"To bring food here." "But who will eat it?" "Whoever seeks the food," they answered. "Who sent it here?" "He who is lord over this land." "Does he by chance come here himself?" "Perhaps, perhaps not. We can tell you no more than this. Tomorrow morning we shall return with different food." "God be with you," answered Daniel, "but first tell me more and direct me to where I might find your lord, so that you will always fare well. I should like to see him now, since he is clearly a most courtly man."

"Do not ask us too much, good sir," they said. "We do not know the slightest thing about this. It has been a year now since he last spoke to us. If he so much as caught sight of any one of us, he would kill us if he were able to catch us. We do not know what troubles him. So disturbed is he that every man whom he sees must die if my lord is at all able to bequeath him such a fate. He was always a courtly man; only this year he has been of such a mind that he allows no one to live. If you wish to see him despite all of this, then a meeting can transpire only on this very spot." Daniel asked God's blessing on them for having told him these things, which, however, were a source of vexation to him.

They then departed quickly. It had by now become so dark that Daniel could scarcely see. He felt a heavy affliction for four reasons: that he was so completely cut off from his comrade; that he could not know whether the count had suffered bodily harm; it further grieved him that he could do nothing to investigate any of this; and finally he did not know how to prevent King Arthur's death at the giants' hands in the land of Cluse. Thus he pondered all of his alternatives. For a time he was about to leave, but then he decided to remain. Gladly he would have been elsewhere, yet nevertheless he tarried nearly a week there in the hope of rescuing or avenging the count of the Bright Fountain. But, by the time King Arthur was to come on horseback into the land of Cluse with his powerful army, no one had yet emerged from the mountain.

Daniel thought to himself: "I have waited as long as I can. Today is the day on which my lord enters the land where death awaits him. Although he will try to defend himself, the giants have skin so hard that he cannot kill them, and they will inflict upon him that which rightly should befall them. I can tarry no longer; I must set out for Cluse now if I am to come to his aid. I place full trust in this sword which fell to my lot at the Dark Mountain. The giants are certainly not so invincible that I cannot deal them enough harm with it that they will never again force any king to surrender his land and then subjugate himself to them. Yet as I now must set out, how shall I ever rescue the count, whom I have lost here? If I leave here without him, I shall be in constant anguish. Furthermore, this worries me greatly: if my lord King Arthur is slain in Cluse, I could never cease to lament his loss. It is better that I leave, and, once victorious in Cluse, that I then return here. There is no use in my further delaying. If I remain here even a bit longer, in truth I am certain to let slip the opportunity both here as well as in Cluse."

Daniel then took his horse and set out boldly on his journey. Great was his chagrin and it was to become still greater, for his heart was heavy at having to depart without the count. Turning around frequently to look back, he said to himself: "God protect you, my comrade! May His grace and His command soon bring us together again in good health!" Off he then galloped in haste, coming quickly to the mountain, since it was but two miles away. Once again the giant was seated there and inquired of Daniel, as he saw him drawing near, where he was going in such haste. Daniel replied straightway: "I am headed for the land through the mountain." "You are a fool," replied the giant; "be silent and cease your childish thoughts. If you ride so much as a foot farther, in truth I say to you, I shall break you into pieces like a twig." "Show me then," said Daniel, "what you are capable of doing, for there is no question of my turning back." The giant jumped to his feet; his body was far from that of a dwarf! Daniel of the Blossoming Valley stood scarcely as high as his knees. Since the giant had never been wounded by any weapon, he did not know that he should defend himself now; unmindful of his coming fall, he raged with anger.

As Daniel of the Blossoming Valley came riding toward him, the giant strode in the direction of his opponent; his fists were clenched in wrath, and he swung at Daniel, who, taking good note of this, angered him by holding out his sword. Irately the giant struck at Daniel's sword, so that it resounded loudly and his hand, as well as a good third of his arm, were lopped off. This was the first misfortune ever to befall him from a sword. Daniel said mockingly: "Tell me, is this by chance the way in which you kill so many men with your hand? Never have I visited a land in which the fighting is done so strangely. Indeed, how would it be if I myself were the twelfth in line to do battle with you? You should have to have a great many fists before you could kill us all. You should also have need, it seems to me, of many good doctors. But unless they are here in an instant, you shall never again go into battle with that hand—on this I shall stake my word!"

Now the giant was highly irritated. He walked over to a massive rock with the intention of hurling it at Daniel, who let him get as far as the rock before lopping off his leg. Nonetheless the giant picked up the rock and cast it at Daniel's shield with such force that his horse fell to the ground with him, causing him great distress. The giant, wishing to avenge himself even further, reached for yet another rock, but was unable to stand any longer on only one leg; down he fell, but still ready to defend himself sitting. And to his great distress, God did not protect him. At that moment the horse on which Daniel was mounted recovered. He then vaulted closer and cut off the giant's other arm, whereupon the monstrous fellow fell helplessly onto his back, with but one leg remaining of his four limbs. He flew into a rage at this and kicked Daniel's horse so hard in its side that it rolled over three times in quick succession. Daniel was nearly injured by this, for he was unaccustomed to falling. Red with anger, he strode up to the giant and cut off his head with these words: "I have, I believe, given you just recompense for that blow. Now you are no longer so huge nor so invincible as before; any man who does battle with you now shall defeat you easily, unless you have a very good doctor indeed!"

King Arthur Slays King Matur

Following Daniel's duel with the giant, King Arthur arrived with a large assemblage of high-spirited knights well prepared for battle. Now three of his comrades had ridden ahead and were close enough to witness the giant's blow to Daniel's horse: Gawein, Parzival, and Iwein. They recognized

Daniel and rejoiced at the giant's death and at Daniel's survival. They were convinced that, if Daniel were anywhere but there on the battlefield with them, they would surely fare ill.

Daniel asked them all to dismount and test their swords, so that they might ascertain whether they could fell the giant's comrade with their blades. They dismounted forthwith, being curious about the truth or untruth of what they had heard about the hardness of the giant's skin. Having drawn their swords, they hacked away at the corpse, but could not pierce the skin at all. All three of them exclaimed: "His brother's words are true indeed. Let us now try your sword, for ours are worthless here." Daniel held out his sword and spoke: "Here it is. I would just as gladly give it to whoever of you wishes it." "Indeed," they answered, "you shall carry this sword yourself. For you are far more worthy of it than is any one of us." Then spoke Sir Gawein: "We cannot linger here any longer; we must ride on."

They all four mounted their steeds and galloped at a fast pace through the mountain. They wasted no time but rode even faster when they spotted the limetree and the golden beast, from whose mouth they then withdrew the banner. Immediately it created such a din that none of them could hear his neighbor. This wailing was still going on when King Arthur entered the land through the mountain. Once hearing the voice of this beast, he made haste toward the limetree, accompanied by his many bold knights, all of whom were set on winning the victory there or else dying in the effort. The giant who had led them to Cluse waited at the foot of the mountain until they had all entered. This he did with the intention of closing the passage behind them until such time as they had fulfilled all that King Matur desired of them. Only as he was about to follow them in at the end of the throng did he discover his brother lying there dead. He made the sign of the cross and raised a loud lament for his brother, saying: "Oh woe, how is it that I have lost you to so strange a death! Your skin was more impenetrable than horn. This could never have happened unless the devil himself did it! Now King Arthur and his men shall all have to sacrifice their lives to me for this. All of them shall pay for your death. Not a one shall ever return alive." He then lowered the rock behind him and galloped after King Arthur's army, for he was angry and in great haste.

As King Arthur and his men quickly assembled around the wailing beast, they realized that all that they had heard about this beast was true, for the din jolted them from their horses as though they had been slain. Each and every one of them lay on the ground before he had a chance to offer any resistance. There was never a clap of thunder to be heard that was this frightful. The noble knight Daniel of the Blossoming Valley, however, recovered and stilled the awful din by hurriedly replacing the banner in the beast's mouth. Save for this, no one would have survived, for it would have been impossible for any of those present to prevent his head from bursting at the deafening roar.

Now King Arthur's army prepared for battle, for they had heard that King Matur would ride up in but a short time. Many a fearless knight began to request the first joust, anxious to perform marvelous deeds with his sword. Since many of them were desirous of the first joust, King Arthur said: "All who were at my court and heard the words of the giant are well aware of his statement that no other king is so excellent as to be able to enter this land: I alone am so fortunate as to be admitted. Now I wish also to determine whether I am so fully blessed that King Matur deems me worthy of fighting a duel against him with sword in hand. You shall, my lords, willingly allow me as much. Inasmuch as he desires me as his subject and bestows upon me a great honor refused to many kings, I will consider it my good fortune if he deigns to joust against me." All present thought it knightly that King Arthur had taken this upon himself.

At that moment they spotted King Matur approaching on a horse trained to obey his every command. Ornately embellished was Matur's clothing, as befitted a king who claimed to have no equal. He held before him his highly ornamented shield whereon stood a Babian, of which I have told you before. Thrusting his lance under his arm, he spurred on his horse until it assumed the proper speed. King Arthur then vaulted forth with the rush of a storm. He bore a crowned eagle on his shield, and his heart pounded with joy that he was about to do battle with this man who desired to subjugate him and take his land. He wished to find out then and there whether he was worthy of this honor, for both men knew full well that the blows of their weapons would reveal the ultimate truth. They came flying at one another so powerfully that both their saddles snapped as they collided. Losing their grip on their horses, both of them fell off backwards and found themselves on the ground! They then made clear what they wished to do: they embarked upon the fiercest sword-play which at that time had ever been witnessed between two men anywhere. How they avenged blow with blow! Each man was valiant and demonstrated skill and strength of body and of sword. As long as the shields held out, they could well protect themselves, but it was unavoidable that the shields should quickly disintegrate, so that soon they were reduced to nothing.

As soon as the shields were destroyed, neither helmet nor armor was spared any longer. They set about hacking at the choice steel of the armor and pressing at one another for well over an hour, so that no one could tell which of them held the advantage. Then King Arthur was fortunate enough to force a blow through King Matur's helmet over his scalp. But Matur parried this straightway with a fearsome blow which came down with such force that King Arthur fell to his knees. Never had this happened to him, and, thinking himself forever disgraced by this, he sprang immediately back to his feet. He then brought about his opponent's downfall, for he dealt King Matur a blow which sealed his doom, since it was sent by Misfortune, from which no man can protect himself. King Arthur struck him on the same spot as the previous blow and lacerated him so badly that his head tore open and fell lifeless onto the grass. King Arthur had survived, and King Matur lay slain.

The First Battle

At this moment they spotted a royal company galloping up—as many as two thousand knights who were required by King Matur's command to engage in a tournament on this day, but were also eager of their own accord. The sight of Matur's corpse angered them greatly, and, discerning King

Arthur there, they dashed forward in full force, whereupon the good knights of the Round Table vaulted out to meet them. Well over a thousand spears were broken into splinters in but a brief lapse of time. Every man who fell was doomed.

The most fearsome wrath of which you have ever heard tell was concentrated on the battlefield that day. Fiercely they hacked away at shield and armor, which flew apart like dust. Many a sturdy helmet was ripped apart by their swords. No man could tell you how the fire flashed forth as one piece of steel penetrated the other. Even a man well protected to withstand the mightiest of sword-blows was on that day naked and bare. Whatever man could maintain himself was blessed with good fortune, but even he had to part with a goodly portion of his bravery. All that has been told us about past battles was a mere trifle in comparison. From both sides there came together youths well versed in the art of combat. Not for the briefest of moments did they cease from the feverish tumult. Whatever they struck was slashed to pieces, and the weapons they bore were sharp beyond all belief, so that the steel burned just as though it were wood.

So grave was their contest and so miraculous the feats they performed that all those present feared that the Day of Judgment was upon them, and that the heavenly conflagration had come over all the earth. Only when they saw that the fire burned upwards, toward the heavens, was this fear allayed, though the heat of the battle caused many a brave man to be uncertain. The combatants on both sides had the strength to carry on indefinitely without either side remaining behind in defeat on the battle-field—except for the fact that Daniel of the Blossoming Valley brought to the ground many a good knight with the sword which had once belonged to the dwarf. More than three times did he ride through the midst of that multitude; many a man was wounded that day who would have otherwise claimed to be invincible in sword-combat. At Daniel's hand, however, even such a man was dealt the blow of death.

Once the battle and all the horror had begun in earnest, they spied trotting toward them the giant who had sealed off the mountain behind them and who was immense both in size and in the anger that he felt toward them. Having once heard the thunder of the battle and being eager to be there himself, he gave spur to his horse, which, however, proved to be so sluggish that he thought it better to proceed on foot (besides, the giant possessed immeasurably long legs!). Thus, he dismounted and took a number of long strides in the direction of King Arthur's army. Thereupon many youthful heroes ran toward him armed with bows and arrows which they had stored in preparation, and with which they took aim at his eyes. Shooting an unceasing barrage of more than a hundred arrows and other missiles, they robbed him in quick measure—this is no untruth—of his eyesight. A frightful wrath overcame him, and whomever he struck, that man was doomed. Angrily he drew up his club and struck with such force that every man whom he could reach lost his life.

Those noble and high-born knights, King Arthur's comrades, in turn breathed revenge at this and were spurred on by their bold valor to seek the victory. Great power they displayed with their trusty swords against the giant, yet however ardently they wished to deal him his death, they remained unable to do so. For this they paid dearly, for once his club was completely knocked to pieces, he picked up and snapped like a twig all whom he found before him. And any man whom he spared from this treatment, he picked up by the leg, regardless of his size, and used him as a club to bludgeon the others. Though they strove to penetrate his skin, they were wholly without success. A great array of swords were tried out on this creature without inflicting any harm at all upon him; and regardless of how many spears were thrust at him, regardless of how many arrows were shot at him, they were not able to injure him a bit.

Realizing the futility of their efforts, they all took pains to flee. This angered him and led him to chase after them wherever he heard them. Whoever came into his hands was doomed to die, for they could only be picked up in pieces afterwards. How could any man escape with his life? What havoc do you expect that this blinded devil would have wreaked, were he still possessed of his eyes (since even without them he slew so many who did yet have their eyesight!)? It would have meant death for all of them! He inflicted such woe upon them that no man dared to approach him. In the face of their failure, they began to take flight from him.

After they had been forced to flee, Sir Keii, who saw the giant, but had not witnessed what had just befallen his comrades, came riding up. He confirmed once more his old reputation, for he enjoyed nothing more than belittling an upright man. So rash was he with words that, even if he knew that his evil tongue should cost him his life, he could not suppress it. Though he himself was unable to win the victory, he never failed to deride those who likewise could not triumph. "What is this, King Arthur?" he said. "If you were sitting safely at home in your court, then you would have around you brave comrades thoroughly capable of felling other knights; these would be given hearty brew to quaff and all would drink to their health, so that they would fight with spear and sword until they avenged any ill that had befallen your family even as long ago as when your father was alive. How is it, however, that these men here are so weak? I see clearly that their opponent is blind; a small child could gain no esteem from doing battle with him. Your men should feel forever shamed for letting themselves be chased about like this. If the Round Table suffers these cowards—whom a blind man, without a sword, drives from their wits in this manner—to be seated at it, then it is not worth a pittance. It is good that I am alive, for I strive after fame. How shall these weaklings refuse me their esteem? I shall now prove to you that I dare to oppose this man alone, whom none of the others can so much as touch."

With these words he leapt forth and broke his spear completely against the chest of the giant, who paid it no notice whatsoever. But, having heard the jangle of the riding equipment of Keii's horse, the giant stepped forward angrily and grasped Sir Keii by the leg, which put an end once and for all to his fighting. He carried Keii quite like a stick, and his armor and tunic fell over his head. So stupefied was Sir Keii that he had nearly had his fill of battle for the rest of his life. The giant thrashed all about him (for his eye sockets were a source of great pain) with the intention of slaying more of the knights with Sir Keii. No man can relate to you how dreadfully he swung. Every man nearby beat a swift retreat, so that the stroke met no one and Sir Keii slipped out of his hand from the force of the swing.

I shall tell you how it came about that he, too, avoided death from the fall: it was near a limetree that Sir Keii escaped from the blind man's hand, and Good Fortune stepped in to prevent him from being broken apart from the fall. For he dropped right onto a branch at the top of the limetree and fell quickly from branch to branch till he finally lay on the ground like a sack! Now you can with pleasure hear tell of how the knights of the Round Table lamented Keii. With one voice they exclaimed: "The devil take this limetree and this blind man for letting him slip away! We have always heard that men who have lost their sight are powerful fellows. This one, however, shall have to forfeit his esteem for this. Why did he allow Keii to escape? Had it not been the devil protecting Keii, he would have surely fallen somewhere other than onto the tree." Yet no matter how great their chagrin, the fact remained that Sir Keii had come away alive. But he, too, was every bit as vexed, for he lay on his back in bed for more than twelve weeks before recovering from the fall.

Thrashing and hacking, the giant avenged the loss of his eyes on King Arthur's men, who would gladly have been elsewhere, but were unable to flee because of the narrowness of the place; so great a throng there was that no man was able to escape. The giant let them come at him and was delighted that no one could flee. There was not a horse among them so high that the giant could not raise his foot above it. Thus he trampled and crushed the horses and all who sat mounted upon them. Moreover, the giant's foot was so heavy that death invariably came to those he stepped on. Listen and I shall tell you just how heavy it was: if it lay upon a man—be he strong or weak—for but a moment, it would suffice to break his back in two.

Thus he scattered all of King Arthur's army from its battle position, save for Daniel of the Blossoming Valley, who was on the other side of the battlefield, among King Matur's men. Daniel could find no escape from them, for however great the damage which he inflicted upon them, he had no choice but to perform their will and remain there in their midst, since they would not let him free. Although they lunged with their swords and let fly their lances, it did them little good, for he knocked them all down with the force of a hailstorm.

Many a man lost the nails on which he carried his shield, and once Daniel came upon him, his death was inevitable. The sword which Daniel bore in his hands helped him out of this dire situation, for he was under fierce attack by all of King Matur's army and had need of a good weapon. Fearsome were his gestures, and he hacked to pieces like a sponge both his opponents and whatever armor protected them. Fortunate was any man who recovered from the wounds inflicted by Daniel, who himself, to be sure, likewise endured great distress. It was a daring venture on his part that he summoned the courage to blaze a trail through two thousand men—a trail which took him so deep into their midst that not one of his comrades saw him to come to his aid.

King Arthur's army began to retreat from the giant once they saw that he would break to pieces as many of them as he could reach. Thus they fled from his clutches toward the enemy, with whom they intermingled in order to escape the giant. He came over to them and as soon as he picked one of them up and was about to crush him, the victim would cry out in despair:

"Stop! I am here with your army!" The giant would believe the man and let him live. This same story they all then told him, from one captive to the next, so that he was deterred from crushing any of them; for he failed to see the truth and was prepared to believe what they told him.

King Arthur's forces then attacked the enemy and were met with a counter-attack. Both sides showed immense fierceness, and only now did the battle really begin. The first battle had been but a trifle, and the sword-play was only beginning now. Authentic combat was seen there as they swung their swords with force enough to cut through helmets and armor. They were youths unafraid to risk their lives and wholly in command of their physical strength, which each of them displayed to all of the others in full and unrestrained measure. There was no man among them so strong that some other failed to make him weak; and many a man who otherwise exercised his skill with equanimity could be seen caught up in the uncontrolled rage of battle. Anyone who wished to come away alive had to perform deeds of wonder.

King Arthur's comrades executed marvelous feats with their swords; the ware which they wished to vend was their life, which they themselves had renounced. Onward they pressed with thrashing swords; they slew great numbers of their opponents, felling some even without wounds when they battered their heads by striking helmets with such force that they were stunned and fell lifeless to the ground. Even those who were well armed felt naked, and the tribulation on both sides was horrendous. No man dared look about him because of the firestorm of blows being exchanged, and no one could say that he had his head about him or even that his head would survive much longer in the torrent of swords. All would have sworn that they had, indeed, already been cut in two. Many a man cried out in anger when he was unable to force his sword to penetrate the steel armor on its own accord. All of them were enduring great tribulation: even the man who was well bred at times forgot his good breeding because of his great distress. What one man spared another, he made three others pay for. Seldom does one win games which have already been lost. At stake that day were both life and reputation—no more and no less—so that he who gambled away both paid a very high price indeed. Because they were loath to lose life and fame, they refused to let this come about.

King Arthur and his followers began to press forward and angrily avenge the harm that had befallen them there. Much give-and-take with the sword could be seen and heard on that battlefield, yet there were no insults exchanged among the men. Although they endured nothing without giving it back in full measure, no one, strangely enough, repaid his opponent with abusive words, no matter what suffering he had endured at his opponent's hands: the sword was the means by which each man insulted his opponent until he had imparted to him a good piece of what he had intended. Such insults no man was able to silence.

King Arthur pushed onward with his three finest kinghts: his nephew Sir Gawein, the noble knight Iwein, and the heroic Parzival. Each of them was an artist skilled in a wondrous sort of drawing, and whatever man received one of his works had but three choices: to lose his life, to meet with death, or not to survive! Each victim soon found which choice was the best. King Arthur and his three companions were excellent scribes whose writing instruments were weighty, for they fashioned such letters as could never be erased or washed off by any man. They, however, washed many a man in such a way that he turned pale with death. Whomever the king wounded, that man had no need of a physician, for no sooner did he fall than he lay dead.

King Arthur now spotted Daniel of the Blossoming Valley far across the battlefield—Daniel, who ranged about in a wide circle and had slain every man within a large radius of himself, performing with his sword such deeds as no man (no matter how fine a sword he had) will ever reproduce for as long as the world exists. All around him he had hacked to pieces a heap of dead men as high as a moat is deep, and he stood upon it defending himself like a great heroic figure. All of the enemy riveted their efforts on doing battle with him, and persevered, as good knights should, until such time as death overcame them.

King Arthur, seeing Daniel's distress, was seized by anger and, with swinging sword, gave spur to his steed and galloped off toward him. All who witnessed King Arthur's actions proclaimed that there never had been a man born into the world whose strength and anger could carry out his will so effectively. We are told that he fought in such a way as to instill fear in the hearts of his opponents. He crafted and performed such feats with the blows of his sword that they all cried out—independent of one another: "There is no doubt—this is the very devil himself. We are all doomed to die!" They had been certain before this that no man could defeat them, but now he convinced them to be fearful of him; they would have sooner dared to come up against a thousand other men than against him alone. The noble King Arthur swung with both hands; there issued forth from his sword a din that penetrated their helmets, so that blood gushed out and his victims lay dead. With a deluge of powerful blows he was able to hew a path through a good thousand defenders. He could be seen maintaining a course through the very midst of the enemy, a course which was a bitter medicine for many of them.

When Sir Daniel became aware that King Arthur was breaking fiercely through the throng toward him, it pleased him greatly and imparted added strength to him. Making his way in King Arthur's direction, he demonstrated beyond doubt that he was glad to hear and see his beloved lord. Death awaited all who were so foolish as to challenge him. Daniel was a great hero and his sword was unique among all swords. He brandished it so that it raged onward, and neither armor nor helmet could offer protection to any man. He became the most awesome forger of metal, and his forging consisted of the following: out of every helmet which he struck he forged, without the use of the blacksmith's fire, two separate helmets—though neither was as useful as the original had been. What I mean to say is that he cleaved it in two. No man whom Daniel struck ever again cried for help, for Daniel hacked him up so badly that he quickly perceived the futility of any hope of being saved. A discouraging situation this was indeed for the enemy! Daniel the knight buffeted them about so that all hope of living escaped them, and their souls departed from them. Not unlike the hunter who rustles the bushes above a rabbit's lair and causes the rabbit to scamper off was Daniel as he beat at the enemy, so that their souls scarcely had time to escape.

Oh, how the sword resounded as Sir Daniel forced his way through the knights toward King Arthur on the battlefield in Cluse! Lustily he swung through their helmets. What he had to dole out was a certain type of sleep-inducing potion; whoever drank of this potion could do nothing to fend off the shades of slumber. The potion was Daniel's sword and the sleep was death. Such sleep was the dreadful visitation which compelled them to lie down against their will and await the Day of Judgment. Daniel hewed a path so wide that he confounded them and broke through their ranks, and all who saw his gestures stood back and made way for him. To any man who hesitated, however, Daniel meted out a most fearsome treasure, so that he fell in great agony and expired even before striking the ground.

As Daniel thrashed and cut his way through men and armor as though they were but water, his sword raged no less turbulently, breaking through steel as though through a mere stream of water. He struck at more and more of the enemy, and the fire burned in the wake of his sword not unlike a flaming flash from the heavens. All were terrified and made the sign of the cross whenever he brandished his sword. So powerful and blinding was its glitter that hard steel broke and split in two on contact. He sawed and crafted his work without the aid of a gauge: Daniel was anything but a delicate craftsman. Whatever he hit shook with the anger of his hatchet.

He now rode through his opponents at will, suffering no harm himself, but dealing out injury to a great many of them; finally he reached King Arthur, who joined with his comrades in showing Daniel good will and bidding him welcome. Though Daniel barely heard their greetings above the deafening roar of frenzied fighting, nonetheless they let him know through words how happy they were to see him unharmed, for they were deeply glad to have him there. The king then lamented to him the great tribulation inflicted upon them by the giant: "Many of our men lie dead upon the battlefield; we cannot harm the giant, beyond putting out his eyes. Since losing them, he has retaliated with such anger against us that we barely escaped him." At this point the king did not yet know who it was who had slain the other giant. He said further: "We are all too weak for this giant; no one can kill him save the one who slew his comrade at the base of the mountain. For this man truly bore a sword with which this second giant could be killed. I would bestow gifts and fiefs upon any of you who is so clever as to find him for us, for otherwise we shall all lose our lives."

Sir Gawein then spoke up: "It was Sir Daniel who slew the giant, and he would have accorded this one the same fate had he been with us. The hardness of his skin would avail him naught, and he would have no hope against Daniel." The king then replied: "If this is so, then I am free of all worry." All three knights said in reply: "Believe us that it was indeed Daniel who did so. We saw him slice off the creature's head neatly with a single swing, and the giant was still wrestling with death as we dismounted nearby. It shall be the second giant's downfall that Daniel still lives, for after he set out alone, he acquired through his valor a sword with which he was able to cut through the giant with the same ease with which one would slice through water."

The king exclaimed in his delight: "Well done, Daniel, glorious hero! Help us bring about a just end to this creature who has today wrought death upon so many of my excellent men." They then joined ranks with one another and, leaving behind all frivolity, returned once more to the raging throng. No man who wished to challenge them there was so fine a warrior that he came away alive. Dead men could be seen falling, and helmets and armor being frightfully cut to bits, as well as manly feats which opened up many a deep gash. King Arthur and his comrades were proven able to deport themselves as knights and to deal powerful and deep blows with their swords. Many a weeping man cried out: "Oh woe that I was ever born!" There arose a battle so grim that no man expected to survive; they were convinced that these were devils on horseback fighting so cruelly.

Daniel's Search for the Count

Daniel spied the giant and proclaimed straightway to his riding-companions: "I shall tarry no more, by God, for I see standing yonder the creature who has inflicted this harm upon us." He put the spurs to his steed and made his sword clank through many a suit of steel armor. All whom he encountered were swiftly cast from their horses. So enraged was Daniel at the sight of the giant that no helmet could offer protection to any man's head, for Daniel ran his sword through it with such fury that not a single victim survived. No matter how well protected a man was, it availed him no more than would a layer of morning dew. Alas, how wretched the man who awaited the blows of Daniel's sword! For Daniel paid him in a currency wherewith he had always been familiar. So remarkable was Sir Daniel's sword that a shirt of flax was just as good a shield against it as was a helmet and armor. Neither iron nor leather could fend it off any differently than would a blanket of shrubbery. Whatever it struck was pulverized as though full of dust.

Thus rode the illustrious hero until he came to the giant, where, holding his trusty sword with both hands, he lopped off both of the giant's legs with one blow. At this, the creature fell like a rock and groaned and roared so painfully that Daniel could bear it no longer and severed the giant's head. The king and his three knights had now drawn close enough to see the giant fall and to hear the din which he raised, and then to see how Daniel fiercely silenced him. The king bowed and offered Daniel his gratitude and his thanks.

In quick measure they returned to the battlefield together, where many a man fell dead that day. The fact that the giant was slain emboldened them so that they killed all who attacked them. They were exuberant and had the enemy completely encircled. The king ordered that the enemy be watched so that none of them might escape. Their numbers became so thin that they perceived the impossibility both of escape and of further fighting. It was a host of splendid warriors against whom they had defended themselves grimly that day. Now that they had been so utterly overwhelmed that the specter of death stared them in the face, they all surrendered to the king's dominion. Only by so doing could they remain alive.

It was around the time of vespers that the horrid battle finally drew to a close. The king then held council to determine whether it was better for them to wait there or to journey onward into the land of Cluse. As all of them were pondering this, Daniel of the Blossoming Valley said: "It is more desirable that we linger here. For if we can hold our ground here, then we will have conquered the entire land. Tell our men to rest for the remainder of the day. You have heard the giant speak of the seven regiments in this land, one of which journeys to this spot each day, having been granted fiefs for that purpose. Thus I am certain that an army every bit as vast as the one with which we have fought today will come riding up on horseback at dawn tomorrow. By summoning them with the beast, we will bring them here with great dispatch. In the meantime, however, we shall rest. I know quite well from my own experience that all of the men have need of respite. It would surely be our death if we were to ride on into the land, for we would be observed immediately. The six remaining armies would join together and attack us all at once. Since this single army held out so long against us today, we should not have long to live."

Daniel's advice was praised by all. Each and every man was pleased to have occasion to rest, and set about making himself comfortable for the night. Many a splendid tent they pitched upon the field, and marvelous stores of food they brought out: wine and bread, meat and fish, both dried and fresh, as well as mulberry wine and clear spice-wine. All of them showed their gratitude to Daniel, who had slain both the giants. Had Daniel not killed them, King Arthur's men themselves would have lain dead on the battlefield. For all of this they thanked him and praised their good fortune. Daniel's own merriness was reserved; he was not unlike one who stifles his vexation and laughs even as his heart is bleeding with care. For never again would he be happy until he could find the count, who had been lost outside of the mountain when the rush of water had driven him back.

As he remained with King Arthur's army until almost midnight, Daniel began to think how he yearned to ride off to the mountain so that he might see whether the boulder was in a raised position; if so, he would search for his comrade who, in his bold valor, had become separated from him there. Daniel would return straightway to King Arthur's camp should the roadway be closed off and would return to the boulder until he found the mountain open and passable.

Now he mounted his horse and set out. It was wise of him that he concealed himself and stole off from the company, so that no one was aware of his secret journey. He was heedful to muzzle his steed insofar as was possible, for he desired to return to the camp without anyone's knowledge of his trip, should he be unable to accomplish his goal. He soon came to a point where the trail was blocked and rendered impassable. This the giant had done by rolling an immense rock into the pathway; none of them had knowledge of this until Daniel saw it. Angrily he said: "Fortune is indeed not with me on this journey. King Arthur and his men have benefited little indeed from the fact that the count became my comrade. So many of these accursed rocks—the devil take them!—stand in my way that I cannot be certain whether I or any man shall be able to come to the count's aid. How I long to find him if it is at all possible! Alas, my good friend! If I ever set eyes on you again, I shall vow to God this very day to renounce all other earthly joy. My life is worthless and despicable to me unless I avenge this distress on the knight who separated us. Little does that knight suspect what is in store for him!"

Daniel dismounted and, driven on by his manliness, strained to lift the rock so that he might continue his journey. But even a hundred men of his strength would have been unable to do so, and he had to leave it where it was. Daniel was angry and troubled at this and drew his sword in a rage, slashing away at the rock with it; for he had heard the Maiden of the Dark Mountain proclaim that the sword would fail to cut nothing which it struck. Wishing to verify this, he swung it with fearsome might. Luck was on his side in every respect, for he hacked the rock apart as though it were made of ice. When Daniel saw that this caused no damage to the sword, he quickened the pace and had in a short time hewn a hole so high and wide that he could lead his horse through it. This seemed to him a stroke of good luck. He mounted his steed and set out in haste to continue his journey. He had but a short distance to traverse, and just before daybreak he arrived at the field near the magnificent tent where he had dined after escaping the flood. Even before arriving there, he discerned that none of the water with which the mountain pass could be closed off was then flowing out.

As he came closer and closer, he spotted approaching him the same man who had previously separated him from his comrade. Daniel's valor admonished him to attack aggressively, and the stranger reciprocated. Both lowered their spears, Daniel on the one side and the stranger on the other. They aimed at each other's chests and crashed together with such force that their spears no longer held together. Thus they reached for their swords and in quick time hacked apart the shields and then each other's armor, so that their very lives were hanging in the balance. Each of them dealt the other many fearsome blows, until the duel reached such a pitch that neither of them had ever before drawn such agony from another man. Daniel's opponent possessed overwhelming strength which he displayed with his skillful swordwork; beneath his armor he wore a durable skin which was precious and dear to him and which had been stripped from the body of a water sprite. This skin helped him to stay alive, for it was steeped in the blood of a dragon, so that he could freely do battle with whomever he wished without sustaining injury.

When Daniel perceived that he could not defeat this knight even with his sword, he began to fear that this very hour would witness his death. Thus he began to mete out fearsome blows with his sword—blows such as might well have been messengers of death, save that he still failed to pierce his opponent's skin. The stranger likewise requited Daniel for this affliction, extracting such a heavy toll that he could hardly be thanked for their both being still alive! Even if they had promised each other under oath equal doses of anguish, they could not have raged any more furiously than they did. Both men strained at the stirrups as they stormed against one another, each breathing the fire of revenge. High into the air they raised their swords, and deeply they arched their backs with the strength of their hearts in order to execute the blows. Both men were valiant fighters. Sir Daniel struck his opponent so savagely that his armor and helmet flew off and fell into the dust in pieces; despite this he still wore the water-sprite's skin, which protected him well.

Finally it was necessary for them to fight on foot, since both horses lay dead. With firm determination each dealt whatever injury he could to the other, until their blows no longer availed them and Daniel began to fear death. Driven on by the urge to live, he sharpened his defense so much the more, and dealt with his sword a blow to the stranger's head that so frightened the latter that he fell stunned before Daniel's feet. Daniel then seized him and commanded him to tell him straightway whether he had killed the count or what had otherwise befallen him. The man refused to speak, although he had not been wounded. His refusal to speak irritated Daniel, since there was no reason for it. Daniel stood over his prisoner and said: "I shall let you live, but I shall determine right now what you have done to my comrade, and the same fate shall be accorded you. This I promise you in truth; only by escaping in the meantime—if you can—will you avoid this!"

Daniel then followed the path into the mountain where the remarkably devised boulder had separated him from his comrade. As he approached, he perceived from the appearance of the rock that he could very likely move it alone. He then lowered it, causing the water to rush forth, for he desired that the stranger cherish no hopes of following him. He was still determined to find the lost count.

Adventure of the Green Meadow

Daniel proceeded on his way until the mountain came to an end, and the path was blocked by an awesome portal. There stood before this portal a fine net, which was so artfully fashioned as to be invisible both by day and by night. Whoever was so foolish as to attempt to pass through this gate— whether entering or exiting—without permission would fall and become so inextricably ensnared in the net that he could (even if placed over a hot fire) move neither his hands nor his feet. Such a straitjacket was this net that its victims could not so much as move back or forth. Unless someone versed in the operation of the net should free them, they would lie there trapped forever. Daniel approached this spot and alas! how stricken with horror he was as he stepped into the net. He fell to the ground and lay there so entangled that he gave up all hope of survival. He was certain that the devil himself had captured him, and he tried to move his hand to cross himself, but was forced to capitulate, unable to budge even a finger. Only his eyes and tongue could he stir at all.

A maiden who had erected the net after the unknown knight's departure spied Daniel in this desolation. Daniel had become entrapped just as she was about to depart but, glancing over her shoulder and seeing him enmeshed, she ran back and exclaimed: "Sir knight, your days are numbered. A more unfortunate journey you could not have chosen to undertake. You have done a wretched job of defending yourself. Alas! what is it that you seek here?" "Noble lady," he replied, "tell me first why I lie here like a piece of lead! What has robbed me of my strength?" "You are trapped in a net," said the maiden, to which Daniel replied: "How is the net so made that I am unable to see it?" "You are indeed spared the sight of it," she answered; "had you been able to see it, you would not have fallen into it. No man can see it. For this very reason it has been the undoing of many men."

Daniel of the Blossoming Valley then responded: "Help me out of this net in exchange for a promise which I make to you with knightly fidelity:

that I will be your prisoner willingly and without any bitterness. I shall shun no suffering, great or small, which you command me to undergo. You shall grant me but one wish, which I ask of your mercy and am willing to beg for at your feet: if I must suffer death, grant me first to avenge any harm done to you by any man still alive on this earth, so that I may sacrifice my life valiantly and not die here like a helpless woman."

The maiden was willing to grant him as much; she accepted his assurance that he would refuse nothing which she alone bade him to do, and she extracted him from the net and, taking him by the hand, led him into a nearby cave. It was a comfortable refuge, but he saw no one there save the maiden and himself; this seemed most strange to him until he later heard what had transpired. The lady then asked him to be seated at a table that stood ready there. If he had refused to do so, he would have broken his word and his fidelity, for he had sworn an oath to her to do all that she ordered until such time as she freed him. There was an abundance of food, but he had no desire to eat it until he could know what was to become of him, and until he heard word of his comrade whom he sought.

His concern for the count deprived him of any appetite. When the maiden saw that he drew no joy from the food, she said: "I wish to lament to you, my lord, the state of affairs in this land, how our heartache has multiplied and deepened, and how our joy has been replaced by sorrow in the last year. In truth, you have never before heard of greater sorrow. My father was the lord of the land and was so courtly that he would have, at a moment's notice, given to any man who desired it all that he owned—no matter how dear—save his own life and that of my mother, his wife. It is he who had the tent erected on the field at the foot of the mountain, and it is he who granted fiefs to the knights who constantly and excellently tend the table inside, which is piled high with foodstuffs suitable for each given day. All of this he did in order that travelers journeying that way and desirous of food should find already prepared whatever they sought. It is arranged so that all of the food which stands there during the day is removed from the tent at nightfall and other dishes are then brought in. These then remain there until daybreak, when once again different food is carried in.

"Since my father had the reputation of being a man who was courtly in so many different respects, a mermaid, whose entire body was as lovely as a rose, once journeyed here. We saw accompanying her a wondrous army both on horseback and on foot, for she was queen in the ocean over all the sea-creatures who stood in her service, each and every one. She remained here for four days exactly, until she could verify, by what she saw and heard, my father's courtly repute. She swore on her life that all that had been told her for so many years about him was true, and she acknowledged the veracity of the report that no more perfect man could be found, save King Arthur. For no man could compare with King Arthur and his court; all men had to defer to him. She then departed, bestowing upon him, as a sign of her esteem, a skin so fine that, once inside it, he is well protected against wounds from all manner of weapons. In addition, she gave him this net, which I erected before the portal here. Never has there been a beast so fearsome—be it wild or tame—that it could avoid ensnarement after once stepping into it. Never was there a sword, moreover, so finely crafted nor so precious that it could be used to cut the net. Along with this the mermaid also gave him a salve so excellent that any man who applies but a small amount to his eyes is no longer prevented from seeing as clearly at night as during the day. Even this net itself is rendered visible. Furthermore, one's eyes would become so very sharp that one could split a small hair into nine pieces lengthwise. This salve I still have in my possession.

"Hear now, for the sake of God, how the devil himself has mocked this land. Our day has turned into a never-ending night. It was but a year ago today, indeed, that the devil sent his messenger to us. He has banished joy from our land and has imposed upon us this great sorrow in which we shall have to live for evermore. No foe who attacked us with the sword or with an army could have dealt us any manner of harm, for our land borders on one side on the sea, and is so safe there that no one can invade us. On the other side, this mountain stands along the border; whenever we close the passageway, we are likewise secure.

"The name of this land is the Green Meadow, and it is two miles across. Many a noble lady has lost her husband here in the last year. Even if all the world had conspired against us, we would easily have survived. Now, however, we shall no longer retain our joy or our good name, for the devil has exerted all his power and has won the victory here. During this past year all of the men whom you ought to see in this land have, in truth, lost their lives—the youths as well as the infants. All male children born here have died immediately. All the men, young and old, have been killed by the power of the devil. Only the women are left alive; the men have so utterly disappeared that, were you to search throughout the land, you would find not even thirty men—alas! no mortal has ever witnessed such wretchedness!—and even these thirty shall lie dead before the passing of this very day.

"As I have related to you, it has been exactly a year today. Yet we were to blame for none of it: it was the malice of the devil. At that time my father was hosting a festival—the grandest which he had ever held—when a man came up, bald-headed and red. All that he ordered the guests to do had to be done: however unjust, they dared not refuse. They were sitting at the tables, caught up in the merriment, when this creature came up and ordered them not to tarry, but to go home on foot and on horseback, and to bring back with them all of the inhabitants of the land, both lords and peasants. Many jumped up, all quick to hurry back to their homes, as he had commanded, and to bring back to him all persons of whom they had knowledge, both rich and poor. Even the sick were put on stretchers on horses, and all returned to the court in such numbers that not a man could be found throughout the land who had failed to journey to the court as ordered.

"When the intruder saw them all assembled, he told them in truth that he intended to remain here a year, for he was afflicted with an illness that required his bathing once a week for an entire year. All of the men in this land were to come to him each day without fail. On the spot he slew— whether this pleased them or not—a hundred men and as many more as he needed to fill a vat with blood. In this vat he was to bathe himself. No man could prevent him from carrying out this massacre, for all who heard him speak were rendered as feeble-minded as geese and were unable to think or act to impair this ogre. Each man whom he ordered to step straight into the fire had no choice but to comply; whomever he commands to stand still, moreover, is incapable of moving an inch from that spot. If he wishes to cut them to pieces, they are forced to endure such treatment. As soon as a week had elapsed, he desired yet another bath. And since that time he has carried this on until now there is not a man left save those whom he intends to kill today. And there are painfully few of them!

"When he came here and his words were heard for the very first time, I happened to be in bed deathly ill, although I was, as he commanded, brought before him sick. My own suffering had so deadened my hearing that I never became aware of his speaking. When I later recovered from my sickness, I saw that all who had heard his words had lost their senses. In addition, this ogre ordered my father to don his armor and to roam about incessantly on horseback, bringing back for the intruder's bath the blood of all whom he defeated in battle. For the selfsame reason the net stands on this spot: whomever my father traps in it is accorded the same fate. A week ago this very day my father set out in the morning in pursuit of booty and attacked a knight, whom he defeated. Just as he was about to return here after this success, he spied two men on horseback. They had found the tent and intended to rob my father of his prisoner and to kill him also, except that he barely escaped them by entering the mountain through the passageway near the boulder. Then he waited until one of them had passed the boulder and cut off the second knight. Had they both found their way in, he would have been unable to defend himself against them. One of them had already proved this by attacking my father near the boulder and bringing him into such distress that he never before had experienced so close a brush with death.

"Whatever fighting my father had ever done before was a pittance in comparison with this battle, and all of his previous opponents were mere children. Throughout the day and into the evening I watched them struggle so fiercely that I could never begin to relate it. Both their steeds were killed, and my father was struck so many times that he lay in bed for four full days and would have lost his life had he fought any longer. But they were near by the entrance to the mountain, into which my father finally fled. He galloped straight for the net, causing the one knight to become entrapped in it. Thus he defeated him and brought him before the diseased ogre, whose words immediately rendered him senseless and tame."

"Tell me in God's name, my lady," Daniel interrupted her, "is this knight still alive?" "This I say to you in all truthfulness," she replied, "his life is worthless, and I shall tell you why: his blood would have been added to the ogre's bath on the same day as their duel, had my father overcome him before the bath had already been accomplished. But they fought on until nightfall, and the knight was captured only after the ogre had already bathed. It is only for this reason that he still lives. But on this very day his blood must be mixed in with the bath. I, too, shall suffer today a sorrow which I shall never be able to forget. God help me that I may never see this day to the end! Four of my brothers are still alive; my father has ridden out in search of them and will soon be returning. Before long the ogre will butcher them all. How shall I ever overcome this grief? You have been too rash in your actions and now stand at my command, which—as you have sworn before God—you shall carry out. I shall now offer you a choice: slay the diseased ogre or endure the same fate that so many before you have suffered here, or cut off my head so that I might give up my life along with my family and not live to experience such heartache. The choices are three, my lord; now make your decision from among them. Whichever of them you may carry out, I shall then free you."

Daniel then answered heroically: "The choice is easily made: I shall avenge you on the diseased ogre. If, however, I am unable to do so, then my blood shall have to be added to his bath before I would ever consent to do you any bodily harm. Never will I agree to kill you. Can you tell me, my lady, is it at all possible for me to come close to the diseased ogre? I have concocted a plan whereby he shall fail to render me senseless, no matter how he may chatter on: I shall obstruct my ears with a well-molded plug of wax. I have in my possession an excellent sword, and if I can draw close to the creature, he will fare the worse for it. Both my sword and my zeal are so sharp as to enable me easily to hack him to pieces."

"You cannot come close to the ogre," the maiden replied; "as soon as he spots you, you will be compelled to stop on the spot, unless he bids you come nearer or goes up to you himself." "Advise me what to do," Daniel then said, "for I shall never slay him if I cannot come closer to him." "I shall tell you in truth," the lady then answered; "if you approach him with your hearing obstructed, he will pose many questions to you, whatever sort he pleases. If you place anything in your ears, you will be unable to hear what answer you must give him. Then he will suffer you to live no longer. So foul a creature is he that he will command you to turn into a stone on that very spot—or an animal, or whatever he pleases. So great is the power that he has from the devil that he is sure to put a curse on you.

"I have fully verified all of this and shall tell you how: twelve weeks ago I captured another man who was willing to avenge me likewise by stopping up his ears. Unfortunately he became so deaf that he heard nothing of what was being said. When the diseased ogre perceived that the knight did not hear his words, he became so enraged that he put a curse on him. Once the creature stopped him in his tracks with the power of the devil, a more martyred man than this could never be found, however long one might search. For he then commanded him to fall to the ground and rendered him both deaf and dumb, as well as blind and crippled. All of this befell that wretched man. I had stolen up close so that I could easily discern his gestures. But I heard nothing of what was said, for I had blocked my ears so that I might not be rendered senseless."

"Then it seems to me from what you say," replied Daniel, "that one must maintain a good distance if one is to stay alive. But pray tell me where I might find this creature now." She replied, "He is nearby." To this Daniel answered: "Now tell me, where are the fine youths whom he intends to kill today? How has he watched over them? And when are they to die?" "They are, as he ordered, by the house located in the orchard," the beautiful maiden replied, "except that he desired to delay the bath and see whether my father might acquire a victim to die along with the others; he is therefore awaiting his return; the bath would already stand prepared, and they would all be dead now—if indeed they are not already! Since my father shows no sign of returning, it may be that he has lost his life elsewhere. And I would not object to this, since he still faces death today from the ogre."

Daniel was greatly alarmed that he might lose not only the count, but also his own life and his reputation. He could think of no plan of action and did not know where to find anyone who could give him protection from the creature's curses. No less than Daniel's life stood in the balance. "I shall go, my lady," he then said, "and allow myself to be slain along with the others and let him bathe in my blood. For I have no hope of inflicting injury upon this man. Since he is able to do battle by means of spells, there is no way for me to seize him. In this manner I shall carry out your commandment."

"No, my lord," said the lady in reply, "for the sake of God not this! You are a most knightly gentleman, and I am but a wretched woman who has lost all of my family, my only source of comfort. I shall gladly let you live, for the purpose of killing me so that I might not experience this grim ordeal. Why would you sacrifice your life, which is far more useful than mine? You must never allow your life to be taken without good cause. I will think no more highly of you for suffering death merely for my sake. When I see that I must live without my brothers and my father, then I wish only to strike myself dead."

She urgently begged him to put an end to her life, but he refused. "In truth, I shall shear off my hair and at once don men's clothing," said the lady; "the ogre will then mistake me for a man. I shall accompany you there, so that death may befall me along with my father and brothers." With all his charm Daniel entreated the maiden to abstain from this, but she refused to grant him as much. "Your tresses are radiant and blond," said Daniel of the Blossoming Valley; "you must not cut them off. If you will for my sake renounce your intention, I shall solemnly promise to do all that I can today, even to death. I would not gladly quit this world; I would prefer to live if possible. Do this for my sake: remain hidden nearby where this nightmare is to take place today, until you see how we shall fare. What need is there now of more words? I shall gladly do all that lies in my power, so that we may remain alive!"

The lady was pleased at such comforting words and promised to do what he bade her and to stand concealed at a certain spot until she saw his fate. She then told Daniel the way to the orchard, which he adroitly entered, quickly finding the good knights who were to suffer torture that day. Wishing at all costs to find his comrade, he looked over the splendid knights one and all until he spied the count, whom he quickly recognized. The assembled knights offered Daniel no form of welcome whatsoever as he approached; they neither spoke nor bowed. Since they were so silent, he, too, fell silent and said nothing, for fear that, should he utter even the first word, the diseased ogre might perchance be near enough to hear it and would foil Daniel's mission. Seeing that no one spoke to him, Daniel perceived that they were utterly robbed of their senses, and he began to imitate them in their gestures. He glanced all about him and carefully observed all that they did, then assumed the same mannerisms himself.

The ogre, wishing to delay no longer, but rather to make preparations for his bath, now came up and ordered all of them over to a vat. They hastened to do his bidding. Daniel of the Blossoming Valley was cunningly hidden in their midst, fearful of being discovered. Beneath his cloak he carried his bare sword hidden from view. Soon they were at the vat, where the diseased creature grabbed the nearest man by the hair and pulled off his garment, till he was as naked as the back of his hand: this was to be the first victim. The ogre stabbed at him as at a swine and raised him over the vat, digging with his grim knife at the man's heart. While the ogre was occupied with this, Daniel slipped up behind him just in the nick of time and lopped off his head. The creature was never again to butcher men or to utter words harmful to their ears. Thus was an end put to his bathing.

All who were standing around him regained their senses and exclaimed: "What has happened to us?" Although they had witnessed everything happening before their very eyes for the entire year, they in fact had no understanding of what had taken place, up until such time as Daniel had saved himself and slain the diseased ogre. He began to relate to them how this creature had dulled their senses from the very outset, what he had done to harm them, and how he had bathed in their blood during the past year. "All of this is so," they replied in unison. "We watched it happen day in, day out, but never once thought of escaping or mustering our courage in common defense. Death was inevitable for us; no one could have fended it off had you yourself not done so."

The Count of the Bright Fountain, meanwhile, had come to his senses and proclaimed: "Welcome in God's name; you are in truth His messenger, and He has sent you here. Your hand has rescued me likewise from the tower in my own land. Both times I would have been lost. Never have I received such great help from one man. I desire nothing more than to be granted the occasion to serve you in return. This indeed would please me." Daniel then replied: "I shall show you an undertaking in which you can easily requite me three times over for the favor I have accorded you." "Onward then!" replied the count; "I have you to thank for the soundness both of my body and of my mind—this I shall evermore proclaim. Show me, for the sake of God, where I might prove myself worthy of all this. See for yourself whether I am worthy of being called a man."

"This man has made us happy once again," cried all the knights with one voice. "We shall all set out with him and most gladly test our fate alongside him, for it is because of him that we are now alive." The lovely maiden who had captured Daniel there came up to him then and gave him a gracious reception unsurpassed by any of which I have ever heard tell. Her eyes became wet with joy. She then went to where she found her mother, to whom she related all that had transpired, and who returned right away and received Daniel, bidding him tell her whether her lord was slain, or, if not, what had befallen him. Daniel told her: "I saw him this very morning as I came here on horseback. When I offered him my salutation, he knocked me to my feet and nearly killed me, save that my good fortune plucked me from his grasp, so that I barely broke away and escaped through the passageway into this mountain. I then closed the entrance before him; otherwise he would have killed me." Daniel did not wish to tell them what had in fact transpired; his heart was seized with joy in great abundance that he had not slain that knight, and that he knew him to be still alive, for it was best thus.

Both knights and ladies proceeded to the field at the foot of the mountain to see what was happening there. The lord of the land then entered the tent, healthy in both body and mind, and his subjects presented Sir Daniel, their source of comfort. "This man has redeemed us," said the lady; "give thanks to him that I still possess my senses. We have all been mindless this past year; not a man has survived save for you and your children and the knights present here. You have this knight to thank for your being still alive."

The lord bowed deeply to Daniel and said: "Show me how or where I can repay you for my life, which you have given back to me. It was my derangement which deceived me into trying to kill you, but even then, sir knight, you defeated me in a most praiseworthy manner, so that I had to surrender my life into your hands. May God reward you for allowing me to live and for helping me to survive this creature who was bent on murdering me. I was utterly doomed, and you have saved me. You must therefore grant to me the chance to make recompense for this. I have nothing but kind intentions to pay you back with, as well I should. You will do well to grant me this much."

"Excellent!" Daniel replied. "You speak with the tongue of a courageous man. Order the horses to be brought here, for I shall take you—if you are willing—to a place where I too must undergo a bath which, if I cannot fend off, is the most deadly that any man ever endured. This bath is none other than death itself, and I have great need of your aid."

"Come then!" the lord said. "Bring up the horses! Coming to the aid of this man is something for which I greatly thirst, for he has rescued me from certain death this very day. If I am able, I shall indeed help him in return."

There then arose a great flurry of activity as his men went after the horses to set out with Daniel. In a very short time they all began to take their leave. The Lady of the Green Meadow took Daniel by the hand and said: "If my land had in it as many knights as a year ago, in truth, they would accompany you now, each and every one. May God Himself be the one to protect you."

Daniel now rode off with twenty-six men who were every bit as valuable to him in their prowess as born kinsmen would have been. They placed in the balance both their lives and all that they possessed. He who gladly does his utmost for others is well deserving of all manner of gratitude, for gratitude sweetens his sense of fulfillment.

As they rode up to the mountain, the giant whom Daniel had slain still lay there hacked to pieces. Daniel's companions marveled greatly at this and exclaimed: "Whoever was able to fell this creature was indeed a hero against whom there could be no defense." Daniel, however, did not betray the fact that he was this same hero. Then they rode on into the mountain and came to the rock, where they all cried out: "Alas! the man who cut this cavity through this rock must indeed wield a marvelous sword!" Sir Daniel comforted them, saying, "He who hewed this hole does whatever I command. He will aid us bravely in our midst even today." And so his comrades declared: "Then no man can resist us and come away alive!"

The Remaining Battles

As the men of this army were approaching through the mountain, they heard the beast wailing with the roar of an abyss opening up over all the land and with a din so deafening that it seemed as though the heavens were about to come crashing down to earth on that very spot. Those who were near the beast soon reached the limit of their endurance and quickly put the banner back in its mouth.

Daniel now came riding up robustly with his followers, whom he was
eager to let show their good will toward him in whatever ways they could.
When King Arthur saw them approaching, he was amazed and exclaimed:
"When did Daniel ride out?" But there was no one in the camp who could
offer an explanation, for Daniel had set out in secret. The king, however,
showed Daniel his good intentions and bade him welcome.

After that greeting there was precious little time for King Arthur to hear
of all that had happened, for at that moment they spotted a good two
thousand knights galloping toward them on horseback. Once having caught
sight of them, they tarried no longer. Many a bold hero leapt into the saddle
without the aid of his stirrup and scarcely waited long enough to grab his
spear and shield. They restrained themselves no longer and took off like a
rush of wind. From the opposite direction came a great many men, fearlessly hurtling toward King Arthur's men. They yearned to be at the very
front ranks of the army, and in their zeal to move ahead of their comrades,
many a man thought his steed too sluggish. There arose a cracking of lances
as though an entire forest were crashing to the ground, and there followed
the clanking of swords banging against the tops of the helmets, just as
though they were all blacksmiths striking on their anvils.

O what powerful blows King Arthur dealt out by the dozens! He acted
as a plow for the others, for he broke through in front and opened up a
furrow wide enough for his men to follow him on their mounts. Both
horses and riders he mowed down, not unlike a farmer who is making a
clearing in the forest and concentrates his every effort on it, cutting down
everything which causes damage, until such time as the field is of value. In
the same way King Arthur slashed down whatever was in his path that
offered him injury, be it horse or man, until he had carved out a wide open
field all around him. Proudly and defiantly did he fight.

Sir Gawein, his sister's son, was among the very finest of knights. He
proved both that same day and at other times that he was a valuable warrior.
For he was able to cast such a spell that all who received it from him fell to the
ground and died: this spell was a mighty sword-blow that cut through bones
and bone-marrow with the force of a wind. Many a youth did he silence on
the battlefield, so that they never made another sound. He struck away at their
skin so fiercely that they had no need of weeping; all throughout the day he
showed his skill at jousting and proved that he was indeed no beginner!

His comrade Sir Iwein cut down so many of the enemy as he broke
through their ranks that every man—however far off—felt far too close to
him and would have preferred to take on any three men other than Iwein
alone. All were doomed as soon as they came within range of his sword. The
bold hero Parzival struck away at the finely-crafted gold embellishments on
his opponents' helmets, so that the skulls beneath split and broke open. Every
man whom he hit, be he never so ardent in battle before, soon turned cold
with death and suffered such utter impoverishment that he lost all he owned,
not only his life and his possessions, but even his very blood until he finally
became something that he had never been before. It was a weighty burden
indeed which Parzival loaded upon the backs of so many of those men.

Daniel of the Blossoming Valley, too, could be seen riding through the
battlefield, which was the most formidable path ever set foot on by any
man; alongside him rode the lord of the Green Meadow, who made not a

single threat which was not followed up by a death-blow. How very happy he was to serve Daniel, who had undergone so much suffering on his account when freeing him from the ogre's bath! Many a man was to atone for that suffering on this day, for the count fought with the fierceness of a lion; all four of his sons, moreover, were distinguished heroes and battled so furiously that Daniel remarked: "Fortunate am I to have set eyes upon you!" And the rest of his companions, how bravely they defended themselves! The Count of the Bright Fountain too gained the chance to prove whether or not he could bring death to other men that day, and whether he himself was worthy of being called a man.

Whatever one does, good or evil, to an upright man, one receives the same in return, but in double measure. The count returned such offerings again and again that day and accomplished all that he had boasted of. He had promised to serve Daniel willingly if it should become necessary, and he was fervently glad that it had come to this. Each and every living man whom he struck met with immediate death. So powerfully did he bang away at his opponents that red juice spurted from their steel helmets. They were utterly incapable of protecting themselves; all who came to him hale and hearty were quickly dispatched infirm and weakly.

Hear now a wondrous thing: however many men were on the battlefield, there was one judge who watched over them all. Whenever one man overcame the other, this judge, as judges are wont to do, separated the two. He could take on ten at a time, and they were all just as totally disengaged from one another, for this judge was called death. The separation was inevitable, yet if they entertained thoughts of stealing away from one another, death stepped in and pitted them against each other. O how they raged on that battlefield! How each man strove after fame! Many a man died, I believe, who had little expected death. What tales were born there of deeds which had never before been told! Many a man became crippled there, many a man was slain; many a man became a coward, many as bold as a wild boar; and many gave vent to their anger. Each showed his courage, which furthered their cause in battle. Since they were of one accord, their undertaking was successful, and they demonstrated all the more clearly that each of them loathed his enemy and would have slain them all at once with his own hands. Those of the enemy who had ridden up haughtily on horseback would have gladly accepted the lowly fate of coming away alive on foot, but even this was denied them.

The harsh were pitted against the harsh in this battle, the strong against the strong, and the sly against the sly. As long as each man was able, whatever blows he dealt out were met with firm resistance. All of them received their fill of this fare, and vast strength was expended in the killing and the frenzied tempest. Anyone who assumed a gentle demeanor there would have been scorned outright and might indeed have incurred injury as a consequence.

These excellent knights, as they kept at each other in desperate self-defense, pressed together until both sides were intermingled. Many then brandished their swords as if desiring nothing less than to kill off all the enemy single-handedly and to bear alone the strength of twelve men or more. No man was victorious who could not fight better and better, more steadfastly, and with might surpassing that of all the others. King Arthur's companions, who had greater endurance, could be seen pressing onward untiringly, spreading death on all sides. All of this was a battle to exceed all battles.

After the battle had raged for a long time, they all converged—Daniel of the Blossoming Valley, King Arthur, and the knights from his court—on horseback at the middle of the battlefield. Fearless youths were these! They all came together and rode in formations through the army of the enemy with a great clamor, freeing many a man from his suffering. The medicine which they dealt out was death itself, with which they were able to punish many opponents. Eventually, however, as their numbers began to thin, they feared death and were compelled to give up all thoughts of victory; thus they surrendered themselves, as was high time, into King Arthur's hands, and the battle came to an end.

King Arthur's men then made preparations to rest for the night, for as you have already heard, they planned to remain there for seven nights (since King Matur had assembled seven armies in his land, each of which journeyed to the tent on separate days). Had all seven armies attacked at the same time, King Arthur's men would have had but little hope of holding up in battle. Thus they camouflaged their encampment, as they planned to do battle five more times with the enemy; only then would they proceed into the land of Cluse. When they had doffed their armor, they were in high spirits because of their success. They laughed and sang and were cheerful and merry. After resting a bit until they overcame their fatigue, they gathered around King Arthur, some sitting and others standing, and all spoke of how Sir Daniel had performed most admirably on the battlefield of Cluse. Daniel, they said, was courageous and wise and was alone responsible for the victory; they would all have died in battle had he not slain the giants. It was because of his valor, others claimed, that such fame had fallen to their lot in Cluse. All present declared Daniel to be indispensable to their triumph.

The king then bade Daniel relate where he had ridden off alone during the night; he also asked Daniel's companions not to keep silent, but to tell him where they had made Daniel's acquaintance. The Count of the Bright Fountain then recounted the story of the dwarf's death at Daniel's hand in the land of the Dark Mountain, how Daniel had acquired the sword from him, and how he had come to the count's aid by rescuing him out of the tower from the creature who carried the lethal head; he related how Daniel had slain the ogre who intended to bathe in their blood, and he finally told the king of all the losses that the lord and the lady of the Green Meadow had suffered from these baths and how desolate their land was, since the only men who had survived were those who had come along on this journey.

When the king had heard all of this, it appeared most amazing to him, and yet very fortunate and indeed a great act of cunning that Daniel had slain opponents whom no other man could withstand. "Of all that I have ever heard tell of brave feats," said the king, "no tale has ever come to me of so monumental a deed as that which Sir Daniel has done." All of the valiant heroes then exclaimed merrily: "May Christ in all His power protect Daniel, for everything about him is upright and courageous, and it is just that he should be acclaimed. For he is able to wrestle with all hardships, as a brave and good knight should. It is good and just that he never encounter failure. Never has there been, and never will there be, a knight with such good cause for joy."

It was the custom of King Arthur's court that no man should tell of his own honorable deeds. Nonetheless such deeds were not left untold, for as soon as another man heard of them, he related them, to the glory of the knight who had performed them. All of them strove, therefore, whenever possible to augment the next man's fame and praise. Sir Daniel's companions then inquired what man it was who bore the sword which had cut down the giants and had hewn the great opening throught the rock. "All wondrous things that have been performed here," said Sir Gawein in reply, "were done by Sir Daniel, who rescued you from adversity in your own land. We would all surely have suffered death had he not slaughtered the giants. It is he too who cut through the rock. Let no man tell you otherwise."

They passed the remainder of the day in this manner and were merry all the night until daybreak; when the hour drew near when their opponents were to arrive, they lured them to the battlefield by once more causing the beast to wail. In a short time they spotted the army galloping up in great haste toward them, and they rushed to welcome them with such a greeting and such a throng and such jousting that many a man had to fix his mind upon saving his life. Each set about giving a sharp rejoinder to the blows of his opponent; they strewed the field all over with dead men, for many a man fell to the ground, never to rise again. They fought in the manner of men giving vent to their anger. Some of them won and some lost, but no one lost as much as those who tasted death. These were the ones who truly lost everything: all else was a mere child's game.

One could see following Daniel of the Blossoming Valley through the midst of the battlefield both the Count of the Bright Fountain and the men with whom he was to be put into the ogre's bloodbath and whom he had assembled in the Land of the Green Meadow, where the maiden had captured Daniel in the net. These men rode here for Daniel's fame and were fighting so fiercely that it was a most honorable thing to see. Those who wished to remain alive had no choice but to give themselves over into his power as captives. Thus the battle ended, and King Arthur's men rested once more.

As the three defeats were besetting the knights of the land of Cluse, they made great haste toward the court, where they heard their queen's deep lament. This occurred on the same day when the third battle came to an end. It was with great impatience that the enemy awaited the dawn of the fourth day. When that time came, all who meant to defend the land rode off to meet King Arthur, swearing fervently either to avenge their king or to leave their land forever. They were greatly pleased that King Arthur, who had played such havoc on their court, was still in the land, for they knew full well where they could avenge their suffering. Out of their hatred of King Arthur was hatched a savage plot in the attack on him: their numbers as they rode off into battle were four times as great as those with whom Arthur's men had previously fought. Now they too, however, were faced with the boldest warriors ever to sit astride their steeds.

King Arthur, bravely leading a forest of spears and swords, now came riding up to the fourth army. Were there any man present that day desirous of death, he would have been granted his wish in quick measure; many a man who desired to live, on the other hand, also lost his life. Spurs dug into the horses on both sides, and they could be seen hurtling toward one another, the spears splintering as they crashed together. Swords were then unsheathed and came cracking down on their opponents' shields.

King Arthur's men bravely took up the fight, raging about with such mighty blows at the enemy that their shields flew to pieces in their very hands. They cut and struggled and struck and fought, until many a man would gladly have been anywhere else than there that day. They forsook all raillery and demonstrated with grimness of purpose what they intended to accomplish and that they would tolerate neither disgrace nor a show of force. The enemy, however, had the same purpose in mind and acted in a similar manner.

A battle of immeasurable compass arose. The way through the battlefield was strewn with the dead, but there was no rest for the living, who exchanged blow after blow. Little did they tolerate anything that could be avenged! Each and every one of them made it burdensome for his opponent, arching frightfully with each sword-blow and forcing his sword through steel and iron. Both horses and men could be seen tumbling to the ground; the blood ran everywhere. The heat of the battle was cause alone for agony. Many a man made the leap from life into death, and every youth, no matter how green in years, turned quickly and inexorably old once he tasted, even briefly, the sort of pleasure enjoyed on that battlefield; a grim day it was indeed. They renounced all idle chatter and spoke only in terse words, chiefly with the sword alone.

In such great quantity did men's armor fly off that even the experienced men among them became frightened. All who could see this took to swords which were strong and sharp and capable of killing a man regardless of what armor he wore. Out of all of this resulted on both sides an epidemic parting of body and spirit. Many a man was forced to do his enemy's bidding and to choose death, which was a formidable command indeed. Renouncing all scorn and contempt, but equally devoid of joy and laughter, they went about this pastime, which was wholly without gentility. Any man who lay weak in bed would have been a fool to partake of such a battle!

Daniel of the Blossoming Valley made no effort to conceal his valor, for he felled the enemy right and left as he rode through their midst. No man could encounter such agony as Daniel meted out with his sword; he did so with such mighty blows that each victim lost all memory then and there of all that had ever happened to him, be it sweet or bitter. For Daniel knocked them senseless and taught them what it was that he bore in his hand. Whatever he struck with that sword was pierced as by a bolt of lightning. I shall tell you why Daniel was able to penetrate so deeply into the enemy ranks: his sword was amazingly sharp, and he himself possessed such great strength and such craftiness, and he swung the sword so zealously that it began to cut ahead, all of its own accord, so that nothing was able to withstand it. It was a grim toll he paid out; even helmets hard as flint were defenseless at his hand. Any man who desired to live had to keep his distance, or Daniel would have slain him in quick measure.

The Count of the Bright Fountain swung a sword covered to the hilt with blood. All whom he encountered had to surrender their bodies and their lives in exchange for death. A grim purchase was this indeed! Both the horses and their riders he mowed down, and he sliced open the skin of all who rode at him, so that they had to forgo not only revenge, but even the utterance of another word. King Arthur's comrades were driven by their bold courage to press onward toward their lord, cutting down a whole host of men along the way and leaving them wholly unaware of the battle that raged on. There were on the battlefield that day both fierceness and hatred, suffering and distress, displeasure and sorrow; there were animosity and lack of moderation, unrest and great power, discomfort, ire, and wrath. Much was lost that was never again recovered.

Those who were able and knew how to fight fared well, so that King Arthur could be seen performing marvelous feats, and the men of Cluse paid dearly. King Arthur's brave helpers proved well their valor and followed him wherever he rode. Many a helmet was made jagged in consequence; this was no undertaking for a coward, for any man who feared his enemy would have fared better elsewhere. They showed such knightliness and were so courageous that any man who wished to do battle with them had to back up his challenge with courage and with feats of bravery. They rode through blood up to the horses' knees, and in which all who were knocked down drowned. But not a one of them displayed cowardice: so great was their collective burden that even those who were mortally wounded dwelt not on their pain, since they yearned fervently on both sides for victory.

King Arthur carried in his hands against the enemy a salve that, once applied to a man, penetrated throughout his body, driving out his soul so that it no longer remained within him. This salve was the sword which he carried and swung so mightily that many a hero lay dead. Never had a living man endured greater tribulation. They hacked away with their swords, so that everything which was on or around them glowed redhot, and whatever their swords touched went up in flames like straw. In the end, there were many among them who would have been happy to escape either dead or alive from this holocaust.

All throughout the long, hot day they battled, until night fell and fatigue sapped their strength so completely that neither side was able to carry out the full vengeance which they were bent on wreaking. A truce was then arranged until the following day. The countless blows which each side had doled out made them glad to put down their weapons and rest for the night. Although both sides had agreed on the truce, King Matur's men nonetheless did not wish to leave the battlefield, but rather dismounted not far from their enemy on the field, where they could see King Arthur's tents already pitched. For they were so bold as to claim that, once having regained their strength, they would easily be the victors. Thus the men of Cluse camped near King Arthur and kept careful watch throughout the night, so that he might not escape them before they were able to overrun him. In fact, there was no need for them to guard against his escape, for even if they had tried to drive him away, he was bent on remaining there until such time as he should either perish or else win the victory.

Late in the night King Arthur went into council with his men to determine the best course of action. The illustrious hero Daniel of the Blossoming Valley spoke up first and said: "If you are willing to follow me in every detail, I have devised a scheme which, if we can carry it out, will reap us the victory and place the enemy at our feet in defeat. It is my belief that they will be forced to concede the victory without even having fought at all. In this way we both will fare well: they for not losing any further lives, as well as we for no longer having to endure the agony of battle. We are killing too many good men who, I think, ought not to die. By my plan, however, they shall preserve their lives and have to surrender to you both themselves and all they possess. Listen now to my plan and see whether it is pleasing to you: we shall all stop our ears before daybreak. When the truce ends, we shall simply remain where we are and let the enemy come to us. Then, as soon as they begin the attack, we shall cause the beast to wail. This will do not the least bit of harm to us, but the din will roar so thunderously through their heads as to deaden both their senses and their bodies. This will be to our advantage, for they will fall to the ground and be compelled to surrender. Thus both the land and its inhabitants will be ours."

The lords all proclaimed Daniel's advice to be wise, and they hastened to carry out what he had proposed. By daybreak they were all prepared, and the truce was withdrawn. King Matur's troops attacked King Arthur, whose men pulled the banner from the beast's mouth, causing it to wail. It raised a din so frightfully overwhelming (as well it could!) that it shot through the heads of all who heard it, and knocked them from their horses onto the ground. The same agony struck all of King Matur's men; not a one could escape, nor defend himself any longer. All who wished to save themselves were forced to surrender their swords and beg for their lives.

Daniel's Coronation

The battle ended in such a manner that King Arthur's men accepted from the enemy both their swords and their oaths of allegiance, whether they wished to give them or not. King Matur's men had met with defeat, but had avoided death in battle. King Arthur's men then replaced the banner and silenced the beast. The men of Cluse approached King Arthur and gave over to him themselves and their land, as well as their children and wives, and were granted it all back from him as a fief. They knelt at his feet and swore an oath that they would never knowingly commit any act which could bring either harm or disgrace upon him. Thus the enemies became good friends. They saw to it before nightfall that the slain King Matur was removed from the battlefield and buried along with all the other dead in a manner befitting his position. A great many priests were quickly procured to help lend the burial propriety in the eyes of God. The king then turned all his thoughts toward a quick end to the animosity between himself and the queen of Cluse.

The king now summoned the knights of that land, who had previously been his enemies, and said: "Now your queen feels enmity towards me; I have, to be sure, not served her well, and cannot therefore reproach her for this. Now, however, you must set about winning me her favor. Tell her of my innocence, and that I came here a prisoner. If her animosity is set aside, I shall—as long as I am as well in body and mind as I am now—treat as my own sons all who aid me in this. I shall compensate you for all the harm I have caused you, and I shall make each of you so happy that you will have to agree that I have treated you well." They were most pleased at King Arthur's words and replied: "This shall indeed be accomplished in quick measure. The queen shall have to put an end to her anger."

They then rode off to the queen and found the noble lady (this was unavoidable) in deep heartache, for she was enduring misery at her dear lord's death. Her lament and her distress and her dire grief had nearly taken her life. Ever since the tidings had come that her lord had been slain, she had lain day and night in misery, doing nothing save for weeping and lamenting, and proving in many ways that no woman had ever undergone greater sorrow. All who heard her words and saw her gestures were certain that such wretchedness had never before befallen a woman. No one thought that she would ever recover from her distress, but that she would have to die of grief.

Her closest counselors, who had advised her all her life as to the right course of action, were at great pains to free her from her suffering. In numerous ways and with great zeal they directed their attention to this. Her very dearest advisors, who well dared to offer their counsel, besought her for the sake of God to be of good cheer, vowing that, as long as she lived, they would serve her willingly and would never abandon her or withdraw their material support. With one voice they proclaimed: "It is our common will that you fall silent. Your lament has been long and excessive, and we beseech you to suppress it. If you grant us this and forsake your weeping, we shall evermore undertake to augment your fame and carry out your will. Moreover, we wish also to inform you that, if you fail to follow our advice, you will incur our displeasure."

Tearfully the lady replied: "Do I not even dare to lament my distress in your presence, my lords, without losing your service and your favor? If so, I shall lose both undeservedly. I can easily see, as well as hear, that a twofold misfortune has beset me: that I must live without my lord and that, in addition, you are to deny me at such quick notice your favor. This I shall always lament to God! I would have none of this to contend with if I still had my lord. Am I supposed to be pleased to hear from all of you so foolish a threat, that if I do not suddenly assume an air of bliss, I shall lose your favor? Any woman whom a lesser burden might befall would certainly be allowed to weep and lament. Yet I have lost the most precious lord the earth has even seen. Never has a woman acquired so good a name by her husband as have I. For this reason I shall never again be happy. If you possessed understanding, you would not reproach me for my weeping. I shall prove to my lord that I cannot forget him and shall weep until the day I die. I shall never again think highly of you, for my grief does not affect you in the least, and you are so quick to oppose me."

One of her vassals, who fully grasped the situation, then said: "This you must believe in all truth: that we too have never and never will suffer so great a loss as this. But what would it avail us to die of grief, since we would gain nothing thereby? Listen carefully therefore to what we have to say, or else you will lose your people and your land and be left quite empty-handed. For this reason you ought not to let yourself scorn our advice so rashly. You are acting in too great haste and may have to abandon your land and your court. What right had our lord to request of King Arthur that he become his vassal? All kings now alive on the earth are but a puff of wind in comparison to Arthur. We had in our army eight thousand knights, but still had to concede the battle: how do you hope to defeat him now? If you wish to be responsible for two more such blights in addition to this one, you will regret it only after it is too late. You should not disregard our advice so contemptuously, for you have long heard the saying that a man who refuses the advice of others cannot be helped by others. Many a man has had to forfeit all his happiness because of a grudge. Consider this, my lady. Your esteem will not be diminished; if you follow our counsel, you stand only to gain in benefit and fame. Your anger toward us is without justification. We shall be every bit as zealous now to do all that will augment and broaden your good name as we once were to carry out whatever my lord commanded us. Consider this advice, which to each of us seems wise, and it shall ever be our intention, both publicly and in private, to perform all that you command."

"Even though your advice may be ill-weighed," said the queen, "I shall now follow it and do what you counsel me, but only because you have always in the past shown nothing save good intentions toward me. May God dispose all of you to maintain your allegiance to me and never swerve from standing by me with full loyalty. Speak now your wish, and I shall have to grant it, for I cannot dispense with your favor."

All of her liegemen then spoke up: "You have only to gain from this, my lady. If our lord had acted in a like manner, he would be alive today. But he would not act according to reason and lies dead as a result. What possible need could he have had to order King Arthur to journey here with the giant and surrender on the spot both himself and his land? When King Arthur refused, the giant took him captive in his own court and in the midst of all his men, and led him off as his prisoner. Now, however, King Arthur has demonstrated the greatness of his valor, of which we have always heard tell. He has slain our lord, along with many a good vassal, but he has acted justly, and so success has smiled upon him. Now he has forced us—those of us who had any remaining will to live—to surrender to his power both ourselves and our possessions, and has allowed us to keep our lives, which we received from him. That which we have done, you must also do. Since we were defeated in battle, we can be glad that he even suffers us to live and to keep what we possess. You are well protected with him, for he is blessed with all good qualities. We have heard from him that he wishes, in truth, to compensate for your loss if you are willing to dismiss from your thoughts all that has happened. It is for this reason that we have been so bold as to attempt to win for him your favor. Now you should, for our sake, abandon all blame, and do as we advise you, if we are dear to you at all."

The queen then replied: "I shall follow you, as I ought, in whatever you advise and do what appears best to you. I have full trust in you that you will not betray me in the end. King Arthur has inflicted great suffering upon me: since I have served all of you well in lamenting my lord, I am now willing to assume a new attitude and to forgo, for your sake, all revenge in order that I not lose my land or your favor. It is indeed an incalculable act of loyalty that you do not abandon me or leave me in the lurch for my having suffered such misfortune. If your advice that I drop all animosity is indeed given in good faith, then you must all promise me here and now that you will remain at my command in word and in deed and never do anything which might bring such adversity upon me again." All of them swore to this, and the queen said: "I shall now permit you to do whatever you want."

   The men of Cluse then rode back to King Arthur and brought him the good news that their lady had undergone a change of heart. Hearing this, the noble King Arthur and his men welcomed them warmly, after which he set out with them in great joy toward the court. When the lady saw him approaching, she arose and greeted him. Her grief, however, still so oppressed her that she was unable to forget all that had happened, and she burst into tears. King Arthur, whose eyes, unbeknown to the others, welled over with tears of sorrow, then said: "Try to take this in good spirit. For in truth, if I am to live, I shall demonstrate to you that indeed all of your suffering touches me to the quick. I would never have inflicted any harm upon your lord here in his own land, except that he left me no choice but to kill him. It was in my eyes a disgrace to surrender to him as long as I could live a free man. Your grief causes me to feel great pity; now, however, you must forgo further sorrow for the sake of my loyalty, and must forgive me my transgressions.

   "I wish to win your favor in a manner that augments your good name. I shall devote myself solely to atoning for your damages and for the death of your husband, so that you will once more become happy. My own heart will have to dwell in the shadow of sorrow until I have devised a means of making your heart glad. I am afflicted and pained by all that I have done to harm you, for I have never before inflicted injury or distress upon a woman. God is my witness that what has transpired could not have been avoided with my good name intact; it had to happen and it did happen. But in truth if you are willing to overlook all that I have done to trouble you, I shall not fail to make amends for your unhappiness. Either I shall rise so high in your favor that you will justly pray that God reward me for it, or else I shall never again wear my crown. Now have no fear of me, for, in truth, all shall turn out well for you."

   "This I shall trust in," said the queen. She was so consoled to hear that it was self-defense which had compelled King Arthur to slay her lord and to hear the promises which he now made to her that she forgot all anger and kissed him on the lips. Listen now and I shall tell you what happiness reigned there, once this sorrow came to an end. King Arthur went into council with all of those whom he had brought from Britain, and said: "I shall tell you all of my plan. Help me now to carry it out with the teaching of your loyal hearts, and advise me how to deal with this lady in a manner commensurate with my good name. Give thought, all of you, and tell me which man it is who can free her of her worries. See to it that your advice is not unwise, for whomever you choose by common consent, to him I intend to give over both the lady and the land. Such a man may indeed call himself happy."

   "I myself wish to offer advice on this matter," said his nephew Sir Gawein: "there is not a man alive today who is right for this land except Daniel of the Blossoming Valley. If you are all willing to follow my counsel, the lady cannot be better cared for. Had Daniel not slain both giants with his own hand, we would never have lived to tell at home the story of what has transpired here. Now we shall requite him for saving our lives; do my bidding therefore and agree that he is well deserving of such reward. None of us could have won the sword from the dwarf as did he nor saved the Count of the Bright Fountain nor the Maiden of the Green Meadow. This land and this lady are well provided for with him."

All of them concurred and asked King Arthur with one voice to grant Daniel of the Blossoming Valley the land and the lady. They were glad to see him rewarded for all that he had done while fighting alongside them. The king praised Sir Gawein's advice, saying: "I myself was disposed toward just what you have counseled me. Since I have now heard your common will, you will be granted it, for you have advised me well in this matter. My life and all that I possess will always be shared with you and ventured for the fame of each and every one of you."

He then inquired of Daniel as to whether he desired the land. Daniel replied merrily: "Indeed I do! May God Himself reward all of you for granting to me alone what we have together won in battle. This is indeed a sign of your faithfulness. I shall prove myself ever worthy of this if I am granted long enough to live."

No other man had ever received a greater benefaction from King Arthur, and this gladdened all their hearts. With a jubilant fanfare the king and his retinue returned to the queen, where King Arthur proclaimed: "My lady, the finest men from all lands seek out my court: the most noble ever to come to me or my court is Daniel, who stands here now, and whom I wish to give to you in atonement. Aside from our heavenly reward, no better lot could befall you. We would never have survived the battle had he not defeated your two huge giants, whose skin was hard as stone. Daniel could have single-handedly vanquished and slain your entire army." King Arthur then began to recount how Daniel had rescued the Lady of the Dark Mountain from the dwarf, how he had consoled the Maiden of the Bright Fountain, and how he had saved the Maiden of the Green Meadow.

"Now tell me," interrupted the lady, "am I to be tainted with disgrace for putting so quick an end to the mourning of my husband? This you must tell me before all else."

King Arthur then replied: "How could it be that you would reap shame from this advice that is urged upon you by all who are intent upon your welfare—both by your kinsmen and by your followers, be they free men or vassals? What shame would there be in doing this? I and my men give you the same advice. Be certain of this: I know of many a brave and upright man, but have heard tell of no knight as excellent as Daniel. Be therefore of good cheer; you can truly speak of good fortune, for you are receiving the finest knight now living."

"Then let there be no further resistance," said the queen. "God will that he should desire me, since you hold him in such high esteem! I shall gladly be joined to him if he wishes me." Present among them were a great many priests, who then gave the queen to Daniel in marriage, granting him thereby more than a wife: the kingdom and the crown. All of this was Daniel's reward.

The Festival Begins

All of the splendid clamor and jubilation brought Daniel of the Blossoming Valley such acclaim that the people received him as lord over the land of Cluse. Then he went aside with King Arthur and sent for all his other comrades, who came up in quick measure. Daniel said in good faith: "I shall no longer conceal the fact that I wish to hold a festival here, since joy has crossed my path and I have become lord over this land. I now desire to bring joy to all whom I can assemble here, both men and women. God willing, you shall now, in keeping with your position of fame, assist me in bringing about my festival. All that you have done on my behalf in choosing me lord here will be for naught if you do not help me further so that I might fulfill all that has been begun. My lady has forgone her grief because of the tales which my lord King Arthur has told of me. Prove now that what one hears is true, namely that King Arthur strives ever for acclaim.

"For when King Matur was ruler in this land, he held a festival every day. Hence the people are accustomed to festivals. If we neglect to make our festival as praiseworthy as the populace is accustomed to witness, then we shall be forever disgraced; nor will I ever be acclaimed or praised in this land. All of the furious fighting which we have carried on in pursuit of worldly reward can be lost very easily, so that no one will ever thank us, but will forever lament King Matur's death all the more. Thus I have need of your aid in acquiring the esteem of the people.

"You have always been courageous and wise and are widely renowned for this. Show now the truth of your reputation. You have all fought and gained this land, and have suffered great adversity before finally winning it by the sword. I now have among my subjects five hundred maidens, who are perfect in all that we have ever heard regarding beauty, both inwardly and outwardly. For they are pure in character and are, in addition, pleasing in appearance; I have never heard tell of women so distinguished. I shall let choose from among these women all of you who desire to remain in this land. No man could count for you how many of them were made widows here, but who nonetheless retain their maidenly beauty. All of you who desire one of them may, in addition, take sufficient land to sweeten the prospect of settling here; thus this festival is yours as well as mine. Let me charge you to act always in a manner favorable to our common esteem. You have been chosen to a circle of the most excellent men ever born and are famed for that excellence. See to it now that you prove the truth of your reputation!"

They all laughed and said: "We shall gladly work to augment your fame, just as you wish and in whatever ways we can." Daniel then made a request of the Count of the Bright Fountain, the Count of the Green Meadow, and the others who had come there with him, leaving their ladies at home, namely that they—so as to prove their friendship and service, and being mindful of the loyalty which Daniel had already shown and still intended to show to them—hasten to journey homeward and bring back their wives. He cherished the hope that the ladies would delight in his joy and in his festival and not begrudge him what he had acquired there. He charged the Count of the Bright Fountain, upon his loyalty, with bringing the Countess of the Dark Mountain, whom he had rescued from the dwarf. This he promised Daniel solemnly.

They tarried there no longer, but took their leave and journeyed until almost noon of the second day. No man, I believe, can know how lavishly they were then received. All things flourished for Daniel of the Blossoming Valley, who had in the meantime dispatched messengers in all directions to bring back his own fellow countrymen. The festival soon began.

All three of the ladies whom Daniel had rescued were seated alongside
the queen. The Maiden of the Dark Mountain recounted to her the story of
the dwarf and lamented her great distress and told her of how many men the
dwarf had slain until Daniel avenged her. The Lady of the Bright Fountain
in turn told the queen of all the harm which she had suffered at the hands of
the creature who carried about the lethal head until Daniel slew it. The
Lady of the Green Meadow related to her all of the misery caused by the
ogre who bathed in blood until Daniel overcame him.

Upon hearing this, the queen immediately became very tearful because of
sorrow, so great was the pity that she felt for them at having endured this
misery. Her heart, however, was most joyous that the same man who had
slain both of the tough-skinned giants had fallen to her lot, for she rejoiced
to hear that others had survived great adversity because of Daniel's efforts.
Thus her joy became so great that she was able to banish her dead husband
from her thoughts.

As soon as Daniel heard that all the people from his land had arrived, a
great array of splendid tents was pitched on a lovely field nearby. Elephants
then came up carrying on their backs a good twenty-four palaces, so that
neither King Arthur nor any other man had ever before seen such lavish
elegance. This took place on a green meadow, which was broad and long,
easily a mile or more wide, which was covered year round with nothing but
flowers and clover and the most beautiful grass that the earth ever bore. The
season was splendid, for this festival began on Whitsunday. The men of the
Round Table were clothed from head to toe in the garb of their land, and
had brought with them the very finest raiments to be found anywhere in all
the world. Early on Whitsunday the vassals of Cluse arrived, and unbounded joy held sway. Daniel of the Blossoming Valley was crowned that
day, and his subjects were anything but scorned for having over them a lord
so excellent. Five hundred maidens were seen standing around about the
queen, and even the least beautiful among them had such beauty that Venus,
standing next to her, would have had to acknowledge the other's beauty as
superior.

After a mass had been sung, mountains of food were served up, and in
such abundance that all of the guests were well cared for and no one was left
wanting for more. After they had eaten on that Pentecost day, the equipment with which they were to ride for the joust glittered with silk and gold
and with precious stones. There arose many forms of entertainment on all
sides, and every game ever devised was played there. The men of the
Round Table strove after praise and entertained the spectators as courtly
knights should. Whatever activity they pursued, their skills seemed flawless
in all respects. The noble maidens observed all of this eagerly; any man who
observed these maidens can forever speak of joy! One could rack one's
brains unendingly and still fail to collect all of the splendid and wondrous
types of garb which they wore. They were as radiant at night as during the
day.

All of the ladies stood pointing their fingers at this knight or that, each
indicating which one she would like, if it should come to this. Above each
of the maidens, protecting them from the sun, hovered a Babian, whose
plumage was clearer than a mirror. Once Daniel was mounted on his steed,
he proved to his lady and to all others present that he was well able to

deport himself as a good king should. All were of one mind: that no man present was Daniel's equal. He then proved his skill in so many different pursuits that the queen could not but praise him, saying that God had in every respect given her compensation for her slain husband. There will never, in my opinion, be a king so engaging as Daniel. The assembled multitude, men and women, all exclaimed to one another: "God has bestowed upon him all that a knight should have. Never has a woman had such good fortune as has our lady." All of them agreed that she could indeed speak of good luck, since she had been made so happy and compensated so soon for her suffering.

When it came time to rest, King Arthur's men dismounted and merrily walked off the grassy field together, to where they were graciously welcomed by the maidens. Sweet laughter could be heard, and many wistful glances of love were to be seen. They observed one another's outward gestures and ways, not failing, however, to take note also of their words and dispositions, until they were each able to find a lady willing to praise them. No man who desired one of them, whether she was a widow or a maiden, was turned down by her, until finally four hundred of the women were chosen to take in marriage all of the knights who had come with King Arthur from Britain. These were the men who were to remain with Sir Daniel there in Cluse. The Duchess of the Dark Mountain chose for herself a duke, who was faithful and good to her. Belamis was his name, and he possessed as much fame as a knight could possibly have. He became her dear husband, was never inconstant to her, and found great reward in exchange for this. The lord and the lady of the Green Meadow had four sons, each of whom soon chose himself a wife well able to gladden him in every way.

Joy unblemished by hatred poured forth from the very bottom of all their hearts, because this festival was carried out on so regal a scale. Daniel of the Blossoming Valley performed in the manner of men who, in the search for the highest acclaim, strive to endow their undertakings with such perfection that Lady Luck, with all her retinue, willingly promises to these men a fitting measure of her favor. Thus their undertakings are praised by all.

Hear now of a most wondrous thing. Daniel of the Blossoming Valley took all of the women aside from the assembled guests and said in a most courtly fashion: "I shall refuse my favor and my salutation to all of those in your midst who have lost their husbands and who refuse to choose another here. There are a great many brave heroes here who are my very dearest friends. As many of you as may take on a husband I shall treat as my very own offspring. Do not dwell on the fact that your lords have been laid to rest during the past seven days. Let whatever disgrace there is be mine alone. You need look no farther than at the queen, who did not disdain to accept this same advice when it was offered her. You have before you the opportunity for happiness; let these men who took your husbands from you make amends so that they in return may be yours in body and in soul. Be free of the fear—whichever of you choose a husband—that this would ever cause you harm. Therefore take a husband, each and every one of you, so that a great host of them will remain here in Cluse. I shall reward you both with gifts and favors. Whoever refuses this and breaks my commandment, however, shall stand in disfavor with me. Accordingly, it is my order that none of you feel ashamed, that there be no disgrace attached to what happens today. My full favor is granted to all who now carry out my wish."

Whatever joy was at first held back was now released in full measure. For the women would have raged angrily in protest except that Daniel had promised that there was no disgrace in what they were to do that day. And so a ceremony was held there which seldom if ever took place anywhere before or since: each lady asked a knight whether he was already trothed to any woman. If he replied no, then the lady asked straightway: "Do you wish me, my lord?" Thus he forfeited both his heart and his mind at her willing offer of love, for which he, not deeming himself worthy of it, would never have dared wish for as long as he should live.

By the time the decree circulated throughout the court that each knight should take whichever lady he wished they experienced for the first time a deep joy which brought tranquility to their hearts. Their discourse and their entreaty on that happy day went on in the following way: the knight approached the lady and, embracing her, said: "Do you wish me, my lady, as your husband?" "Indeed my lord, and I shall give praise to God if you have set your heart upon me." "Yes, my lady, you may be certain that my love for you is even stronger than yours for me." Thereupon they kissed one another in a manner wholly devoid of disgrace. O when was there ever another day so resplendent with joy! Such a day will, I am convinced, never again occur.

He who was to be lord in that land was courtly and brave; this he demonstrated in numerous ways. For even when he became wanting in knights before making recompense to all of the women for their lost husbands, he quickly devised a remedy for making amends to them: he took aside six hundred of his squires, all of whom were nephews of King Arthur's comrades, and striving to mobilize his land, he dubbed them knights on the spot; he also bestowed upon them, once having found the proper moment, garments so beautifully radiant that all who beheld them said aloud that the angels in heaven would be forever joyous if God clothed them in such gowns. Moreover, Daniel ordered them presented with such horses that no one who desired to be at all generous of heart could deny Daniel his praise. Wherever one expected wood or iron on the riding equipment, there stood pure silver. The men of the Round Table beheld these marvelous gifts and agreed amongst themselves that although they had seen in many lands splendid riding accoutrements and lavish clothing in which the highest mastery was evident, all of this had been but a trifle in comparison.

As the young knights rode together to court, many a tongue spoke of how no man had ever beheld clothes as rich and as elegant as those which they wore. The horses, whenever they touched them, glistened brightly with the reflection of the sun; so blindingly did they sparkle and burn, in fact, that those charged with attending to the horses were scarcely able to endure the brilliant shimmer. These youths, in their newly acquired order of knighthood, deported themselves so skillfully and decorously that no one who viewed them could deny that they fulfilled every demand of perfection. The ladies of Cluse for this reason held their new husbands dear; and as the ladies saw to it that their spouses had all that they required, many a courtly stranger in that land was accorded the welcome reserved for the head of a household. It had turned out well for both the men and the women that they were to remain together.

Once the widows were provided for, and once all their lamenting had been duly banished, all the sights and sounds of entertainment and games which one expects at a festival were evident in great abundance there. Lady Bliss was granted her will in many ways, for it was she who was praised and esteemed and wore the crown upon her head that day.

Arrival of the Giants' Father

Then suddenly Bliss was rudely struck, so that the crown fell from her head and she fell sprawling before the throne, landing in a puddle of water. In her place, uninvited, sat Care, trampling Bliss beneath her feet. Just as all the guests were caught up with joy, there came walking up a most peculiar man who wore but a silken tunic and silken breeches. He was neither unduly large nor unduly small; his complexion was most radiant, and his hair was well-kempt, gray and white and with curls. As he strode into the court, he carried a club in his hand and knocked the people away from him, commanding them to clear a path. Everyone who saw him quickly made way for him, until he finally came before the throne. He cried out and commanded them to be silent; then he asked the way to the loftiest man among them. Sir Gawein was the first to point him to where King Arthur was sitting, for he was undisputedly the most exalted of them all.

The awesome man then said: "Make room for me, all of you, for I wish to show you a game which you will all agree is unfamiliar to you. I well believe that no man has ever seen a game so unusual." This they thought an amusing sport, and they stepped back to make room. The man then said: "I must be able to see the field, or else it cannot be done." They now cleared a path for him in the proportions which he himself prescribed.

Hear now what happened then: the man walked up to King Arthur and, placing his arm around him, jerked him up like a wisp of straw (a most amazing theft!) and carried him off right under their noses. So quickly did he run off that there was no one in their midst able to catch up with him on horseback, although many made the attempt. This game was not only disagreeable to King Arthur's men, but also loathsome. Daniel and Gawein, Parzival and Iwein were soon off in hot pursuit. They were, with their lowered spears, most eager to pay him back for this by robbing him of his life.

The man who carried the king away ran with great speed—like the very wind itself! The giants who had been slain there had been his sons. Not even a bird could have outflown him as he ran. Nonetheless King Arthur's men kept up their pursuit in the hope of capturing him once they came to the mountain. But they soon perceived that the man was carrying King Arthur up onto the mountain. Seeing this, they were filled with desolation, as they were unable to pursue him on such terrain. They quickly dismounted from their horses and were about to climb after him. Those who wished to live were forced to give up this idea, since no man could do so without falling to his death. They were all left standing there gaping sadly! The climb to the spot where he brought the king would have been dizzying even for an ape. Had it been of any use, there stood a great number of archers who could have shot the man, but no good would have come of that, as both King Arthur and his abductor would have plunged to their death. Thus, they preferred to let him carry the king off than to kill them both.

Once the intruder had fled up the mountain, he set King Arthur down on a frightening ledge from which he could move neither up nor down nor to one side or to the other. Had he budged at all from that ledge, he would have suffered a fall which he could not have survived even if he were made of steel. The assembled men down below watched all of this, and many a man and woman became immensely despondent. The old man then climbed back down the same dizzying path until he was near enough for them to hear what he said. He commanded them to fall silent, and not one made a sound, for great was their distress as to how the king should ever get back down and why he had been abducted.

The old man then said: "As long as I have the use of my God-given senses, you shall all pay with your lives, you who are to blame for my dear sons' having been hacked to pieces so horribly. I shall not rest until I avenge this on you and shatter your joy as you have done to me. The loss of my sons will be of no benefit to you." They were about to shoot him, but Daniel admonished the foolish people against this course of action. "The king has been put on a ledge," he said to them all, "from which he will fall to his death unless we can peacefully convince this man to bring him back down to us. If you have any sense at all, you will refrain from shooting him. As long as he has the king, I advise you to let this man live, regardless of what may happen to us in consequence."

Daniel then turned to the old man and said: "You can, it seems, use any means you wish against us. Your armor is so fine that you will easily withstand us no matter how long the king is to sit up there. If we, however, should win him back, you will have to show us how it is that your better instincts lead you to appear before us unarmed and to threaten an entire army single-handedly. Why do you intend to harm the king, and how do you wish to slay us?"

The old man then replied: "I shall tell you this: I shall carry each of you onto this mountain and set you down on a spot where you will grow old and gray before any man devises a scheme to bring you back down again. You will all die of starvation first. This is how you will have to perish—as many of you as I can catch—and believe me, I shall gladly endeavor to capture a great many of you! Since the ground is so well washed with the blood of my sons, whom you have slain, the wind will parch and emaciate as many of you on this mountain as are allotted to me. If there is any one among you who is of such a mind that he dares come alone and unarmed close enough to the rock so that I can grab him by the hand, let him determine whether he be able to pull me down, or whether I have the strength to pull him up to a spot where he will be bereft of all help. Is any one of you so brave as to approach me and put this to the test?"

Many a volunteer cried out: "Yes, I will go, I will go!" They all shouted, but nothing came of it, and this is why: none was willing to let the next man go, and as a consequence they all had to forgo the challenge. The old man, seeing this, demanded their silence: "You are all free of fear. Now tell me in truth, where is the finest man amongst you? Such a man should certainly thirst for the fame to be acquired here."

There was not a man who presumed to speak up, for it would have been unfitting to say: "I am the finest." They likewise were aware that it would be improper to name any other man as capable of taking on such responsibilities. For if that man died in pursuit of fame, or even if he encountered great tribulation, others might twist it around and perhaps claim that he who named him did so out of animosity. Thus for a good while many a mouth was kept closed. Finally Parzival broke the ice of good breeding; he was too courageous to leave the king trapped on the mountainside, and said: "I am the most valued man here. I have no witness for this, but rather wish to praise myself. If this is considered madness on my part, I shall do battle with you." Leaving his sword behind, he walked boldly in his armor toward the old man, who, seeing this, hastened down from the mountainside. A battle, free of swords, then took place, but was of short duration. For the old man leaped down from the rock and, grabbing Parzival with one arm, climbed back up where he had come from. Parzival was outraged at having to follow the man. Furiously he defended himself, but this was to be the cause of great distress for him, for the old man, angered at this, hurled him onto a rock, a blow which left Parzival pallid as though with death. The impact was so great that his heart nearly burst in two.

There then arose a clamor down below; all of them, save Daniel alone, cried out that the man should be killed. Why did they let him live? Daniel entreated them to forgo this and to wait for him on the spot, for he would bring back help. He then set out in haste, for it was his plan to request and be granted a truce, once he had in his hands the net in which the Maiden of the Green Meadow had found him trapped. To this end he departed in haste to acquire the net. It was a journey of two miles, and the steed raced along obeying nothing but Daniel's spurs. His steed was obedient, and in a short time Daniel arrived at the Green Meadow, where the maiden spotted him as he was riding up to the court. There he received, in truth, a most worthy reception: she came running (not walking) out to meet him. Before he had even fully dismounted, she embraced him most nobly, bade him welcome in the name of God, and, kissing him sweetly, pressed him to her bosom, with the words: "I wish to raise a lamentation to God that neither I nor anyone else can fully appreciate the service which you have shown me; for I would gladly serve you if only I knew how!"

The knight Daniel then said in reply: "If what I have done for you is pleasing, then show me so! For you now have occasion to acquire my favor fully, if you help me out of the distress which has overcome me." "How has this happened?" she asked; "is my father still well?" "I left him this very hour," he replied, "free of care."

He then told her the story of how the awesome man had captured King Arthur and afterwards Parzival. Then he said: "Hasten now and go there with me. There is so much at stake for me that I can never—for as long as I shall live—hope to requite you for your good will. You never needed me as urgently as I now need you. I feel quite certain that if you bring your net to that spot and place it in the path as he descends, you will end his climbing." "Fear not," she answered; "I shall capture him for you in an instant." Then she addressed her maidens, ordering them to bring her a horse. Once helped

into the saddle, she set out at a fast amble that was in fact almost a trot. For
she was well aware from what he had said that, no matter how quickly they
could arrive there, it would not be soon enough for him. Daniel whipped his
horse on harder and harder, and she was greatly pained by the deep concern
which he displayed for King Arthur's safety. Thus they arrived at Cluse in
a very short time, finding assembled at the foot of the mountain both the
men of the Round Table as well as all in the land who could rightly
distinguish between honor and shame.

King Arthur's men were all lamenting the harm that had so viciously
fallen upon their noble king. They feared that he might have to send home
to Britain a dismal tale, for the distress which he was suffering deprived
them of the hope that he might survive. They were grieved not only at this
ill fortune, but also at the fact that no one knew how to bring him down
from the ledge uninjured. In the midst of their woe Daniel and the Maiden
of the Green Meadow came up on horseback. Her father, having spotted
them, cried out with unbounded joy: "Welcome, both of you," to which
the assembled knights and ladies followed suit. Wasting no time, they set
about the preparations: as soon as she had dismounted, she made ready her
net. Daniel led her to the spot where she was to set it up. Gladly she went
about doing so, spurred on by her sense of duty and by Daniel's bidding!
No one, however, could see what she was doing, save her mother and
father, both of whom Daniel told to say nothing until such time as they
should see the old man entangled in the net.

All of those present had been frightened by the sight of Parzival being
pulled so roughly up the mountain. Since then the old man had been
standing there fiercely taunting them with questions as to whether anyone
else wished to try his luck there. No one dared go near the old man since
they had all just witnessed the apparent death-blow to Parzival. This was
the excuse which they all proffered: "There is no man among us who is
brave enough. Wait, however, until King Daniel returns. He will take you
on immediately." The old man then sat down on the face of the cliff,
waiting for Daniel's arrival, so that he might slay him. Daniel was informed
of this, and he remained silent for the sake of safety, not revealing himself
until he heard the maiden say: "The net is now in place. Go and stand at
that spot, and bid him to descend. He will be unable to lay a hand on you!"
At this Daniel of the Blossoming Valley shouted at the old man: "I am told
that you wish to engage in a tug-of-war with me. Can you assure me that
this is so? They also say that you intend to inflict misfortune upon me. Are
you still of such a mind?" "Indeed I am," he replied. "Then on with it!"
said Daniel, who then ordered his sword carried off.

This was to the old man's utter satisfaction, and he ordered the people to
stand back, flying at Daniel at an immense speed, heading like a blind man
straight for the middle of the net. He would gladly have taken Daniel as his
third captive, but a different outcome was awaiting him: he became so
thoroughly entangled in the net that he lost all hope of survival and was in
such agony that he cried out for help and thrashed about in an attempt to rip
the net apart. But try as he would, he had to abandon all hope of so doing.
He would not, however, refrain from his outburst until he had rendered
himself incapable of moving even his hands or feet in this straitjacket hold.
He was completely held in its fetters. Once again, though, his heart, which

was robust and wrathful, smoldered with anger at being so crippled, and he squirmed like a netted fish, until he finally was reduced, in all his strength, to such timidity that he lay there as if dead, so overwhelming a nightmare was this for him.

Whatever man has cunning at his beck and call is deserving of all the more praise from both men and women. For one man alone can accomplish with cunning that which a thousand men, however strong they might be, could never do together. See this exemplified in the old man: had he been able to maintain himself, he would have carried Daniel up the mountainside, where all of his helpless lamentation would never have done him any good. If the old man had proceeded to use cunning, all of their strength combined would have been powerless. It was a fruitful use of cunning which Daniel employed.

Hear now of what they did once they saw the old man in the net: they ran amid great clamor and praised in unison both God and the maiden. A reception a thousand times greater than the first one was then bestowed upon the maiden, and they would have gladly lifted her onto their shoulders with gratitude had they been asked to. They were all beside themselves with joy. All of those present offered their obedience to her, and she was acclaimed in a manner befitting a god.

Queen Danise, who wore the crown in Cluse, rendered the maiden proper thanks for having arrived so gallantly and for having freed them from the old man. "If I shall live to see it," said the queen, "this service which you have rendered us will be for you a shield against all care. I shall not rest until such time as I have amply demonstrated my appreciation for this favor which you have done me." Thus, the Maiden of the Green Meadow came to be praised highly for the rest of her life.

The fine knights, as they raced there, caused such an uproar that it could be heard far and wide. So deafening a racket it was that one could not even hear it well until it was finally silenced upon command. Then a hush fell over the gathering, and Daniel addressed the old man: "You have inflicted great misery upon us. Since we now hold you prisoner, why should we spare your life? We ought rather to bring about once and for all a safe peace from your wiles. You have so ruthlessly wrought death upon us that you yourself will indeed reap the same reward. If you could hold us captive as we do you, then you would certainly deal us the final blow. Therefore, you must likewise suffer death. If my sword does not penetrate your skin, then I shall turn it around and bash in your skull with the hilt, before I will ever allow you to live. You have practiced intemperance against us, and since we have captured you, you will indeed die for having dealt in death yourself."

The old man then replied: "You will be forever laden with my ingratitude if I live as much as half a day. I prefer to die, and I ask nothing of you save death. Since you have turned my life into such deep anguish, do not prolong my suffering. I shall be glad the sooner you end it. It is foolish of you to fail to do so, for if you do let me live, your own death will be inescapable."

Daniel, displeased by these words, then replied: "You are indeed a man of good sense! How is it that you could ever be so foolish? How do you dare request to be killed? You yearn for a woe which no man should hasten to experience. It is fitting that a wise man know what he speaks; even if for twenty-four days on end he spoke the wisest words ever uttered, nonetheless, if but a single word of that were false, others would take note of the falsely spoken utterance a thousand times more keenly than of all his wisdom, and he would thereby incur the loss of his acclaim and of his good name. I condemn you most vehemently for your lack of wisdom in counseling your king, whether out of sincere loyalty or out of desire for some reward, to undertake the base scheme of sending your son to King Arthur and ordering him captured in a most disgraceful manner in his own court. We are not like you, who wish to surrender your life voluntarily. We endured great hardship in order to vanquish your sons once they attacked us and extracted violently a great toll of life. They offered us death, and we refused it; we wreaked no further revenge save to fight off the army which then came, but only in self-defense and with but a narrow margin of victory. I wish to say in all truth that none of this would have come about, except that their very iniquity slew them and forbade them to win from us in their haughtiness either our lives or our possessions. God has given them just recompense for that. Any man who finds blame with us for this is a fool. Now tell me in truth—if God and your loved ones be at all dear to you—was it at your advice that King Matur committed this act of immoderation against us?"

The old man then said in response: "If my lord had asked for my advice (and he did not do so), I would not have permitted this to happen. Even if I had been unable to prevent their plan, I would have sooner delayed its inception than helped to carry it out. If what you claim is true—that my sons were in pursuit of you—and if they forced you to kill them, you had no choice but to retaliate as you have done—there was no other way. Since this is so, I shall now gladly embrace my salvation from death. For if you desire a reconciliation, I shall not be the one to refuse it, inasmuch as it was King Matur who sent my sons, as well as himself and many a bold hero, off to their death. It had been my belief that it was your arrogance which brought you here. I was, to my misfortune, not informed of their plan and knew not that it was being carried out, until I saw my children lying dead. Since I have lost them because of my lord, I shall forgo my anger. Grant to me now your gracious favor as recompense for my great loss and as evidence of your goodness. For you have greatly impaired my joy and can reap lasting fame by now treating me with much more favor if I forswear my wrath. I can prove myself well deserving of this in whatever way necessary. If you are now in need of counsel, I can offer you advice right away which will bring a good name upon you."

Daniel rejoiced at this and asked the maiden to make haste to release the man at once and disentangle him from the net. His command was soon fulfilled, and the old man, once freed, asked: "What is this, noble lady? Do tell me more of it." "It is a net," she replied; "any man, be he strong or weak, suffers the same fate as you once I set it for him." "Are you able to see it?" he asked. "Indeed, how could I do anything with it if I could not see it?" "How is it then that I am so blind?" he said; "this I ask of you: can everyone here see this net?" "There are but three persons present who can see it." "If it could ever come to pass," the old man responded, "that I were to be so blessed as to see this net, I would be happy beyond all measure."

"If it pleases you at all," she said, "I shall not refuse you this request. I have with me here an ointment more excellent than any other that you or I have ever seen. If I apply but a small amount of it to your eyes, your eyesight will become so sharp that even the blackest of nights will be to you like a summer day, and the net will thereby be rendered clear and visible."

The old man answered: "I would be ungrudging with everything over which I have dominion—a thousand marks in gold, and more—I would gladly give it all in order that these two objects, the net and the ointment, might belong to me. If they were for sale, I should give half the world, if it were mine, in exchange for them."

The Maiden of the Green Meadow then said in answer: "Keep your possessions and bring down for us your captives from atop the cliff. As soon as that has come about, I shall give you both the net and the ointment, that we may all live in friendship with you and in an everlasting bond of loyalty unmarred by animosity."

When the old man heard that he was so close to possessing what he prized so highly, he bowed down at her feet as a sign of his willingness to aid her, and then vaulted off with the swiftness of a hart. He then applied all his zeal to the benefit of those to whom he had previously refused his favor and whom he had disgraced. Thus his scorn became loyal friendship, for he willingly brought the king back down from the cliff. Then he hastened back up and carried Parzival down.

All were full of joy that these two were freed from their torture, and King Arthur said: "All favors which I have ever incurred were as naught compared to this. Only now do I know what true bliss is, for so overjoyed am I now that I shall evermore be happy. It is a godsend that I have been so graciously rescued from the mountain; only barely did I come away unharmed in body and in mind." The king then turned to the old man and said: "I shall give thanks to God and shall gladly reward you for bringing me down from this cliff. Know likewise that you will never leave here before I offer recompense, of whatever manner you please, for the suffering which you have undergone." The maiden then gave the old man both the net and the ointment. Sir Daniel then said to him: "You have now done well, so that no act of service more pleasing than this has been performed at any time or in any place. If I am at all able, I shall prove to you the truth of this."

They tarried no longer, but returned on horseback to the throne. No man who has ever read of joy has ever experienced such joy as befell them there. They bestowed upon Bliss a yet more splendid welcome than before and placed her once again on her lofty throne of grandeur. Her dominion then assumed such alacrity that all of the courtiers obeyed her command before it was even given.

Conclusion of the Festival

Daniel, who was host in that land, saw to it that they were well contented, for he made certain that they were lacking in nothing. Yet the joy still seemed to him incomplete; he therefore said most decorously to King Arthur: "You have done me great honor here in Cluse by making me lord over this land. Now aid me in banishing any remaining traces of shame, and I shall be justifiably grateful to you for evermore. Only then will I have both material good as well as a good name."

"I should be highly pleased," replied King Arthur, "and would gladly help you to confirm your reputation to the extent that no man would take note of any imprudence of which you might henceforth be guilty, or which might perhaps be vexing to another man. I would gladly see done whatever may seem fitting to you. Tell me now, what is it that you desire?"

"That my comrades and I might ride to Britain to Queen Guinevere in order that she should witness the bliss now reigning over my land. In so doing, she will in turn bring such good fortune upon me that all of my countrymen whose esteem I seek will grant to me an even larger measure of that esteem. Thus, I shall fare well in all respects."

"I am well disposed toward you," answered the king. "If you do not possess sufficient stores of gold and precious stones and silken clothing here in Cluse, then I shall give you this advice, which will be to your advantage: when you arrive in Britain—this will be no loss to me—order my courtiers to load twenty-four beasts of burden so that you need not make your land empty of such goods."

"Have my thanks for this," Daniel laughed, "but I need to import neither gold nor fine clothing. For so great are my stores that I am well furnished with everything that is sought after in all the world." Daniel then asked as many of his comrades as were present and still without wives that they willingly ride with him to Britain. This was a request easily fulfilled, for they did whatever he bade them. "I entrust it to you," said Daniel to the king, "to see to it that the guests are wanting for nothing that is required for their enjoyment." Whereupon King Arthur replied: "I shall indeed insure that."

Hear now how many men Daniel selected to accompany him: there were six hundred of them who made the journey with him. He allowed to remain in Cluse all who had recently taken wives. This he did not do out of any ill-feeling, but only that the festival might proceed in full joy in anticipation of his return. Daniel was a man well able to cultivate his own good name. He bade these men meanwhile, as a favor to him, to allow their wives to accompany the queen on the journey, and all promised to do so without objection. Thus they rode with great hubbub into the land of Britain. Once there, they wasted little time before setting out on the return journey. Lanzelet and Sir Erec were now at court, as well as the others whom King Arthur had had to leave behind because they were out on diverse paths in search of adventure. They now lamented the fact that fate had neglected to bring word to them of King Arthur's campaign.

Another brave hero, whose mind was dominated by a thirst for fame, had in the meantime arrived at King Arthur's court; this man was the Duke of Zone, and he had come there because he had often heard tell that any man who had once been in Britain would become so blessed that the shadow of dishonor would never darken his path, regardless where it might take him thereafter. This thought he could not banish from his mind, and he had often fancied at home in his own court that the powerful King Arthur might dub him a knight. It was to this end that he had journeyed to Britain; Beladigant was his name.

When Daniel saw him, he inquired as to his name and his business there; this Beladigant at once told Daniel and added that he was a man who strove for great repute, and that he would like to enhance his reputation at King Arthur's court. He was prepared, he said, to do whatever was necessary for this if the king would receive him into his fellowship of knights.

"Have no misgivings," replied Daniel, "about having departed from your land in search of this. You have not come too late, indeed you have arrived at an opportune moment. Since you have set out in search of reward and fame, I shall take it upon myself that you find all of this in ample measure."

"You give me good cause for comfort, my lord," replied Beladigant. "May God reward you for this. I shall gladly show myself worthy of it."

Once Daniel saw that his comrades had brought their ladies there, they all set out with him on the return journey. With much jubilation Queen Guinevere (a lady unparalleled in excellence) joined them with eighty maidens. A splendid entourage they were, arriving joyously in Cluse without incident. The guests all hurried out to greet the ladies, as was wholly befitting their lofty name. For they were greatly pleased at Guinevere's arrival. The festival then got underway with still greater jubilation than before Queen Guinevere's coming. Daniel's esteem likewise was heightened by her having come there for his sake. Any man who struggles undauntedly in the search for fame will attain his goal; for this reason they spoke that day of Daniel's good fortune. Thus thanks and appreciation are due both to God and to Daniel that King Arthur was able to celebrate in Cluse the same sumptuous festival which he had in previous years always held in Britain.

As soon as King Arthur heard that Sir Beladigant wished to be inaugurated into knighthood, he gladly granted him his request and dubbed him a knight on the spot. The strains of music swelled up, of the fiddle and the flute, playing in all the chords ever devised to please the ear. There were three hundred French fiddlers present, and they were both skilled and renowned. These I have selected, for they were masters of their art. Sixty German minstrels, unequaled in their art, were heard there blowing their strings, and the jangle of tambourines with little bells filled the air. Flutes of diverse types melted away all the cares of the guests, and a hundred harpists fashioned a most exquisite melody, for which they were well rewarded. And twenty vocalists sang songs of love to banish all distress. People were seen engaged in extraordinary dances, and lances were being hurled. What man could fail to enjoy this? Pages scurried about to win prizes; no one was in an ill humor amongst that gathering, and readings were given from various works in French. Physical prowess is likewise a worthy pastime, and it was common to see a man able to lift with one arm a fortress of immeasurable girth. Whoever tired of looking at this could watch men who were able to run with the speed of a bird. The entertainment was augmented by bows and cross-bows which fired off arrows and bolts.

Not to be missed were the knightly jousts with the crack of splintering lances. The horses cantered about high-spiritedly; pages cried out, and all manner of board games were played. Falcons and sparrowhawks likewise flew about. Beautiful tales were told of knights in combat, and they all wore wreaths and garlands of fragrant flowers. They held the widest round-dance of which I have ever heard tell in all my days; more than two

thousand knights and ladies partook thereof. Lady Bliss was awakened and
forbidden to fall back asleep.

The ladies all had shade from the beautifully plumaged Babians, which
always hovered above them. The elephants which bore palaces on their
backs were driven here and there. The blaring peal of trumpets was to be
heard far and wide, so that a man could whisper into his neighbor's ear
and—as long as his neighbor was not deaf—not be overheard by anyone
else. If ever you have heard anyone who has been present at knightly
festivals claim to have witnessed one more splendid than this, surely he is a
liar, or else he has beheld the realm of heaven itself. Such a festival as this
will, I believe, never be equalled. Great was the bliss attendant upon them
all.

Sir Beladigant's knighthood was recognized here as exceptional, so that
King Arthur, who along with Sir Daniel watched Beladigant riding his
steed, exclaimed that Beladigant indeed possessed all manly attributes. The
whole crowd saw the truth of this. Thus he acquired the reputation of being
one of the most excellent of knights—a reputation which no man present
was able to overturn.

The king sent for him, and Sir Beladigant hastened to the assembly of
knights. Their words were warm with friendship from the outset, and
Beladigant was seated between Daniel and King Arthur, who inquired of
him: "Have you yet taken a lady in marriage, sir knight?" "No," came the
reply; whereupon King Arthur inquired further, saying: "Tell me this: if
you are of such a mind that you wish it, then I shall grant you a wife,
material goods, and abundant joy."

"My happiness would be drowned in folly," he answered, "if I should
refuse such a kind offer. I am most ready to receive gladly all that you do in
my behalf. It is true what they say, that no man who comes to your court in
search of material reward shall fail to attain his goal. For you are truly a
noble lord; that I have always heard. A fortunate man I am to see my own
name so aggrandized as a consequence."

King Arthur then had the Maiden of the Green Meadow sent for, since
he wished to reward her for having purchased his life with her net and for
having given his life back to him by rescuing him just when he was so
thoroughly drowned in distress. The Maiden of the Green Meadow, whose
name was Sandinose, came before King Arthur. She possessed the beauty of
a rose fashioned expertly with hues of red and white. No man who wished
to possess a maiden embellished with perfection could ever in a thousand
years imagine a damsel crowned with more excellence or more exquisitely
adorned with beauty than was she. When King Arthur had seen her, he said
to the knight Beladigant: "What do you think of this damsel?" "In truth,"
he replied, "I would be blind in all my senses were I to refuse her." "How
does this knight please you, my lady?" "Very well, my lord," she said.
This made King Arthur happy, and he gave them to one another with his
own hand, commanding that Beladigant be made duke over the land of
Cluse.

King Arthur thereby proved to the maiden his ability to give a generous
reward. He was said to have at his disposal a thousand different crowns. So
manifold was his goodness that, even if he has suffered physical death, his
name has never perished, but rather lives on in lofty acclaim for as long as a

single upright man shall live. For King Arthur was ever inclined toward the brave and rewarded them well for doing their best and acquiring both happiness and fame. Once having rewarded the lovely lady so well for her net and for her efforts, he inquired as to where the old man was, and ordered that he be summoned without fail. This was quickly done, and the old man, upon hearing this, came at once before King Arthur with these words: "What do you desire of me?" The king had him sit right beside him and inquired astutely as to what he possessed of material goods. "Are you of such a mind," asked King Arthur, "as to return with me to Britain? If so, you will never leave my side. If that is not your will, then whatever I possess—far or near—is yours for the asking regardless of how dear it is to me. I do not reward you for dragging me up the mountain, for this seemed to me an act of immoderation and caused me great discomfort. I shall gladly reward you, however, for bringing me back down. Tell me now what reward you desire from me."

"I ask for nothing of what you possess," he answered, "save that you allow me to retain the fief which King Matur, who never denied me his friendship, once granted me. He was always well disposed toward me. Would that he had refrained from leading my sons astray and seducing them from my precepts! He never disregarded my advice, save for this one time, which was to be his downfall. Beyond the mountain there lies a land which he granted as a fief to me with his own hand. This land is a mile wide and is encircled by mountains which are so craggy and so high that nothing—wild or tame—which I have brought here has ever escaped. Nor can any man enter into this land; I alone am agile enough to be able to come and go as I please. I have taken there all kinds of things which I enjoy as entertainment and as game. Prove your goodness and grant it to me at this time as a fief, since it has now fallen to you. I shall gladly serve you in return, as has been my wont."

King Arthur then said in reply: "Since no man save you alone can enter or leave this land, I would be a most evil man to refuse this request. Hear now what I mean: I would rather own the most frivolous trinket than two such inaccessible lands. Take my hand as a pledge that this land is your own forever, and that you are relieved of the service which you have until now performed in exchange for it. For you shall receive this land as a reward for having cast me into the straits of death and then having helped me out of my tribulation."

The old man was joyful and bowed most decorously at King Arthur's feet, giving him heartfelt thanks and saying: "My cares are now at an end." Arthur, the mighty king, was a just man indeed. How could his praise and his fame ever die out? How could they fail to endure for evermore and be deservedly proclaimed both far and wide?

Thus the festival lasted exactly four weeks. The guests parted in a courtly fashion and rode off in high spirits. So richly rewarded were the minstrels that, had they lived forever, they would have remained evermore wealthy. Oh! How fully had King Arthur garnered the praise of all those present! The Queen of Cluse embraced him just as he was about to take leave of her, and said to him: "May God's blessing be with you. I could not have wished for a finer husband than Daniel, even if all the kingdom of earth were mine and I were in my youth and possessed the finest excellence of all women. Never has a woman received a more splendid reward than that which you have granted me. I, as well as all whom you leave behind here, stand at your command." He now entrusted her to God and departed merrily. Twelve hundred of his cherished men, who had taken wives in the land of Cluse, remained behind.

I am always amazed that King Arthur was so generous a man and the lords nowadays are so miserly. King Arthur did well to relinquish so readily such a rich land, for he granted it to a man who always performed his will, and of whom he never needed to make a request, since they often rode together in pursuit of adventure. Whenever the king had need of him, Sir Daniel was already present without having to be summoned. Thus King Arthur did not relinquish the land of Cluse, but rather retained his vassal Daniel, who dwelt in bliss ever after with a never-ending festival there in his land of Cluse. His life remained spotless, and he invested his subjects with the same fiefs which the slain King Matur had granted them in order that they might every day engage in tournaments. Daniel presented them with even more, so that they would strive yet more zealously than they had in the past; and indeed they fulfilled his will in this regard.

Never has there lived a man to whom God has granted a more excellent existence in this world than Daniel, whose life was lived amid acclaim and without the slightest taint, until the day he died. For this reason he was, and is even now, counted among the finest of knights; hence his praise spread far and wide. Now must I make an end to my story. You have heard all that has reached my ears. May God vouchsafe that we should all enter into His kingdom. AMEN.

chapter *VIII*
SPANISH

TWO LANCELOT BALLADS

Harvey L. Sharrer

In Spain by the late fifteenth century ballads (called *romances* in Spanish) had replaced the oral epic poem as a form of popular entertainment. Few Spanish ballads survive today in medieval manuscripts, but at the courts of Castile and Aragon the genre received respectability by the 1450s, and it achieved great aesthetic height during the sixteenth century, when a large corpus of traditional ballads was printed in songbooks (*cancioneros* or *romanceros*) and in broadsides or chapbooks (*pliegos sueltos*). Across the centuries learned Hispanic poets would gloss and imitate the content and form of the ancient texts. But many of the old ballads also survive down to the present day in oral tradition, not only in Spanish but also in Catalan and Portuguese, with variant versions still being sung in remote parts of Spain and Portugal, in the Americas, and among Sephardic Jews (expelled from Spain in 1492) in North Africa, the eastern Mediterranean, and the New World. The traditional Hispanic ballad varies in length, but the better ones contain much dramatic tension, pathos or mystery, produced through a process of oral composition, called *fragmentismo* (fragmentism) by modern critics, which shortens the narrative to its bare essentials, sometimes beginning the story *in medias res*. The result is often a song of great beauty and fairy-tale charm. The meter of the Hispanic ballad, normally octosyllabic lines with alternate monorhyming assonance, is closely related to that of the traditional medieval Spanish epic.

Three Spanish ballads are thought to derive from the thirteenth-century French Arthurian prose romance cycles or their Hispanic translations: "Herido está don Tristán" ("Sir Tristan is wounded"), from the *Prose Tristan*; and the two ballads included here in English translation: "Nunca fuera caballero" ("Never was a gallant Knight") and "Tres hijuelos había el rey" ("Three tender striplings had the King"), from the *Lancelot* branch of the Vulgate Cycle. Spanish balladry also preserves various other texts that indicate possible Arthurian origin, among them ballads containing the names of Ginebra (Guinevere) and Galván (Gawain), but the connections here with the Matter of Britain are remote.

The ballad "Nunca fuera caballero" does not correspond to any one episode of the Vulgate *Lancelot*. However some critics have seen a close relationship between it and the story of Lancelot's killing of the evil Meleagant, who abducted Queen Guinevere, which was retold in the cycle's prosification of Chrétien de Troyes's *Lancelot*, or *The Knight of the Cart*. Even less clear is the origin of the figure of Quintañona as Guinevere's maid and go-between, for Guinevere never employs such a person in her love affair with Lancelot. There may, however, be a parallel with the story of Isolde's young maid and companion Brangain, who gives Isolde and Tristan the philter that eternally cements their love; but in Spanish "Quintañona" implies an old go-between, more precisely one who is 100 years old. In the Vulgate *Lancelot* a maid called Brisane, said to be perhaps 100 years old (or more than 100 in *Lanzarote de Lago*, the Spanish translation of the romance), purposely serves Lancelot a wine that causes him to think that he is sleeping with Guinevere when in reality it is the daughter of King Pelles. The Spanish ballad thus seems to conflate separate, unrelated episodes of the prose romance. Four versions of the ballad survive from the sixteenth century, in printed songbooks and a manuscript anthology, and it was also glossed in the same period by two court poets, Luis Milán and Martín de la Membrilla Clemente. In Chapter 13 of Part I of *Don Quixote* (1605), Miguel de Cervantes' burlesque hero mentions Quintañona's role in the loves of Lancelot and Guinevere and cites the first four lines of the ballad, referring to it as well-known and frequently sung in Spain.

"Tres hijuelos había el rey" survives in a mid-sixteenth-century songbook. It too is a fragmented and contaminated ballad. That it was once much longer seems evident from its three changes in assonance (the English translation uses many more). One modern critic, William J. Entwistle, has interpreted the poem's enigmatic situation as follows: the king, perhaps on his deathbed, cursed his three illegitimate sons, who become metamorphosized into beasts (one as a heathen Moor); his daughter and lawful heir finds her lands devastated by the eldest son, now a white-footed stag, and seeks the help of a knight in return for her hand. Lancelot undertakes the adventure but without accepting the marriage offer. Taking along his hounds or hunting dogs (strangely rendered as "boots" in the translation), he comes across a hermit (a common interpreter of mysteries in the Vulgate Cycle) who shows him the stag in the company of seven lions and a whelped lioness that has killed seven counts. The hermit then denounces the lady (confused with Quintañona) who sent Lancelot on such a dangerous mission.

The Spanish *Prose Lancelot*, extant only in a mid-sixteenth-century manuscript copy, the *Lanzarote de Lago*, does not contain this material, nor do the surviving versions in French. But much of the ballad's mystery, as Entwistle and others have pointed out, can be explained by a study of the ballad's close affinity with the twelfth-century French *Lai de Tyolet* and the thirteenth-century Dutch verse romance *Lanceloet en het hert met de witte voet* (*Lancelot and the White-footed Stag*), interpolated within a verse translation of the last three branches of the Vulgate Cycle. That "Tres hijuelos había el rey" is an ancient ballad is attested by several variant lines (in different assonances) of the dialogue between Lancelot and the hermit as cited by the late fifteenth-century Spanish grammarian Antonio de Nebrija. In the early sixteenth century lines from the same passage in the ballad are included in a poem by Jerónimo Pinar in the *Cancionero general* (1511) and in the anonymous *Comedia Thebayda,* and they are also echoed in various other court lyrics of the period. The ballad survives in a much altered state (even Lancelot's name is changed to Baltasar) in twentieth-century oral tradition, versions having been collected in Andalusia and the Canary Islands.

The translations of Spanish ballads by James Young Gibson, a Scotsman who visited Spain in 1871–1872, are still considered among the best available and show that alternating rhyme can replace assonance with some success in English. His version of "Nunca fuera caballero" is a literal translation, but one that makes Lancelot's rendezvous with Guinevere more discreet than in the original, has Quintañona serve Lancelot mead rather than wine, and, in the last line, turns a third-person narration of the Queen's reception of her knight into direct speech. Gibson's translation of "Tres hijuelos había el rey" is also a faithful one, but as pointed out above, he renders the Spanish word for "hounds" (*sabuesos*) as "boots." In the last two lines he also alters the original lament for unnamed knights who lost their lives because of Quintañona ("dueña de Quintañones" in the Spanish), thereby keeping the attention focused on Lancelot. Gibson based his translations on versions in the *Cancionero de romances* (Antwerp, 1550).

Bibliographic note: Gibson's translations were published posthumously and are cited here from the second edition, *The Cid Ballads and Other Poems and Translations from Spanish and German,* ed. Margaret Dunlop Gibson (London: Kegan Paul, Trench, Trübner & Co., 1898). Recent translations are by W. S. Merwin in *Some Spanish Ballads* (London: Abelard-Schuman, 1961), and by Roger Wright, in his bilingual anthology *Spanish Ballads* (Warminister: Aris & Phillips, 1987).

For a modern edition of the Spanish texts and a good introduction to the genre as a whole, see C. Colin Smith, ed., *Spanish Ballads* (Oxford: Pergamon Press, 1964). A detailed introduction can be found in Entwistle's *The Arthurian Legend in the Literatures of the Spanish Peninsula* (1925; rpt. New York: Phaeton, 1975), up-dated to 1959 in María Rosa Lida de Malkiel's essay "Arthurian Literature in Spain and Portugal," in *Arthurian Literature in the Middle Ages,* ed. Roger Sherman Loomis (Oxford: Clarendon, 1959), pp. 406–18; and to 1986 in my article "Spanish and Portuguese Arthurian Literature," in *The Arthurian Encyclopedia,* ed. Norris J. Lacy (New York: Garland, 1986), pp. 516–21. See also my *Critical Bibliography of Hispanic Arthurian Material, I. Texts: the prose romance cycles,* Research Bibliographies and Checklists, 3 (London: Grant & Cutler, 1977); and "Notas sobre la materia artúrica hispánica, 1979–1986," *La Corónica* [Oxford, Ohio], 15 (1986–87), 328–40.

Two Lancelot Ballads

"Nunca fuera caballero"

Never was a gallant knight
Served by damosel or dame
As the good Sir Lancelot,
When from Britain forth he came.

Ladies took his armour off,
Damsels waited on his steed,
And the Lady Quintañona
Poured him out the foaming mead.

Sweet and fair Queen Guinivere
Took him to her secret bower,
Being in the better humour,
That she had not slept an hour;

There the Queen with beating breast
Told her sorrow in his ear:
"Lancelot, Sir Lancelot!
Hadst thou but been sooner here!

Never had that shameless knight
Said to me the words he said:
That in spite of thee, Señor,
He would come to me in bed!"

Furious rose Sir Lancelot,
Armed himself with double speed;
To his lady bade adieu,
Took the road upon his steed.

Underneath a shady pine
There he found the knight he sought;
First they couched and broke the lance,
Then with battle-axe they fought.

Lancelot with heavy stroke
Laid the caitiff on the green;
Cut his head from off his shoulders,
Fairer stroke was never seen.
Homeward rode Sir Lancelot;
"Welcome, welcome!" quoth the Queen.

"Tres hijuelos avia el rey"

Three tender striplings had the King,
Three striplings and no more;
And for the wrath he bore to them
He cursed them loud and sore.

The first of them became a deer,
The next a dog turned he,
The last he turned a Moorish man,
And sailed across the sea!

Upon a time Sir Lancelot
Among the dames did play;
"Sir Knight," quoth she, the boldest one,
"Be on your guard this day!

For were't my luck to wed with thee,
And thine to wed with me,
I'd ask the bonnie white-foot deer
As wedding-gift from thee!"

"With all my heart, my lady fair,
I'd bring him safely here,
If I but knew the far countrie
Where herds that bonnie deer!"

Sir Lancelot he rode along
For many a weary day;
His boots hung at his saddle-bow,
And all to hunt the prey.

He clambered up among the hills,
And there he found a cell,
Where far from any living man
An Eremite did dwell.

"God keep thee!" quoth the Eremite,
"Thou'rt welcome here to me;
And by the boots thou bearest there,
A huntsman thou may'st be."

"Now tell to me, good Eremite,
Thou holy man austere,
Now tell to me where I may find
The bonnie white-foot deer."

"Come take thy rest with me, my son,
Until the night hath flown;
I'll tell thee all that I have seen,
And all that I have known."

And as they talked the live-long night,
And whiled the time with cheer,
There passed, two hours before the light,
The bonnie white-foot deer;

And with him seven lions, and
A lioness with young;
Full seven counts had she laid low,
And many a knight and strong.

"Wherever be thy home, my son,
God shield thee with His arm!
Whoever sent thee here this day
Had thought to do thee harm!

Shame, Lady Quintañona, shame,
Hell-fire thy portion be!
If such a brave and gallant knight
Should lose his life for thee!"

(Translated by J. Y. Gibson)

INDEX